Visual Perception
and Cognition in Infancy

Carnegie Mellon Symposia
on Cognition

David Klahr, Series Editor

Anderson: Cognitive Skills and Their Acquisition

Carroll/Payne: Cognition and Social Behavior

Clark/Fiske: Affect and Cognition

Cole: Perception and Production of Fluent Speech

Farah/Ratcliff: The Neuropsychology of High-Level Vision: Collected Tutorial Essays

Granrud: Visual Perception and Cognition in Infancy

Gregg: Knowledge and Cognition

Just/Carpenter: Cognitive Processes in Comprehension

Klahr: Cognition and Instruction

Klahr/Kotovsky: Complex Information Processing: The Impact of Herbert A. Simon

Lau/Sears: Political Cognition

MacWhinney: Mechanisms of Language Acquisition

Siegler: Children's Thinking: What Develops?

Sophian: Origins of Cognitive Skills

VanLehn: Architectures for Intelligence

Visual Perception and Cognition in Infancy

Edited by

Carl Granrud
Carnegie Mellon University

LEA **LAWRENCE ERLBAUM ASSOCIATES, PUBLISHERS**
1993   Hillsdale, New Jersey   Hove and London

Lawrence Erlbaum Associates, Inc., Publishers
365 Broadway
Hillsdale, New Jersey 07642

Library of Congress Cataloging-in-Publication Data

Visual perception and cognition in infancy / edited by Carl Granrud.
    p.   cm. – (Carnegie Mellon symposia on cognition)
    Includes bibliographical references and indexes.
    ISBN 0-8058-0705-5 (cloth). – ISBN 0-8058-0706-3 (paper)
    1. Visual perception in infants–Congresses. 2. Cognition in
infants–Congresses. I. Granrud, Carl. II. Series.
    [DNLM: 1. Cognition–in infancy & childhood–congresses.
2. Visual Perception–in infancy & childhood–congresses. WW 105
V83413]
BF720.V57V57 1993
155.42'2214–dc20
DNLM/DLC
for Library of Congress   92-30246
                                        CIP

Books published by Lawrence Erlbaum Associates are printed on acid-free
paper, and their bindings are chosen for strength and durability.

Printed in the United States of America
10 9 8 7 6 5 4 3 2 1

Contents

Preface   vii

1   **Spatial and Chromatic Visual Efficiency
in Human Neonates**
Martin S. Banks and Elizabeth Shannon   1

2   **Motion Nulling Techniques and Infant Color Vision**
Davida Y. Teller and Delwin T. Lindsey   47

3   **What Can Rates of Development Tell Us
About Underlying Mechanisms?**
Richard Held   75

4   **Perception of Visual Direction in Human Infants**
Richard N. Aslin   91

5   **Kinematic Foundations of Infant Visual Perception**
Philip J. Kellman   121

6   **Infants' Perception of Biomechanical Motions:
Intrinsic Image and Knowledge-Based Constraints**
Bennett I. Bertenthal   175

v

7 Infants' Sensitivity to Motion-Carried Information
   for Depth and Object Properties
   Martha E. Arterberry, Lincoln G. Craton, and Albert Yonas   215

8 Future-Oriented Processes in Infancy:
   The Case of Visual Expectations
   Marshall M. Haith   235

9 The Object Concept Revisited: New Directions in the
   Investigation of Infants' Physical Knowledge
   Renée Baillargeon   265

10 Commentary: Extending the Ideal Observer Approach
   Velma Dobson   317

11 Commentary: Cheers and Lamentations
   Robert S. Siegler   333

   Author Index   345

   Subject Index   353

Preface

The chapters in this book are based on papers presented at the 23rd Carnegie Mellon Symposia on Cognition, held in Pittsburgh, June, 1990. This symposium was an exciting event. Speaker after speaker presented new discoveries about infants' visual perception in areas ranging from sensory processes to visual cognition. It was apparent from the talks that this field is continuing to make significant progress in understanding the infant's perceptual world.

Several advances have come from the development of new methods for exploring infant perception and cognition that have brought new empirical findings. Outstanding examples of these advances can be seen throughout this volume. Teller and Lindsey describe the "motion-nulling" technique that has allowed them to make precise measurements of infants' chromatic discriminations. Haith presents the innovative method that he has used to investigate infants' expectations about future events. Baillargeon describes the methods she has used to reveal young infants' object permanence. Kellman reviews a number of methods that led to discoveries about infants' object perception abilities; and Arterberry, Craton, and Yonas present new methods that they developed for studying infants' perception of object properties that are specified by motion.

Advances have also been made in understanding the mechanisms underlying perceptual development. Banks and Shannon report findings from "ideal observer" models indicating that immaturities in the retina are a major cause of newborns' poor visual acuity, contrast sensitivity, and chromatic vision. Aslin describes simulations that shed light on the processes involved in the development of accurate saccadic eye movements. Held discusses evidence that development in the visual cortex plays an important role in perceptual development; and Bertenthal investigates the processes involved in perceiving biomechanical motion. In their commentaries, Siegler applauds these advances and urges us to do more work aimed at discovering underlying mechanisms, and Dobson points out future directions for ideal observer modelling.

I want to thank all of the authors for the excellent chapters they have contributed to this volume and for the superb symposium talks that they gave. Their work makes me confident that we will continue to see many exciting discoveries in infant perception and cognition in the years to come. I also want to thank the people who helped in putting together the symposium and this book: David Klahr and Bob Siegler provided valuable advice on how to organize a symposium and edit a book; Betty Boal worked tirelessly to make the symposium a success: The Carnegie Mellon Psychology Department provided financial support for the symposium; Christopher Pecci did excellent editorial work on the book; and Erica Sekuler and Cathy Reed helped compile the book's subject index. I am grateful to you all.

—Carl Granrud

1

Spatial and Chromatic Visual Efficiency in Human Neonates

Martin S. Banks
Elizabeth Shannon
University of California at Berkeley

The early stages of vision are primarily serial. Visual stimuli pass sequentially through the eyes' optics, which are responsible for forming the retinal image; the photoreceptors, which sample and transduce the image into neural signals; and two to four retinal neurons, which transform and transmit those signals to the optic nerve and eventually to the central visual pathways. Considerable information is lost in these early stages of the visual process as evidenced by the close correspondence between the filtering properties of the optics and receptors, and some measures of visual sensitivity (e.g., Banks, Geisler, & Bennett, 1987; Coletta, Williams, & Tiana, 1990; Pelli, 1990). In this chapter, we examine how immaturities among these early stages of vision limit the spatial vision and the color vision of human neonates.

It is well established that human neonates see poorly. In the first month of life contrast sensitivity (a measure of the least luminance contrast required to detect a visual target) and visual acuity (a measure of the finest detail that can be detected) are at least an order of magnitude worse than in adulthood (reviewed by Banks & Dannemiller, 1987). Chromatic discrimination (the ability to distinguish targets on the basis of their wavelength composition) is much reduced, too (reviewed by Teller & Bornstein, 1987). One would think that the anatomical and physiological causes of such striking functional deficits would have been identified, but the specific causes are still debated. Some investigators have proposed that optical and retinal immaturities are the primary constraint (Jacobs & Blakemore, 1988; Wilson, 1988), whereas others have emphasized immaturities in the central nervous system (Bronson, 1974; Brown, Dobson, & Maier,

1

1987; Salapatek, 1975; Shimojo & Held, 1987). Our purpose is to establish as well as possible the limitations imposed by optical and receptor immaturities and to discuss how those limitations should be incorporated into our descriptions and theories of vision in early life. We conclude that much, but not all, of the spatial and chromatic deficits exhibited by neonates can be explained by optical and receptor immaturities. Immaturities among post-receptoral mechanisms are responsible for the unexplained portion of the deficits.

The approach we use relies on ideal observer theory. By definition, the performance of an ideal observer is optimal given the built in physical and physiological constraints (Green & Swets, 1966). Ideal observers have been useful tools in vision research because their performance provides a rigorous measure of the information available at chosen processing stages (Barlow, 1958; Geisler, 1989; Pelli, 1990; Watson, Barlow, & Robson, 1983). For instance, the performance (e.g., contrast sensitivity or visual acuity) of an ideal observer with the optical and photoreceptor properties of an adult eye reveals the information available at the receptors to discriminate various spatial and chromatic stimuli. Similarly, comparing the performance of two ideal observers with different optics and receptors reveals how changes in those properties affect the information available for visual discrimination. In this sense, ideal observer analyses allow an atheoretic assessment of constraints imposed by various stages of visual processing.

Unlike more conventional neural theories that assume specific neural mechanisms at different ages (e.g., Bronson, 1974; Salapatek, 1975; Wilson, 1988), we attempt to reduce assumptions to a minimum. An ideal observer is derived here with the optical and photoreceptor properties of the human neonate (see also Banks & Bennett, 1988). The properties of the young fovea are now understood well enough to minimize the number of necessary assumptions. The performance of this ideal observer is then computed for various spatial and chromatic tasks. Its performance is the best possible for a visual system with the front-end of the newborn system. Moreover, comparisons of the performance of newborn and adult ideal observers reveal the information lost by optical and photoreceptor immaturities across the life span. We will show that much, but not all, of the deficits human neonates exhibit in contrast sensitivity, grating acuity, and chromatic discrimination can be understood from information losses in the optics and photoreceptors.

OPTICAL AND PHOTORECEPTOR DEVELOPMENT

This section briefly reviews the literature on the development of the eye and its optics and on the development of the photoreceptors. More detail is provided in Banks and Bennett (1988).

The eye grows significantly from birth to adolescence, with most of the growth occurring in the first year. For instance, the distance from the cornea, at the front of the eye, to the retina, at the back (the axial length), is 16 to 17 mm at birth, 20 to 21 mm at 1 year, and 23 to 25 mm in adolescence and adulthood (Larsen, 1971; Hirano, Yamamoto, Takayama, Sugata, & Matsuo, 1979). Shorter eyes have smaller retinal images. So, for example, a 1° target subtends 204 μ (microns) on the newborn's retina and 298 μ on the adult's (Banks & Bennett, 1988). Thus, if newborns had the retina and visual brain of adults, one would expect their visual acuity to be about two thirds that of adults.

Another ocular dimension relevant to visual sensitivity is the diameter of the pupil. The newborn's pupil is smaller than the adult's, but this difference probably has little effect, if any, on visual sensitivity because the eye is shorter, too. More specifically, the eye's numerical *aperture* (the pupil diameter divided by the focal length of the eye) is nearly constant from birth to adulthood (Banks & Bennett, 1988); so, for a given target, the amount of light falling on the retina per degree squared should be nearly constant across age.

Still another ocular factor relevant to visual sensitivity is the relative transparency of the ocular media. Two aspects of ocular media transmittance are known to change with age: the optical density of the crystalline lens pigment and that of the macular pigment. In both cases, transmittance is slightly higher in the young eye, particularly at short wavelengths (Bone, Landrum, Hime, Fernandez, & Martinez, 1987; Werner, 1982). Thus, for a given amount of incident light, the newborn's eye transmits slightly more to the photoreceptors than does the mature eye.

The ability of the eye to form a sharp retinal image is yet another relevant ocular factor. This ability is typically quantified by the *optical transfer function*. There have been no measurements of the human neonate's optical transfer function, but the quality of the retinal image almost certainly surpasses the resolution performance of the young visual system (see Banks & Bennett, 1988, for details). Thus, it is assumed here that the optical transfer function of the young eye is adult-like. This assumption is not critical for our purposes because moderate changes in optical quality would not affect the main conclusions of this chapter.

If optical imperfections do not contribute significantly to the visual deficits observed in young infants, receptoral and postreceptoral processes must. The retina and central visual system all exhibit immaturities at birth (for reviews, see Banks & Salapatek, 1983; Hickey & Peduzzi, 1987), but recent work has also found striking morphological immaturities in the fovea, particularly among the photoreceptors.

The development of the fovea in the first year of life is dramatic, but subtle morphological changes continue until at least 4 years of age (Yuodelis & Hendrickson, 1986). To illustrate some of the more obvious developments, Figs. 1.1 and 1.2 display Yuodelis and Hendrickson's micrographs of retinas at different ages. Figure 1.1 shows low-power micrographs of the fovea at birth, 4 years, and adulthood. The black lines and arrows mark the rod-free portion of the retina,

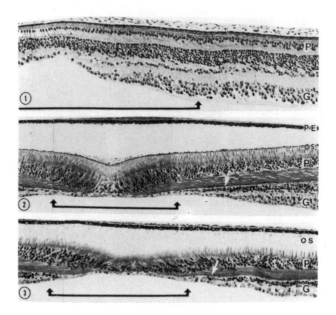

FIG. 1.1.   Low-power micrographs of the human fovea at birth (1), 45 months
(2), and 72 years (3). The black lines and arrows mark the width of the rod-free
foveola. Because at birth the foveola is very wide, only half of it is shown. The
most central cone synaptic pedicles are indicated by a white arrow in (2) and (3).
P, photoreceptor nuclei; G, ganglion cell layer; OS, outer segment of photoreceptors; PE, pigment epithelium. From Yuodelis and Hendrickson (1986).

the so-called *foveola*. The diameter of the rod-free zone decreases from roughly 5.4° at birth to 2.3° at maturity.

   Figure 1.2 displays, at higher magnification, the human foveola at birth and
adulthood. An individual cone is outlined for clarity in each panel. The cones'
outer segments are labelled OS. The inner segments are just below the outer
segments.

   In the mature cones, the inner segment captures light, and through waveguide
properties, funnels it to the outer segment where the photopigment resides.
As the light travels down the outer segment, many opportunities are provided
to isomerize a photopigment molecule and thereby create a visual signal.

   The micrographs of Fig. 1.2 illustrate the striking differences between neonatal and adult cones. Neonatal inner segments are much broader and shorter, and, unlike their mature counterparts, they are not tapered from the external
limiting membrane to the interface with the outer segment. The outer segments
are distinctly immature, too, being much shorter than their adult counterparts.

   In order to estimate the efficiency of the neonate's lattice of foveal cones,
we calculated the ability of the newborn's cones to capture light in the inner

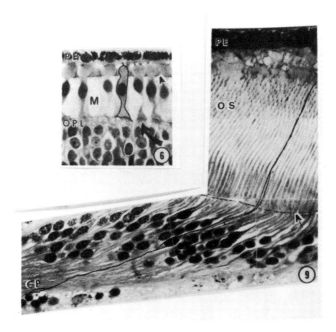

FIG. 1.2. Development of human foveal cones illustrated by light micrographs. A single cone is outlined in both figures; magnification is constant. Ages: (6) = 5 days postpartum; (9) = 72 years. PE, pigment epithelium; OPL, outer plexiform layer; M, Muller glial cell processes; CP, cone pedicles; OS, outer segments. From Yuodelis and Hendrickson (1986).

segment, funnel it to the outer segment, and produce a visual signal (Banks & Bennett, 1988). We began by estimating the effective collecting area of cones at different ages. We found that the newborn inner segment cannot funnel light to the outer segment properly: The inner segment is so short and broad that light rays approaching and reflecting off the inner segment wall at acute angles cannot reach the outer segment.

If the funneling property of the inner segment does not work, the effective aperture or collecting area of newborns' cones must be the outer segment. Taking the smaller size of the newborn eye into account, the angular diameter of the effective collecting area is about 0.35 minutes of arc. The dimensions required to compute this value are given in Table 1.1. The effective aperture of adult foveal cones is, of course, the inner segment because its funneling properties are rather good. Thus, the aperture of adult cones is about 0.48 minutes.

Calculations were also made of the average spacing of cones in the newborn and adult fovea from Yuodelis and Hendrickson's data (see Banks & Bennett, 1988, for details). Table 1.2 shows the cone-to-cone distances in minutes of

TABLE 1.1

Factor	Source	Neonate Central Fovea	Neonate Foveal Slope	15 Months Central Fovea	Adult Central Fovea
Pupil diameter	Salapatek & Banks (1978)	2.2 mm	2.2 mm	2.7 mm	3.3 mm
Axial length	Larsen (1971) Stenstrom (1946)	16.6 mm	16.6 mm	20.4 mm	24.0 mm
Posterior nodal distance	from axial length ratios	11.7 mm	11.7 mm	14.4 mm	16.7 mm
Receptor aperture	Yuodelis & Hendrickson (1986) Miller & Bernard (1983)	0.35 min arc	0.35 min arc	0.67 min arc	0.48 min arc
Receptor spacing	Yuodelis & Hendrickson (1986)	2.30 min arc	1.66 min arc	1.27 min arc	0.58 min arc

arc. Cone-to-cone separation in the center of the fovea is about 2.3 min, 1.7 min, and 0.58 min in neonates, 15-month-olds, and adults, respectively. It is very important to note that these lattice dimensions impose a limit on the highest spatial frequency that can be resolved without distortion or aliasing (Williams, 1985). This highest resolvable spatial frequency is called the *Nyquist limit*. From cone spacing estimates, Nyquist limits of 15, 27, and 60 c/deg were calculated for newborns, 15-month-olds, and adults, respectively. Adult grating acuity is similar to the Nyquist sampling limit of the foveal cone lattice (Green, 1970; Williams, 1985). One naturally asks, then, whether a similar relationship is observed in newborns. The answer is evident from a comparison of Table 2.2 and Fig. 1.7. Although newborn Nyquist limits are much lower than adult, they are not nearly as low as the highest grating acuity observed early in life. Thus, in human newborns the Nyquist sampling limit of the foveal cone lattice far exceeds the observed visual resolution, implying that coarse sampling by widely spaced receptors is not a major cause of low acuity in newborns.

TABLE 1.2
Nyquist Limits

Assuming regular hexagonal lattice:		
Nyquist limit in c/deg $= \dfrac{60}{\sqrt{3*D}}$	*where D = center-to-center distance (min arc)*	
	D	*Nyquist Limit*
Neonate central fovea	2.30 min arc	15.1 c/deg
Neonate foveal slope	1.66 min arc	20.9 c/deg
15 month central fovea	1.27 min arc	27.2 c/deg
Adult central fovea	0.58 min arc	59.7 c/deg

We used the information listed in Table 1.1 to construct model receptor lattices for newborns and adults; these are shown in Fig. 1.3. The white bars at the bottom of each panel represent 0.5 minutes of arc and serve as references. The light gray areas represent the effective collecting areas: the cone apertures. Nearly all of the light falling within these apertures reaches the photopigment and is, therefore, useful for vision. The effective collecting areas cover 65% and 2% of the retinal patches for the adult and newborn foveas, respectively. Consequently, the vast majority of incident photons are not collected within newborn cone apertures and are, therefore, not useful for vision.

The next factor to consider is how efficiently the outer segment—where the photopigment resides—absorbs photons and produces the isomerization that

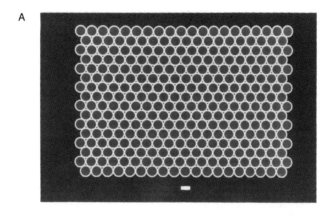

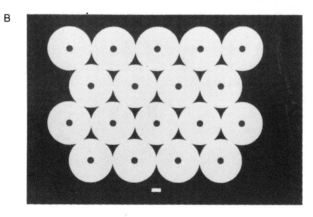

FIG. 1.3. Schematics of the receptor lattices used in (a) adult and (b) neonatal ideal observers. The white bars represent 0.5 min arc. Light gray areas represent the inner segments; dark gray areas represent effective collecting areas. The effective collecting areas cover 65% of the adult central fovea but only 2% of the newborn central fovea.

triggers the visual process. As can be seen in Fig. 1.2, the lengths of newborn and adult outer segments differ substantially. In the central fovea, for instance, the ratio of adult to newborn outer segment length is about 16:1. Intuitively, longer outer segments should provide more opportunities for a photon to produce an isomerization. We calculated the proportion of photons incident on the outer segment that produce an isomerization (see Banks & Bennett, 1988, for details). The 16:1 difference calculated between adult and newborn outer segment lengths produces about a 10:1 difference in the number of isomerizations for a given number of incident photons. These calculations imply that once photons are delivered to outer segments, newborn cones are much less efficient than mature cones in producing isomerizations.

One can see from these calculations that the cone lattice of the newborn fovea is quite inefficient in delivering photons to the photopigment-laden outer segments. Moreover, because the path length of the outer segment is short, its efficiency is low, too. Taking into account the age-related changes in the factors listed in Table 1.1, we estimate that the adult foveal cone lattice absorbs 350 times more quanta than the newborn foveal lattice. Stated another way, if identical patches of light are presented to newborn and adult eyes, roughly 350 photons are effectively absorbed in adult foveal cones for every photon absorbed in newborn cones.

Ideal observers were built for the adult fovea and newborn fovea. The properties built into these observers are listed in Table 1.1. All of the ideal observers had three receptor types—SWS (short-wavelength-sensitive or blue), MWS (medium-wavelength-sensitive or green), and LWS (long-wavelength-sensitive or red) cones—with adult spectral sensitivities (Estevez, 1979; Walraven, 1974). SDE software developed by Geisler (1984) was used to compute the performance of these observers for various spatial and chromatic tasks. As mentioned earlier, ideal observers employ an optimal decision rule to discriminate stimuli on the basis of different effective photon catches among photoreceptors. Thus, they allow one to assess, without assumptions about subsequent neural mechanisms, the limitations optical and receptoral properties place on the detection and discrimination of spatial and chromatic stimuli. Likewise, the performance of the neonatal ideal observer relative to the adult is a measure of the extra information lost by immature optics and photoreceptors.

CONTRAST SENSITIVITY

The *contrast sensitivity function* (CSF) represents the visual system's sensitivity to sinusoidal gratings of various spatial frequencies. The CSF is a reasonably general index of visual sensitivity because any two-dimensional pattern can be represented by its spatial frequency content (Banks & Salapatek, 1981; Cornsweet, 1970). Thus, an understanding of how optical and receptoral immaturities limit contrast sensitivity should offer insight into how they limit spatial vision in general.

Before discussing infant contrast sensitivity, consideration is given to how optics and photoreceptor efficiency affect contrast sensitivity in adults. Banks et al. (1987) and Crowell and Banks (1991) used the ideal observer whose properties are detailed in Table 1.1 to calculate the best contrast sensitivity the human fovea could possibly have given the quantal fluctuations in the stimulus (photon noise), the optics of the eye, and the size, spacing, and efficiency of the foveal cones. They also included considerations of a postreceptoral factor: the functional summation area for gratings of different spatial frequencies (Howell & Hess, 1978). (Summation experiments suggest that the intermediate- to high-frequency detecting mechanisms summate information over a constant number of grating bars or cycles.)

Figure 1.4 displays the CSF of the ideal observer for sinewave gratings of a constant number of cycles. Different functions illustrate the contributions of various pre-neural factors. The function labeled *quantal fluctuations* represents the performance of an ideal machine with no optical defocus and arbitrarily small and tightly packed photoreceptors. This function has a slope of -1, which is to say that contrast sensitivity is inversely proportional to patch width. The inverse proportionality is a manifestation of the square-root law behavior of ideal machines (Banks et al., 1987; Barlow, 1958; Rose, 1942). The function labeled *aperture and quantal fluctuations* represents performance when the photoreceptors are given the dimensions of the adult foveal cones; comparing it to the one above it reveals the contribution of the finite aperture of foveal cones (which has the effect of attenuating high spatial frequencies slightly). The solid lines represent performance with all pre-neural factors included; the difference between this function and the one above it represents the contribution of optical defocus (Campbell & Gubisch, 1967). The other solid lines represent the contrast sensitivities for luminances of 340, 34, and 3.4 cd/m². As expected for ideal machines, these functions follow the square-root law: Reducing luminance by a log unit produces a half log unit reduction in contrast sensitivity.

Figure 1.5 shows the performance of real adult observers when they are presented the same targets as the ideal observer. The data points are contrast sensitivities for gratings of 5 to 40 c/deg for two adult observers. As is normally observed, contrast sensitivity is greater for high than for low luminances. As expected, the contrast sensitivity values for the real adult observers are substantially lower than those of the ideal observer.

The solid lines are the three ideal functions of Fig. 1.4 shifted vertically as a unit to fit the real observer's data. The ideal functions fit the experimental data reasonably well, which shows that the shapes of the ideal and real CSFs are similar. The similarity of shapes demonstrates that the high-frequency roll-off of the human adult's foveal CSF for gratings with a fixed number of cycles can be explained by the operation of optical and receptoral factors alone. This observation implies, in turn, that neural efficiency—the efficiency with which information at the outputs of the receptors is transmitted through the rest of

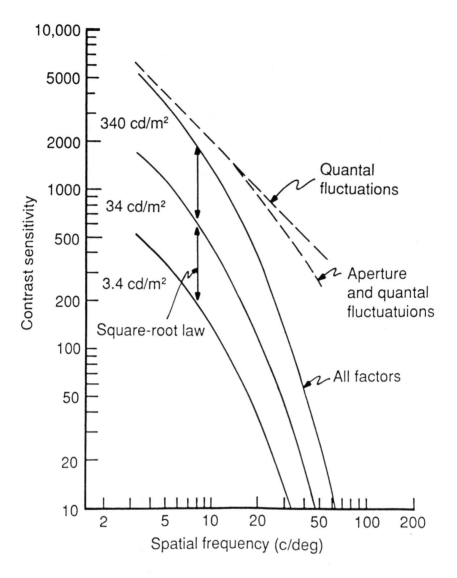

FIG. 1.4. CSF of an ideal observer incorporating different properties of the human adult fovea. Contrast sensitivity is plotted against the spatial frequency of fixed-cycle sine-wave grating targets. The highest dashed curve shows the contrast sensitivity of an ideal machine limited by quantal noise, ocular media transmittance, and photoreceptor quantum efficiency. The slope of -1 is dependent on the use of sine-wave gratings of a constant number of cycles. Space-average luminance is 340 cd/m^2. The lower dashed curve shows the contrast sensitivity with the receptor aperture effect included. Finally, the highest solid curve shows the sensitivity with the optical transfer function added. The other solid curves represent the contrast sensitivities for 34 and 3.4 cd/m^2. From Banks, Geisler, and Bennett (1987).

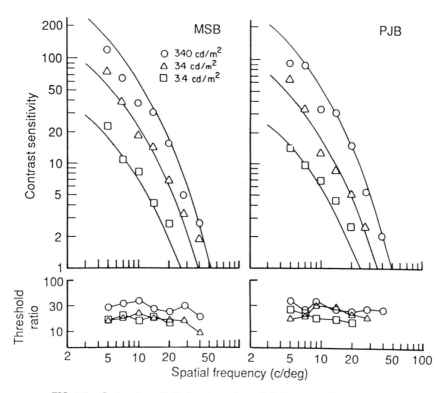

FIG. 1.5.   Contrast sensitivity functions of two adult observers. The top graphs
plot contrast sensitivity as a function of spatial frequency for three luminance levels tested. The solid lines are the contrast sensitivity of the ideal observer (from
Fig. 1.4), shifted downward by 1.33 log units for MSB and 1.43 log units for PJB.
The bottom graphs plot threshold ratios as a function of spatial frequency. The
ratios are the human observers' contrast threshold divided by the ideal observer's thresholds. From Banks, Geisler, and Bennett (1987).

the visual system—is constant from 5 to 40 c/deg for adult foveal vision.
Moreover, the luminance dependance of intermediate- and high-frequency sensitivity is similar for real and ideal adult observers, which means that adults exhibit square-root behavior just like ideal observers. These two observations—that
the spatial-frequency dependence and luminance dependence of human adult contrast sensitivity is similar to those exhibited by an ideal observer placed at the
receptors—are important in our analysis of contrast sensitivity development:
They legitimize comparisons of ideal and real observer performance at different
ages.

Figure 1.6 displays neonatal and adult CSFs. Contrast sensitivity is obviously quite low in newborns. Peak sensitivity, whether measured by forced-choice
preferential looking (FPL; Atkinson, Braddick, & Moar, 1977; Banks & Sala-

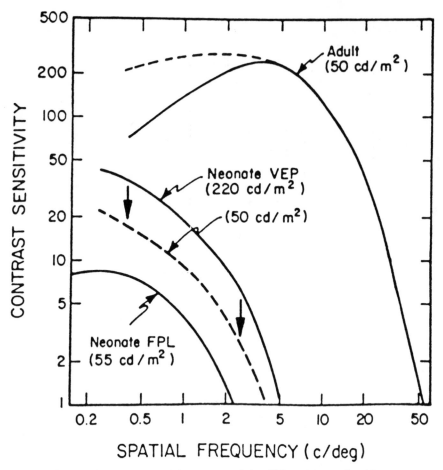

FIG. 1.6. Empirically determined adult and infant CSFs and the predicted loss
of sensitivity caused by optical and receptoral factors. The function labeled Neonate FPL is from Banks and Salapatek (1978). The function labeled Neonate
VEP is from A. M. Norcia (personal communication, 1988). The dotted line indicates the expected location of the VEP function at 50 cd/m^2, assuming the square-
root law holds. The function labeled Adult is from Campbell and Robson (1968);
the dashed extension to it indicates the presumed sensitivity for counterphase
flickering gratings like those used in VEP studies.

patek, 1978) or by the visual evoked potential (VEP; Norcia, Tyler, & Allen,
1986; Pirchio, Spinelli, Fiorentini, & Maffei, 1978), is substantially lower than
that of adults. One can also see that visual acuity in neonates is very limited,
being 12 to 25 times worse than that of normal adults (Dobson & Teller, 1978;
Norcia & Tyler, 1985).

    To examine the extent to which the development of contrast sensitivity can
be explained by optical and receptoral maturation, CSFs of the ideal neonatal

and adult observers were computed for gratings of a fixed number of cycles. The space-average luminance was 50 cd/m². The ideal CSFs are shown in Fig. 1.7. As in Fig. 1.4, these functions reflect performance limitations imposed by quantal fluctuations in the stimulus, ocular media transmittance, optical transfer, and the aperture spacing, efficiency, and spacing of photoreceptors. Notice that the ideal sensitivity is higher at the margin of the newborn's foveola than in the central 250 μ because of the greater efficiency of foveal slope cones (that is, cones roughly 2.7° from the center of the fovea; see Table 1.1 and Banks & Bennett, 1988, for details).

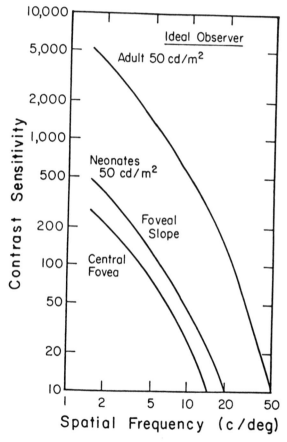

FIG. 1.7. CSFs for ideal observers incorporating the pre-neural factors of the adult and neonatal central foveas and the neonatal foveal slope. As in Fig. 1.4, the stimuli were grating patches of a constant number of cycles, in order to incorporate changes in summation area with spatial frequency (Banks, Geisler, & Bennett, 1987; Howell & Hess, 1978). Space-average luminance is 50 cd/m². The differences between adult and neonatal sensitivities are due primarily to the reduced quantum capture of the neonate's cone lattice. From Banks and Bennett (1988).

Most noteworthy are the differences between the contrast sensitivities of the adult and neonatal ideal observers. They are substantial. For example, the ratio between adult sensitivity and neonatal central foveal sensitivity at 5 c/deg is about 21:1 (1.32 log units). The major cause of decreased sensitivity in the newborn is the reduced photon capture of its cone lattice.

Of course, neither adults nor newborns are ideal observers, so one naturally asks whether these predicted differences in sensitivity can explain the differences observed between real adult and real newborn performance. If the visual systems of newborns and adults were identical except for the observed differences in eye size, and in cone aperture, efficiency, and spacing, one would expect the neonatal CSF to be simply a vertically shifted version of the adult. To examine this possibility, empirically determined adult and newborn CSFs were compared. Figure 1.8 displays an adult CSF at 50 cd/m^2 along with neonatal CSFs obtained at similar luminances with FPL and VEP. The vertical arrows indicate the amount of shifting one would expect if the visual systems of adults and newborns were identical except for the optical and receptoral factors listed in Table 1.1. The vertical shifts correspond to information lost by small eye size and inefficient photon capture and photoisomerization. As already mentioned, the fact that ideal and real adult contrast sensitivities are affected in similar ways by changes in spatial frequency and luminance makes plausible the implicit assumption behind vertical shifting. In keeping with this, the adult function was not shifted at frequencies below 3 c/deg because Banks et al. (1987) and Crowell and Banks (1991) were unable to show that differences between real and ideal contrast sensitivity below 3 c/deg can be explained by the factors considered.

The shifting accounts for a substantial fraction of the observed newborn–adult disparity, but not all of it. Evidently, additional factors contribute to the newborn contrast sensitivity deficit. The disparity between the real newborn CSF and the shifted adult function will be called the *postreceptoral gap*. It is illustrated in Fig. 1.9. Our analysis suggests that the postreceptoral loss is roughly 7-fold (0.85 log units) at 3 c/deg and 22-fold (1.34 log units) at 5 c/deg. What factors, not considered in our analysis, determine the magnitude and shape of the postreceptoral gap? There are, of course, numerous candidates including intrinsic neural noise (such as random addition of action potentials at central sites), inefficient neural sampling (such as lack of appropriate cortical receptive fields for detecting sinewave gratings), poor motivation to respond, and so forth.

A caveat is warranted before concluding this section. Despite the fact that the fovea subtends a large area at birth, newborns may use extrafoveal loci in contrast sensitivity experiments. There are no quantitative data on the morphological development of extrafoveal cones, so it is possible that the extrafoveal cones are actually more efficient than foveal cones at birth (Abramov et al., 1982). If this were the case, the disparity between predicted and observed contrast sensitivity (the postreceptoral gap) would be greater than indicated in Figs. 1.8 and 1.9. There is some evidence, however, that suggests, but by no means

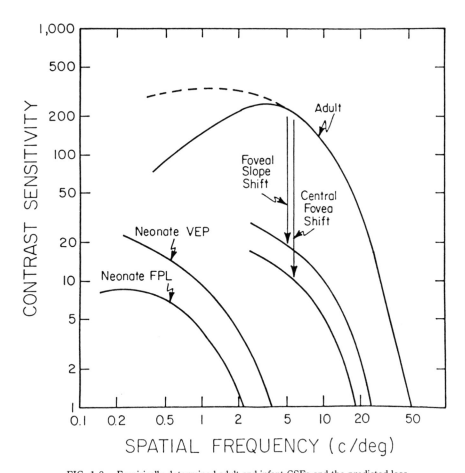

FIG. 1.8. Empirically determined adult and infant CSFs and the predicted loss of sensitivity caused by optical and receptoral factors. The curve labeled Neonate FPL is from Banks and Salapatek (1978) and was collected at 55 cd/m². The curve labeled Neonate VEP is derived from data from A. M. Norcia (personal communication, 1988). The VEP data were collected at a space-average luminance of 220 cd/m², so we shifted the functions downward by 0.32 log unit to indicate its expected location at 50 cd/m² (under the assumption that the square-root law holds). The curve labeled Adult represents data from Campbell and Robson (1968) that were collected at 50 cd/m². Each vertical arrow represents the ratio of the ideal neonate sensitivity to the ideal adult sensitivity at each spatial frequency. The reductions in contrast sensitivity indicated by the arrows represent the effects of smaller image magnification, coarser spatial sampling by the cone lattice, and less efficient photoreception in the neonate. The curves at the bottom of the arrows are the CSFs that one would expect if adult and neonatal visual systems were identical except for pre-neural factors. From Banks and Bennett (1988).

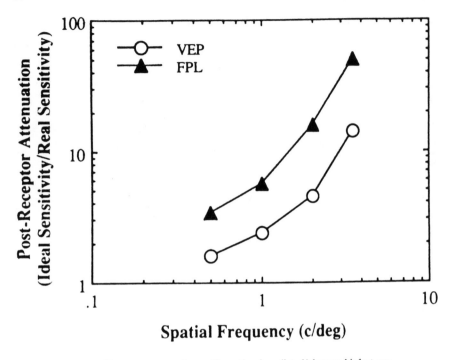

FIG. 1.9. The postreceptoral gap. The ratio of predicted/observed infant contrast sensitivity is plotted as a function of spatial frequency. The predicted sensitivities are the shifted curves in Fig. 1.8 and represent the contrast sensitivities
one would expect if the only loss of information infants suffer relative to adults
is due to immature optics and photoreceptors.

proves, that newborns fixate visual targets foveally. Hainline and Harris (1988),
Slater and Findlay (1975), and Salapatek and Kessen (1966) all showed that neonates use a consistent retinal locus when fixating a high-contrast target. They
could not, however, prove that this locus is the fovea because of uncertainties
about the location of the visual axis with respect to the optic axis. Other evidence relevant to the issue of peripheral and foveal viewing concerns the relative sensitivity of foveal and peripheral vision in neonates; some of this evidence
is from macaques, and some is from humans. Retinal and central nervous development in macaques and humans is similar, except that macaques are somewhat more advanced at birth and mature more rapidly (Boothe, Williams,
Kiorpes, & Teller, 1980; Hendrickson & Kupfer, 1976; Kiely et al., 1987). Blakemore and Vital-Durand (1980) measured the visual resolution of lateral geniculate cells supplied by different retinal regions. In newborn macaques, the acuity
of foveal cells was similar but higher than the acuity of peripheral cells. Thus,
in macaque infants, the highest resolution is likely to be observed with central
vision. The same appears to be true for human infants. Lewis, Maurer, and

Kay (1978) found that newborns could detect a narrower light bar against a dark background when it was presented in central vision than when it was presented in the periphery. More recently, Allen, Norcia, and Tyler (1989) showed that VEP acuity is higher in central than in peripheral vision in infants as young as 2 months. These observations suggest that the newborn contrast sensitivity and acuity estimates are manifestations of central rather than peripheral processing, but more direct experimental evidence is needed to show that central fixation is the same as foveal fixation in such young infants.

In conclusion, within the assumptions of the analysis just presented, much but not all of the contrast sensitivity and acuity deficits observed early in life can be accounted for by small eye size and by photoreceptor immaturities in and around the fovea. The major constraint is the poor photon catching of the newborn's foveal cone lattice. The unexplained portion of the sensitivity deficit—the postreceptoral gap—must reflect immaturities among postreceptoral retinal circuits and central visual pathways.

CHROMATIC VISION

We next investigated whether changes in visual efficiency, as indexed by the comparison of human neonate to ideal observer performance, offer much insight into the development of chromatic vision.

Infants less than 8 weeks of age do not consistently demonstrate the ability to discriminate stimuli that differ in hue only. Older infants, however, make such discriminations quite reliably (Clavadetscher, Brown, Ankrum, & Teller, 1988; Hamer, Alexander, & Teller, 1982; Packer, Hartmann, & Teller, 1984; Peeples & Teller, 1975; Teller, Peeples, & Sekel, 1978; Varner, Cook, Schneck, McDonald, & Teller, 1985). Here we consider three sorts of hue discriminations—Rayleigh, tritan, and neutral-point—because they are particularly interesting theoretically.

The *neutral-point* test is based on the observation that color-normal, trichromatic adults are able to distinguish all spectral (monochromatic) lights from white; that is, they do not exhibit a neutral point. In contrast, color-deficient observers, such as dichromats, exhibit distinct neutral points. Peeples and Teller (1975) and Teller et al. (1978) used a neutral-point test to examine 8-week-olds' color vision. They examined both white-on-white luminance discrimination and discrimination of a variety of chromatic targets from white. The stimulus conditions are listed in Table 1.3 and the colors of the test targets and background are represented in Fig. 1.10, which is a chromaticity diagram. Eight-week-olds discriminated many colors from white: red, orange, some greens, blue, and some purples (see also Table 1.3). They did not, however, discriminate yellow, yellow-green, one green, and some purples from white. Thus, 8-week-old infants seemed to exhibit a neutral zone running from short wavelengths to yellow and

TABLE 1.3

Experiment	Age	Task	Stimuli	Results	Ratio	Predicted Weber Fraction	Accurate Prediction
Hamer et al. (1982)	4 weeks	Chromatic	Red on yellow	Fail	3.49	1.92	+
			Green on yellow	Fail	3.14	1.73	+
	8 weeks	Chromatic	Red	Marginal	3.49	1.27	+
			Green	Marginal	3.14	1.13	+
	12 weeks	Chromatic	Red	Pass	3.49	0.63	+
			Green	Pass	3.14	0.57	+
Packer et al. (1984)	4 weeks	Intensity	Yellow(8°×8°)	Threshold = ± .27 lu			
		Chromatic	Red(8°×8°)	Fail	3.49	1.61	+
		Intensity	Yellow(4°×4°)	Threshold = ± .35 lu			
		Chromatic	Red(4°×4°)	Fail	3.49	1.92	+
		Intensity	Yellow(2°×2°)	Threshold = ± .55 lu			
		Chromatic	Red(2°×2°)	Fail	3.49	2.51	+
	12 weeks	Intensity	Yellow(8°×8°)	Threshold = ± .11 lu			
		Chromatic	Red(8°×8°)	Pass	3.49	0.54	+
		Intensity	Yellow(4°×4°)	Threshold = ± .18 lu			
		Chromatic	Red(4°×4°)	Pass	3.49	0.63	+
		Intensity	Yellow(2°×2°)	Threshold = ± .31 lu			
		Chromatic	Red(2°×2°)	Marginal	3.49	1.08	+
		Intensity	Yellow(1°×1°)	Threshold = ± .40 lu			
		Chromatic	Red(1°×1°)	Fail	3.49	1.40	+
Peeples & Teller (1975)	8 weeks	Intensity	White(14°×1°)	Threshold = ± .12 lu			
		Chromatic	Red on white	Pass	2.58	0.62	+

Study	Age	Condition	Stimulus	Result			
Teller et al. (1978)	8 weeks	Intensity	White (14°×1°)	Threshold = ± .12 lu			
		Chromatic	Red on white	Pass	2.58	0.62	+
			Orange	Pass	4.13	1.00	+
			Yellow 1	Marginal	12.26	2.95	+
			Greenish-yellow	Fail	7.10	1.71	+
			Yellowish-green	Fail	4.17	1.01	+
			Green 1	Marginal	3.29	0.79	–
			Green 2	Pass	3.23	0.78	+
			Greenish-blue	Pass	2.90	0.70	+
			Blue	Pass	2.52	0.61	+
			Bluish-purple	Pass	7.35	1.78	–
			Purple 1	Fail	10.32	2.49	+
			Purple 2	Marginal	9.94	2.39	+
			Reddish-purple	Pass	3.42	0.83	+
Varner et al. (1985)	4 weeks	Intensity	Green (4°×4°)	Threshold = ± .16 lu			
		Chromatic	Violet on green	Fail	0.04	0.01	–
	8 weeks	Intensity	Green	Threshold = ± .10 lu			
		Chromatic	Violet on green	Pass	0.07	0.01	+
Clavadetscher et al. (1988)	3 weeks	Intensity	Green (8°×8°)	Threshold = ± .40 lu			
		Chromatic	Violet 1 on green	Fail	0.04	0.02	–
		Chromatic	Violet 2 on green	Fail	0.07	0.04	–
		Chromatic	Blue on green	Fail	0.84	0.50	–
		Chromatic	Red on green	Marginal	1.98	1.19	+
		Chromatic	Blue on red	Marginal	2.85	<1.71	+
	7 weeks	Intensity	Green (8°×8°)	Threshold = ± .20 lu			
		Chromatic	Violet 1 on green	Pass	0.04	0.01	+
		Chromatic	Violet 2 on green	Marginal	0.07	0.02	–
		Chromatic	Blue on green	Pass	0.84	0.31	+
		Chromatic	Red on green	Pass	1.98	0.73	+
		Chromatic	Blue on red	Pass	2.85	<1.05	+

19

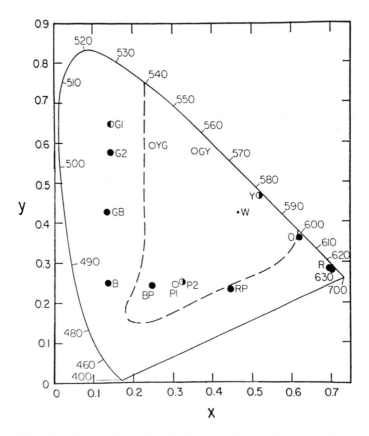

FIG. 1.10. Chromaticities of the stimuli used in the neutral-point experiment
of Peeples and Teller (1975) and Teller et al. (1978). Subjects in both experiments were 8-week-old infants. Filled symbols represent stimuli that all infants
reliably discriminated from white (W); open symbols represent hues that all infants failed to discriminate from white; half-filled symbols represent hues that some,
but not all, infants discriminated from white. The dashed curve represents the
boundary between hues that should and hues that should not be discriminated
from white according to the visual efficiency hypothesis. Hues falling outside the
triangular area bounded by the dashed curve should be discriminable from white,
and those falling within the area should not. From Banks and Bennett (1988).

green. Although they included other possibilities, Teller et al. (1978) hypothesized from these results that 8-week-olds may have deficient SWS cones because the neutral zone was somewhat similar to that exhibited (in color parlance)
in tritanopia or tritanomalous trichromacy.

A *tritan* test is designed to examine the function of SWS cones. By presenting two lights that activate MWS and LWS cones equally, the test isolates the
SWS cones. Varner et al. (1985) asked whether 4- to 8-week infants could distinguish two such lights. Specifically, they presented violet targets in a green

surround. Table 1.3 lists the conditions. Eight-week-olds distinguished the two lights at all luminances, so they must have at least minimally functional SWS cones. Four-week-olds, on the other hand, did not discriminate the two lights reliably, suggesting an SWS cone defect or a postreceptoral defect involving the circuits serving the SWS cones.

Rayleigh discrimination tests involve the discrimination of brightness-matched, long-wavelength lights, such as red and green. They are diagnostically important because adults with the most common color defects—*deuteranopia* (lacking MWS cones) and *protanopia* (lacking LWS cones)—are unable to make such discriminations. Hamer et al. (1982) and Packer et al. (1984) examined the ability of 4-, 8-, and 12-week-olds to make Rayleigh discriminations. The stimulus conditions are described in Table 1.3. Either a green or a red target was presented at one of a variety of luminances on a yellow surround. The results were clearcut: Most 8-week-olds and essentially all 12-week-olds made these discriminations reliably. This is clear evidence that most infants have at least minimally functional LWS and MWS cones by 8 weeks of age. In contrast, the majority of 4-week-olds did not exhibit the ability to make either discrimination. Packer et al. also found a significant effect of target size. Twelve-week-olds were able to make Rayleigh discriminations with 4° and 8° targets, but not 1° and 2° targets. These results imply that the color vision of 4-week-olds differs from that of color-normal adults, perhaps due to an absence of MWS and/or LWS cones or to an inability of postreceptoral circuits to compare MWS and LWS cone signals. The target-size effect in older infants suggests that the stimulus must be salient for them to demonstrate their chromatic ability.

More recently, Clavadetscher et al. (1988) re-examined the conditions tested by Hamer et al. (1982), Packer et al. (1984), and Varner et al. (1985) along with some new conditions. Specifically, they used the same paradigm employed in the previous work to examine 3- and 7-week-olds' ability to distinguish pairs of monochromatic lights. The conditions are listed in Table 1.3. In the first experiment, test lights of 645 nanometers (nm) (red), 486 nm (blue), 446 nm (blue), or 417 nm (violet) were presented against a 547 nm (green) background. In the second experiment, a light of 486 nm was presented against a broadband red background. Thus, there were five hue pairings tested in all. Three-week-olds did not discriminate any of these pairings reliably, but they gave evidence of a modest ability to discriminate the 645/547 nm and 486 nm/red pairings. Seven-week-olds discriminated all of the pairings reliably. Thus, the observations of Clavadetscher et al. (1988) confirm the earlier reports in that their neonates did not exhibit the ability to make Rayleigh (e.g., 645/547 nm) nor tritan (417/547 nm) discriminations reliably. They extend these observations, however, by showing that neonates also fail to discriminate other hue pairings reliably.

We should add, because it is important for the theoretical analyses described later in this section, that Teller and her colleagues also measured luminance discrimination thresholds in each of the aforementioned experiments by measur-

ing the smallest luminance increments and decrements required to elicit a reliable response.

Teller and her colleagues have drawn the following conclusions from this constellation of data: First, most infants are probably trichromatic by 12, if not 8,
weeks of age; that is, they have three functional cone types and the postreceptoral machinery required to preserve and compare their signals. Second,
at 4 weeks of age, the majority of infants fail to make both Rayleigh and tritan
discriminations and therefore have some form of color deficiency. Teller and
her co-workers raised the possibility that younger infants' discrimination failures
may be due to the absence or relative immaturity of different cone types or
because of relative immaturities among postreceptoral chromatic channels.

In sum, there are no rigorous demonstrations that the majority of infants
4 weeks of age or younger make hue discriminations. The absence of such evidence is consistent with the hypothesis that human neonates are generally color
deficient. Two sources of such deficiency are possible: First, neonates may track
only one or two cone types or one or two of their cone types may be insensitive
relative to the other cone types. Second, neonates may lack postreceptoral chromatic channels or have less sensitive chromatic channels compared to their luminance channels.

There is, however, another possibility. Perhaps neonates have a full complement of functional, although inefficient, cone types and the requisite neural
machinery to preserve and compare their signals, but their overall visual efficiency is simply too poor to allow them to demonstrate their chromatic capabilities. Similarly, older infants may exhibit reliable chromatic discrimination because
of increased visual efficiency. For the purposes of this hypothesis, we define
visual efficiency as the discrimination performance of a visual system limited by
optical and photoreceptor properties (see Tables 1.1 and 1.2) plus a general
postreceptoral loss. This definition will be made clearer further on.

The visual efficiency hypothesis is evaluated by using the ideal observer whose
properties are given in Table 1.1 and a measure of visual efficiency. To introduce
the approach, adults' luminance and chromatic discrimination is first discussed.
Mullen (1985) measured adults' luminance contrast sensitivity with monochromatic gratings (yellow and black stripes) of various spatial frequencies and chromatic sensitivity with isoluminant (equally bright) red/green and blue/yellow
gratings. She found that luminance contrast sensitivity exceeded chromatic sensitivity by a factor of 4 to 5 at most spatial frequencies. An important question
is whether reduced chromatic contrast sensitivity at intermediate to high spatial frequencies reflects reduced sensitivity among post-receptoral chromatic
channels as opposed to luminance channels or whether it simply reflects reduced
cone contrast (the variation in photon catch from one cone to the next), due to
the overlapping spectral sensitivities of different cone types.

To address this question, Geisler (1989) computed the performance of an
adult ideal observer for the conditions of Mullen's experiment. The observer

had a full complement of LWS, MWS, and SWS cones with adult properties. Naturally, the contrast sensitivity of the ideal observer was much higher than the sensitivity of Mullen's observers, but the effects of spatial frequency and chromatic versus luminance contrast were quite similar: The shapes of real and ideal luminance CSFs and real and ideal chromatic CSFs were nearly identical across a wide range of spatial frequencies. Moreover, ideal luminance sensitivity was consistently 3.5 times greater than ideal chromatic sensitivity for the colors chosen. Geisler concluded, therefore, that the contrast sensitivities of real and ideal adult observers are affected similarly by the spatial frequency and chromatic content of the stimulus. Because the ideal observer had no postreceptoral channels devoted to luminance or chromatic contrast, this observation shows that different efficiencies among such channels need not be hypothesized to explain the difference between luminance and chromatic contrast sensitivity.

Why is the ideal observer's sensitivity poorer for an isoluminant chromatic grating than for a luminance grating? The main cause is the extensive spectral overlap of cone photopigments.[1] Because of the overlap, the modulation of LWS and MWS cone outputs is significantly reduced for isoluminant chromatic gratings as compared to luminance gratings composed of the same components. The diminished cone response is bound to reduce ideal sensitivity because ideal observers utilize all the information in the matrix of cone signals. The fact that real observers show similar sensitivity losses over a wide range of spatial frequencies suggests that the extensive spectral overlap of cone types is a major constraint on human adult chromatic contrast sensitivity, too.

Geisler's conclusion can be expressed in a simple fashion: The ratio of adult chromatic sensitivity to adult luminance sensitivity is equal to the corresponding ratio of ideal sensitivities. This same reasoning can be applied to infants' color vision: The visual efficiency hypothesis, described earlier in a qualitative fashion, can now be stated quantitatively: Infant chromatic sensitivity divided by infant luminance sensitivity is also equal to the corresponding ratio of ideal sensitivities (and, therefore, to the ratio of adult sensitivities).

We adapted the ideal observer analysis to ask whether the visual efficiency hypothesis is consistent with empirical observations of early chromatic vision and its development. First, the sensitivity of the infant ideal observer was computed for the experimental conditions of Teller and her colleagues. The observer

---

[1]To explain this, it is useful to consider an isoluminant red/green grating divided into its two components: a red/black grating and a green/black grating. Consider, in particular, the outputs of LWS cones to each grating component. When the red component is presented, LWS cones respond in rough proportion to the luminance variation from the peak to the trough of the grating. They also respond in this way to the green component, although their responses at peaks and troughs are somewhat reduced. When the red and green grating components are added in phase—producing a yellow/black grating—the LWS cone modulations due to each component add, producing a large overall modulation. However, when the components are combined in opposite phase—producing an isoluminant red/green grating—the LWS cone modulations of each component cancel to some degree and the overall modulation is smaller. The same reasoning obviously applies to the MWS cones.

was identical to the one whose properties are given in Table 1.1. In keeping with the hypothesis that infants have a normal complement of cone types, we built in SWS, MWS, and LWS cones in adult proportions and with adult spectral sensitivities (see Banks & Bennett, 1988, for details), but each cone type was made less efficient than its adult counterpart in keeping with the earlier observations on contrast sensitivity.

After constructing the infant ideal observer, the spectral characteristics of each stimulus were encoded and the corresponding activations of SWS, MWS, and LWS cones calculated. This allowed us to compute the infant ideal observer's thresholds for the luminance and chromatic discrimination tasks of the five experiments listed in Table 1.3. Ideal luminance discrimination threshold was expressed as the just-detectable luminance decrement divided by the background luminance. To compute ideal chromatic discrimination performance, we constructed a stimulus composed of the uniform background, a decrement in the background, and an increment of the appropriate color. For example, the computer version of the Rayleigh stimulus of Packer et al. (1984) consisted of a uniform yellow background and a square region of the same luminance with a yellow decrement and a red increment. The increment was added in various proportions around the presumed equiluminance point in order to find the luminance ratio for which threshold was highest. While maintaining isoluminance, the magnitudes of the decrement and increment were manipulated in order to establish the infant ideal observer's chromatic discrimination threshold. This threshold was expressed as a Weber fraction: the magnitude of the background decrement (in this case, the yellow decrement) divided by the background luminance. Finally, the ratio of the ideal Weber fraction for chromatic discrimination divided by the ideal Weber fraction for luminance discrimination was computed. The ratios for each age group and experimental condition are given in Table 1.3. Higher ratios mean higher chromatic thresholds. The ratios vary widely from color to color. The smallest was 2.52, for blue-on-white discrimination, and the largest was 12.3, for yellow-on-white discrimination.

The ideal observer's luminance discrimination thresholds were much lower than those of Teller's infants. Furthermore, the neonate ideal observer was able to make all of the chromatic discriminations when the contrast of the target (background decrement/background luminance) was 1.0 as it was in Teller's experiments. Thus, as with contrast sensitivity and grating acuity, the infant ideal observer exhibited notably better performance than real neonates. Earlier, this performance disparity was attributed to postreceptoral losses.

The visual efficiency hypothesis outlined earlier incorporates such postreceptoral losses. It states that young infants' inability to make chromatic discriminations is a manifestation of low visual efficiency rather than some deficit among chromatic mechanisms per se. In other words, luminance and chromatic sensitivity should, according to this hypothesis, follow similar growth curves. Predictions of the visual efficiency hypothesis are obtained simply by multiplying the observed luminance discrimination thresholds (the Weber fractions measured by Teller and her colleagues) by the ratio of ideal chromatic to ideal luminance threshold. In equations, the predictions are:

$$CT_n/LT_n = CT_i/LT_i \qquad (1)$$
$$CT_n = CT_i*(LT_n/LT_i) \qquad (2)$$

where CT_n and LT_n are the chromatic and luminance thresholds (Weber fractions) for neonates and CT_i and LT_i are the same for the ideal observer. For examples of these predictions, refer to Table 1.3. In the Packer et al. (1984) experiment, for instance, the observed luminance discrimination threshold of 4-week-olds was 0.27 log units, a Weber fraction of 0.46. The ratio of ideal chromatic/luminance threshold was 3.49. So the chromatic discrimination Weber fraction (or threshold contrast) predicted by the visual efficiency hypothesis is simply 0.46 × 3.49, or 1.61. But for Teller's stimuli (background decrements replaced by increments of a different hue), contrasts greater than 1.0 are not physically realizable, so the hypothesis predicts a discrimination failure. The predicted thresholds vary with age, luminance, and target size because the luminance discrimination thresholds reported by Teller and her colleagues varied with those factors. Consequently, the hypothesis makes the unsurprising prediction that chromatic discrimination improves with increasing luminance, target size, and age. The predictions varied with the colors of the background and test target, too, because the ratios of ideal chromatic to ideal luminance threshold depended on the spectral composition of the stimuli. Thus, some discriminations, such as yellow from white, are expected to be more difficult than others, like blue from white.

The predicted Weber fractions for the neutral-point tests of Peeples and Teller (1975) and Teller et al. (1978) are given in the next to last column of Table 1.3. The visual efficiency hypothesis predicts discrimination failures for predicted Weber fractions greater than 1.0 and successes for smaller fractions. Figure 1.10 depicts the neutral-point predictions and data in the format of the chromaticity diagram. The data points represent the stimuli and the dashed line the predictions. The filled data points represent colors that were always discriminated by 8-week-olds, and unfilled points represent those colors that the infants always failed to discriminate. Half-filled points are those colors that were occasionally discriminated. Colors within the line should, according to the hypothesis, be indiscriminable from white, and colors outside the line should be reliably discriminated. The zone of theoretically indiscriminable stimuli is broad and, as expected, it does not resemble confusion zones for any standard dichromatic observer because the infant ideal observer has three cone types. The predictions match the observations tolerably well. We conclude that 8-week-olds' performance in the neutral-point experiments of Peeples and Teller (1975) and Teller et al. (1978) is largely consistent with the predictions of the visual efficiency hypothesis.

The predictions for the Rayleigh discrimination experiments (Hamer et al., 1982; Packer et al., 1984) are also given in Table 1.3 and illustrated in Figs. 1.11 and 1.12. Consider the experiment of Packer et al. first. Again, empirical measurements of luminance discrimination thresholds were multiplied by the ratio of ideal chromatic to ideal luminance threshold to estimate the Weber fractions, which, according to the hypothesis, would be needed for reliable discrimination (see Banks & Bennett, 1988, for details). These fractions are plotted in Fig. 1.11 and listed in the next to last column of Table 1.3. The dotted line represents chromatic contrasts of 1.0, the value presented in the Packer et al. experiment. Filled symbols represent those conditions in which discriminations were made reliably and unfilled symbols conditions in which discriminations were consistently not made. Half-filled symbols represent conditions in which the discrimination was made occasionally. All of the fractions for 4-week-olds are greater than 1.0, so the hypothesis correctly predicts discrimination failures for all target sizes at that age. The 12-week data and predictions are more complicated.

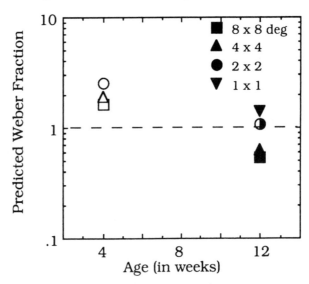

FIG. 1.11. Data and predictions for the Packer et al. (1984) experiment. Predicted Weber fractions are plotted as a function of age in weeks. Open symbols represent conditions in which infants did not reliably discriminate the test pair. Filled symbols represent conditions in which infants exhibited reliable discrimination, and half-filled symbols represent conditions in which some infants exhibited reliable discrimination and some did not. Different symbol shapes represent different target sizes. The dashed line represents the contrasts of the stimuli presented in this experiment. The vertical placement of the symbols corresponds to the Weber fractions predicted by the visual efficiency hypothesis. Thus, symbols above the dashed line represent conditions in which discrimination failures are predicted, and symbols below the line represent conditions in which reliable discrimination is predicted.

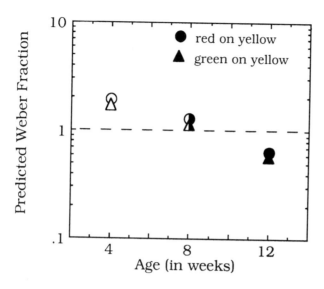

FIG. 1.12. Data and predictions for the Hamer et al. (1982) experiment. Conventions are the same as in Fig. 1.11, except that different symbols represent green-on-yellow and red-on-yellow discriminations.

The fractions are less than 1.0 for 4 ° and 8 ° targets, so the hypothesis predicts reliable discrimination for those targets. The fraction is slightly greater than unity for the 2 ° target, so a near miss is predicted. Finally, the fraction is well above unity for the smallest target, so a discrimination failure is predicted. The efficiency hypothesis, therefore, correctly predicts the results in all three conditions at 4 weeks and all four at 12 weeks.

Now consider the other Rayleigh discrimination experiment by Hamer et al. (1982). Figure 1.12 displays the empirical observations and the predictions of the efficiency hypothesis. The predicted Weber fractions are well above unity for 4-week-olds, so the efficiency hypothesis correctly predicts clear discrimination failures for red and green targets at that age. The fractions are slightly greater than 1.0 for 8-week infants, so near misses are predicted. Finally, the fractions are well below unity for the oldest infants, so consistent discrimination is correctly predicted for both colors at that age.

The predictions of the visual efficiency hypothesis are consonant with the pattern of Rayleigh discriminations observed by Hamer et al. (1982) and Packer et al. (1984). Recall that the neonatal ideal observer used in deriving predictions has three equally functional cone types and uses optimal strategies to compare their outputs. Stated another way, the efficiency hypothesis assumes no deficit among chromatic mechanisms relative to luminance mechanisms. Thus, poor Rayleigh discrimination performance early in life does not necessarily imply deficiencies among chromatic mechanisms per se. The pattern of discrimination failures observed among the youngest children and for small targets among the older children can be explained by the operation of optical and receptoral factors, and changes overall visual efficiency alone.

We have shown that two hypotheses can account for neonates' inability to make Rayleigh discriminations. The first, which we call the *chromatic deficiency hypothesis,* claims that neonates lack MWS and/or LWS cones, or one is much less efficient than the other, or have a deficit among their red/green postreceptoral chromatic mechanisms. The second, the *visual efficiency hypothesis,* claims that neonates have functional MWS and LWS cones and the requisite red/green mechanisms, but that these are too insensitive to support Rayleigh discriminations.

The chromatic deficiency hypothesis predicts that Rayleigh discrimination performance should improve with age more than luminance discrimination performance: specifically, that the ratio CT/LT (see equation 2) decreases with age. The cause of the decrease could be receptoral or postreceptoral in origin. A receptoral cause would be the absence of one or two cone types or lower efficiency in one or two cone types compared to the remaining ones. A postreceptoral cause would be the absence of the red/green and/or blue/yellow chromatic mechanism or lower sensitivity among one or two chromatic mechanisms relative to the luminance mechanism.

The visual efficiency hypothesis predicts that chromatic and luminance sensitivities should both increase with age, but the ratio of sensitivities should remain constant. The visual efficiency hypothesis states that the ratio of efficiencies among cone types is similar across age (all are less efficient than their adult counterparts) and that the ratio of sensitivities of postreceptoral chromatic and luminance mechanisms is similar across age (all less efficient than adult mechanisms). In order to distinguish these two hypotheses, more sensitive measurements of chromatic discrimination are needed.

To this end, Allen, Banks, Norcia, and Shannon (1990) used VEPs, which provide higher contrast sensitivities than FPL, and optimal spatiotemporal stimuli to examine luminance and Rayleigh discriminations at different ages. The stimuli consisted of two spatial sinusoids of equal contrast: one produced by modulating a saturated green stimulus (thus creating a green/black grating) and the other by modulating a saturated red stimulus (creating a red/black grating). The two sinusoids were added in spatial counterphase (the bright red bars of one sinusoid being positioned in between the bright green bars of the other). They then varied the ratio of $R/(R+G)$, where R and G are the mean luminances of the red and green sinusoids. $R/(R+G)$ ratios of 0, 0.5, and 1.0 yielded green/black, red/green, and red/black sinusoids, respectively.[2]

---

[2]The stimuli were created by modulating the green and red guns of a Conrac 7300 display. Allen et al. placed an amber filter in front of the CRT screen in order to minimize the contribution of SWS cones and to insure that the stimuli were in the Rayleigh region, above 550 nm. The CIE chromaticity coordinates of the filtered green and red phosphors were (0.42, 0.57) and (0.65, 0.34), respectively. Space-average luminance was 8 cd/m^2.

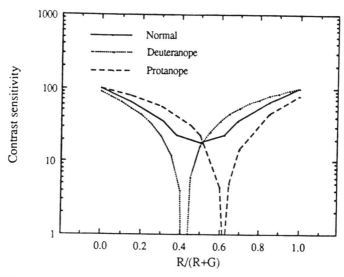

FIG. 1.13. Predictions of contrast sensitivity as a function of the amount of red in a red/green sinusoidal grating. The solid line is the predicted sensitivity of a normal trichromatic observer. The prediction was calculated from an ideal observer with SWS, MWS, and LWS cones in the ratio of 1:16:32. The dotted line is the prediction for a deuteranope and the dashed line is the prediction for a protanope. The prediction is that the grating will be undetectable by the deuteranope at an R/(R + G) value of .42 and undetectable by a protanope at a value of .62. From Allen et al. (1990).

Figure 1.13 displays the contrast sensitivity values one predicts for color-normal and color-deficient observers. The solid line represents the predicted contrast sensitivity for a normal trichromatic observer. The prediction was calculated from the adult ideal observer with a full complement of SWS, MWS, and LWS cones. The dotted line represents the predicted sensitivities for a deuteranope, a person who lacks MWS cones, and the dashed line represents the predicted sensitivities for a protanope, who lacks LWS cones. Allen et al. (1990) found that the psychophysical and VEP data of color-normal adults are consistent with the predictions for a color-normal observer.

Figure 1.14 displays the sensitivity values obtained in three color-defective adults. Panel A shows data from two protanopes. The open circles are psychophysical thresholds and the squares are thresholds obtained with VEPs. These protanopes showed a large decrement in performance at the predicted R/(R + G) ratio of 0.62. Panel B shows the data for a protanomalous observer who also shows a performance dip in the expected region, but because she has some functional LWS cones, the dip is not as large as the protanopes'.

The visual efficiency hypothesis predicts that the shapes of the solid-line functions in Figs. 1.13 and 1.14 will be the same in neonates and normal adults, but that the neonatal functions will be displaced downward on the log sensitivity

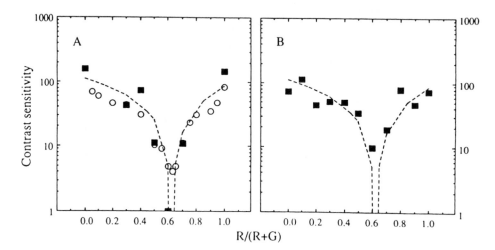

FIG. 1.14.   Contrast sensitivity in color-deficient adults. Panel A shows thresholds
from two protanopic adults. The open circles are psychophysical thresholds and
the closed squares are thresholds estimated from sweep VEP recordings. The
dashed line is the predicted sensitivity for a protanope. The data point on the
x-axis at 0.6 represents the absence of a VEP signal at that value. Panel B shows
VEP thresholds from a protanomolous adult. Like the protanope, the protanomolous
adult has a dip in sensitivity close to the value predicted for an observer lacking
LWS cones. However, at this value VEPs are measurable in the protanomolous
adult. From Allen et al. (1990).

axis. The chromatic deficiency hypothesis, on the other hand, predicts that the
shapes of the functions will differ for neonates and adults: The dip should be
larger in neonates, more like the color-deficient adults in Fig. 1.14.

Allen et al. (1990) tested neonates from 2 to 7 weeks of age using the VEP.
The data from 4 of these children are displayed in Fig. 1.15 along with the prediction for a color-normal individual. In each case, the data are consistent with the
predictions for a color-normal observer and clearly inconsistent with those for
protanopes and deuteranopes. The data from 13 infants who completed at least
six threshold measurements are shown in Fig. 1.16. Again, these data are inconsistent with predictions for a protanope or deuteranope. The data are also
inconsistent with the idea that the red/green postreceptoral chromatic mechanism in neonates is less mature than the postreceptoral luminance mechanism;
if it were less mature, the dip in these functions would be larger in neonates
than in adults.

Allen et al. (1990) concluded that infants as young as 2 weeks of age demonstrate a clear cortical response to an isoluminant red/green grating. This observation is consistent with the visual efficiency hypothesis that young infants'
inability to demonstrate chromatic discriminations behaviorally (e.g., Hamer et
al., 1982) is due to generally poor visual sensitivity rather than to a loss of LWS

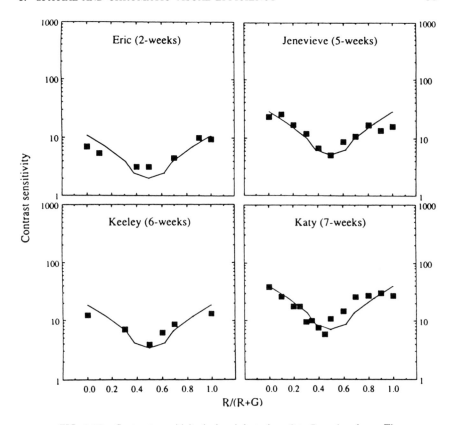

FIG. 1.15. Contrast sensitivity in four infants from 2 to 7 weeks of age. The spatial frequency of the grating was 0.8 c/deg. The solid lines are the predicted sensitivity of a normal trichromatic observer. Thresholds were obtained from sweep VEP recordings. From Allen et al. (1990).

or MWS cones or a specific immaturity of the postreceptoral red/green mechanism. Thus, human neonates appear to have functional MWS and LWS cones and the postreceptoral neural machinery to preserve and compare their signals.

We now turn to a discussion of tritan discriminations, which isolate the functioning of SWS cones, and, to some extent, the postreceptoral blue/yellow chromatic mechanism. Varner et al. (1985) reported that few 4-week-olds and most 8-week-olds demonstrate the ability to make a tritan discrimination. We again examined the performance of the infant ideal observer in the conditions of this experiment. In contrast to the Rayleigh and neutral-point discriminations discussed earlier, chromatic performance near isoluminance actually exceeded luminance performance. That is, the threshold Weber fraction of the ideal observer was lower for discrimination of violet from green near isoluminance than for discrimination of a green decrement alone. This behavior occurred because the ideal observer used a different strategy in this chromatic task than it had in the

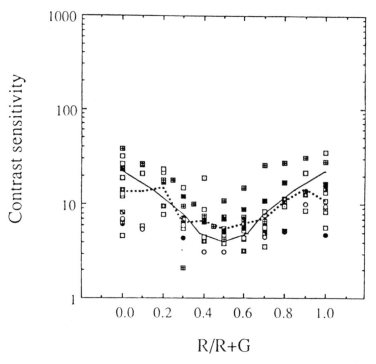

FIG. 1.16. Contrast sensitivity for 13 infants from 2 to 7 weeks of age. The solid line is the predicted sensitivity of a normal trichromatic observer. The dashed line connects the means at each value of R/(R + G). From Allen et al. (1990).

others. Color-normal adults actually exhibit similar behavior (for details, see Banks & Bennett, 1988), so the visual efficiency hypothesis cannot predict the pattern of results observed in 4-week-olds. The prediction failure for 4-week-olds is indicated by the minus sign in the rightmost column of Table 1.3. This observation implies that infants may well have a tritan color defect: dysfunctional or relatively insensitive SWS cones or relatively insensitive blue/yellow chromatic mechanisms. Of course, this prediction failure does not affect our interpretation of the Rayleigh discrimination experiments because they do not involve SWS cones.

To examine further the possibility that infants 4 weeks of age or less have a tritan defect, we looked at the results of Clavadetscher et al. (1988). They reported that 3-week-olds fail to discriminate a variety of lights (417, 448, 486, and 645 nm) from green, and blue (486 nm) from red. Seven-week-olds in their study made all of these discriminations reliably. The predictions of the visual efficiency hypothesis were computed as before and they are listed in Table 1.3 and displayed in Figure 1.17. The figure plots the predicted Weber fraction

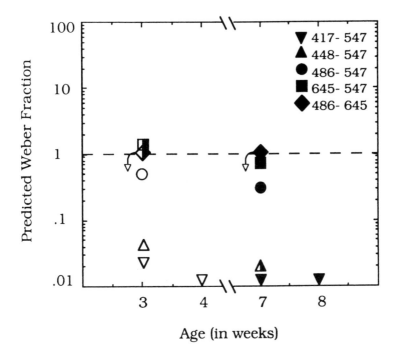

FIG. 1.17. Predictions of the visual efficiency hypothesis for the experiments of Clavadetscher et al. (1988) and Varner et al. (1985). Predicted Weber fractions are plotted for each of the test pairs used in those experiments. Conventions are the same as in Fig. 1.11 except that different symbols represent the different hue pairings. The solid arrows indicate that the predicted Weber fractions for those two points should be somewhat lower; see text for explanation.

(stimulus contrast required to elicit reliable discrimination) for each of the presented hue pairings. The horizontal line represents the stimulus contrast Clavadetscher et al. actually presented. Points above the horizontal line represent those conditions in which discrimination failures are predicted and those below the line the conditions in which discrimination successes are predicted. The filled symbols represent conditions in which discriminations were made reliably and unfilled symbols those conditions in which discriminations were consistently not made. Half-filled symbols represent those conditions in which there was some evidence for discrimination. The arrows next to the symbols for the 486/645 pairing (and the "less than" sign in Table 1.3) indicate that the predicted Weber fraction should be lower than the indicated values; Clavadetscher et al. presented the 486/645 pair at a higher luminance than the others. Decrement sensitivity probably improves with increasing luminance, changing the term LT_n in equations 1 and 2 presented earlier, which, in turn, would decrease the predicted Weber fraction. Clavadetscher et al., however, did not measure intensity discrimination at the higher luminance, so we do not know how much the predictions should be displaced downward.

One can see from Fig. 1.17 that the hypothesis accurately predicts 7-week-olds' ability to distinguish four of the five hue pairings presented in the study. The hypothesis does not predict the 3-week data, however. It predicts correctly that 3-week-olds' ability to discriminate 645/547 and 486/red pairings should approach reliability, but it predicts incorrectly that these infants should discriminate the other pairings—417/547, 448/547, and 486/547—reliably. It is significant that these three pairings are the ones that most involve SWS cones. Consequently, as with Varner et al. (1985), we are forced to reject the visual efficiency hypothesis as an explanation for hue discriminations that involve the SWS cones. Instead, it looks like neonates have either relatively insensitive SWS cones or a relatively insensitive postreceptoral blue/yellow mechanism that subserves SWS cones.

The constellation of results suggests that the visual efficiency hypothesis accounts accurately for the development of hue discriminations that involve MWS and LWS cones, but fails to account for the development of discriminations that involve SWS cones. Thus, we hypothesize that human neonates have a tritan defect due to dysfunctional SWS cones or possibly to delayed development among the blue/yellow, postreceptoral chromatic mechanism. To pursue this idea, we created a neonatal ideal observer with no SWS cones in order to simulate a tritan defect. We then used exactly the same procedure, as outlined in equations 1 and 2, to generate predictions of discrimination performance in the conditions of Varner et al. (1985) and Clavadetscher et al. (1988). The visual efficiency hypothesis for an observer with a tritan defect predicts an inability to discriminate the 417/547 nm pairing in Varner et al. and Clavadetscher et al. because those lights stimulate MWS and LWS cones in the same ratio, so discrimination has to be based on differential activation of the SWS cones. The other predictions are portrayed in Fig. 1.18 (see also Table 1.4). As in previous figures with this format, the predicted Weber fraction (or stimulus contrast) needed to discriminate the lights is plotted for each hue pairing. The horizontal line represents the stimulus contrast actually presented in the Clavadetscher et al. study, so any points plotted above the line represent predicted discrimination failures and those below the line represent predicted discrimination successes. Filled symbols represent conditions in which infants made the hue discrimination reliably and open symbols the conditions in which they reliably did not make the discrimination. Half-filled symbols represent conditions in which there was modest evidence for discrimination.

Clearly, the tritan-defective predictions are accurate for the 3-week data, but, as expected, inaccurate for the 7-week data. They are therefore supportive of the idea that infants 4 weeks of age or younger have a tritan defect and

TABLE 1.4

Experiment	Age	Task	Stimuli	Results	Ratio	Predicted Weber Fraction	Accurate Prediction
Varner et al. (1985)	4 weeks	Intensity	Green(4°×4°)	Threshold = ± .16 lu			
		Chromatic	Violet on green	Fail	24.26	7.52	+
Clavadetscher et al. (1988)	3 weeks	Intensity	Green(8°×8°)	Threshold = ± .40 lu			
		Chromatic	Violet 1 on green	Fail	24.26	14.60	+
		Chromatic	Violet 2 on green	Fail	2.79	1.67	+
		Chromatic	Blue on green	Fail	3.44	2.07	+
		Chromatic	Red on green	Marginal	2.00	1.20	+
		Chromatic	Blue on red	Marginal	2.87	<1.72	+

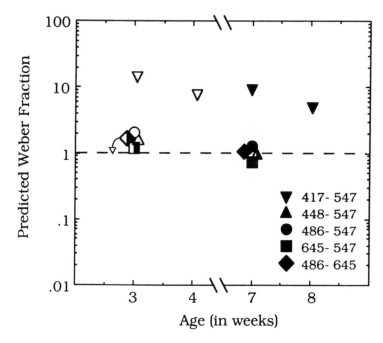

FIG. 1.18. Predictions for the visual efficiency hypothesis when SWS cones are assumed to be nonfunctional. Conventions are the same as in Fig. 1.17.

older infants do not. The early defect could be due to relative insensitivity among SWS cones or among postreceptoral blue/yellow chromatic mechanisms.

In summary, the predictions of the visual efficiency hypothesis are consistent with the pattern of Rayleigh and neutral-point discriminations observed by Teller et al. (1978). Moreover, Allen et al. (1990) have shown empirically that the chromatic information required to make a Rayleigh discrimination is transmitted to the cortex of infants as young as 2 weeks of age. Consequently, Rayleigh discrimination and most neutral-point failures observed among the youngest children and for small targets among the older children do not imply differential deficiencies among chromatic mechanisms per se. Rather, the ratio of chromatic to luminance sensitivity remains constant across age, as shown empirically by Allen et al. (1990) for Rayleigh discriminations, suggesting that neonates' apparent inability to make chromatic discriminations that depend solely on MWS and LWS cones is caused by an overall deficit in visual efficiency. The predictions of the visual efficiency hypothesis are not consistent with the tritan discriminations observed by Varner et al. (1985) and Clavadetscher et al. (1988). Modifying the visual efficiency hypothesis to include a tritan defect at 3 and 4 weeks allowed us to predict all of the data with reasonable accuracy. Therefore, young infants may, in fact, possess some form of color anomaly invoking a deficiency among SWS cones or cone pathways fed by them.

DISCUSSION

Ideal observer analyses were used to estimate the information available at the photoreceptors for the discrimination of spatial and chromatic stimuli. The information is much reduced in the human neonate compared to the adult mainly because of immaturities among neonates' photoreceptors. This reduction in the information available for discrimination sets an upper bound on the visual performance human neonates are capable of given their optics and photoreceptors. Real newborns can do no better than the neonatal ideal observer. The discrimination information lost by inefficient photoreception accounts for a substantial fraction of the gap between adult and infant contrast sensitivity, grating acuity, and chromatic discrimination. Nonetheless, the magnitude of the information gain with age is insufficient by itself to account for the entire developmental gap in these tasks.

In this section, we consider various hypotheses about the sources of the postreceptoral loss and the sorts of visual tasks for which this analysis is likely or unlikely to yield useful insights.

Contributors to Postreceptoral Loss

The performance of the neonatal ideal observer was much better than that of human neonates in all of the tasks considered. This is hardly surprising given that human adult performance does not equal ideal performance in these same tasks. More interestingly, the gap between real and ideal neonate values is significantly larger than that between real and ideal adult values (see Figs. 1.8 and 1.9). This means that neonates, although significantly limited by optical and receptoral deficiencies, use the information that is available at the photoreceptors less efficiently than adults do. What postreceptoral factors contribute to this additional developmental deficit? Some of the obvious candidates are considered here.

Before considering mechanistic explanations of postreceptoral loss, we should entertain a methodological explanation: Perhaps the sensitivity of the young visual system is actually better than believed, so the postreceptoral loss is properly ascribed to motivational deficiency. There is no good theory of how motivation should affect visual performance, so unfortunately, it is difficult to know where to look for its effects. For the sake of argument, though, suppose that behavioral estimates of visual thresholds are uniformly higher than true sensory thresholds. This would imply that the postreceptoral gap is smaller than our estimates. Behavioral procedures, like FPL, rely on an infant's willingness to perform the appropriate looking behavior. It is well known that infants tend to preferentially fixate patterned over unpatterned stimuli, but their looking preference is entirely voluntary and certainly not mandated whenever they detect a target. The VEP technique used in infant vision studies only requires that the infant look in the direction of the target for fairly brief periods. For these reasons, it has been assumed that the FPL measurements are more subject to motivational deficits. VEP measurements commonly reveal greater sensitivities than behavioral measurements. For instance, grating acuity measured by VEP is typically an octave higher (Dobson & Teller, 1978). If this argument is accepted, it should be noted that VEP estimates of neonatal contrast sensitivity and grating acuity still fall well short of the values predicted from the front-end losses as plotted in Fig. 1.8.[3] That is to say, whether one relies on FPL or VEP measurements of visual sensitivity, one cannot explain all of the difference between neonatal and adult performance from front-end losses alone.

There are a number of possible explanations involving inefficient neural processing that might explain age changes in the postreceptoral loss. Real observers' deviations from ideal performance are characterized by two general factors: the level of internal noise and the efficiency with which the observer utilizes available stimulus information. These two factors have been called *intrinsic noise* and *sampling efficiency,* respectively (Legge, Kersten, & Burgess, 1987). Here the possibility is discussed that one or both of these causes of less-than-ideal performance contribute to the postreceptoral loss observed in neonates.

Intrinsic noise refers to sources of random error within the visual system. In an audio system, an example is a noisy amplifier. There are numerous sources of noise within the visual system that could degrade visual performance. Let us discuss one plausible example because it might be particularly important in developing systems. A consistent and striking physiological observation is that cells in the visual cortex of kittens respond sluggishly compared to adult cells (Bonds, 1979; Derrington & Fuchs, 1981; Hubel & Wiesel, 1963). Their response latency, fatigability, and peak firing rate are much lower than those found in mature neurons. The firing rates of retinal ganglion cells, in contrast, do not differ markedly across age (Hamasaki & Flynn, 1977). Peak firing rates also decrease at successive sites in the geniculostriate pathway of adult cats, but the effect is more dramatic in kittens. Thus, it appears that peak firing rate drops dramatically in the ascending visual pathway of kittens. The human visual cortex appears to be quite immature early in life, too (Atkinson & Braddick, 1981; Braddick & Atkinson, 1987; Naegele & Held, 1982), so the same drop in firing rate may occur in human neonates. Reduced firing rates from retina to cortex, if caused by random or nearly random dropping of spikes from one cell to the next, would decrease the total number of spikes in an unpredictable

---

[3]This discussion makes an important and incorrect assumption that the thresholds obtained with VEP are comparable to those obtained with FPL. The means of estimating VEP thresholds involves signal averaging and extrapolation of data, which are not used in FPL. We do not know how much averaging and extrapolation decreases the estimated threshold (i.e., increases estimated sensitivity), so one is really comparing apples and oranges in such a discussion. Our only point is that even with those enhancements, VEP estimates still fall short of ideal observer performance (which does not involve this sort of averaging and extrapolation).

way. If the spike trains are Poisson distributed (an approximation to the binomial distribution) or nearly so, a drop in the mean number of spikes reduces the signal-to-noise ratio. It is equivalent to adding noise and, therefore, is best thought of as a source of intrinsic noise. Thus, successive reductions in firing rate may well be a significant source of information loss in the young visual system.

Poor sampling efficiency may also contribute significantly to the postreceptoral loss. The optimal strategy in detecting a visual stimulus is one that extracts the greatest signal information possible while keeping the effects of external or internal noise to a minimum. When the parameters of the signal are known, the optimal strategy is implemented, for all intents and purposes, by a weighting function that matches the profile of the expected signal (for a rigorous treatment, see Geisler, 1989). This is probably accomplished in the visual system by monitoring the activity of neurons whose receptive fields nearly match the profile of the expected signal. The newborn visual system might exhibit poorer sampling efficiency than the adult for two reasons. First, because of the immaturity of the visual cortex, neurons with receptive fields that match experimental stimuli (e.g., sinewave gratings) may be rare or non-existent. Second, and perhaps most importantly, in behavioral experiments the situation is surely quite different for a neonate compared to an adult. The adult can be coached to anticipate the spatial configuration and temporal characteristics of the signal to be detected. Thus, an adult observer can choose more wisely which neurons to monitor. Newborns, on the other hand, cannot be coached in such a fashion. The experimenter has to rely on the general orienting response of the child to salient or novel targets. The child presumably has to monitor the activity of a very large number of neurons, any of which could indicate the appearance of a salient or novel event. The consequence is a reduction in sampling efficiency.

The contributions of intrinsic noise and sampling inefficiency to the postreceptoral gap can be distinguished by the so-called *equivalent noise paradigm* (Legge et al., 1987; Pelli, 1990). In this paradigm, observers are asked to detect targets embedded in a noise masker. The logic of the paradigm is portrayed in the left panel of Fig. 1.19. Hypothetical contrast thresholds for detecting a sinusoidal grating are plotted as a function of noise intensity. An ideal observer has no intrinsic noise and is able to sample the stimuli to be discriminated optimally; its contrast thresholds are proportional to noise spectral density. Real observers possess some amount of intrinsic noise and sample stimuli with less than perfect efficiency. One can see the effects of these two sources of information loss in the real observer curve in the left panel of the figure. At low noise intensities, the threshold-elevating effects of intrinsic noise are larger than those of the noise masker, so real observer thresholds at low noise levels are flat and elevated relative to ideal observer thresholds. As the intensity of the noise masker is increased, however, the elevating effects of the masker begin to override those of intrinsic noise. The noise level at which this occurs is called the *equivalent noise* because it is the level at which the masker's effects are

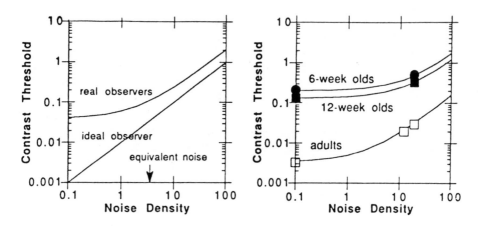

FIG. 1.19. Predicted and observed data in equivalent noise paradigm plots. Both panels plot contrast threshold for detecting a sinewave grating as a function of the strength of a noise masker. The left panel shows the expected functions for an ideal observer with no intrinsic noise and perfect sampling efficiency and that for a real observer with some intrinsic noise and imperfect sampling efficiency. The estimate of the equivalent noise strength is indicated by the arrow. The right panel shows the observed functions from an experiment by Banks, Stephens, and Hartmann (1985) for 6-week-olds, 12-week-olds, and adults.

equivalent to the effects of intrinsic noise. Finally, at high noise intensities, threshold becomes proportional to masker level. The gap between real and ideal performance here is a measure of sampling efficiency uncontaminated by intrinsic noise.

Banks, Stephens, and Hartmann (1985) provided some data relevant to measuring intrinsic noise and sampling inefficiency in young infants. This experiment, however, was conducted for another purpose, so there are too few measurements to draw any firm conclusions. Nonetheless, it is interesting to consider their findings. Banks et al. presented sinewave gratings with and without a noise masker to 6-week-olds, 12-week-olds, and adults. We have replotted their data in the right panel of Fig. 1.19. The data points on the left side of the figure are the contrast thresholds when the noise was not present and those on the right are the thresholds when different noise maskers were present. The key finding is that adults exhibited a significantly larger masking effect than did 6- or 12-week-olds. That is to say, the presence of the noise elevated threshold much more in adults than in infants. As shown in the plot in the right panel, this implies that the 6- and 12-week-olds have more intrinsic noise than adults do; stated another way, the equivalent noise in infants appears to be higher than in adults. It also appears from these plots that infant and adult curves will not superimpose at high noise levels, which if true, implies that infants' sampling efficiency is poorer, too.

As stated earlier, the spatial and chromatic visual deficits infants exhibit are due to both front-end and postreceptoral immaturities. The postreceptoral immaturities—whose effects are evidenced by the postreceptoral gap shown in Fig. 1.9—may well be caused by both elevated intrinsic noise and low sampling efficiency.

Developmental Findings That Do and Do Not Lend Themselves to Ideal Observer Analyses

According to Occam's razor, scientific explanations should be sought first in terms of known qualities. We have followed this philosophy by examining the information available at the photoreceptors for making a variety of spatial and chromatic discriminations and by calculating how the information at the photoreceptors changes with age. Thus, more complicated explanations involving different growth rates among retinal and cortical mechanisms (e.g., Shimojo & Held, 1987) are not required. We also found that neonates' inability to make a variety of chromatic discriminations is consistent with analyses of the information at the receptors. Consequently, explanations involving delayed development of chromatic mechanisms are not necessary (at least for LWS and MWS cones and for the red/green chromatic mechanism).

Only a subset of the spatial and chromatic tasks in the infant literature has been examined here. Indeed, the tasks chosen are ones in which real observers are most likely to behave similarly to ideal observers. This analysis would be inconsistent with observed behavior in a large number of other spatial and chromatic tasks. For example, spatial frequency and orientation masking (Blakemore & Campbell, 1969; Campbell & Kulikowski, 1966) occur at postreceptoral sites, so their development (Banks et al., 1985; Braddick, Wattam-Bell, & Atkinson, 1986) would not be evident in ideal observers like ours. Increment threshold functions (Barlow, 1958) follow Weber's law across a wide range of stimulus conditions. This lawful behavior is in part a manifestation of the operation of adaptation mechanisms, a factor not considered in this analysis. Consequently, an important aspect of the development of increment threshold functions (Dannemiller & Banks, 1983; Hansen & Fulton, 1981) will not be reflected in age changes in front-end limitations. Finally, the sensitivity roll-off and Weber's behavior of the low-frequency end of the mature CSF (Kelly, 1977) is commonly attributed to the operation of lateral interactions among retinal network mechanisms, another factor not considered here. Thus, the development of this property of the CSF (Atkinson et al., 1977; Banks & Salapatek, 1981; but see Movshon & Kiorpes, 1988) will also not be manifest in ideal observer performance.

The development of numerous spatial and chromatic capabilities, therefore, will not be evident in analyses of age changes in the information at the photoreceptors. Nonetheless, ideal observer analyses might still be quite helpful in investigation of such capabilities. As pointed out by Watson (1987), even departures of real observers' performance from ideal are important clues about the structure of processing. Such departures show that human visual performance is influenced substantially by postreceptoral processes. Similarly, developmental changes in the departures between real and ideal performance indicate how post-receptoral contributions vary with age.

SUMMARY

We examined the contributions of pre-neural factors to the differences between neonatal and adult spatial and chromatic vision. Ideal observers were constructed that incorporated reasonable estimates of the optics, ocular media, and photoreceptor aperture, efficiency, and spacing of adult and neonatal foveas. Comparison of the performance of these ideal observers allowed us to estimate reasonably rigorously the contribution of optical and receptoral immaturities to the deficits in neonates' spatial and chromatic vision. There were two main findings:

1. Immaturities in pre-neural mechanisms alone (primarily reduced eye size and changes in photoreceptor morphology) predict a 1.3 log unit decrease in contrast sensitivity and 2-octave (.6 log unit) decrease in grating acuity. Although these are substantial effects, they are smaller than the observed differences: Grating acuity for 4-week-old infants, for example, is typically 3.5 to 4.5 octaves lower than the mature values. Therefore, we conclude that pre-neural mechanisms account for much, but not all, of the differences between neonatal and adult contrast sensitivity and grating acuity. The remaining difference must reflect the contribution of postreceptoral mechanisms.

2. The failure of infants younger than 7 weeks to make a variety of chromatic discriminations may be caused by poor visual efficiency rather than differential immaturities among cone types or chromatic channels. In addition, improvements in chromatic discrimination observed from birth to 12 weeks may reflect improvements in visual efficiency rather than in chromatic mechanisms. The hypothesis fails, however, to predict the inability of infants younger than 7 weeks to make chromatic discriminations that depend on SWS cones. We showed that those discrimination failures and subsequent improvements can be explained by assuming that SWS cones, or the postreceptoral circuits that serve them, are quite immature during the first weeks of life.

ACKNOWLEDGMENTS

This research was supported by NICHHD Research Grant HD-19927 to Martin S. Banks. We thank David Shen for his assistance in the preparation of the manuscript and Andrew Eisman for programming assistance. We are also grateful to Davida Teller and Carl Granrud for helpful comments on the manuscript.

REFERENCES

Abramov, I., Gordon, J., Hendrickson, A., Hainline, L., Dobson, V., & LaBossiere, E. (1982). The retina of the newborn human infant. *Science, 217,* 265–267.

Allen, D., Banks, M. S., Norcia, A. M., & Shannon, E. (1990). Human infants' VEP responses to isoluminant stimuli. *Investigative Ophthalmology and Visual Science, 31* (Suppl. 4), 10.

Allen, D., Norcia, A. M., & Tyler, C. W. (1989). Development of grating acuity and contrast sensitivity in the central and peripheral visual field of the human infant. *Investigative Ophthalmology and Visual Science, 30* (Suppl. 4), 311.

Atkinson, J., & Braddick, O. (1981). Development of optokinetic nystagmus in infants: An indicator of cortical binocularity? In D. F. Fisher, R. A. Monty, & J. W. Sanders (Eds.), *Eye movements: Cognition and visual perception* (pp. 53–64). Hillsdale, NJ: Lawrence Erlbaum Associates.

Atkinson, J., Braddick, O., & Moar, K. (1977). Development of contrast sensitivity over the first three months of life in the human infant. *Vision Research, 17,* 1037–1044.

Banks, M. S., & Bennett, P. J. (1988). Optical and photoreceptor immaturities limit the spatial and chromatic vision of human neonates. *Journal of the Optical Society of America A, 5,* 2059–2079.

Banks, M. S., & Dannemiller, J. L. (1987). Infant visual psychophysics. In P. Salapatek & L. B. Cohen (Eds.), *Handbook of infant perception: From sensation to perception* (pp. 115–184). New York: Academic Press.

Banks, M. S., Geisler, W. S., & Bennett, P. J. (1987). The physical limits of grating visibility. *Vision Research, 27,* 1915–1924.

Banks, M. S., & Salapatek, P. (1978). Acuity and contrast sensitivity in 1-, 2-, and 3-month-old human infants. *Investigative Ophthalmology and Visual Science, 17,* 361–365.

Banks, M. S., & Salapatek, P. (1981). Infant pattern vision: A new approach based on the contrast sensitivity function. *Journal of Experimental Child Psychology, 31,* 1–45.

Banks, M. S., & Salapatek, P. (1983). Infant visual perception. In M. M. Haith & J. J. Campos (Eds.), *Handbook of child psychology* (pp. 435–571). New York: Wiley.

Banks, M. S., Stephens, B. R., & Hartmann, E. E. (1985). The development of basic mechanisms of pattern vision: Spatial frequency channels. *Journal of Experimental Child Psychology, 40,* 501–527.

Barlow, H. B. (1958). Temporal and spatial summation in human vision at different background intensities. *Journal of Physiology, 141,* 337–350.

Blakemore, C., & Campbell, F. W. (1969). On the existence of neurons in the human visual system selectively sensitive to the orientation and size of retinal images. *Journal of Physiology, 203,* 237–260.

Blakemore, C., & Vital-Durand, F. (1980). Development of the neural basis of visual acuity in monkeys: Speculation on the origin of deprivation amblyopia. *Transactions of the Ophthalmological Society of the United Kingdom, 99,* 363–368.

Bonds, A. B. (1979). Development of orientation tuning in the visual cortex of kittens. In R. Freeman (Ed.), *Developmental neurobiology of vision* (pp. 31–41). New York: Plenum.

Bone, R. A., Landrum, J. T., Fernandez, L., & Tsarsis, S. L. (1988). Analysis of the macular pigment by HPLC: Retinal distribution and age study. *Investigative Ophthalmology and Visual Science, 29,* 843–849.

Booth, R. G., Williams, R. A., Kiorpes, L., & Teller, D. Y. (1980). Development of contrast sensitivity in infant *Maccaca nemestrina* monkeys. *Science, 208,* 1290–1292.

Braddick, O., & Atkinson, J. (1987). Sensory selectivity, attentional control, and cross-channel integration in early visual development. In A. Yonas (Ed.), *Perceptual development in infancy: The Minnesota Symposium on Child Psychology* (pp. 105–143). Hillsdale, NJ: Lawrence Erlbaum Associates.

Braddick, O., Wattam-Bell, J., & Atkinson, J. (1986). Orientation specific cortical responses develop early in infancy. *Nature, 320,* 617–619.

Bronson, G. W. (1974). The postnatal growth of visual capacity. *Child Development, 45,* 874–890.

Brown, A. M., Dobson, V., & Maier, J. (1987). Visual acuity of human infants at scotopic, mesopic and photopic luminances. *Vision Research, 27,* 1845–1858.

Campbell, F. W., & Gubisch, R. W. (1966). Optical quality of the human eye. *Journal of Physiology, 186,* 558–578.

Campbell, F. W., & Kulikowski, J. J. (1966). Orientation selectivity of the human visual system. *Journal of Physiology, 187,* 437–445.

Clavadetscher, J. M., Brown, A. M., Ankrum, C., & Teller, D. Y. (1988). Spectral sensitivity and chromatic discrimination in 3- and 7-week-old human infants. *Journal of the Optical Society of America A, 5,* 2093–2105.

Coletta, N. J., Williams, D. R., & Tiana, C. L. M. (1990). Consequences of spatial sampling for human motion perception. *Vision Research, 30,* 1631–1648.

Cornsweet, T. (1970). *Visual perception.* Orlando, FL: Harcourt Brace Jovanovich.

Crowell, J. A., & Banks, M. S. (1991). *The efficiency of foveal vision.* Manuscript submitted for publication.

Dannemiller, J. L., & Banks, M. S. (1983). The development of light adaptation in human infants. *Vision Research, 23,* 599–610.

Derrington, A. M., & Fuchs, A. F. (1981). The development of spatial-frequency selectivity in kitten striate cortex. *Journal of Physiology, 316,* 1–10.

Dobson, V., & Teller, D. Y. (1978). Visual acuity in human infants: A review and comparison of behavioral and electrophysiological techniques. *Vision Research, 18,* 1469–1483.

Estevez, O. (1979). *On the fundamental data-base of normal and dichromatic color vision.* Unpublished doctoral dissertation, University of Amsterdam, The Netherlands.

Geisler, W. S. (1984). Physical limits of acuity and hyperacuity. *Journal of the Optical Society of America A, 1,* 775–782.

Geisler, W. S. (1989). Sequential ideal-observer analysis of visual discriminations. *Psychological Review, 96,* 267–314.

Green, D. G. (1970). Regional variations in the visual acuity for interference fringes on the retina. *Journal of Physiology, 207,* 351–356.

Green, D. M., & Swets, J. A. (1966). *Signal detection theory and psychophysics.* New York: Robert E. Krieger.

Hainline, L., Harris, C. M., & Krinsky, S. J. (1990). Variability of refixations in infants. *Infant Behavior and Development, 13,* 321–342.

Hamaski, D. I., & Flynn, J. T. (1977). Physiological properties of retinal ganglion cells of 3-week-old kittens. *Vision Research, 17,* 275–284.

Hamer, R. D., Alexander, K., & Teller, D. Y. (1982). Rayleigh discriminations in young human infants. *Vision Research, 22,* 575–588.

Hansen, R. M., & Fulton, A. B. (1981). Behavioral measurement of background adaptation in infants. *Investigative Ophthalmology and Visual Science, 21,* 621–629.

Hendrickson, A., & Kupfer, C. (1976). The histogenesis of the fovea in the macaque monkey. *Investigative Ophthalmology, 15,* 746–756.

Hickey, T. L., & Peduzzi, J. D. (1987). Structure and development of the visual system. In P. Salapatek & L. B. Cohen (Eds.), *Handbook of infant perception: From sensation to perception* (pp. 1–42). New York: Academic Press.

Hirano, S., Yamamoto, Y., Takayama, H., Sugata, Y., & Matsuo, K. (1979). Ultrasonic observations of eyes in premature babies: Part 6. Growth curves of ocular axial length and its components. *Acta Societatis Ophthalmologicae Japonicae, 83,* 1679–1693.

Howell, E. R., & Hess, R. F. (1978). The functional area for summation to threshold for sinusoidal gratings. *Vision Research, 18,* 369–374.

Hubel, D. H., & Wiesel, T. N. (1963). Receptive fields of cells in striate cortex of very young, visually inexperienced kittens. *Journal of Neurophysiology, 26,* 994–1002.

Jacobs, D. S., & Blakemore, C. (1988). Factors limiting the postnatal development of visual acuity in the monkey. *Vision Research, 28,* 947–958.

Kelly, D. H. (1977). Visual contrast sensitivity. *Optica Acta, 24,* 107–129.

Kiely, P. M., Crewther, S. G., Nathan, J., Brennan, N. A., Efron, N., & Madigan, M. (1987). A comparison of ocular development of the cynomolgus monkey and man. *Clinical Visual Science, 3,* 269–280.

Larsen, J. S. (1971). The sagittal growth of the eye: IV. Ultrasonic measurement of the axial length of the eye from birth to puberty. *Acta Ophthalmologica, 49,* 873–886.

Legge, G., Kersten, D., & Burgess, A. E. (1987). Contrast discrimination in noise. *Journal of the Optical Society of America A, 4,* 391–404.

Lewis, T. L., Maurer, D., & Kay, D. (1978). Newborns' central vision: Whole or hole? *Journal of Experimental Child Psychology, 26,* 193–203.

Movshon, J. A., & Kiorpes, L. (1988). Analysis of the development of contrast sensitivity in monkey and human infants. *Journal of the Optical Society of America A, 5,* 2166–2172.

Mullen, K. T. (1985). The contrast sensitivity of human color vision to red/green and blue/yellow chromatic gratings. *Journal of Physiology, 359,* 381–400.

Naegele, J. R., & Held, R. (1982). The postnatal development of monocular optokinetic nystagmus in infants. *Vision Research, 22,* 341–346.

Norcia, A. M., & Tyler, C. W. (1985). Spatial frequency sweep VEP: Visual acuity during the first year of life. *Vision Research, 25,* 1399–1408.

Norcia, A. M., Tyler, C. W., & Allen, D. (1986). Electrophysiological assessment of contrast sensitivity in human infants. *American Journal of Optometry and Physiological Optics, 63,* 12–15.

Packer, O., Hartmann, E. E., & Teller, D. Y. (1984). Infant color vision: The effect of test field size on Rayleigh discriminations. *Vision Research, 24,* 1247–1260.

Peeples, D. R., & Teller, D. Y. (1975). Color vision and brightness discrimination in two-month-old infants. *Science, 189,* 1102–1103.

Pelli, D. (1990). Quantum efficiency of vision. In C. Blakemore (Ed.), *Vision: Coding and efficiency* (pp. 3–24). New York: Cambridge University Press.

Pirchio, M., Spinelli, D., Fiorentini, A., & Maffei, L. (1978). Infant contrast sensitivity evaluated by evoked potentials. *Brain Research, 141,* 179–184.

Rose, A. (1942). The relative sensitivities of television pick-up tubes, photographic film, and the human eye. *Proceedings of Institute of Radio Engineers, 30,* 293–300.

Salapatek, P. (1975). Pattern perception in early infancy. In P. Salapatek & L. B. Cohen (Eds.), *Infant perception: From sensation to cognition* (pp. 133–234). New York: Academic Press.

Salapatek, P., & Kessen, W. (1966). Visual scanning of triangles by the human newborn. *Journal of Experimental Child Psychology, 3,* 155–167.

Shimojo, S., & Held, R. (1987). Vernier acuity is less than grating acuity in 2- and 3-month-olds. *Vision Research, 27,* 77–86.

Slater, A. M., & Findlay, J. M. (1975). Binocular fixation in the newborn baby. *Journal of Experimental Child Psychology, 20,* 248–273.

Teller, D. Y., & Bornstein, M. H. (1987). Infant color vision and color perception. In L. B. Cohen & P. Salapatek (Eds.), *Handbook of infant perception: From sensation to perception* (pp. 185–236). New York: Academic Press.

Teller, D. Y., Peeples, D. R., & Sekel, M. (1978). Discrimination of chromatic from white light by two-month-old infants. *Vision Research, 18,* 41–48.

Varner, D., Cook, J. E., Schneck, M. R., McDonald, M. A., & Teller, D. Y. (1985). Tritan discriminations by 1- and 2-month-old human infants. *Vision Research, 25,* 821–832.

Walraven, P. L. (1974). A closer look at the tritanopic convergence point. *Vision Research, 14,* 1339–1343.

Watson, A. B. (1987). The ideal observer concept as a modeling tool. In *Frontiers of visual science: Proceedings of the 1985 Symposium* (pp. 32–37). Washington, DC: National Academy of Sciences.

Watson, A. B., Barlow, H. B., & Robson, J. G. (1983). What does the eye see best? *Nature, 31,* 419–422.

Werner, J. S. (1982). Development of scotopic sensitivity and the absorption spectrum of the human ocular media. *Journal of the Optical Society of America, 72,* 247–258.

Williams, D. R. (1985). Aliasing in human foveal vision. *Vision Research, 25,* 195–206.

Wilson, H. R. (1988). Development of spatiotemporal mechanisms in infant vision. *Vision Research, 28,* 611–628.

Yuodelis, C., & Hendrickson, A. (1986). A qualitative and quantitative analysis of the human fovea during development. *Vision Research, 26,* 847–876.

2

Motion Nulling Techniques and Infant Color Vision

Davida Y. Teller
Delwin T. Lindsey
University of Washington

Since the 1970s, a variety of studies of infant chromatic discriminations and related topics have been carried out (reviewed by Brown, 1990; Teller & Bornstein, 1987). Most of the studies of chromatic discrimination have been motivated by classical trichromatic color theory, and the paradigms used have been guided by an interest in probing the functional maturity of the very earliest stage of chromatic processing in the visual system, that is, the photoreceptors.

The logic has been as follows: The initial encoding of wavelength information is made possible by the presence in the human retina of three different types of photoreceptors, the long-wavelength-sensitive (LWS), mid-wavelength-sensitive (MWS), and short-wavelength-sensitive (SWS) cones.[1] Moreover, certain classes of adults, called *dichromats,* demonstrate highly specific losses of chromatic discrimination that stem from having only two, rather than all three, functional classes of cones. In adults, there are diagnostic tests for these color discrimination deficiencies. The most straightforward of these are called *Rayleigh* discriminations, which are possible only if the observer has both LWS cones

---

[1]The nomenclature used in color vision is confusing, and has undergone changes with time. Historically, cone types have sometimes been referred to by color names (e.g., *blue, green,* and *red* cones). However, most modern color theorists reserve color names to refer to color appearances or sensations, and not to elements of the neural substrate. Some modern theorists use the initials B, G, and R to refer to cone types, because they have mnemonic value in relation to the more familiar color names. Other color vision theorists prefer the terms S or SWS (short-wavelength-sensitive), M or MWS (mid-wavelength-sensitive), and L or LWS (long-wavelength-sensitive) cones, respectively.

and MWS cones, and *tritan* discriminations, which are possible only if the observer has SWS cones in addition to one other cone type. (For a more extended treatment, see Boynton, 1979; Teller & Bornstein, 1987.)

The earliest studies of infant color discrimination were designed to determine the earliest age at which infants can make Rayleigh discriminations and tritan discriminations. That is, at how early an age can infants provide the classical evidence that their LWS, MWS, and SWS cones are functional? A brief answer to this question is that, in general, 1-month-olds perform poorly at chromatic discrimination tasks, including both Rayleigh and tritan discriminations, whereas 2-month-olds generally succeed at both when large color differences are used. Thus, we have evidence that the minimal neural machinery—including in particular the photoreceptors—necessary for these tasks is present and functional in most 2-month-olds. In 1-month-olds, a critical immaturity somewhere in the system prevents these discriminations from being performed.

But what kind of immaturity is this? One-month-olds do not seem to be dichromats; that is, they do not demonstrate the highly specific patterns of chromatic confusions shown by specific kinds of adult dichromats. They do not tend to fail on tritan discriminations while succeeding on Rayleigh discriminations, or vice versa; rather, they seem to demonstrate a generalized color weakness across both diagnostic tests. Thus, the data provide no support for the idea that infants suffer from a differential loss of any particular photoreceptor type with respect to the others. Moreover, discrimination failures are negative results, and they provide no information concerning whether the critical immaturities leading to the discrimination failures are receptoral, postreceptoral, or both. (See Banks & Bennett, 1988; Banks & Shannon, this volume; Brown, 1990, for further critical reviews and interpretations of this work.)

During the past few years, we have been developing an alternative approach to studying infant color vision. Our reasons for doing so are first, that the preferential looking techniques used in earlier studies are laborious, and second, that we have become interested in setting studies of infant color vision in a wider and more complete theoretical context. In theories of adult color vision, it is widely agreed that the signals initiated by the different photoreceptor types do not remain separated for very long, but instead are combined by summing and differencing into at least three postreceptoral channels: one luminance channel and two chromatic channels (described further on). We believe that experimental paradigms designed to probe the maturation of these channels are likely to provide a broad range of interesting data about the development of color vision.

Our approach involves the use of a color video-based visual display system. The video system is programmed to allow modulation of the luminance and chromaticity of the stimuli in any direction in a three-dimensional color space and to allow spatially modulated patterns to be moved across the video screen. To date, we have carried out several studies on adult subjects (Lindsey, 1990; Lindsey & Teller, 1988, 1989, 1990; Teller & Lindsey, 1990). We have also carried out two studies on infant subjects using motion nulling techniques made possible by the new video equipment, and using optokinetic nystagmus (OKN) as the response measure (Teller & Lindsey, 1988, 1989).

In the present chapter, we first describe OKN motion nulling techniques as we use them with infants. A brief, informal introduction to some concepts from color theory will then be presented, with emphasis on the concepts of three-dimensional color spaces, postreceptoral channels, and null plane analysis. Although a complete technical account is beyond the scope of this chapter, and although some aspects of this treatment are still controversial among color theorists, we hope to provide the reader with both an intuitive feel for the uses and limitations of three-dimensional spaces in thinking about infant color vision and a translation of some concepts from older work in infant color vision into this context. A more advanced treatment of these concepts can be found in Teller and Lindsey (in press).

The first two experiments we have undertaken on infants using the new system are then described. These experiments deal with infants' luminance matches and with infants' sensitivity to color versus luminance variations.

MOTION NULLING TECHNIQUES

The Motion Nulling Paradigm

Motion nulling techniques were introduced into systematic studies of adult color vision by Anstis and Cavanagh (1983; Cavanagh, MacLeod, & Anstis, 1987). In addition, the present work owes a great debt to Maurer, Lewis, Cavanagh, and Anstis (1989), who first used these techniques on human infants.

The stimulus paradigm involved in motion nulling is shown schematically in Fig. 2.1. The subject views a video display on which are presented two stimulus components, superimposed on each other, moving in opposite directions. In the example shown in Fig. 2.1, the two components are a white (i.e., white/black) sinusoidal grating of fixed space-average luminance and contrast, moving in one direction, and a red (i.e., red/black) sinusoidal grating of fixed space-average luminance but variable contrast, moving in the opposite direction. The fixed stimulus component (here, the white) is called the *standard* stimulus, and the variable stimulus component is called the *test* stimulus.

Under such circumstances, for an adult subject, the perceived direction of motion depends upon the contrast of the test stimulus. If the contrast of the test grating is very low, the perceived direction of motion will be dominated by the standard grating; if the contrast of the test grating is very high, the perceived direction of motion is dominated by the test grating. If the contrast of the test grating is varied systematically, there will exist a contrast level somewhere in the middle, at which neither stimulus component dominates the other.

MOTION NULLING PARADIGM

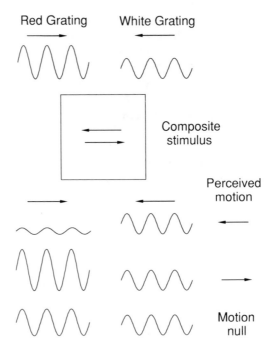

FIG. 2.1. Motion nulling paradigm (schematic). The paradigm involves two stimulus components moving in opposite directions, here a red grating moving rightward and a white grating moving leftward (first row). Both gratings are sinusoidal:
that is, the schematic sinusoid indicates the variation of luminance (*y* axis) across
space (*x* axis), and variations in the vertical extent of the schematic sinusoid
represent variations of the contrast of the grating. Each of the stimulus components looks like a set of fuzzy or blurred stripes.

    The two components are combined and the composite stimulus is displayed
on a color video screen (second row). The contrast of one grating, here the red,
is varied. When the contrast of the red grating is low (third row), the white grating dominates and leftward motion is perceived. When the contrast of the red
grating is high (fourth row), it dominates and rightward motion is perceived. At
some intermediate contrast value (fifth row), the effects of the two stimuli are
balanced, and neither direction of motion is perceived; this value is the motion null.

The subject's perceptions at this point may be complex: For example, he or
she may report that the stimulus appears to shimmer, and/or that it reverses
direction from one moment to the next. However, there will be no single,
predominant direction of motion. This value defines the motion null point.

    Why would motion null points be interesting? The general theoretical notion
is that there is some neural analyzer or circuit that determines our perception
of the direction of motion under these conditions, and that whichever stimulus

component produces the larger signal for this mechanism will control the perceived direction of motion. At the null point, it is as though the test and standard components contribute equal and opposite signals to this motion analyzer, so that they exactly balance, and neither direction of motion can be perceived. The goal of the research is to find sets of such null values, and use them to constrain theories about the inputs to the neural circuits that control the perception of motion under these conditions.

Optokinetic Nystagmus (OKN) as a Response Measure

A close analogue of motion null points can be measured in infant subjects, using the pattern of eye movements known as optokinetic nystagmus, or OKN. If a boldly patterned stimulus is moved in front of an infant, the infant's eyes (like those of an adult) will track in the direction of motion of the stimulus, then saccade back, track and saccade back, and so on. If the stimulus is moving rightward, the slow tracking phase of the eye movements will be to the right, and vice versa. An adult observer can watch the infant's eye movements on a video monitor, and judge the presence or absence, and the direction, of the OKN, or make a forced-choice judgment as to whether the stimulus is moving leftward or rightward (Hainline, de Bie, Abramov, & Camenzuli, 1987; Maurer et al., 1989; Teller, 1979).

Maurer et al. (1989) showed that motion nulls can be measured readily in this way in infant as well as adult subjects. They also asked adult subjects to report the perceived direction of motion of the grating, and these reports agreed with the judged direction of the OKN on virtually every trial. So, at least in adults, the OKN measure is perfectly correlated with the perceived direction of motion, and this correspondence adds some face validity to the OKN measure as an indicator of infant motion perception.

Unfortunately, OKN nulling techniques have three major limitations for studies of color vision (Teller & Lindsey, 1989). The first is that OKN is best elicited when the stimulus fields are very large, such that the stimuli cover large regions of the retina, rather than being confined to a small area at a single retinal eccentricity. This is a problem because the retina is not homogeneous, and in adult subjects the characteristics of color vision vary across the retina. The second is that the only feasible way to make these stimuli—particularly the sinusoidal gratings, which are important for our purposes—is to use a color video system. The color video system we have used produces only moderate brightness levels; and the range of colors—the color gamut—that can be produced by any color video system is limited. Third, of course, one can only use OKN techniques to study *moving* stimuli—a generally non-traditional approach to color vision. These limitations influence the range and precision of experiments, and complicate the interpretation of the data.

COLOR THEORY AND NULL PLANE ANALYSIS

As already discussed, the initial encoding of wavelength information is made possible by the fact that the human retina contains three different types of cone photoreceptors: the LWS, MWS, and SWS cones. However, the signals initiated by the different photoreceptor types do not remain separated for very long, but instead are combined by summing and differencing into at least three postreceptoral channels (Hurvich & Jameson, 1957). Most recent theorists assume that there is one *luminance* (or brightness) channel, in which signals from different cone types are summed, and two *chromatic* (or opponent) channels, in which differences are taken between signals from different cone types.

There is not yet universal agreement among color theorists concerning the exact pattern of the initial postreceptoral recoding. However, there is a simple, rather generic theory (see Boynton, 1979), which we adopt for the present purposes. This theory posits that there is a single, spectrally non-opponent luminance channel, made by summing the inputs from LWS and MWS cones. There are also two spectrally opponent chromatic channels, made by differencing the signals from different cone types: an r/g (for red/green) channel, made by taking a difference between LWS and MWS cones, and a tritan channel, made by taking a difference between SWS cones and the sum of LWS and MWS cones.[2]

This particular chromatic recoding scheme receives some psychophysical support from the differing degrees to which stimuli along these two chromatic axes support the perception of borders (Tansley & Boynton, 1976), and from the relatively high degree of independence of adaptational influences between stimuli modulated along the two chromatic axes (Krauskopf, Williams, & Heeley, 1982). It has also received some support, at the physiological level, in that single cells recorded at early levels of the visual system appear to conform, at least partially, to this code (Derrington, Krauskopf, & Lennie, 1984).

Of course, outside the central fovea the retina also contains a fourth photoreceptor type, the rods. Rod-initiated signals do not enter into foveal color vision. However—and here is the problem—when one uses large stimulus fields of moderate luminance, as we must in these studies, there is always a possibility that these signals also contribute to the observed behavior.

---

[2]The use of color names for the postreceptoral channels in color theory can also result in confusions. Such problems are avoided here by using the terms *r/g* and *tritan* to refer to the theoretically derived postreceptoral channels specified in the three-dimensional model.

Earlier versions of opponent process theories of color vision (e.g., Hurvich & Jameson, 1957) have differed from this scheme. One major difference is that in the earlier models the two chromatic axes were defined to coincide with the axes formed by the two mutually exclusive pairs of unique hues: red/green and blue/yellow. The present r/g axis differs very little from the classical red/green axis, but the tritan axis differs substantially from the earlier blue/yellow axis. These differences are of major importance in color theory, but will be set aside for the present purposes.

There is general agreement from a variety of sources that rod-initiated sig-, nals do not have their own pathway out of the retina. Thus, if these signals are to have any visual effect they must be combined into one or more of the three channels already described. It is quite universally agreed that rods contribute to the extrafoveal luminance channel. There is no agreement about whether or how rod signals enter the other two channels, and for present purposes this possibility will be ignored.

A Geometrical Model of the Postreceptoral Channels

Color theorists find it useful to employ three-dimensional geometry to represent visual stimuli in terms of the responses of each of the three cone types (e.g., Cornsweet, 1970), or in terms of the responses elicited in each of the three putative postreceptoral channels. We here digress to consider the characteristics of such three-dimensional representations in some detail, because such representations allow some very interesting logical characteristics of chromatic processing to be understood readily at the intuitive level. Moreover, these characteristics provide the motivation for the infant experiments to be discussed further on.

A three-dimensional postreceptoral channels space, with the signals in the luminance, r/g, and tritan channels represented on the three axes, and with possible rod inputs omitted, is shown in Fig. 2.2A (modified from Derrington et al., 1984). The vertical axis represents activity in the luminance channel. The two chromatic axes define a horizontal plane, with the r/g axis defined as 0° and the tritan axis as 90° within that plane. Because this plane is perpendicular to the luminance axis, all stimuli represented within it have the same luminance, or are *isoluminant*. The origin of the space is the *white point*, which represents an achromatic stimulus that is matched in luminance to the other (chromatic) stimuli that fall in the isoluminant plane.

Light of any given color and brightness will provide a specific signal in each cone type, and thus, by sums and differences, a specific signal in each of the three postreceptoral channels. Thus, visual stimuli, including the red, green, and blue video phosphors[3] used to generate our moving gratings, can be represented as points in this space. Such a representation makes explicit the signal that each stimulus will generate in each of the three putative postreceptoral channels.

---

[3]A minor exception to the rule of using color names only to describe color appearances is that we refer to the three video phosphors by the terms *red, green,* and *blue*. Because video phosphors have exactly defined spectra, their locations can be plotted exactly in Fig. 2.2. The determination of color appearance is complex, and not wholly dependent on spectral composition, so the locations of lights that have particular color appearances are only approximate.

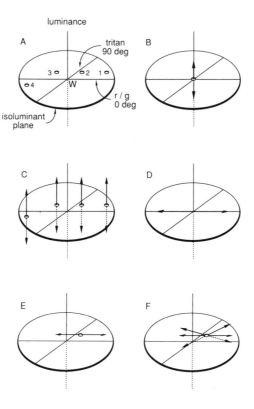

FIG. 2.2. Three-dimensional representation of postreceptoral color space, modified from Derrington et al. (1984). A: The putative luminance, r/g, and tritan responses are plotted on three orthogonal axes, with the origin at a nominal "white" point W. Any visual stimulus will provide a specific signal in each cone type, and thus a specific signal in each of the three putative postreceptoral channels. The plane defined by the two chromatic axes, perpendicular to the luminance axis, is the isoluminant plane. The numbers 1, 3, and 4 represent the locations of the (luminance-matched) red, green, and blue video phosphors, respectively, used to generate the stimuli. A set of isoluminant red-, yellow-, green-, and blue-appearing stimuli would be represented approximately at locations 1, 2, 3, and 4, respectively.

Schematic representations of modulations along various axes in color space. B: Luminance modulation through the "white" point (representing the standard stimulus for Experiment I). C: Luminance modulations of isochromatic stimuli: red, green, and blue (representing the test stimuli for Experiment I) and yellow (representing the standard stimulus for Experiment II). D: Chromatic modulation along the r/g axis. E: Chromatic modulation of a red/green grating, parallel to the r/g axis (representing the test stimulus for Experiment II). F: Variations of "elevation" for the red/green grating, in and slightly out of the isoluminant plane (representing the variations of relative luminance of the red/green grating used in Experiment II).

Null Plane Analysis

One of the logical characteristics that arises from such a plot is that *null planes* exist for each of the three channels. That is, the optimal variation in the activity of a given channel will be generated by using a spatial pattern (say, a set of stripes or a sinusoidal grating) made up of a set of lights represented along the axis corresponding to that channel (or a line parallel to it). In contrast, a spatial pattern made up of a set of lights that fall within any plane perpendicular to a given axis will make no spatial variation in the signal in the channel represented by that axis.

Thus, within the context of this theoretical approach, by judicious choice or custom designing of stimuli, it should be possible to create spatial patterns that we see with only one or two of our color/luminance channels, but not all three. Thinking in terms of the photoreceptor level, we can design spatial patterns that we see only with LWS cones, or only with LWS and MWS cones, and so on. In fact, the Rayleigh and tritan diagnostic tests for classical color deficiencies, described in the introduction, are based on exactly this principle.

In addition, thinking in terms of putative postreceptoral channels, we can design spatial patterns that we see only, for example, with our luminance channel, or only with our r/g or tritan channel; or, alternatively, with both r/g and tritan channels but not with the luminance channel. In this way we can ask what the properties of vision are when we "see" only through each individual channel, or when two or all three channels are used in various combinations.

Using these concepts from three-dimensional geometry, it becomes easy to think about a whole realm of perceptual experiments. Suppose that the signals in the three different putative channels were to be separated and were to travel in completely different pathways (or processing "streams") in later stages of visual processing. Suppose that the three different signals were to access different sets of processing modules and be involved in sustaining different visual functions.

If signals carried in, say, the tritan channel did not participate in the analysis of borders, then stimuli custom-designed to be "seen" through only the tritan channel should not sustain the perception of borders. Or if signals in the chromatic channels did not access face recognition, then faces should be unrecognizable using stimuli that make only chromatic signals. From such a perspective we might predict failures of particular visual functions—perhaps dramatic failures—to occur when particular, highly specific stimuli selected to fall within particular null planes are used. Such losses would provide an exact analogy to the dramatic, highly specific failures of discrimination that occur in dichromats because of a loss of an individual cone type, but would be caused by the loss of access of a postreceptoral channel to a particular functional element of the neural processing machinery.

Empirical Null Planes.   Some of these ideas appear to work out in practice, as demonstrated by the adult literature on the use of isoluminant stimuli.
The horizontal plane perpendicular to the luminance axis in Fig. 2.2A is a plane
in which color varies but luminance remains constant, or in the current jargon,
an *isoluminant plane.* By using isoluminant stimuli—spatial or temporal patterns
made up of lights of different colors, all of which fall within an isoluminant plane—
one can examine the characteristics of vision sustained solely by the chromatic
channels in the absence of a differential signal from the luminance channel.

Experiments with isoluminant stimuli are currently attracting a great deal of
interest in color vision and perception research. The reason for this interest
is that a variety of perceptual functions, including motion perception, may be
poorly sustained at isoluminance. For example, suppose one were to make a
spatial pattern out of red and green stripes, set it in motion, and vary the luminance of the green with respect to the red. As the luminance of the green
stripes approaches that of the red, the perceived motion slows down or even
stops completely (Cavanagh, Tyler, & Favreau, 1984; Lindsey & Teller, 1990).
Or, when two stimuli are nulled against each other in motion nulling paradigms,
such as the one described earlier, the motion null turns out to occur when the
two stimuli are isoluminant (Anstis & Cavanagh, 1983; Cavanagh et al., 1987).
In addition to motion, many other visual functions, including stereopsis, border
perception, and accommodation, show distinct perceptual minima at or near
isoluminance.[4]

Alternative Coding Schemes and Infant Development.   What if the
luminance, r/g, and tritan channels do not actually provide a correct description
of the chromatic/luminance code, and/or what if color/brightness information
is recoded later into a different set of channels? If such recodings were to occur, then null planes could occur in locations not predicted from this particular
model, cutting through this space at unpredicted angles. Conversely, if they
do exist, the locations of such planes for a particular visual function (say, some
aspect of the perception of motion) could be taken to reveal the neural coding
at the level of that particular functional stage (e.g., a particular motion processing module).

Finally, what if infants had differential immaturities in one or another channel, or a novel chromatic code that differs from ours? Then, by the same logic,
infants should show performance failures or performance minima at novel loci

---

[4]The term *isoluminance* is used with at least two meanings. Technically, one would specify the
lights that fall in the isoluminant plane by use of an international standard such as V_λ (Boynton,
1979), and then ask how closely the observed perceptual minima conform to the V_λ-defined
isoluminant plane. However, in informal usage the perceptual minimum is also often called the
isoluminance point.

Brief reviews and access to the developing literature on vision at isoluminance can be found
in Troscianko (1987) and Lindsey and Teller (1990).

in color space, and their pattern of failures or performance minima should help to reveal the nature of their color/brightness code. It is these ideas that have excited us and motivated our experiments in both infant and adult vision.

Stimulus Modulation in Color Space

One final concept that requires explication is that of stimulus *modulation* in a particular direction or along a particular axis in color space. The concept of modulation refers to spatial or temporal variation or change. A square-wave grating made of black and white stripes, or a sinusoidal grating varying in luminance (white–grey–black–grey–white), is said to be *luminance-modulated*. In three-dimensional channels space, the spatial components of this stimulus would differ from each other solely along the luminance axis, as shown in Fig. 2.2B. In theory, such a stimulus makes a spatially varying signal solely in the luminance channel; the other two channels "see" no spatial variation, but only a homogeneous field of light. A white, luminance-modulated grating is used as the standard grating in Experiment I (described further on).

Similarly, but perhaps counterintuitively, a red grating, even though described by a color name, is also predominantly luminance-modulated. As shown in Fig. 2.2C, it is represented by modulation along a line that passes through the isoluminant plane at a point displaced from the origin, but still parallel or nearly parallel to the luminance axis. It thus makes its main spatially varying signal in the luminance channel. The same will be true of any *isochromatic* stimulus; that is, any stimulus made by spatial luminance modulation of a light that retains a single color (or more properly, a single spectral composition). Thus, red, green, blue, or yellow gratings are all predominantly luminance-modulated. In Experiment I, red, green, and blue luminance-modulated gratings are used as test gratings, and nulled against the white standard grating. In addition, a yellow luminance-modulated grating appears as the standard grating in Experiment II.

In contrast, a grating made solely of spatial variations in color (or more properly, spatial variations in spectral composition but not luminance) is said to be *chromatically modulated*. Such stimuli could be modulated along the r/g axis, as schematized in Fig. 2.2D, or along the tritan axis, or in general along any line that falls within the isoluminant plane, on or off the major axes. A red/green-appearing, chromatically modulated grating, made by modulating along a line slightly displaced from the r/g axis but nearly parallel to it, is shown in Fig. 2.2E. This stimulus is used as the test grating in Experiment II.

Because the infant's isoluminant plane is not exactly known, one cannot specify a priori the stimuli that will fall within it. Thus, in Experiment II a series of different stimuli are used, representing slight variations of the relative luminances of the red and green bars of the red/green test grating. In three-dimensional channel space, these stimuli are represented as modulations along a set of axes that take on a series of different tilts above and below the nominal isoluminant plane, as shown in Fig. 2.2F. These stimuli, and all stimuli modulated along an axis other than the luminance axis or axes within the isoluminant plane, are modulated in both chromaticity and luminance simultaneously to varying degrees.

Experiments With Infants

In sum, infants can be tested with a motion nulling paradigm, using OKN as the behavioral response, with pairs of stimuli modulated along carefully chosen lines in a theoretically derived color space. Such experiments can be used to infer the relative sensitivity of the infant to the two stimuli that are nulled against each other, and thus to pose specific questions about the infant's luminance/color vision.

Two experiments carried out in this conceptual framework are described here. Experiment I explores the infant's relative sensitivity to luminance-modulated gratings of different spectral composition, and defines the infant's isoluminant plane. Experiment II explores the infant's ability to respond to red/green, purely chromatic modulations, and the infant's relative sensitivity to luminance-modulated versus red/green chromatically modulated gratings.

In fact, these new experiments ask old questions (Teller & Bornstein, 1987), albeit within a more theoretical context and with new stimuli. Experiment I, which concerns definition of the infant's isoluminant plane, is analogous to earlier experiments on infant spectral sensitivity (e.g., Peeples & Teller, 1978); that is, on variations in sensitivity with the wavelength composition of the stimulus.

In Experiment II, the red/green chromatic grating is used to address the question of discrimination within the isoluminant plane. This experiment is analogous to earlier experiments on infant chromatic discriminations (e.g., Peeples & Teller, 1975). Moreover, the introduction of small luminance modulations into the red/green grating in Experiment II—tilts of the axis of modulation slightly out of the nominal isoluminant plane—are analogous to the small variations of relative luminance used in earlier experiments on chromatic discrimination. In both cases, these luminance variations are introduced in order to avoid being fooled by infant "brightness mismatches," or deviations of the infant's isoluminant plane from that of adults, whether such deviations are caused by rod intrusion into the luminance channel or by other factors.

EXPERIMENT I: INFANT ISOLUMINANCE

In our first experiment (Teller & Lindsey, 1989), infants were tested with each of three luminance-modulated, isochromatic test gratings—red, green, and blue—made from the three phosphors of the color video system. The test grating moved across the color video screen in one direction. It was nulled against a fixed-contrast, white standard grating moving in the opposite direction. As illustrated in Fig. 2.1, the luminance modulation of the red, green, or blue test grating was varied to find the contrast needed to null the white standard grating.

All gratings were 0.3 c/deg sinusoids moving across the screen at a velocity of 25 deg/sec (7.5 Hz). The field size was approximately $50° \times 50°$ at the 30 cm test distance used. The space-average luminance of each component grating was fixed at 2.6 cd/m² (candela per square meter), so for both together it was 5.2 cd/m². The contrast of the white standard was fixed at 50% with respect to its *own* space-average luminance (25% when both gratings are present), while the contrast of the red, green, or blue test grating varied from trial to trial.

On each trial, the observer judged the presence or absence, and the direction, of OKN. OKN was usually judged to be present; the few judgments of no OKN have been divided equally between directions for simplicity in the following graphs. We used five trials per point, which turned out to be adequate to generate steep and monotonic psychometric functions that span the range from 0% to 100%.

Figure 2.3 shows psychometric functions from five infants and five adults tested with red, green, and blue test gratings. The abscissa shows the luminance

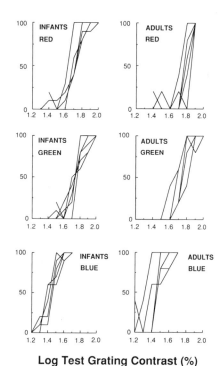

FIG. 2.3. Results of Experiment I. Individual psychometric functions are shown for five infants and five adults, tested with broadband red (top), green (middle), and blue (bottom) test gratings. Each test grating was nulled against a 50% contrast (1.7 log percent contrast) white standard grating. The abscissa shows the log contrast of the test grating. The ordinate shows the percent of trials on which the subject's OKN was judged to occur in the direction appropriate to the test grating. The contrast required to produce OKN in the test direction on 50% of the trials is taken as the motion null value.

% OKN in Test Direction

Log Test Grating Contrast (%)

modulation (contrast) of the red test grating, and the ordinate shows the percent of trials on which the OKN was judged to go in the direction appropriate to the test grating. As the contrast of the test grating increases, the percent of OKN in the test direction goes from near 0% to near 100%. For both infants and adults, the psychometric functions are quite steep and regular, even with only five trials per point. Remarkably, the functions from the infants look virtually as steep and regular as those of adults, and the individual differences among infants are, if anything, smaller than those among adults.

For each group of subjects, the psychometric functions were shifted along the abscissa to align with the group mean, and then averaged. Figure 2.4 shows the group averages for all three conditions, and summarizes the results from Experiment I. These data have several interesting features. First, for each test stimulus, infants and adults are remarkably similar in the amount of contrast that it takes to null a standard white grating. That is, by this large-field, motion-based measure, they have very similar or identical isoluminant planes. There is a small difference for the red grating, in that infants seem to require a little less contrast than adults, but this difference is not statistically significant.

Second, there is an interesting variation in the absolute values of contrast that are required for the nulls. The contrast of the standard grating was 50%, for a log percent contrast value of 1.7. So, if equal contrasts were always required for the isochromatic gratings to null the white standard grating, the value required would be 1.7 in every case, as marked by the arrows in Fig. 2.4. This

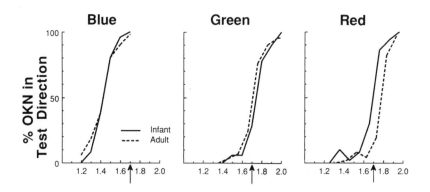

Log Test Grating Contrast (%)

FIG. 2.4.   Group averages for Experiment I. Axes as in Fig. 2.3. The arrows on the abscissae show the predicted null values if a contrast of 50% (log contrast of 1.7) were required for each chromatic test stimulus to null the 50% contrast white standard stimulus. Infants and adults give very similar performance for all three test stimuli. For red and green test stimuli the null values occur near 1.7 log contrast units, but for the blue test stimuli less contrast is required for the motion nulls.

prediction works for the red and green gratings, but interestingly, for the blue grating it doesn't work. Both infants and adults require a smaller than predicted contrast of the blue grating to null the white.

To account for these data, we developed a quantitative model of motion nulls. The details are presented elsewhere (Lindsey, 1990; Teller & Lindsey, 1989). Because the stimuli used are modulated mainly along the luminance dimension, it is assumed that all responses are mediated by the luminance channel. The heart of the model is the assumption mentioned earlier: that, at the motion null, the two stimuli being nulled against each other set up equal and opposite amplitudes of spatiotemporal variation in whatever neural circuit is controlling the perception of motion. We then calculated the null points that would be expected, based on a variety of different assumptions about the influences of LWS cones, MWS cones, and rods, and the absorption of light by the two preretinal pigments: lens pigment and macular pigment. These preretinal pigments are important because they absorb different wavelengths of light differentially, before the light gets to the photoreceptors; these preretinal filters can thus have an important impact on the shapes of empirical spectral sensitivity curves.

The predicted values are shown in Fig. 2.5. The abscissa of Fig. 2.5 shows the three test gratings: blue, green, and red. The vertical bars show the ranges of null values obtained for the five infants, with the group average values plotted at 0 on the ordinate. The adult values are very similar, and are not plotted. The ordinate shows the deviations of predicted values from the actual values obtained for the infants. The lines show the predictions from each of a series of different combinations of photoreceptor inputs and assumed densities of lens and macular pigments. If a particular analysis yielded predictions that were perfectly consistent with the data, all of the deviations would be 0.

Two simple hypotheses can be ruled out immediately. The curve labeled V_λ is the standard foveal photopic luminosity curve (as modified by Judd, 1951), which in adult color theory is usually modeled by the sum of inputs from LWS and MWS cones, and thus corresponds to our luminance axis. Compared to this prediction, both adults and infants are clearly too sensitive to modulations of the blue phosphor, so the model that the motion nulls are based purely on nulling inputs to a standard luminance channel can be rejected. Similarly, the curve labeled V'_λ shows the predictions based on rod inputs alone, and obviously this model can also be rejected.

What about preretinal filters? The curve labeled *lens* is (adult) V_λ corrected for the reduced density of the infant's lens pigmentation (Hansen & Fulton, 1989). As it turns out, the differences between the average lens density of infants and adults predict only very small differences in null values, with the largest difference expected for the blue phosphor. Even the difference for the blue phosphor is almost negligibly small, and in fact, no trace of it can be seen in the data of Figs. 2.3 and 2.4.

The curve labeled *MP* represents a calculation correcting (adult) V_λ to re-

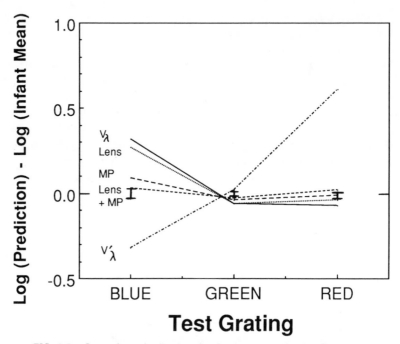

FIG. 2.5. Comparison of null values for the three test stimuli in Experiment I to predictions from a variety of adult luminous efficiency curves. Zero on the ordinate represents the infant average null values; vertical bars show ranges. Adult values were similar and are not plotted. The curves show predictions from standard adult rod-based (V'_λ) and foveal luminance-based (V_λ) spectral sensitivity curves, and for various corrections for lens and macular pigment variations. Both V_λ and V'_λ fail to fit the data. Corrections for lens and macular pigment provide a sufficient fit, but rod inputs cannot be ruled out.

move the effects of the macular pigment, a preretinal pigment found primarily near the fovea. As it happens, V_λ is originally defined through the use of small, foveally viewed stimuli, so the effects of the macular pigment are already built into V_λ. To predict spectral sensitivity for large fields, such as those used here, we have removed the effects of macular pigment by a mathematical correction that effectively reduces its density to 0. This correction makes a major improvement in the fit of the predicted curve to the data. The curve labeled *lens + MP* makes both corrections, and it may or may not improve the fit a little more. In any case, calculations that take the appropriate densities of preretinal filters into account provide reasonable fits to the data.

This outcome suggests that a standard LWS + MWS cone-based luminance channel, dominated by inputs from the peripheral retina and thus escaping the effects of the macular pigment, controls the null values seen in this experiment (cf. Maurer et al., 1989). On the other hand, a small assumed input from rod-initiated signals would also allow a good fit. Because there are only three degrees of freedom to the fit, the data do not have the statistical power to guide a decision regarding a variety of weightings of LWS cones, MWS cones, and rods, and additional evidence will be needed to reduce the options further.

In summary, the first experiment involved establishing the infant's isoluminant plane by nulling luminance-modulated isochromatic gratings—red, green, and blue—against white gratings. The experiment showed that OKN motion-nulling techniques can yield remarkably well-behaved data. Maurer et al.'s result, that infants and adults have highly similar isoluminant points when tested with such nulling techniques, proved to be well-replicated. All of these factors encouraged us to continue the use of the OKN nulling technique; and we undertook a second experiment, using a different form of modulation in color space and asking a different set of questions.

EXPERIMENT II: CHROMATIC
VERSUS ACHROMATIC SENSITIVITY

The previous research in infant color vision (Clavadetscher, Brown, Ankrum, & Teller, 1988; Teller & Bornstein, 1987) has made clear that very young infants respond very poorly to isoluminant chromatic stimuli. One-month-olds rarely demonstrate chromatic discrimination, and 2-month-olds require large color differences. Given their poor performance, it is tempting to wonder whether very young infants might have some kind of differential, specific weakness in the processing of purely chromatic, isoluminant stimulus patterns.

However, there is another alternative. Infants' sensitivity to luminance modulations is also poor (reviewed by Banks & Dannemiller, 1987), so (cf. Banks & Bennett, 1988; Brown, 1990) the question can be posed: Do infants suffer from a differential loss of sensitivity to purely chromatic stimuli, or from a uniform loss of sensitivity to both chromatic and luminance-modulated stimuli? In the context of color theory, do the chromatic channels lag behind the luminance channel during development, or are there uniform developmental sensitivity deficits that apply equally to both chromatic and luminance channels?

Motion-nulling techniques may provide an especially direct way to address this issue. To use motion nulling, one could superimpose a luminance-modulated grating moving in one direction and a chromatically modulated grating moving in the other direction, and ask which direction of motion dominates the OKN. If the chromatic grating is much more readily nulled by the luminance-modulated grating in infants than it is in adults, one would have support for a differential loss of chromatic sensitivity; if motion nulls turn out to be the same for infants as for adults, one would have support for the notion of uniform losses that apply to both luminance and chromatic channels.

This experiment is made conceptually complex by the fact that the coincidence of any given infant's (or adult's) isoluminant plane with the nominal isoluminant plane of Fig. 2.2 cannot be taken for granted; it may deviate from the nominal isoluminance of the idealized color space. For this reason, the chromatic grating has to be presented not only at nominal isoluminance (i.e., modulated in the nominal isoluminant plane), but also in combination with each of a series of values of luminance modulation (i.e., at various tilts out of the isoluminant plane). As will be seen, performance minima provide an internal check on the isoluminance value.

The stimuli for Experiment II are schematized in Fig. 2.6. The red and green components of the red/green grating were made from the isolated red and green phosphors of the color video, modulated out of spatial phase; the yellow/black gratings were constructed by modulating the same two phosphors in phase (i.e., superimposing the red and green bars). To keep the chromatic contrast high, the red and green components of the red/green grating were each always modulated at 100% (50% when both gratings are present), and their average luminances were traded off to vary the luminance difference between the red and green bars of the grating. In consequence, the color of the combined stimulus field varied slightly from one red/green luminance contrast to the next.

Infants of two ages, 4 weeks and 9 weeks, were tested. To take the infant's acuity limits into account, we used spatial frequencies of 0.15 c/deg for 4-week-olds and 0.3 c/deg for 9-week-olds. The adult data were also taken at 0.3 c/deg, but spatial frequency doesn't make much difference in this range for adults.

As the first phase of the experiment, we began by collecting extensive motion-nulling data on several individual pilot subjects. Two of these subjects are shown in Fig. 2.7. The abscissae in Fig. 2.7 show the luminance contrast between the red and green bars in the test grating. At the left the green bars are brighter than the red, at the right the red are brighter than the green, and 0 indicates the nominal isoluminance point. At isoluminance, the stimulus contains only

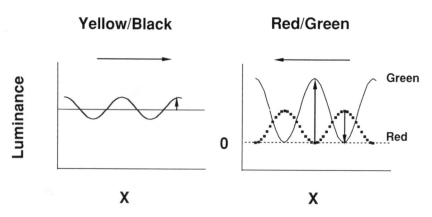

FIG. 2.6.   Stimuli for Experiment II. Axes as in Fig. 2.1. The vertical arrows represent the amplitudes of sinusoidal modulation. Yellow/black and red/green gratings were tested individually, and then nulled against each other.

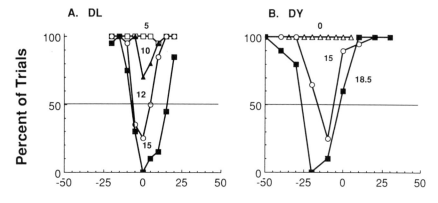

**Luminance Contrast (Percent)
in Red / Green Grating**

FIG. 2.7.   Illustrative results for the preliminary nulling phase of the experiment. In this phase of the experiment, extensive data were collected from individual subjects. Yellow/black and red/green gratings were nulled against each other. The abscissa shows the percent luminance contrast added to the red/green grating (i.e., the tilt out of the isoluminant plane of Fig. 2.2). Zero on the abscissa represents adult isoluminance. The ordinate shows the percent of trials on which the subject's OKN was judged to occur in the direction of the red/green grating.

A: Results for a single subject, DL, for various contrasts of the yellow/black nulling grating. The parameter on the curves is the contrast in the yellow/black grating. When the contrast of the yellow/black grating is low, the red/green gratings drive OKN, but they are weakest in the vicinity of isoluminance. At 15% contrast, the yellow/black grating dominates the subject's responses at isoluminance on all trials.

B: Results for a second subject. Note similarity to DL.

chromatic modulation; at any other value, it contains both chromatic and luminance modulation. The ordinate is the percent of trials on which the subject produces OKN in the direction dictated by the motion of the red/green grating. The parameter on the curves is the percent contrast of the yellow/black grating moving in the opposite direction: 0%, 5%, 10%, 12%, 15% or 18.5%.

The data of Fig. 2.7A are from one of the authors (DL), a color-normal adult. With the yellow/black grating at 0 contrast, the subject always showed OKN in the red/green direction. These data have been omitted for clarity. The same is true at 5% contrast. But as the contrast of the yellow/black grating increases, the subject stops producing OKN in the red/green direction, for a range of red/green luminance contrasts near nominal isoluminance. Instead, the subject produces OKN in the yellow/black direction on a greater and greater fraction of the trials. For this subject, the *equivalent achromatic contrast* of the red/green grating—the percent contrast of the yellow/black grating needed to reduce the response to the red/green grating to 50%—is between 10% and 12%. Thus, this particular red/green grating and a 10% to 12% contrast luminance grating null each other, or, by our model, produce equal spatial modulations in the neural mechanism that is controlling the motion null.

As the contrast of the yellow/black grating is increased further, the fraction of responses in the direction dictated by the red/green grating can be reduced to 0. For subject DL, 15% contrast in the yellow/black grating reduced this fraction just to 0 at isoluminance. For a second subject, DY, shown in Fig. 2.7B, 15% contrast of the yellow/black grating was not quite sufficient, but 18.5% contrast brought the minimum of the curve to 0.

Similar results from several color-normal adults tested with the 15% contrast yellow/black grating are shown in Fig. 2.8A. The 15% yellow/black contrast systematically brings color-normal subjects down to somewhere between 0% and 50% responding in the direction of motion of the red/green grating in the vicinity of isoluminance. Thus, for color-normal subjects, use of the 15% yellow/black grating allows use of the whole range of possible response percentages, and thus maximum statistical power. This 15% yellow/black grating was therefore the one we chose to use later, in the main experiment.

Figure 2.8B shows the results of the same experiment for a red/green color-deficient subject (in technical terms, an extreme deuteranomalous trichromat).

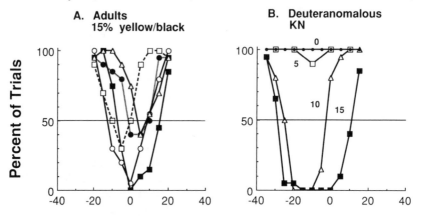

**Luminance Contrast (Percent)
in Red / Green Grating**

FIG. 2.8.   Additional results from preliminary nulling experiments.

A: Results for several adult subjects, tested with 15% contrast of the yellow/black grating. For color-normal adults, the 15% contrast yellow/black grating dominates the subjects' responses on the majority of trials over a narrow range in the vicinity of isoluminance. The 15% contrast yellow/black grating was used in the main experiment.

B: Results for a color-deficient (extreme deuteranomalous) adult subject. For this subject, the 15% contrast yellow/black grating virtually eliminates the response to the red/green grating over a wide range around isoluminance. Results from 0, 5%, and 10% contrast yellow/black gratings are also shown.

For this subject, the 15% yellow/black grating erases the response to the red/green grating over a substantial range of red/green luminance contrasts around isoluminance. We interpret this result as showing a differential loss of sensitivity in a chromatic as opposed to a luminance channel. So, the question becomes, what will a 15% yellow/black nulling grating do to infants? Will infants respond as the color-normal adults do, and lose the response to the red/green grating only in the immediate vicinity of isoluminance? Or will infants have the response to the red/green grating erased over a broad range, as the color-deficient subject does?

The main experiment consisted of three parts. First, we presented the yellow/black gratings alone, and measured luminance contrast thresholds. Second, we presented the red/green gratings alone, and measured responses to red/green gratings with a range of concomitant luminance modulations. Third, we tested red/green versus yellow/black gratings moving against each other in the full-blown nulling paradigm, using the 15% yellow/black grating chosen from the preliminary experiments.

For simplicity, the results are presented as group averages. Figure 2.9 shows the results for the first stimulus condition (the yellow/black grating) for 4-week-olds, 9-week-olds, and adults. The upper curves show the percent of trials on

Yellow / Black

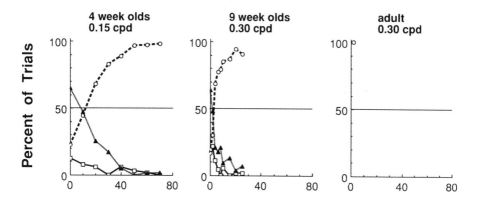

FIG. 2.9. Group average results for yellow/black gratings alone, for 4-week-olds, 9-week-olds, and adults. The abscissa shows the contrast in the yellow/black grating, and the ordinate shows the percent of trials on which OKN was judged to be in the direction of the yellow/black grating (○), or in the opposte (wrong) direction (□), or on which no OKN was judged to occur (▲). Infants, especially 4-week-olds, show lowered contrast sensitivity to the yellow/black grating.

which OKN was in the yellow/black direction, as a function of the contrast of the yellow/black grating. The adults showed yellow/black-appropriate OKN on 100% of the trials, even with 2% contrast, which was the lowest we could produce. The 9-week-olds showed a threshold contrast at about 3%, and the 4-week-olds required about 12%. We find, then, in agreement with the prior literature, that infants' contrast thresholds are elevated above those of adults, and 4-week-olds' above those of 9-week-olds.

The results for the second stimulus condition, red/green gratings alone, are shown in Fig. 2.10. For all luminance differences, for both adults and 9-week-olds, red/green-appropriate OKN occurred on virtually 100% of the trials, even at isoluminance. That is, for adults and 9-week-olds, isoluminant red/green gratings drive OKN when these large test fields are used. For 4-week-olds, however, this performance falls apart. Gratings that contain high luminance contrasts still produced appropriate OKN, so the response itself is robust, but in a broad range around isoluminance, only slightly over half of the trials yielded OKN in the direction of the motion of the chromatic test grating.

This result is consistent with earlier studies: One-month-olds respond only weakly, if at all, to isoluminant chromatic stimuli. However, the OKN is judged to go in the appropriate direction more frequently than in the wrong direction, so these infants must be said to be showing a marginal response to isoluminant red/green gratings.

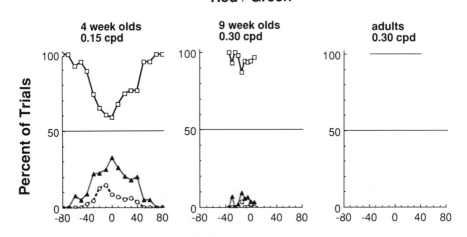

Red / Green

FIG. 2.10. Group averages for red/green gratings alone. The abscissa shows the luminance contrast in the red/green grating. The ordinate shows the percent of trials on which OKN was judged to be in the direction of the red/green grating (□), or in the opposite (wrong) direction (○), or on which no OKN was judged to occur (▲). Four-week-olds show lowered sensitivity to the red/green grating

Finally, the results for the nulling experiment are shown in Fig. 2.11. For all three groups, at the extremes of the red/green luminance range, we still get responses in the red/green direction, but in the middle, the red/green-appropriate OKN occurs on only somewhat less than half of the trials. The 15% contrast yellow/black grating nulls the red/green grating for all three age groups, and brings the responses down to minima below 50% for all three. In fact, of the three groups, the 4-week-olds showed the most robust response to the red/green gratings at the point of minimum response.

The curves for the three age groups also differ in breadth; in particular, the 4-week-olds required much larger changes in luminance contrast in the chromatic grating to produce substantial changes in the response than did the older age groups. This result doubtless stems from the fact that, as shown in the first part of the experiment (Fig. 2.9), the 4-week-olds are much less sensitive to small changes in luminance contrast than are the older subjects. To a first approximation, the slopes of their luminance curves in Fig. 2.9 correspond well to the slopes of each group's nulling curves—the sides of the U—in Fig. 2.11. Quantitative analysis of these aspects of the data remain to be carried out.

The results of Experiment II can be summarized as follows. First, tested with yellow/black gratings alone, as expected, young infants have a lowered sen-

Red / Green vs. Yellow / Black

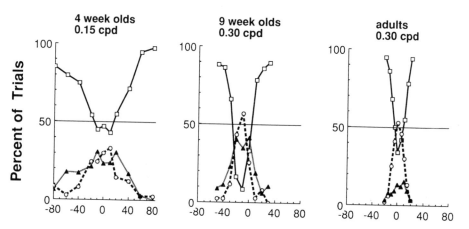

Luminance Contrast (Percent)
in Red / Green Grating

FIG. 2.11. Group averages for the nulling experiment. The ordinate shows the percent of trials on which OKN was judged to be in the direction of the yellow/black grating (○), or the red/green grating (□), or on which no OKN was judged to occur (▲). In all cases the yellow/black nulling grating was set to 15% contrast. The isoluminant red/green grating sustains control of the direction of OKN at least as well for 4-week-olds as it does for 9-week-olds and adults.

sitivity to luminance contrast. Second, tested with red/green gratings alone, 4-week-olds are much worse than 9-week-olds at making chromatic discriminations. Third, these sensitivity losses are at least approximately balanced, in that all three age groups produce similar minima when red/green gratings are nulled against yellow/black gratings. Quantitative justification of this conclusion, however, awaits more extensive data and theoretical analysis.

Finally, while we were doing the nulling experiment, we were lucky enough to encounter a 9-week-old "superbaby," DY, who produced enough trials to allow us to test her with several different contrasts of the yellow/black grating. Her data bear a remarkable resemblance to those of DL, and were in fact shown next to DL's in Fig. 2.7B. Most readers will doubtless have allowed themselves to be fooled into believing that DY was an adult! This degree of similarity between adult and infant data is rare in the infant vision literature.

In summary, the results of this experiment are difficult to reconcile with the idea that infants have any differential, specific loss of red/green chromatic processing. They are consistent with the idea of a generalized loss of sensitivity that applies to both r/g and luminance channels. These results also serve to emphasize a major advantage of the motion-nulling paradigm: It apparently provides a comparatively low-noise approach to evaluating the relative effectiveness of two stimuli, and can be used to sort specific losses of sensitivity to one stimulus from generalized losses that apply uniformly to both.

Given the ideal detector analysis of infant color vision presented by Banks and his co-workers (Banks & Bennett, 1988; Banks & Shannon, this volume), the obvious next step is to try this experiment with tritan stimuli. If Banks' analysis is correct and general, then tritan stimuli, unlike red/green stimuli, should be more readily nulled in infants than in adults.

SUMMARY AND CONCLUSIONS

In summary, we have been developing and using quantitative OKN and OKN nulling techniques, in the theoretical context of null plane analysis, to study infant color vision. So far, we have done two studies. In the first, we showed that infant and adult isoluminance points are similar for large, moving gratings. In the second, we showed that 4-week olds, 9-week-olds and adults are similar in the contrasts of luminance-modulated and red/green-modulated gratings required for motion nulls. In both experiments, the data from infants are remarkably well-behaved, and approach the quality of data generated by adult subjects. The relatively low noise level of the data provides a welcome change, at least in comparison to data generated by the forced-choice preferential looking techniques with which one of us has previously worked. The quantitative elegance of the data encourage us to continue, and to develop a program of research on infant color vision using OKN and OKN nulling techniques.

The first two experiments generated with the new techniques and stimuli yield remarkable similarities between infants and adults. One must, however, remember that this outcome may be specific to the large-field OKN paradigm. That is, the neonatal fovea is markedly immature, whereas the peripheral retina is relatively mature (reviewed by Banks & Bennett, 1988; Banks & Shannon, this volume). When large fields are used, the responses of both infants and adults are, in all probability, dominated by signals originating in the peripheral retina, so that similarities between infants and adults are reasonable. On the other hand, techniques specialized to test the infant fovea (when they are invented) might well reveal a different pattern of differences between infants and adults.

We close with the reminder that, despite all their advantages, OKN nulling techniques are subject to important limitations as tools for studying color vision. Color vision has classically been studied with small, foveally fixated, stationary fields. Classical trichromatic theory has been largely developed to account for the results of such experiments. As such, classical trichromatic theory makes no routine provision for rod inputs or motion processing, and it may or may not stretch readily to accommodate these factors.

When we work in this theoretical context, we therefore run the risk of working in an incomplete interpretational context for the OKN nulling data. The challenge of the field is to modify color theory to accommodate the rules for combining motion signals from all four photoreceptor types over broad retinal regions, and/or to design important experiments in the face of these theoretical limitations.

ACKNOWLEDGMENTS

This chapter was prepared with the support of NIH Grants EY 04470 and EY 02920 to Davida Y. Teller. We thank Corinne Mar, Cynthia Ames, and Kathy Cox for technical assistance and assistance in testing infants.

REFERENCES

Anstis, S. M., & Cavanagh, P. (1983). A minimum motion technique for judging equiluminance. In J. Mollon & L. T. Sharpe (Eds.), *Colour vision: Physiology and psychophysics* (pp. 475–481). London: Academic Press.

Banks, M. S., & Bennett, P. J. (1988). Optical and photoreceptor immaturities limit the spatial and chromatic vision of human neonates. *Journal of the Optical Society of America A, 5,* 2059–2079.

Banks, M. S., & Dannemiller, J. L. (1987). Infant visual psychophysics. In P. Salapatek & L. B. Cohen (Eds.), *Handbook of infant perception: From sensation to perception* (pp. 115–184). New York: Academic Press.

Boynton, R. M. (1979). *Human color vision.* New York: Holt, Rinehart & Winston.

Brown, A. M. (1990). Development of visual sensitivity to light and color vision in human infants: A critical review. *Vision Research, 30,* 1159–1188.

Cavanagh, P., MacLeod, D. I. A., & Anstis, S. M. (1987). Equiluminance: spatial and temporal factors and the contribution of blue-sensitive cones. *Journal of the Optical Society of America A, 4,* 1428–1438.

Cavanagh, P., Tyler, C. W., & Favreau, O. E. (1984). Perceived velocity of moving chromatic gratings. *Journal of the Optical Society of America A, 1,* 893–899.

Clavadetscher, J. E., Brown, A. M., Ankrum, C., & Teller, D. Y. (1988). Spectral sensitivity and chromatic discriminations in 3- and 7-week-old human infants. *Journal of the Optical Society of America A, 5,* 2093–2105.

Cornsweet, T. N. (1970). *Visual perception.* New York: Academic Press.

Derrington, A. M., Krauskopf, J., & Lennie, P. (1984). Chromatic mechanisms in lateral geniculate nucleus of macaque. *Journal of Physiology, 357,* 241–265.

Hainline, L., de Bie, J., Abramov, I., & Camenzuli, C. (1987). Eye movement voting: A new technique for deriving spatial contrast sensitivity. *Clinical Vision Sciences, 2,* 33–44.

Hansen, R., & Fulton, A. B. (1989). Psychophysical estimation of ocular media density of human infants. *Vision Research, 29,* 687–690.

Hurvich, L. M., & Jameson, D. (1957). An opponent-process theory of color vision. *Psychological Review, 64,* 384–404.

Judd, D. B. (1951). Report of U.S. Secretariat Committee on Colorimetry and Artificial Daylight. Proceedings of the Commission Internationale de l'Eclairage, Paris. Vol. 1, Part 7.

Krauskopf, J., Williams, D. R., & Heeley, D. W. (1982). Cardinal directions of color space. *Vision Research, 22,* 1123–1131.

Lindsey, D. T. (1990). Linear analysis of eccentricity-dependent changes in the null-based isoluminant plane. *OSA Technical Digest, 15,* 166.

Lindsey, D. T., & Teller, D. Y. (1988). Spatio-temporal phase characteristics of moving gratings synthesized from isoluminant red and green components. *Investigative Ophthalmology and Visual Science,* (Suppl. 29), 302.

Lindsey, D. T., & Teller, D. Y. (1989). Influence of variations in edge blur on minimally distinct border judgments: A theoretical and empirical investigation. *Journal of the Optical Society of America A, 6,* 446–458.

Lindsey, D. T., & Teller, D. T. (1990). Motion at isoluminance: Discrimination/detection ratios for moving isoluminant gratings. *Vision Research, 30,* 1751–1761.

Maurer, D., Lewis, T., Cavanagh, P., & Anstis, S. M. (1989). A new test of luminous efficiency for babies. *Investigative Ophthalmology and Visual Science, 30,* 297–303.

Peeples, D. R., & Teller, D. Y. (1975). Color vision and brightness discrimination in two-month-old human infants. *Science, 189,* 1102–1103.

Peeples, D. R., & Teller, D. Y. (1978). White-adapted photopic spectral sensitivity in human infants. *Vision Research, 18,* 49–53.

Tansley, B. W., & Boynton, R. M. (1976). A line, not a space, represents visual distinctness of borders formed by different colors. *Science, 191,* 954–957.

Teller, D. Y. (1979). The forced-choice preferential looking procedure: A psychophysical technique for use with human infants. *Infant Behavior and Development, 2,* 135–153.

Teller, D. Y., & Bornstein, M. H. (1987). Infant color vision and color perception. In P. Salapatek & L. B. Cohen (Eds.), *Handbook of infant perception: From sensation to perception* (pp. 185–236). New York: Academic Press.

Teller, D. Y., & Lindsey, D. T. (1988). OKN isoluminance points and equivalent achromatic contrasts in infants and color-normal and -abnormal adults. *OSA Technical Digest, 11,* 64.

Teller, D. Y., & Lindsey, D. T. (1989). Motion nulls for white vs. isochromatic gratings in infants and adults. *Journal of the Optical Society of America A, 6,* 1945–1954.

Teller, D. Y., & Lindsey, D. T. (1990). Motion photometry: Additivity and the isoluminant plane. *OSA Technical Digest, 15,* 166.

Teller, D. Y., & Lindsey, D. T. (in press). Infant color vision: OKN techniques and null plane analysis. In K. Simons (Ed.), *Infant vision: Laboratory and clinical research*. New York: Oxford University Press.

Troscianko, T. (1987). Perception of random-dot symmetry and apparent movement at and near isoluminance. *Vision Research, 27,* 547–554.

What Can Rates of Development Tell Us About Underlying Mechanisms?

Richard Held
Massachusetts Institute of Technology

Many investigators of visual development have attributed the appearance and/or changes in sensitivity of discrimination performance with age to neuronal developments in higher visual centers, the cortex in particular (Atkinson, 1984; Bronson, 1974; Held, 1989; Maurer & Lewis, 1979). The attribution of function to cortex is convincing when based on knowledge of the visual nervous system and its development as studied in animal preparations (Spillmann & Werner, 1990). Such knowledge provides grounds for asserting that many of the processes that account for properties of visual perception must go on in the cortex. For example, the neuronal equipment for analyzing stereoptic stimuli—single cells responsive to binocular disparities—is not found prior to cortex, but arguments of this kind do not necessarily prove that the changes essential for the development of such properties actually occur at the same loci in the cortex or other higher centers. As Banks and Shannon (this volume) and other investigators have argued, some of these developmental changes may be accounted for at least equally well by lower level (retinal or otherwise) increases in the efficiency of signal processing with resulting increases of the information processing capabilities (resolution and discrimination) of higher level systems that may not have changed. Colleagues and I have suggested just such a possibility in an earlier report on the oblique effect, discussed further on (Gwiazda, Brill, Mohindra, & Held, 1978). How might decisions be made between these alternatives, given the state of current knowledge? I attempt here to answer this question.

Banks and Bennett (1988) applied the logic of sequential ideal-observer analysis, which Geisler spelled out in a recent review (1989), to the development

of vision. This analysis assumes strictly sequential processing from retinal receptor to cortex in a well-established series of cascaded levels. If visual performance varies with change in stimuli similarly in both real and ideal observers,
then the performance variation may be attributed to the variation in information
available at the level of the ideal observer. So far the ideal observer analysis
of visual development has not been extended beyond the photoreceptors. Yet,
the outcomes even at that level already resemble psychophysical results from
human observers for some of the spatial acuities and chromatic sensitivities
provided that allowance is made for across-the-spectrum losses of information
in the transition from the locus of the ideal observer to the response. An account of these losses is called the *relative efficiency* method or the *dark-glasses*
hypothesis. The implication of this work is that, although the absolute level of
information available to the ideal observer—in this case at the photoreceptors—is
degraded in its path through the brain, its spectral (both spatial frequency and
light wavelength) variation remains available to the response system of the human observer. Developmental changes in the retina during infancy increase its
sensitivity and hence the information available from signals arriving at the level
of the ideal observer. Some of this increase is available to the real observer
and can account, at least in principle, for some of the changes in vision observed
during infancy and childhood. Following this reasoning, Banks and Bennett (1988)
argued that in infancy both grating and vernier acuity increase monotonically
with age because of the increased efficiency of detection at the photoreceptor
level. Moreover, from these considerations they predicted a more rapid rate
of increase in vernier acuity compared to grating acuity (see section on development of vernier acuity further on).

The characteristic curves of Fig. 3.1a represent this process. In the plots

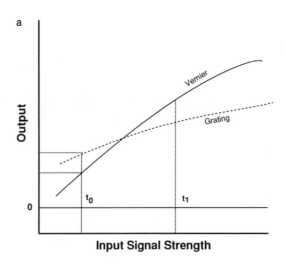

Input Signal Strength

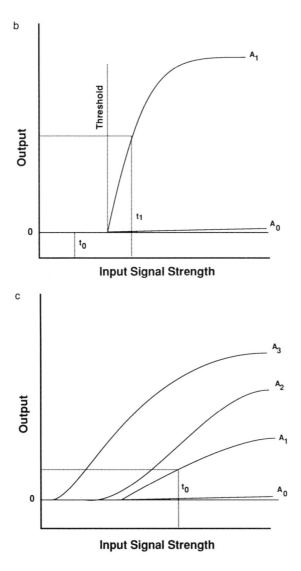

FIG. 3.1. Operating characteristics of higher level processors (t_0, t_1: signals of increasing strength). (a) Differing slopes of processors for grating and vernier acuities. (b) A_0: Flat characteristic with near zero output. A_1: Characteristic with threshold and steeply rising slope. (c) A_0, A_1, A_2, A_3: Successive operating characteristics with decreasing thresholds and increasing slopes.

of Fig. 3.1, the strength of the input signals to higher level analyzers (t values) are represented on the abscissa increasing to the right. The output signal strength (resolution, in these cases) of the analyzers as a function of input strength are represented as increasing upward on the ordinate. In the case of grating and vernier acuities (Fig. 3.1a), consider input strength proportional to the output of the photoreceptors.

Can this argument be applied to the onset and development of other visual functions? For example, can the well-documented abrupt onset of stereopsis at several months of age (reviewed in Held, 1991) be accounted for in this manner as the outcome of increases in sensitivity at the retinal level? The answer could be affirmative if the stereosystem in cortex had a threshold requirement for input signal strength. Then, we might predict the sudden initiation of stereopsis at the age when strength of input to the stereosensitive system reaches and exceeds that threshold value. This condition is depicted as curve A_1 in Fig. 3.1b. When input strength (t_0) is below threshold, no output is produced (zero resolution). When it is above threshold (as in t_1), stereopsis is present. Once above threshold stereoacuity increases rapidly because of a very steep operating characteristic (A_1) inherent in the stereosystem. In other words we might suppose that the stereosystem has a highly nonlinear input–output response characteristic, which would account for its abrupt onset and subsequent rapid increase in acuity with age. This hypothesis contrasts with my attribution of the initiation of stereopsis to an actual neuronal change in striate cortex, namely, segregation of the ocular dominance columns (Held, 1985; Shimojo, Bauer, O'Connell, & Held, 1986). My colleagues and I have argued that this segregation is a necessary, but not sufficient, condition for stereopsis because further neuronal connections are necessary to compute disparities. Under this assumption, during the prestereoptic period, the operating characteristic of the system would be flat (depicted as A_0, in Fig. 3.1b) with zero output at any value of input, such as either t_0 or t_1. However, at the completion of segregation of the ocular dominance columns, the characteristic curve would have acquired a positive slope (like A_1) and would now show an output contingent upon input (stereopsis). In other words, instead of reaching a nonzero output by increasing signal strength, as in Banks' proposal, the characteristic curve changes and can thereby produce a nonzero output despite constant input.

Hypothetically, both column segregation and suprathreshold signal strength might be required and might even develop at the same age. Thus, as shown in Fig. 3.1c, a very young infant might have a characteristic curve such as A_0. No input value t would produce an output. Later the characteristic might become A_1 which requires a suprathreshold value of t such as t_1 to yield an output value. With age the threshold input might lower and the slope increase as shown by A_2 and A_3.

Let us return to the question of how we might distinguish developmental change resulting from the low level (retinal) increases in information from more central structural and functional changes. One approach consists in examining rates of change in both locations. Following Geisler's lead, Banks and Bennett (1988) performed an analysis of the theoretical effects of improved front-end efficiency on increases in vernier and grating acuities. It predicts that the former should increase as the square root of signal strength while the latter increases as the fourth root (depicted in Fig. 3.1a). Psychophysical data bear out this prediction within limits. Banks and Bennett applied this analysis to the developing grating and vernier acuities of young infants and concluded that the rate differential could result from the increases in signal strength with age available from the cone receptors. This analysis of relative rates suggests a method for isolating the higher level effects. Suppose that the output of the retina is kept constant. Then, any improvement in higher level function would have to be attributed to change at some other locus, presumably at a higher level. Accordingly, as in Fig. 3.1c, if the operating characteristic changes with age, a subthreshold stimulus at an early age (t_0 at A_0) would elicit close to zero output, whereas at a later age it would produce a significant output (t_0 at A_1).

Banks and Bennett (1988) and Wilson (1988) argued convincingly that grating acuity rises with the developing efficiency of receptor processing. Other developmental changes causing increased acuity may occur at higher levels in the visual system. If during some period of development, however, no change occurs in grating acuity, one may conclude that no change relevant to grating acuity is occurring at any level of the visual system including that of the receptors. The only exception would be the unlikely case in which such changes exactly balance each other. If during that period some other visual function showed significant change, one would have to attribute it to some level of the visual system beyond that of the receptors. A more direct approach would consist in manipulating the visual stimulus so as to keep constant the information processed by the receptors. The sort of computations provided by Banks and his collaborators should make that possible, and then any changes in visual function would be attributable to higher processes. In this manner the rates of development of each of the two visual functions may provide some information about the underlying mechanisms.

In the following pages I survey aspects of visual development in order to see if current knowledge allows us to distinguish lower and higher level developmental contributions. In each case we must first establish that a particular visual performance entails higher level (cortical) change and then examine what we know of lower level changes and how they may influence the higher level function.

GRATING ACUITY

The course of development of grating acuity in the infant is by now well established (Mohn & van Hof-van Duin, 1991). Measured in the neonate by behavioral methods, it begins at or below a spatial frequency of 1 c/deg (Snellen 20/600) but rises steadily over the course of the first year and beyond. Much of this development can plausibly be accounted for by Banks' proposal. Changes in the packing density of foveal cones and their sensitivities in the retinas of infants and children can considerably increase the spatial frequency of sampling and the efficiency of light capture.

At some time during the first few months we begin to see evidence for the *oblique effect* (Appelle, 1972), the observation that oblique-edged targets for measuring acuity have, in general, higher thresholds than those composed of edges oriented on the horizontal and vertical. We do not know the precise reason for this difference but it does reveal a differential effect contingent upon selectivity for edge orientation. There appears to be neither a retinal mechanism nor one in the lateral geniculate responsive to differences in edge orientation. Fine-grained orientational selectivity begins at the striate cortex. Consequently, although we may attribute the general improvement in acuity to increases in sensitivity at the retinal level, the variations in acuity with orientation must be contributed by a cortical mechanism. But is the onset of the oblique effect attributable to change in that cortical mechanism or to increases in the signal strength entering the cortex that exceed a threshold for expressing the oblique effect?

The oblique effect in normal adult observers is restricted to patterns of a spatial frequency exceeding at least 4 to 5 c/deg (Campbell, Kulikowski, & Levinson, 1966; Freeman & Thibos, 1975), yet in infants it has been observed first at 6 weeks of age when viewing square wave gratings with a fundamental frequency of 0.75 c/deg (Gwiazda et al., 1978; Leehey, Moskowitz-Cook, Brill, & Held, 1975). This observation corresponds to the finding that, in very young infants, the entire contrast sensitivity function is shifted toward lower frequencies and lower sensitivities with a peak at a frequency less than 1.0 c/deg (Pirchio, Spinelli, Fiorentini, & Maffei, 1978). It led us to infer (Gwiazda et al., 1978) that:

> . . . the (orientational) anisotropy in the visual system, evidenced by the oblique effect, antedates in time the changes that result in increased acuity during the first year of life. . . . If the increase in acuity with age results from subcortical changes, then we can conceive of the accompanying increases in contrast sensitivity, in the spatial frequency at maximum contrast sensitivity, and in the cutoff frequency (acuity) as the result of increasing resolution at the subcortical levels that feed into the anisotropic cortex. (p. 1563)

In other words, we proposed that the oblique effect was inherent in the cortical mechanism from early in infancy. It did not appear at all before at least 6 weeks of age. When it did appear, it was seen at a frequency lower than ever reported in adults. The oblique effect implies orientational selectivity. In recent years, the onset of this selectivity and its development in infants have been studied in several laboratories, including our own. The results are more extensively discussed further on. For now, it will suffice to state that orientational selectivity appears to have its onset between the ages of 1 and 2 months, in agreement with the age of onset of the oblique effect. This agreement suggests that whatever process is responsible for the beginnings of orientational tuning may also be responsible for the onset of the oblique effect.

ORIENTATIONAL SELECTIVITY

Orientational selectivity in the human infant has been claimed by various investigators to begin anywhere from birth to many weeks of age. (The literature is briefly reviewed by Slater, Morison, & Somers, 1988.) We have tried to develop a procedure that would yield quantitative estimates of orientational tuning. To that end we have used a masking paradigm incorporated in a two-alternative forced choice procedure. The two parts of the display each had a masking grating of low spatial frequency (typically 0.37 c/deg) presented at a common nonvertical orientation. On one side a vertical test grating of the same spatial frequency was superimposed on the mask with appropriate adjustment to equate luminance on the two sides. This test grating was counterphased at 0.5 Hz to provide a source of apparent motion, which attracts the infant's attention when the motion is visible. We varied the contrast of the grating to find the threshold of detectability as a function of the orientation of the mask to the test grating.

Note that in this procedure we used motion generated by the counterphasing of the test grating. We are assuming that when the contrast level of the test grating falls below its masked threshold, the motion will have disappeared. In terms of mechanism, we assume that the contrast-determined edge must be above threshold for the appearance of motion by counterphasing. I like to think of the alternative as the Cheshire cat problem defined by Lewis Carroll in *Alice in Wonderland*. You will remember that the Cheshire cat has a fixed smile on its face. The face slowly fades out (read: is reduced in contrast) until all that remains is the smile! (read: motion). In other words, the alternative to the assumption just made is that the threshold for motion could require less contrast than that for visibility of the edge. We have assumed that these thresholds are roughly the same, that contrast edge processing precedes the detection of motion based on the displacement of such edges. (Parenthetically, I should add that we are not alone in making this assumption. Many of the experiments using masking share it, e.g., Campbell et al., 1966; Phillips & Wilson, 1984.)

Using the masking procedure on a group of infants, average responses do not show a significant difference between the thresholds with masks at 10° and 90° at 1 month, but by 2 months of age the results show significantly lowered thresholds with masks rotationally displaced 90° from the test grating compared to masks at 10° from the target orientation (Held, Yoshida, Gwiazda, & Bauer, 1989). Intermediate masking orientations show intermediate thresholds at several months of age (Yoshida, Gwiazda, Bauer, & Held, 1990). These results agree in part with those of Braddick, Atkinson, & Wattam-Bell (1986), who reported orientational discrimination by 6 weeks of age using a visually evoked potential method. In a few of our infants who were repeatedly measured at two-week intervals, the transition to significant orientational selectivity occurred from one measurement session to the next. This result suggests that the onset of such selectivity may be just as abrupt as that of stereopsis and binocular rivalry, which occurs within a one- to two-week interval.

The results are consistent with the evidence already discussed above for an oblique effect commencing at 6 weeks of age (Gwiazda et al., 1978; Leehey et al., 1975), because orientational discrimination appears to begin between 1 and 2 months. Both of these results can, in principle, be accounted for either by increasing sensitivity at the retinal level or by development of orientational selectivity in the cortex. The orientationally selective mechanism might require signals that, prior to 1 month or so of age, are too weak to activate it. Alternatively, they both could be accounted for by the sharpening of orientational tuning at the cortical level. I argue for the latter account, for reasons elaborated further on in the section on stereopsis and binocularity.

VERNIER ACUITY

Shimojo, Birch, Gwiazda, & Held (1984) developed the motion-sound display procedure in order to measure vernier acuity in infants. A section of a square wave grating is displaced so as to produce an aligned set of vernier offsets at the edges of the bars of the grating. The section is displaced periodically parallel to the edges of the carrier grating. Apparent motion is induced by the displacements of the vernier offset. As in the case of orientation masking, we tacitly assumed that displacements of offsets smaller than would be detectable in static displays would not induce motion and hence produce spuriously low thresholds for the offset. From a mechanism point of view, we assumed that the motion process utilizes the information coming from the outcome of processing the offset. Adult observers showed no difference in threshold between moving and static displays, and we believe that our assumption was justified by the outcome.

We documented three results of interest here:

1. Vernier acuity develops very rapidly relative to grating acuity. This result was also reported by Manny and Klein (1984) and confirmed with monkey subjects by Kiorpes and Movshon (1988).

2. By keeping a suprathreshold vernier offset constant while varying the spatial frequency of the carrier grating, we showed, not surprisingly, that it was

the grating acuity threshold that determined visibility of the vernier (Shimojo et al., 1984). This result confirmed what is probably obvious: that edge processing is a requisite of vernier offset processing, just as the motion we induce for detection requires a detectable vernier offset. We have found that although the advantage of binocular over monocular viewing for grating acuity in infants is small, the advantage for vernier acuity is on the order of three times (Bauer, Gwiazda, Held, & Thorn, 1988). This is not the case in adult vision.

3. We also found that significant sex differences occur during months 4, 5, and 6 (Held, Shimojo, & Gwiazda, 1984). We have not found them in grating acuity. They suggest two alternative explanations. The absence of sex differences in the development of grating acuity suggest that they arise after retinal processing. Alternatively, as M. S. Banks has pointed out (personal communication, 1991), if receptor efficiency is greater during this period in females, it would boost vernier acuity much more than grating acuity and so yield the sex difference.

The development of hyperacute vernier acuity parallels that of hyperacute stereoacuity (Shimojo et al., 1984). Moreover, if vernier acuity and stereoacuity are scaled with respect to grating acuity, we see similar differences in the timing of acquisition of hyperacuity between the sexes. What can these results tell us? The process responsible for vernier acuity has attributes that differ from that responsible for grating acuity and has been attributed to cortex. In this case, the evidence for a cortical process is strong but so is Banks' argument.

BINOCULARITY

There is little question but that interocular interactions must be processed after convergence at the cortical level. We have studied the development of two forms of binocular vision involving interactions between inputs to the two eyes: stereopsis and rivalry. The most striking finding in the case of stereopsis is its apparent absence prior to about the age of 3½ months. This result has also been found by a number of other laboratories using different procedures (reviewed in Held, 1991). When testing was performed at two-week intervals, the appearance of a preference for disparate over non-disparate stimuli occurred within two weeks of its not even having been present (Birch, Gwiazda, & Held, 1982; Held, Birch, & Gwiazda, 1980; see Fig. 3.2). Following onset, stereoacuity rose rapidly, so that within a few weeks it had risen to the limits of resolution of our apparatus (½ to 1 minute of disparity). Moreover, once stereoptic discrimination was shown at a coarse level of acuity, infants rarely reverted either to lower acuity values or to the absence of stereopsis.

Highly correlated with stereopsis in age of onset is the aversive response to binocularly rivaling stimuli (Birch, Shimojo, & Held, 1983). Longitudinal studies

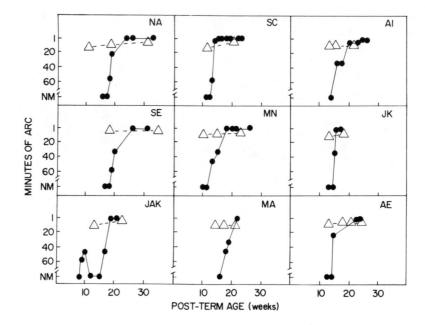

FIG. 3.2. Concomitant development of stereo (circles) and grating (triangles) acuities, measured on the same nine subjects. Stereoacuity data reported from Birch et al., 1982; grating acuity data recorded by J. Gwiazda (unpublished).

were performed in which binocular combinations of orthogonal gratings were paired with binocular combinations of parallel gratings (Shimojo et al., 1986). The initial preference was clearly for the orthogonal gratings, but it shifted to the parallel gratings (fusible) at the same age as the onset of stereopsis (Gwiazda, Bauer, & Held, 1989; Shimojo et al., 1986), and the two measures are highly correlated. When measured weekly, the preference usually shifted from one week to the next and rarely reverted.

Can these abrupt onsets be accounted for by the relatively slow and continuous growth of sensitivity as reflected in the contrast sensitivity function (CSF) and grating acuity? Yes, but only if we assume that some threshold is crossed by the slowly growing sensitivity (Fig. 3.1b). However, measurements taken of the onset of stereopsis and the course of development of grating acuity (see Fig. 3.2), on the same subjects, show that there may be little or no change in the latter during this period. If grating acuity is taken as a measure of the efficiency of retinal processing and of the signal strength arriving at cortex, then the absence of a change can hardly account for the onset of stereopsis. We may then have a test case for deciding between the two alternative interpretations of development. The result favors developmental change at the cortical locus. The argument for a cortical locus of change is stronger in the case of the fusion–rivalry shift. The timing of this shift (i.e., the age of the subject) is not only highly correlated with the onset of stereopsis but is also predictable from our speculative model (Held, 1985; Shimojo et al., 1986). Moreover, this shift does not appear to be dependent upon increasing sensitivity to other properties, such as orientation, contrast, and high spatial frequency because the stimuli are always well above the thresholds for these properties.

Other evidence of cortical processing includes the different ages of onset of crossed compared with uncrossed stereopsis (Birch et al., 1982; Held et al., 1980). It is doubtful that this effect could be produced by lower level information, although the differential in age of onset could result from different threshold requirements. That is to say, crossed stereopsis may require less information than uncrossed and therefore appear when output from the retina is adequate for the former but not the latter. The sex differences that we have already discussed in connection with vernier acuity are also seen in the measures of binocular vision (Bauer et al., 1986; Gwiazda et al., 1989), but in neither grating acuity nor orientational selectivity (Held et al., 1984; Yoshida et al., 1990). They have also been found in the precedence effect in the development of sound localization in infants by Muir, Clifton, and Clarkson (1989). These differences appear to occur in the development of some but not all cortical processes.

Taken together, this evidence confirms the view that mature binocularity entails a very well-marked visual process, which has a component of developmental change occurring at or beyond striate cortex.

MODEL OF STEREOPTIC DEVELOPMENT

Believing that the results favor a central development interpretation, we proposed that this process could be accounted for by a stage in the segregation of the ocular dominance columns, which would allow recombination and analysis of the information from the two eyes (Held, 1985). As already mentioned, we have tested the implication that before segregation, superimposition of inputs from the two eyes would occur, thereby producing the appearance of a plaid when orthogonal gratings are presented to separate eyes. The results bore out this implication (Shimojo et al., 1986). Similar timing has been shown in the comparison of VEP onsets of correlation–decorrelation and stereopsis with dynamic random dot stereograms. These results argue that the same mechanism produces both the abrupt onset of stereopsis and the change in response to binocularly rivaling stimuli. In recognition of the transition, we have distinguished pre-stereoptic binocular interaction from the post-stereoptic state by calling the latter *mature binocularity* (Held, 1988, 1991). Both stereoptic and rivalry processes must utilize this mechanism even though considerable evidence, both psychophysical and neurophysiological, suggests that they become separate and independent at a later stage (Logothetis & Schall, 1990; Wolfe, 1986), but see Blake and O'Shea (1988) as well.

Concerning the sex differences, our hunch is that they are not necessarily cortical as such but arise during intense synaptogenesis, perhaps modulated by the neurotrophic effects of the males' high levels of plasma testosterone. The combination of intense synaptogenesis (Huttenlocher, de Courten, Garey, & van der Loos, 1982) and high testosterone level (Forest, Cathiard, & Bertrand, 1973) yields a window in time during which sex differences may develop (Held, Bauer, & Gwiazda, 1989). This window happens to occur during one stage of cortical development.

CONCLUSION

If our reasoning about sequential processing is correct, then further stages of processing of information may also carry the earmarks of earlier processing. For example, the sex differences that arise at the hyperacuity level of processing should also show up in whatever next stages require information from the lower level.

To reiterate, the fact that we can attribute function to a particular locus in the visual system does not necessarily imply that development at that locus can account for onset of the function. As Banks has argued, in the cases of grating and vernier acuity, increased signal strength from lower levels may account for the changes and their differential rates. Even the abrupt onset of mature binocularity might be accounted for in that manner: The operating characteristic of the binocular processing mechanism may require a minimum signal intensity (threshold) not available prior to an age of about 3½ months. The potential for activation may be present at least from birth, but its actualization may be delayed until lower level mechanisms are adequate (until the output of those mechanisms reaches the operating range of the binocular mechanisms). How might such proposals be further tested?

We might try to produce higher levels of signal strength at an abnormally early age by increasing the stimulus intensity beyond normal levels and thereby show precocious function. However, much testing of infants has already been carried out with relatively intense stimuli. Testing at still higher levels might entail unacceptable risks. Moreover, the adaptational mechanisms of the retina might very well attenuate the effects of such intense stimuli. On the other hand, if testing is done with a signal strength kept below the presumedly effective levels during the normal ages of development, evidence for function should not appear. If it did, despite the absence of change in the input signal, that appearance obviously could not be attributed to the contribution of lower level changes in signal strength. We would have reason to claim, then, that the development occurred at the higher level, as we have in the case of stereopsis. On the other hand, if signal strength determines onset, then the Banks generalization holds, and we may entertain an interesting possibility.

Suppose that the operating characteristic of some visual function remains more or less constant with age. If so, even the adult system would fail to function if the input signal were degraded back to early infantile levels. More generally, if the operating characteristics of cortical processes are set very early in life, but their operation is not evident until much later in development when signal strength is adequate, then sufficient reduction in signal strength in the adult should yield infant-like responses. This proposal is a direct interpretation of the dark-glasses hypothesis of Banks and Bennett (1988) and Brown, Dobson, and Maier (1987). In fact, sufficient reduction of retinal illuminance in adult observers can reduce contrast sensitivity and grating acuity to infant-like levels (Van Nes & Bouman, 1967). Under these conditions, will the oblique effect appear at very low spatial frequencies, such as 1.0 c/deg? If grating acuity is reduced to the 2- to 3-month infant levels, will vernier acuity be hypoacute? Will sex differences appear as they do in infants? These may sound like bizarre predictions, but they are logical implications of the previous reasoning about the neuronal loci of developmental change, and must be addressed.

ACKNOWLEDGMENTS

Joseph Bauer, Jane Gwiazda, and Jeremy Wolfe reviewed this manuscript and made many useful comments, as well as materially contributing to the research reported. Research from our laboratory has been supported by grants from the National Institutes of Health Nos. 2RO1-EY-1191, SP30-EY02621, and BRSG 2S07RR0747.

REFERENCES

Appelle, S. (1972). Perception and discrimination as a function of stimulus orientation: The "oblique effect" in man and animals. *Psychological Bulletin, 78,* 266–278.

Atkinson, J. (1984). Human visual development over the first 6 months of life: A review and a hypothesis. *Human Neurology, 3,* 61–74.

Banks, M. S., & Bennett, P. J. (1988). Optical and photoreceptor immaturities limit the spatial and chromatic vision of human neonates. *Journal of the Optical Society of America, 5,* 2059–2079.

Bauer, J. A., Gwiazda, J., Held, R., & Thorn, F. (1988). Two eyes are much better than one in infant vernier acuity but not in infant grating acuity. *Investigative Ophthalmology and Visual Science, 29* (Suppl. 3), 24.

Bauer, J., Shimojo, S., Gwiazda, J., & Held, R. (1986). Sex differences in the development of binocularity in human infants. *Investigative Ophthalmology and Visual Science, 27* (Suppl. 3), 265.

Birch, E. E., Shimojo, S., & Held, R. (1983). The development of aversion to rivalrous stimuli in human infants. *Investigative Ophthalmology and Visual Science, 24* (Suppl.), 92.

Birch, E. E., Shimojo, S., & Held, R. (1985). Preferential looking assessment of fusion and stereopsis in infants aged 1 to 6 months. *Investigative Ophthalmology and Visual Science, 26,* 366–370.

Blake, R., & O'Shea, R. (1988). "Abnormal Fusion" of stereopsis and binocular rivalry. *Psychological Review, 95,* 151–154.

Braddick, O., Atkinson, J., & Wattam-Bell, J. (1986). Orientation-specific cortical responses develop in early infancy. *Nature, 320,* 617–619.

Bronson, G. W. (1974). The postnatal growth of visual capacity. *Child Development, 45,* 873–890.

Brown, A. M., Dobson, V., & Maier, J. (1987). Visual acuity of human infants at scotopic, mesopic and photopic luminances. *Vision Research, 27,* 1845–1858.

Campbell, F. W., Kulikowski, J. J., & Levinson, J. (1966). The effect of orientation on the visual resolution of gratings. *Journal of Physiology, 187,* 427–436.

Forest, M. G., Cathiard, A. M., & Bertrand, J. A. (1973). Evidence of testicular activity in early infancy. *Journal of Clinical Endocrinology and Metabolism, 37,* 148–150.

Freeman, R. D., & Thibos, L. N. (1975). Contrast sensitivity in humans with abnormal visual experience. *Journal of Physiology, 247,* 687–710.

Geisler, W. S. (1989). Sequential ideal-observer analysis of visual discriminations. *Psychological Review, 96,* 267–314.

Gwiazda, J., Brill, S., Mohindra, I., & Held, R. (1978). Infant visual acuity and its meridional variation. *Vision Research, 18,* 1557–1564.

Gwiazda, J., Bauer, J., & Held, R. (1989). Binocular function in human infants: Correlation of stereoptic and fusion-rivalry discriminations. *Journal of Pediatric Ophthalmology and Strabismus, 26,* 128–132.

Held, R. (1985). Binocular vision: Behavioral and neural development. In J. Mehler & R. Fox (Eds.), *Neonate cognition: Beyond the blooming buzzing confusion* (pp. 37–44). Hillsdale, NJ: Lawrence Erlbaum Associates.

Held, R. (1988). Normal visual development and its deviations. In G. Lennerstrand, G. von Noorden, & E. Campos (Eds.), *Strabismus and amblyopia* (pp. 247–257). London: Macmillan.

Held, R. (1989). Development of cortically mediated visual processes in human infants. In K. von Euler (Ed.), *Neurobiology of early infant behaviour* (pp. 155–164). London: Macmillan.

Held, R. (1991). Development of binocular vision and stereopsis. In J. R. Cronly-Dillon (Series Ed.) & D. Regan (Ed.), Vision and Visual Dysfunction: Vol. 9 (pp. 170–178). London: Macmillan.

Held, R., Bauer, J., & Gwiazda, J. (1988). Age of onset of binocularity correlates with level of plasma testosterone in male infants. *Investigative Ophthalmology and Visual Science, 29*(Suppl. 3), 60.

Held, R., Birch, E. E., & Gwiazda, J. (1980). Stereoacuity of human infants. *Proceedings of the National Academy of Sciences* (USA), *77,* 5572–5574.

Held, R., Shimojo, S., & Gwiazda, J. (1984). Gender differences in the early development of human visual resolution. *Investigative Ophthalmology and Visual Science, 25*(Suppl. 3), 220.

Held, R., Yoshida, H., Gwiazda, J., & Bauer, J. (1989). Development of orientation selectivity measured by a masking procedure. *Investigative Ophthalmology and Visual Science, 30*(Suppl. 3), 312.

Huttenlocher, P. R., de Courten, C., Garey, L. J., & van der Loos, H. (1982). Synaptogenesis in human visual cortex: Evidence for synapse elimination during normal development. *Neuroscience Letters, 33,* 247–252.

Kiorpes, L., & Movshon, J. A. (1988). Development of vernier and grating acuity in strabismic monkeys. *Investigative Ophthalmology and Visual Science, 29* (Suppl.), 9.

Leehey, S. C., Moskowitz-Cook, A., Brill, S., & Held, R. (1975). Orientational anisotropy in infant vision. *Science, 190,* 900–902.

Logothetis, N. K., & Schall, J. D. (1990). Binocular motion rivalry in macaque monkeys: Eye dominance and tracking eye movements. *Vision Research, 30,* 1409–1419.

Manny, R., & Klein, S. (1984). The development of vernier acuity in infants. *Current Eye Research, 3,* 453–462.

Maurer, D., & Lewis, T. L. (1979). A physiological explanation of infant's early visual development. *Canadian Journal of Psychology, 33,* 232–252.

Mohn, G., & van Hof-van Duin, J. (1991). Development of spatial vision. In J. R. Conly-Dillon (Series Ed.) & In D. Regan (Ed.), Vision and visual dysfunction: Vol. 10 (pp. 179–211). London: Macmillan.

Muir, D. W., Clifton, R. K., & Clarkson, M. G. (1989). The development of a human auditory localization response: A U-shaped function. *Canadian Journal of Psychology, 43,* 199–216.

Phillips, G. C., & Wilson, H. R. (1984). Orientation bandwidths of spatial mechanisms measured by masking. *Journal of the Optical Society of America, 1,* 226–232.

Pirchio, M., Spinelli, D., Fiorentini, A., & Maffei, L. (1978). Infant contrast sensitivity evaluated by evoked potentials. *Brain Research, 141,* 179–184.

Shimojo, S., Bauer, J. A., O'Connell, K. M., & Held, R. (1986). Prestereoptic binocular vision in infants. *Vision Research, 26,* 501–510.

Shimojo, S., Birch, E. E., Gwiazda, J., & Held, R. (1984). Development of vernier acuity in infants. *Vision Research, 24,* 721–728.

Slater, A. M., Morison, V., & Somers, M. (1988). Orientation discrimination and cortical function in the human newborn. *Perception, 17,* 597–602.

Spillmann, L., & Werner, J. (1990). *Visual perception: The neurophysiological foundations.* New York: Academic Press.

Van Nes, F. L., & Bouman, M. A. (1967). Spatial modulation transfer in the human eye. *Journal of the Optical Society of America, 57,* 401–406.

Wilson, H. R. (1988). Development of spatiotemporal mechanisms in the human infant. *Vision Research, 28,* 611–628.

Wolfe, J. M. (1986). Stereopsis and binocular rivalry. *Psychological Review, 93,* 269–282.

Yoshida, H., Gwiazda, J., Bauer, J., & Held, R. (1990). Orientation selectivity is present in the first month and subsequently sharpens. *Investigative Ophthalmology and Visual Science, 31* (Suppl. 3), 8.

4

Perception of Visual Direction in Human Infants

Richard N. Aslin
University of Rochester

> One of the most obvious characteristics of the visual world is its stability. The world does not rotate as you turn around (you would become badly disoriented if it did) nor does it shoot from side to side or up and down as you shift your fixation from one object to another. This fact is so obvious that most of us take it as a matter of course and do not realize that there is any need for explanation. And yet it is really a very astonishing fact. Things possess a direction-from-here not with respect to the margins of the visual field but with respect to a fixed visual world—an external frame of reference which seems unexplainable on the basis of the retinal picture.
>
> —J. J. Gibson (1950, p. 31)

This quotation from Gibson describes the puzzle of *position constancy*; that is, how do objects maintain an invariant perceived direction despite variations over time in the projection of the object's image onto different retinal locations? This is the question that I will turn to in the second half of this chapter. First, however, it seems appropriate to ask a more fundamental question, which Gibson did not address explicitly: How does the visual system correctly assign discrete visual directions to each location on the retina? In other words, given a single immobile eye centered in the orbit, how does the visual system assign a directional value of zero or straight ahead to that portion of the retinal image that falls in the center of the fovea? Why is the foveal stimulus not incorrectly assigned a directional value of "20° to the right"? Similarly, why are the topographic relations of the objects around us isomorphic with the topographic relations of our perceptions? Why do points in the retinal image maintain the property of adjacency when transformed into the perception of visual direction?

These questions may seem ridiculous because we all know that light travels in straight lines and that the retinal image is a point-for-point transformation of object-space that maintains all topological relations. Thus, it would surprise no one if I simply stated as fact, as did Ewald Hering (1880/1942) in the late 19th century, that each retinal "local sign" is linked innately with a specific visual direction relative to the fovea. Hering "borrowed" this notion of innate retinal local signs from R. H. Lotze (1852), who coined the term *Localzeichen* to refer to the analogous concept in the tactile-kinaesthetic modality. Lotze also applied the concept of local signs to the retina, but he specifically rejected the notion that the assignment of directional values was innate. Rather, he proposed that the relation between eye movements and their resulting visual stimulation acted to calibrate the spatial metric of the retinal image, and that there is no physiological possibility that each and every retinal receptor has a unique and innate visual direction (paraphrased from Walls, 1951a).

In some sense, both Hering and Lotze were correct. Gordon Walls, in a marvelous three-part series that appeared in the *American Journal of Optometry* in 1951 (Walls, 1951a, 1951b, 1951c), described the results from a little known experiment published in 1902 by a German ophthalmologist named Schlodtmann. Schlodtmann recognized that the literature on individuals with restored sight was subject to the criticism that only the very *first* postoperative visual image could provide a definitive test of innate perception of visual direction. This literature, subsequently reviewed by Senden (1960), is difficult to interpret, and Walls (1951a) described Schlodtmann's opinion of it as "a total loss" (p. 176). So, Schlodtmann decided that a definitive test of the innateness of visual direction would require subjects who were still congenitally blind!

He selected subjects with the following characteristics: (a) congenital blindness, (b) having a normal retina, (c) only capable of distinguishing light from dark, and (d) incapable of judging the direction of a light source. Three such individuals were found. The test of visual direction was remarkably simple. It consisted of inducing "pressure phosphenes" with a small wooden dowel at various locations on the eyeball. On every trial, all of the subjects reported that the perceived direction of the phosphene corresponded to a location contralateral from the pressure point on the eyeball, just as in normally sighted adults who view the phosphenes with eyes closed. Of course, it is possible that these "innate" percepts of visual direction required some earlier nonvisual interactions in a spatially ordered world, but at least these data on phosphenes in congenitally blind subjects demonstrate that visual inputs per se are not required for the perception of visual directions.

Although Schlodtmann's (1902) demonstration showed that visual directions are assigned innately on a coarse scale (i.e., right, left, up, down), it by no means demonstrated that all 1 million or so retinal ganglion cells have receptive fields with an innate assignment of visual direction. Such a claim, which was dismissed by Lotze, *could* be true, but there is compelling evidence that any innate assignment of visual directions to individual retinal locations must be plastic enough to accommodate *some* reassignment during early postnatal visual development.

Two factors argue for developmental plasticity in the assignment of visual directions to individual retinal locations (see Aslin, 1987; Banks, 1987). First, there are significant changes in the optics of the eye during the first two postnatal years (Larsen, 1971a, 1971b, 1971c, 1971d). Second, there is a migration of photoreceptors toward the fovea that continues at least into the second postnatal year (Yuodelis & Hendrickson, 1986). Taken together, these factors indicate that a point located 10° from the fovea in a newborn would stimulate a photoreceptor whose ultimate position on the adult retina would be only 6.7° from the fovea (Aslin, 1987). A variety of evidence from adults also indicates that some plasticity remains, so that small optical distortions introduced by spectacles and even some forms of retinal damage can be adapted to successfully (Welch, 1986). Thus, although the general coordinate structure of visual directions may be innate, the fine-tuning of each retinal location appears to require some form of visual experience.

How could we measure the initial process of calibrating visual directions in early infancy? In adults, the task might consist of judgments of equal spatial intervals in all directions from the fovea. Adults' performance on bisection acuity tasks indicates that they are extremely good at such judgments, with thresholds scaled in proportion to the density of receptive fields across the retina (Bedell & Flom, 1981, 1983; Bedell, Flom, & Barbeito, 1985). Asking infants to perform an analogous psychophysical task will likely prove impossible because of our inability to control precisely the location on the retina to which discrete targets are presented.

Alternatively, one could ask infants to make a motor response, like reaching, to localize a visual target (Hofsten, 1982). Reaching is not an ideal response, however, for three reasons: (a) manual responses are under rather poor control in early infancy; (b) a given retinal direction would require specification of eye position unaltered by subsequent eye movements, thereby demanding the use of flashed targets, which may not elicit a complete reaching response; and (c) the infant must base the reach on visual information about the target location without the aid of visual information about the location of the hand.

Eye movements themselves would seem to be a more direct and tractable method for measuring retinal visual directions in young infants. Saccadic eye movements are present from birth; they can be reliably elicited by a single small visual target, even from newborns; and several recording techniques allow for fairly precise measures of their direction and magnitude. Moreover, we know that saccadic eye movements in adults can not be corrected in mid-flight. Thus, the retinal error signal specified by the distance and direction from the fovea to the target's image on the peripheral retina must be converted into a motor command that rotates the eye to place the target's image on the fovea without the aid of feedback *during* the saccade itself.

What do we know about infant saccades? First, we know that they are almost always initiated in the appropriate direction to bring the peripheral target's image closer to the fovea (Harris & MacFarlane, 1974; Lewis, Maurer, & Kay, 1978; MacFarlane, Harris, & Barnes, 1976). Thus, just as Hering surmised and Schlodtmann confirmed, there is no need for visual experience to "teach" the oculomotor system the coarse directional values for right, left, up, or down. A similar coarse directional innateness is present in the olfactory (Rieser, Yonas, & Wikner, 1976) and auditory modalities (Clarkson, Clifton, & Morrongiello, 1985; Muir & Field, 1979).

Second, we know that the magnitude of saccades in very young infants is grossly hypometric; that is, until at least the fourth postnatal month infant saccades undershoot the peripheral target whenever the initial retinal error is 10° or more (Aslin & Salapatek, 1975). This undershoot stands in marked contrast to adult saccades, which bring the fovea within 10% or less of the initial retinal error specified by the peripheral target (see Fig. 4.1).

I have been interested in these multiple undershooting saccades since I first observed them in 1973. Over the next 15 years, I have entertained a variety of hypotheses about why they are present in early infancy; these include attentional deficits, motor limitations, and poorly specified sensory information. For example, perhaps young infants cannot make large saccades. We know this is not true because in the dark infants often make saccades as large as 30°. Perhaps the oculomotor apparatus itself is immature, leading to "sloppy" saccades. The six extraocular muscles are controlled by paired innervations delivered via the brainstem. For a given muscle pair, the agonist or pulling muscle receives a brief burst of innervation while the innervation of the antagonist muscle ceases. At the end of this paired burst–pause interval, both muscles receive a new innervation that holds the eye in its final orbital position. Several types of mis-

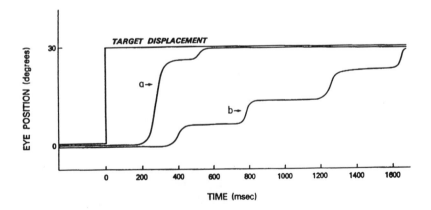

FIG. 4.1.   Schematized saccadic eye movements of an adult (A) and a 2-month-old (B) to a 30° displacement of a target. Reprinted from Aslin (1987).

matches could occur in the timing and magnitude of innervation delivered to these muscle pairs, but we do not see these mismatches in young infants; only the hypometric nature of saccades is observed. Thus, it appears that the intrinsic command structure of the saccadic system is quite mature at birth, except for the magnitude of a particular type of error.

The hypothesis that I have favored is that multiple saccades are a reflection of a poorly coordinated linkage between the retinal local sign stimulated by a peripheral target and the motor command required to rotate the eye so that the image of the target is positioned on the fovea. What seems to change during development is the precise mapping of neuromotor command *strength* onto specific peripheral retinal locations. This is a problem of motor learning. But is it relevant to the perception of visual direction? It is possible that oculomotor errors reflect a faulty visual-direction system. Alternatively, specification of visual direction may be accurate, but oculomotor errors may result from a faulty translation into motor commands. I describe here a line of reasoning that has led me to provide an alternative account of the presence of multiple saccades in early infancy, but first, I will consider how the developing oculomotor system might accomplish the motor learning task of calibrating the saccadic system.

SIMULATIONS OF SACCADIC CALIBRATION

The purpose of conducting the following series of simulations was to help me understand what type of learning procedure could be operating during the calibration of the saccadic system in early infancy. The point of these simulations was to build a model consistent with known empirical findings on infant saccades and with the least number of assumptions about innate mechanisms. The idea was to find a subset of models that are plausible so that further empirical research could be directed to tests of competing alternatives within this subset.

To begin, consider the following set of assumptions: First, the coarse direction of a peripheral target is specified innately. Second, the visual system "knows" when a target is foveated. This second assumption is supported by a variety of scanning studies that have shown that newborns use a consistent line of sight to fixate small contours in the visual field (see Haith, 1980). Third, the metric of space along a given retinal meridian is not known. That is, if a target is imaged on the peripheral retina and creates an error signal x, and a saccade changes that error signal to y, the visual system only has access to the sign (direction) and not to the magnitude of that error signal. We know that this assumption is unlikely to be correct, but it provides a more stringent test of the model than if a topographic mapping of the retina onto a motor command surface is assumed. It also avoids, for the moment, the logical problem of assuming what we are trying to explain. Recall, for example, the debate in the philosophical literature about the dilemma of the inverted retinal image. The concern over the orientation of the retinal image with respect to the "real world" was clearly a pseudo-issue unless one assumed the operation of an homunculus. As succinctly put by Boring (1942), "To say that the image is inverted would be to know the relation of the retinal image to the actual external object of which it is an image" (p. 225). Similarly, if the metric of retinal errors is already specified, then there *is* no problem of sensory-motor calibration.

The model I will describe is analogous to the following situation. Imagine that you are playing a video game whose goal is to learn how to destroy any possible attacking space ship before it crashes into you. You know that the ships are attacking one at a time on a direct collision path from any of 100 possible (and randomly determined) directions. You are armed with a single weapon initially centered among the 100 possible directions, with 50 to the left and 50 to the right. An arrow tells you whether the attacking ship is on the left or the right as well as its location, but its location is specified as an arbitrary code number for the angular rotation required to aim your weapon at the attacker. You first press either the *Left* or the *Right* button to turn your weapon, then enter a number from 1 to 50 on a keypad to rotate your weapon by that magnitude, and finally press the *Fire* button. Feedback consists only of the following three categories: *Destroyed, Missed Left,* or *Missed Right.* If you managed to destroy the attacker, a memory screen displays the left–right direction and the command from 1 to 50 that you last entered, along with the code that specified the attacker's last location. If you missed the attacker, you note the direction of the miss and choose another command from 1 to 50, checking your memory screen for a command that managed to destroy a previous attacker when it was in that same location. Your goal is to see how quickly you can fill up the screen that lists the commands required to destroy an attacker approaching from any of the 100 possible directions.

The actual simulation, of course, dealt with saccadic eye movements (see Fig. 4.2). The visual field consisted of 100 locations along the horizontal axis, 50 to the left of the fovea and 50 to the right of the fovea when the eye was centered in the orbit. Each location was defined as 1° apart because the maximum size of adult saccades from central orbit is approximately 50°. For simplicity, no vertical locations or vertical eye movements were considered. Each trial consisted of the displacement of a luminous target on an otherwise dark background to 1 of the 100 horizontal locations. The target remained at that location until it was foveated. Saccades were always initiated in the direction of the target because the left–right nature of the error signal was assumed to be known.

The goal of the simulation was to fill a look-up table that initially contained pairs of retinal error "codes" and unspecified motor commands (see Fig. 4.3). That is, each target location had a unique spatial "tag," but neither the angular distance between these locations nor their ordering within the look-up table were known. When a saccade resulted in a zero retinal error (i.e., the target was

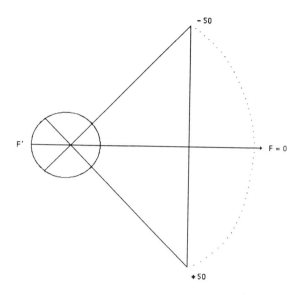

FIG. 4.2. Configuration of the saccadic simulation. A single eye was positioned in central orbit with 50 potential stimulus locations to the right and 50 to the left of the fovea (F′).

Error Signal	Motor Command
Location "A"	-36
Location "B"	+17
Location "C"	-13
-	-
-	-
-	-
Location "99"	+49
Location "100"	+50

FIG. 4.3. Sample look-up table for the saccadic simulation containing pairs of errors signals (in random order) and motor commands.

foveated), this final command was entered into the look-up table. Once the look-up table was filled, any target displacement could be foveated with a single saccade. The question was how many target displacements and how many saccades would be required to fill the look-up table.

The initial simulation allowed the motor commands to range from 1° to 50° in either direction. Figure 4.4 illustrates how a typical trial might proceed with a "fresh" look-up table. Notice that each saccade was in the appropriate direction, but that the sequence of saccades tended to oscillate around the actual location of the target until the retinal error signal eventually resulted (by chance) in a zero error. This final saccade command and its immediately preceding retinal error code were entered into the look-up table for future use.

The results of three separate simulations, each using a different randomization sequence, are shown in Fig. 4.5. Notice that after about 100 target displacements, only 20% of the look-up table entries were filled, that after 1,000 displacements about 50% of the look-up table was filled, and that between 10,000 and 100,000 target displacements were required to fill the complete look-up table.

The results of 100 such simulations, each with a different randomization sequence, are summarized in Fig. 4.6. Note that approximately 40,000 trials were required on average to fill the look-up table, and that the total number of saccades was only slightly greater than the total number of target displacements. This is because after 50% of the look-up table was filled, almost all of the target displacements could be foveated with either one or two saccades. Thus, much

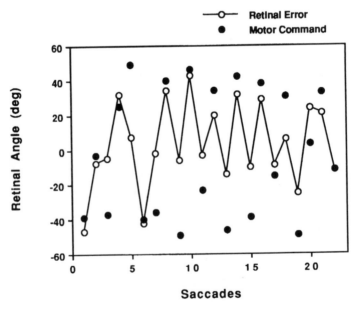

FIG. 4.4.   Sample trial in the 1° to 50° simulation illustrating a sequence of retinal errors and randomly selected motor commands, which eventually lead (by chance) to foveation.

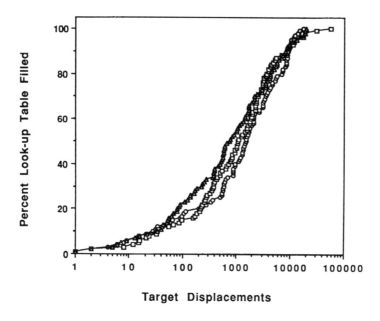

Target Displacements

FIG. 4.5. Three separate simulations illustrating the number of target displacements required to fill the 1° to 50° look-up table.

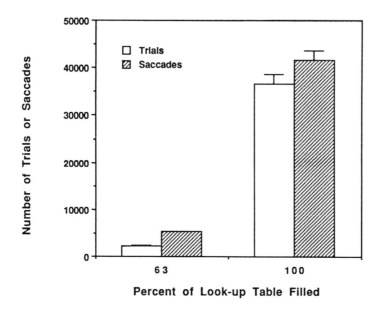

Percent of Look-up Table Filled

FIG. 4.6. Mean number of trials (target displacements) and saccades required to fill either 63% or 100% of the 1° to 50° look-up table (based on 100 separate simulations). Error bars = 1 S.E.M.

of the delay in filling the look-up table was associated with waiting for the random pairing of a target displacement and a saccade magnitude that was not already stored in the look-up table. Perhaps a more realistic measure of "filling" the look-up table was a value of 63%, which corresponds to the time constant of the exponential rise describing the process of filling up the look-up table. Note that only about 5,000 saccades were required to reach this level of matching retinal errors to saccadic commands.

A total of between 5,000 and 40,000 saccades seems a small price to pay for calibrating a sensory motor system, but recall that the simulation was limited to the horizontal axis. If the number of locations was expanded from 100 along the horizontal axis to all pairs of horizontal and vertical locations in a 100 by 100 matrix, then the 40,000+ saccades required to fill the look-up table must be squared. Assuming a rate of 2 saccades per second, this full 100 by 100 look-up table would require more than 27 years to fill! Even the more reasonable measure of filling only 63% of the look-up table would require over 24 weeks of saccades, with no breaks for sleeping, eating, or other things that infants are known to do other than making saccades.

This initial simulation, then, was simply a way of setting a baseline for the time required to calibrate the saccadic system without incorporating at least one known property of infant saccades; namely, the fact that they are hypometric. If we add this constraint by assuming that infant saccades are restricted to a range of 3° to 8° rather than 1° to 50°, the pattern of retinal errors and motor commands shown in Fig. 4.7 is obtained. This is the same initial target displacement as shown in Fig. 4.4, but now the initial saccade only reduces the retinal error by 3° to 8° because of the limit on saccade magnitudes. Notice that once the retinal error is reduced to 8° or less, the simulation undergoes oscillations until a random saccade foveates the target.

Is this use of small hypometric saccades an efficient way to calibrate the saccadic system? First, it should be clear that the entire look-up table can never be filled when the magnitude of saccades is limited to 8°. There are retinal errors from 9° to 50° that will never trigger a single saccade large enough for foveation. However, one can ask the question of efficiency under two conditions: (a) when the look-up table is not used at all (i.e., without memory for the results of previous saccade commands), and (b) when the lookup table is used, but with a fixed number of target displacements. Figure 4.8 shows the results of 100 simulations run with each of the two ranges of saccade magnitudes on 1,000 trials per simulation. Note that *without* the use of the look-up table, saccades limited to 3° to 8° resulted in approximately one third the total number of saccades across 1,000 trials than when saccades ranged from 1° to 50°. This is because hypometric saccades are less likely to lead to grossly *hyper*metric responding; that is, a sequence of overshoots. However, when the look-up table was used, there was no advantage to hypometric saccades. This is because once the look-up table in the 1° to 50° case was partially filled (63%),

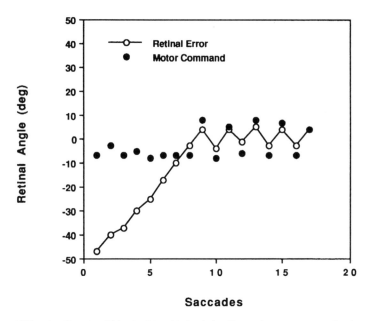

FIG. 4.7. Sample trial in the 3° to 8° simulation illustrating a sequence of retinal errors and randomly selected motor commands, which eventually lead (by chance) to foveation.

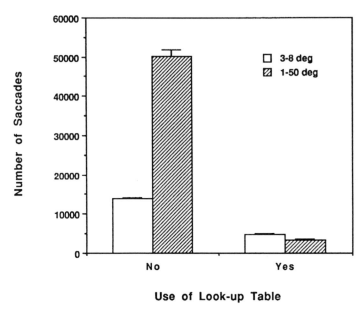

FIG. 4.8. Mean number of saccades required to foveate a target (across 1,000 trials) when saccade magnitudes ranged from 3° to 8° or from 1° to 50°, when the look-up table was and was not used (based on 100 separate simulations). Error bars = 1 S.E.M.

the greater efficiency of 3° to 8° saccades was overcome by the fact that only 1 to 3 saccades were required to foveate the target on later trials.

At this point one must ask whether these simulations represent a plausible scheme for calibrating the saccadic system in young infants. There are some obvious problems with these simulations. First, these simulations are noise-free, both at the sensory level, which registers the retinal error, and at the motor level, which initiates the saccadic command. Second, the manner in which the look-up table is filled assumes perfect memory for pairs of retinal errors and saccadic commands. Obviously, these are idealized simulations. Both noise and imperfect memory would lengthen the calibration process. Perhaps more importantly, however, is the simulated visual environment. Recall that the target consisted of a single luminous spot on a completely dark background. Perhaps we should consider the implications of adding structure to the visual environment.

The next simplest visual environment consists of two luminous targets on a dark background. Given the assumption that the scaling of retinal error magnitudes is initially unspecified, it is possible, with two targets in the visual field, to execute a command to one target and foveate the other. If the goal of the saccadic system were simply to place *any* target on the fovea, then foveating the "wrong" target would be fine. However, there is good evidence that infants make saccades to the *nearer* of two targets (Bronson, 1982). Thus, if the goal were to foveate the nearer target and the result of the saccade were to foveate the farther target, storage of this pair of retinal error code and saccadic command would be incorrect, especially because any future use of that pair (e.g., when only a single target was present) would fail to foveate the target.

Figure 4.9 shows the results of simulations in which two targets were initially placed at two randomly selected locations (between 1° and 50°) on the same side of the fovea. Again, 1,000 trials were presented in each of 100 simulations for saccades ranging from 3° to 8° and from 1° to 50°, and no entries were placed in the look-up table because saccades larger than 8° were never executed in the 3° to 8° simulations. Note that, as in the case of the single-target simulations (replotted for comparison), the use of hypometric saccades resulted in a much more efficient pattern for foveating one of the two targets.

Perhaps more important, however, was the percentage of errors in these simulations. Each random saccade that resulted in a foveation of the *farther* of the two targets was counted as an error. Figure 4.10 shows that approximately 40% of the saccades that resulted in foveating one of the two targets in the 1° to 50° simulations would have been an incorrect entry in the look-up table. In contrast, only 12% of the entries in the look-up table would have been incorrect when saccades were limited to 3° to 8°. Thus, smaller saccades are less likely to lead to errors in foveating one of two or more targets when the goal of the saccade is the nearest target.

The final simulation was an attempt to model the single-target environment in a more realistic manner. The following assumptions were made: First, retinal

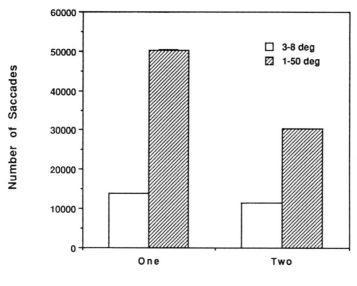

Number of Targets

FIG. 4.9. Mean number of saccades (across 1,000 trials) required to foveate either one target, or one of two targets when a saccade was directed to the nearer target, using either 3° to 8° saccades or 1° to 50° saccades (based on 100 separate simulations and no look-up table). Error bars for 1 S.E.M. are too small to be visible.

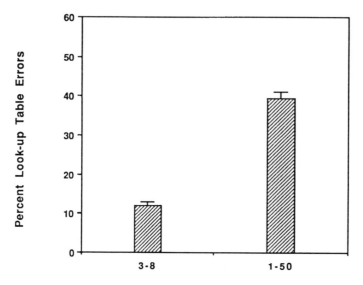

Range of Saccade Magnitudes (deg)

FIG. 4.10. Mean percent of errors (defined as foveating the *farther* of two targets) in the simulation described in Fig. 4.9 when saccade magnitudes ranged from either 3° to 8° or from 1° to 50°. Error bars = 1 S.E.M.

103

errors smaller than 3° were ignored because there is little evidence that saccades in infants are reliably initiated to such small target displacements. Second,
3° to 8° saccades were used to fill up only this "near foveal" portion of the
look-up table. Third, the remainder of the full look-up table (i.e., retinal errors
from 9° to 50°) was filled with the aid of a simple integration algorithm. That
is, 3° to 8° saccades were used to foveate targets beyond 8° from the fovea,
but a running sum of all saccade magnitudes in a localization sequence was stored
until the target was foveated; then that sum was entered in the look-up table
for the retinal error of the initial target displacement. Thus, once the initial portion of the look-up table was filled, any retinal error between 3° and 8° required
only a single additional saccade because these values were already stored in
the look-up table. Then, when a target was displaced to a location between 9°
and 50° from the fovea, a random sequence of 3° to 8° saccades was executed
until the fovea was within 8° of the target, followed by a final calibrated saccade
drawn from the partially filled look-up table.

As shown in Fig. 4.11, if the initial target displacement was 27° to the right
of the fovea, and the first four saccades were +4°, +7°, +5°, and +3° (randomly selected), then the fovea would be within 8° of the target. This retinal
error has already been stored in the look-up table and triggers the final 8° saccade that results in foveation. The sum of this sequence of five saccades, which
is equal to a saccade magnitude of 27°, is then also stored in the look-up table.

Figure 4.12 shows the results of this simulation. Approximately 1,200 saccades were required to fill up the 3° to 8° portion of the look-up table, and less
than 800 additional saccades were required to fill up the remainder of the look-
up table using the integration algorithm.

The first question to ask about this simulation is whether it is plausible as
a timeframe for infant saccadic calibration. We know that infant saccades are
hypometric at least into the fourth postnatal month, and that they begin to look
more adultlike by 6 months of age. The 1,203 saccades required to fill up the
3° to 8° portion of the look-up table, when expanded to include vertical as well
as horizontal locations, would require approximately 200 hours (at a rate of 2
saccades/sec). Given some rough estimates of the number of waking hours during
which infants *could* make saccades, 200 hours would entail approximately 2 to
3 months after birth. Thus, the model falls within a plausible timeframe.

However, the model still suffers from the implausibility of an idealized system with no noise and perfect memory. The model also underestimates by a
factor of 2 the age at which the saccadic system would become fully calibrated
using the integration algorithm (1934^2 saccades = 519 hours or approximately 13 weeks). The model also simplifies the task by not considering the added
complexity of the nonlinear nature of the oculomotor plant; that is, that the force
required to rotate the eye a given angular extent varies with starting orbital
position. Moreover, the complex attachment of the six extraocular muscles to
the eyeball implies that any saccade, even along the horizontal axis, must in-

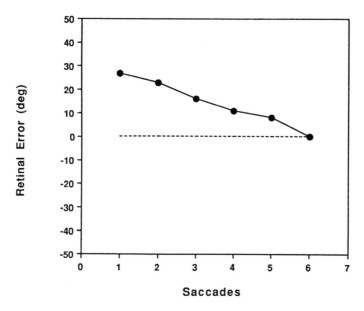

FIG. 4.11. Sample trial after the central (3° to 8°) portion of the look-up table was filled, illustrating the reduction in retinal error using randomly selected 3° to 8° saccades and the final calibrated saccade selected from the look-up table. The integration algorithm then entered the initial retinal error from this trial along with the sum of the series of saccadic magnitudes into the look-up table.

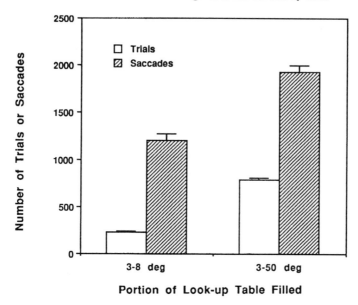

FIG. 4.12. Mean number of trials (target displacements) and saccades required to fill the 3° to 8° portion of the look-up table (without the integration algorithm) and the remaining 9° to 50° portion of the look-up table using the integration algorithm. Error bars = 1 S.E.M.

volve a complex configuration of motor commands whose timing and magnitude are not a simple linear sum of the forces required to move the eyeball from one point in (x, y) space to another point. Finally, the integration scheme introduced in this final simulation is unrealistic *not* because integration is not performed by neural systems (such integrations are, in fact, quite common in brainstem areas known to control the mature oculomotor system), but because these integrators are not perfect. Rather, most neural integrators "leak" or fail to hold the sum of their inputs for more than a few seconds (Robinson, 1989).

Despite these caveats, the model does offer a starting point for a very "dumb" system of sensorimotor calibration. A look-up table is the simplest and least elegant method of motor learning (Atkeson, 1989). I chose such a scheme over a more symbolic or algorithmic one, such as expressing the retinal error signal as the sine and cosine in a Cartesian coordinate system, for two reasons: First, it is not apparent to me how the visual system could employ a symbolic representation of retinal error signals without already having a calibrated system. My contention is that a look-up table representation offers a simple learning mechanism that, with a sufficient amount of data (gathered from pseudo-random sensorimotor activity), could act as the input to a more general symbolic algorithm. Once the algorithm was induced from a partial data set via the look-up table, all possible eye movements could be generated according to a few simple rules rather than with reference to the look-up table itself.

Second, as pointed out by Atkeson (1989), a look-up table is very fast and only locally affected by neural damage. In contrast, a symbolic representation tends to require computations that can be time-intensive, and if these computations are localized in a specific brain region, the entire system can be disabled by a small amount of neural damage. Moreover, if the algorithm does not have access to critical information, it will fail to compute the "correct" answer in many cases. Less built-in structure is required in a tabular representation, but it is less flexible and shows poor generalization to novel conditions.

A final but critical aspect of these simulations of saccadic calibration must now be revealed. I finessed the issue of topographic structure in the look-up table. If sequences of saccadic commands are integrated to yield a command for large retinal errors not already entered in the look-up table, then the summation of commands implies a topographic representation. If the retinal errors were randomly arranged in the look-up table, the property of adjacency would not yield integrated commands that would foveate targets with retinal errors between 9° and 50°. Thus, the final simulation, which was motivated by my goal of incorporating the known oculomotor behavior of young infants (i.e., multiple saccades), forced me to admit that the topographic structure of the retinal error signal is an essential feature of motor learning in the saccadic system. Once that assumption is incorporated into the model, one is forced to ask why the infant saccadic system takes so *long* to calibrate itself. Perhaps all of the other simplifying assumptions that I made in these simulations are unrealistic, and the effect of complicating factors such as noise, imperfect memory, and "leaky" integration delays the saccadic calibration process by several months. Although these are plausible explanations, I now believe that they account for only part of the lengthy postnatal period of hypometric saccades.

THE DEVELOPMENT OF POSITION CONSTANCY

I now discuss the hypothesis that I currently favor as the explanation for multiple saccades during early infancy. I still believe that the saccadic system must calibrate itself via oculomotor experience and that hypometric saccades are a more efficient way to perform such a calibration, but I now think that the primary reason for hypometric saccades in early infancy is the problem of *position constancy*. That is, how does the visual system compensate for the change in retinal information resulting from a saccade so as to maintain an invariant percept of the direction of stationary objects in space? This is not a trivial problem because the eyes are in nearly continuous motion resulting from movements of the body, the head, and the eyes themselves. If the same retinal stimulation can result from movements of some part of the observer or from movements of some part of the visual world, then how does the visual system differentiate object-movement from self-movement? In this section, I argue that an important, but largely overlooked, source of information about the direction and magnitude of eye movements—optic flow—could be used with other information about oculomotor commands to solve the problem of position constancy.

There are two classic views of the mechanism that enables the adult visual system to maintain position constancy across saccades (see Fig. 4.13). *Inflow* refers to a proprioceptive signal that senses the position of the eyeball in the orbit. *Outflow* refers to an efferent command to the extraocular muscles that rotates the eyeball by an expected amount. If the visual system could monitor precisely the position of the eyes in the orbits, either by proprioception or by knowledge of motor commands, then changes in the retinal image created by self-movement could be subtracted from changes in the retinal image created by object-movement, thereby yielding a veridical perception of visual direction. Both of these models, of course, beg the question as to how either inflow or outflow information becomes calibrated. Constraints on that calibration process are, I believe, the primary reason for hypometric saccades in early infancy.

The inflow model has had few proponents over the past century, even though there are muscle spindles in the extraocular muscles that could mediate a stretch reflex analogous to that used in the spinal motor system to signal limb position. Moreover, Steinbach (1987) has summarized recent evidence from patients whose eye muscles have been surgically reattached, suggesting that inflow signals *are* used in the perception of visual direction.

In contrast, the outflow model has been championed by nearly every the-

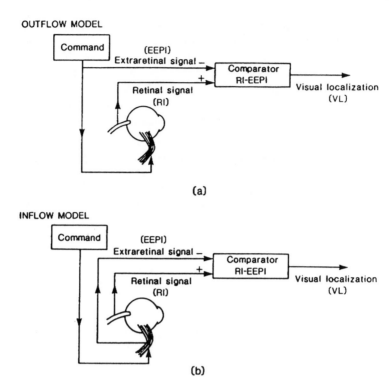

FIG. 4.13. Two models that have been proposed as explanations for position constancy during eye movements. From L. Matin (1986).

orist since Helmholtz (1925). Evidence in support of outflow is twofold. First, rotation of the eye by external means, such as pressure from a finger, leads to the perception of a change in visual direction for all points in the visual field. The explanation for this anomalous percept is that outflow signals, which normally accompany a saccade, are not present to be subtracted from the expected effect of the eye movement. Thus, the change in position of the retinal image is registered as a change in visual direction. Second, if the eye is prevented from rotating despite the presence of a saccadic command, then the apparent visual direction of all points in the visual field also changes. Again, the explanation for this anomalous percept is that the saccade activates a signal, referred to as an *efferent copy* or *corollary discharge*, in expectation of the change in position of the retinal image. When this compensatory signal is not matched by a rotation of the eye and its resultant change in retinal information, the unchanged retinal information is assigned a new set of visual directions.

There is absolutely no argument with these observations in support of a role for outflow. They have been replicated many times, most recently in a series of eye press experiments by Bridgeman and his colleagues (Bridgeman & Delgado, 1984; Ilg, Bridgeman, & Hoffmann, 1989; Stark & Bridgeman, 1983), and in a series of paralyzed eye muscle experiments by L. Matin and his colleagues (L. Matin et al., 1982; see also L. Matin, 1986). The eye press experiments reveal not only that displacement of the retinal image in the absence of a saccadic command induces an anomalous percept of a change in directional values, but that a slow eye press, which is compensated for by additional innervation to keep the retinal image stabilized, results in a shift in apparent visual direction. The paralyzed eye muscle experiments clearly indicate that an unsuccessful attempt to make a saccade results in a shift in apparent visual direction. However, this apparent shift in visual direction is not reflected in judgments that use a *head*-centered reference (e.g., setting a point to "straight ahead") when the entire visual field is illuminated. That is, the paralyzed eye muscle effect is only consistent with the outflow model when the target is a single luminous spot on a dark background. The absence of the effect under normally illuminated conditions has been labeled *visual capture* and has been assumed to involve knowledge of the typical appearance of visual images under nonparalyzed conditions as well as the visibility of parts of the body in the retinal image (e.g., the nose and orbits or the hands and feet).

What is missing from these models of position constancy, in addition to an account of how inflow or outflow signals become calibrated during development, is a consideration of the *visual* information that is present during a saccade. Most theorists have dismissed this visual information because of the blur of the retinal image during a saccade and because of saccadic suppression. These are, admittedly, serious counterarguments. However, one must consider the quality of retinal information required to extract a change in eye position during a saccade. Whatever the process, even if it does not involve visual information, it must be fairly elementary because it is present in virtually every organism that has a movable eyeball. Thus, it must be that highly detailed spatial resolution is not required to determine how far and in what direction the eye has rotated. The infant visual system is just such a low spatial frequency organism. Moreover, saccadic suppression is only on the order of 0.5 log units. Adults can clearly localize targets *during* a saccade. In fact, one of the modern classics on the role of outflow in position constancy is a paradigm developed by L. Matin, E. Matin, and Pearce (1969), which asks subjects to judge the visual direction of a flash presented during a saccade. These experiments have shown that in total darkness, the apparent visual direction of a flash begins to change just prior to the saccade and continues to change for up to several hundred milliseconds after the saccade. Interestingly, these experiments have not provided clear evidence of a similar change in perceived visual direction due to outflow when they are conducted in a normally illuminated environment (O'Regan, 1984).

What visual information is present in a normally illuminated environment that *could* be used to specify the direction and magnitude of a saccade? Gibson (1950), and several others in more recent years, including Lee (1974) and Banks (personal communication, February, 1989), have pointed out that the retinal image motion induced by a saccade is unique. First, it consists of changes in the position of *all* elements in the visual field. Second, for objects at a constant viewing distance, all elements move rigidly. That is, there is no differential velocity or shearing motion induced by a saccade. Third, the change in position occurs over very brief durations. A typical 10° saccade in adults lasts only about 30 to 40 msec.

This last fact, the very brief duration of saccades, suggests that some form of autocorrelation operates on the pre- and post-saccadic images. Figure 4.14 illustrates two samples from a "visual field" just before and just after a saccade. A form of pattern-matching could determine how far the image was displaced by "counting" the displacement in units of retinal local sign.[1]

If an autocorrelation is performed on the image, then by what mechanism is this autocorrelation implemented? The classic view of motion detection (Reichardt, 1961; see also Santen & Sperling, 1985) is a form of autocorrelation. The motion detector shown in Fig. 4.15 delays the output of one receptor so that its signal coincides in time with the output of an adjacent receptor that is stimulated by a target moving from receptor #1 to receptor #2 during the delay interval. If the motion is faster or slower than the delayed output of receptor #1, or if the target moves in the opposite direction, the output of the motion detector will be less than optimal.

It seems clear that the output from the entire retina is, at some level of the visual system, passed through a motion-analyzing network consisting of local motion detectors. These motion detectors are spaced differently as a function of retinal eccentricity and/or the spatial frequency (size) of targets. For example, several investigators (Baker & Braddick, 1985; Burr, Ross, & Morrone, 1986; Burt & Sperling, 1981) have shown in adults that the direction of motion can be extracted, either in the periphery or in central vision, with low spatial frequency (i.e., large) stimuli moving at velocities exceeding 100°/sec. These are velocities that for high spatial frequency (i.e., small) stimuli would lead to the perception of blur and little or no directional information. What seems to characterize these motion detectors is a relative invariance of the delay element between spatially adjacent receptors. Thus, if one extrapolated from these adult experiments (see Fig. 4.16), it is quite possible that in the far periphery there are receptors sensitive to extremely low spatial frequency stimuli (i.e., separated by large retinal distances) and to very high velocities. What I am proposing here is a *direct* motion-sensitive mechanism that performs the autocorrelation of pre- and post-saccadic images "on-line" during a saccade.

Clearly, if the velocity of a saccade were very high, the motion signal could saturate and provide inaccurate information about the change in eye position.

---

[1]Of course, this pattern-matching task would also have to solve the problem of contrast variation induced by changing the receptive fields over which corresponding image positions were located before and after the saccade. This could be done by the zero-crossing approach suggested by Marr (1982) or by some sort of gradient approach.

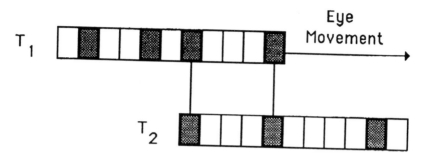

FIG. 4.14. Schematized one-dimensional retinal images before (T_1) and after (T_2) a saccade.

What would facilitate this process of extracting velocity information during saccades are *small* saccades. Small saccades have lower peak velocities, and for adults, peak velocities of saccades less than $10°$ in magnitude are $200°/sec$ or less. Data from Hainline, Turkel, Abramov, Lemerise, & Harris (1984) on saccades in infants (see Fig. 4.17) indicate not only that saccades are typically less than $10°$ in magnitude, but that their peak velocities are less than $200°/sec$, much like those of adults.

If infants extracted eye velocity from retinal information during saccades, how would they convert that velocity signal into a change in position? The answer is *integration*. The integral of velocity is position. Thus, a neural integration process, which is clearly performed in other areas of the visual system (see Robinson, 1989), could provide the kind of position information needed to specify the direction and magnitude of a saccade.

As with any preliminary hypothesis, there are several potential problems with this model. First, I simplified the velocity information present in the moving

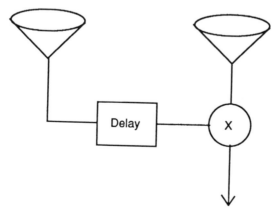

FIG. 4.15. Idealized rightward motion detector consisting of two receptors, a delay, and a multiplier.

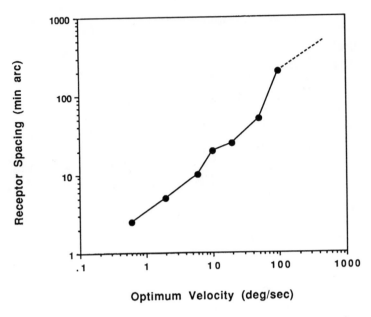

FIG. 4.16. Relation between optimal velocity sensitivity and receptor spacing in human adults based on data from the retinal periphery and from the fovea using gratings of optimal spatial sensitivity. Dashed line is a linear extrapolation into the region of peak saccadic velocities. Redrawn from Nakayama (1985).

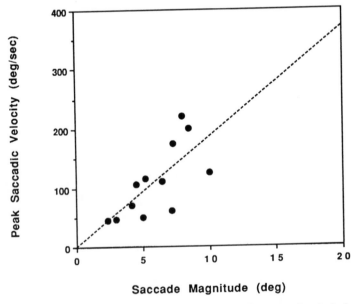

FIG. 4.17. Relation between saccadic magnitude and peak saccadic velocity in a 65-day-old human infant who was freely scanning a two-dimensional visual display. Redrawn from Hainline et al. (1984).

retinal image during a saccade. As shown in Fig. 4.18, the rotation of the eyeball creates a gradient of velocities, which is highest at the meridian perpendicular to the axis of rotation and lowest at the two endpoints of the axis of rotation. Thus, for a horizontal saccade the highest velocities are along the "equator" and the velocities at the two "poles" are zero. Second, it is not clear how these different velocities would be combined into a single value that could be integrated to yield a measure of the change in eye position.

One potential solution to these problems involves the process by which motion information is extracted from the optic flow present in the retinal image during a saccade. If the output of all the local motion detectors distributed over the entire retina were simply summed, they would provide a signal at least proportional to eye velocity. Motion detectors with receptors spaced close together only send a signal when stimulus velocity is slow. Thus, for these detectors, the rapid stimulus velocities induced by a saccade would be invisible because of saturation. Only those motion detectors with velocity sensitivity matching the velocity of the saccade would respond. Because of the gradient of retinal velocities from one "pole" to another, the direction of the saccade would be defined by the meridian of greatest velocity.

This scheme does not explain how the velocity signal and its integrated position signal become calibrated during development. It merely points out the possibility that information exists in the changing retinal image during a saccade to specify the direction and magnitude of a saccade. What seems undeniable is that the visual system must learn the correlation between these visual signals and the efferent commands that triggered the saccade. Two points are important to note here. First, each and every saccade provides the infant with an opportunity to extract that correlation between retinal and extraretinal information. There may be noise in the extraretinal information and in the retinal

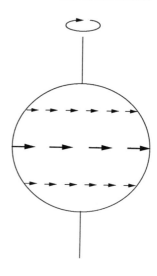

FIG. 4.18. Schematic of the posterior view of the retinal image during a rightward eye movement. The length of each vector is proportional to image velocity.

information, but the *pattern* of velocities across the retinal image is precisely the same for every saccade; only the direction and magnitude of the velocity gradient changes across saccades. Second, Hein, Vital-Durand, Salinger, and Diamond (1979) have provided compelling evidence in cats that the absence of correlated retinal and extraretinal signals prevents the normal development of spatially guided behaviors. Thus, the "meaning" of retinal and extraretinal signals must be extracted through self-produced interactions with the visual world. This enables the organism to differentiate retinal motion created by object movement from retinal motion created by movement of the eye.

Finally, there are some other aspects of adults' perception of visual direction during saccades that seem, on the surface, to contradict the scheme that I am proposing. For example, Bridgeman and his colleagues (Bridgeman, Hendry, & Stark, 1975; Stark et al., 1976) have shown that a structured visual field can be moved up to 30% of the magnitude of the saccade *during the saccade* without the subject being aware of the visual displacement. Recently, Shioiri and Cavanagh (1989) reported that adults are insensitive to displacements of a 30° × 30° random-dot field during a saccade, suggesting that the low-level motion system is suppressed during saccades.

If position constancy is based on retinal information acquired during the saccade, then how can adults be so insensitive to these image displacements? I think two factors are involved. First, although the size of the visual stimuli in the Bridgeman et al. (1975) and Shioiri and Cavanagh (1989) studies were relatively large (13° × 13° and 30° × 30°, respectively) compared to earlier studies, which used a single point of light, the subjects had peripheral retinal information specifying that the visual environment had *not* moved during the saccade. Thus, peripheral retinal information specifying the stability of the visual world may outweigh the central retinal information specifying a mismatch between retinal position and the expected outcome of a saccadic command. This interpretation is supported by Bridgeman and Fisher's (1990) finding that detection of image displacement during a saccade is poorer near the fovea than in the peripheral visual field. Moreover, as pointed out by Shioiri and Cavanagh (1989), "The visual system can simplify its task of extracting a stable visual world during saccades if it totally ignores motion information from finer image details. Whether or not motion information from larger scale image features are analyzed remains to be seen" (p. 927).

Second, even under reduced conditions, adults' perceptions of visual direction are resistant to recalibration. For example, a number of experiments (e.g., McLaughlin, 1967; Miller, Anstis, & Templeton, 1981) have shown that the adult saccadic system can quickly alter its mapping of retinal error onto motor commands. The paradigm consists of displacing a target to a given peripheral location and moving that target during the saccade as one attempts to bring its image onto the fovea. If the target is moved toward the fovea, adults make a normal saccade that lands beyond the distance of the target. If this target movement is presented over several dozen trials, the saccadic system recalibrates itself and makes a smaller than normal saccade so that the fovea is directed to the "new" target location based on its "old" retinal error signal. Despite the ease with which the gain of the saccadic system can be altered in this paradigm, the perceived visual direction of the target is altered very little (Moidell & Bedell, 1988). Thus, as pointed out by Bridgeman, Lewis, Heit, and Nagle (1979), there appear to be two different systems for position constancy: a motor system that can be rapidly recalibrated, and a cognitive system that is resistant to recalibration even when the motor recalibration is largely complete.

The critical question is whether this dissociation of motor and cognitive recalibration observed in adults is also present in early infancy. Given the protracted period required for initial calibration of the saccadic system, it is possible that the perception of object position in early infancy is also initially uncalibrated. However, once the correlation between retinal and extraretinal information for change in eye position has become established during early infancy, the system can function quite well even under impoverished conditions. For example, adults can correctly localize targets in the dark when no visual information is present during the saccade to specify the direction and magnitude of the eye movement. The system, once calibrated, appears to retain a memory of the expected effects of saccadic commands. However, a systematic alteration of the correlation between retinal and extraretinal information for change in eye position can lead to a rapid remapping of the motor system, even though the cognitive system remains largely unchanged. Presumably, extensive adaptation experience would eventually lead to a total recalibration of the motor and cognitive systems, but such long-term experiments have rarely been attempted.

SUMMARY AND CONCLUSIONS

In this chapter, I have attempted to outline two fundamental reasons why young infants require an extended period of postnatal visual experience to calibrate the magnitude of their saccadic eye movements. The first reason involves the matching of specific neural command signals directed to the eye muscles with the angular rotation of the eye that is required to bring the image of a peripheral target onto the fovea. Apparently, some minimal amount of oculomotor experience is necessary for the saccadic system to become calibrated. Although a point-by-point (look-up table) learning algorithm could, in principle, succeed in calibrating the saccadic system, it appears that some form of rule-structure is required to speed up the calibration process, given the known time-course of the development of saccadic accuracy in infancy. Moreover, it appears that the topographic relations inherent in the retinal image must be preserved as this sensory information for target location is transformed into oculomotor commands for foveation.

The second reason that saccadic calibration extends over several postnatal months concerns the mechanism by which the developing visual system maintains position constancy during saccades. I argued that both inflow and outflow information, which could in principle specify the magnitude and direction of a saccade, must be calibrated by utilizing the optic flow information present in the retinal image *during* a saccade. The accuracy of this retinal information is enhanced when the velocity of saccades is reduced. Small-magnitude saccades have lower velocities, and these small saccades are very common in early infancy. Thus, the optic flow information extracted during small saccades could be used, along with the knowledge that a saccade had been initiated, to calibrate the *visual* outcome of specific saccadic commands. This learned correlation between the visual consequences of saccades and their preceding neural commands would then form the basis for position constancy under reduced conditions when outflow or inflow provides the only means for specifying perceived visual direction.

Many of these ideas require empirical tests. For example, it is not clear whether adults are sensitive to shifts in the location of the visual image during a saccade when the visual information in the far periphery is altered. It also is not clear whether precise position information can be extracted from the integration of velocity signals. In addition, the mechanism by which velocity signals are extracted from whole-field image motion has not been worked out. Nevertheless, the mechanism that enables the developing visual system to map retinal coordinates into object coordinates, given a freely moving head and eyes, is a puzzle that merits further empirical and computational study.

ACKNOWLEDGMENTS

During the preparation of this chapter, I was supported in part by a fellowship from the John Simon Guggenheim Memorial Foundation, by the Center for Advanced Study in the Behavioral Sciences, and by NSF grant BNS 87-00864 to the Center for Advanced Study in the Behavioral Sciences. Computer consultation provided by Patrick Goebel is gratefully acknowledged, as are the helpful comments provided by Bruce Bridgeman, Marshall Haith, and Sandy Shea.

REFERENCES

Aslin, R. N. (1987). Anatomical constraints on oculomotor development: Implications for infant perception. In A. Yonas (Ed.), *The Minnesota symposia on child psychology: Vol. 20. Perceptual development in infancy* (pp. 67–104). Hillsdale, NJ: Lawrence Erlbaum Associates.

Aslin, R. N., & Salapatek, P. (1975). Saccadic localization of visual targets by the very young human infant. *Perception and Psychophysics, 17,* 293–302.

Atkeson, C. G. (1989). Learning arm kinematics and dynamics. *Annual Review of Neuroscience, 12,* 157–183.

Baker, C. L., & Braddick, O. J. (1985). Eccentricity-dependent scaling of the limits for short-range apparent motion perception. *Vision Research, 25,* 803–812.

Banks, M. S. (1987). Visual recalibration and the development of contrast and optical flow perception. In A. Yonas (Ed.), *The Minnesota symposia on child psychology: Vol. 20. Perceptual development in infancy* (pp. 145–196). Hillsdale, NJ: Lawrence Erlbaum Associates.

Bedell, H. E., & Flom, M. C. (1981). Monocular spatial distortion in strabismic amblyopia. *Investigative Ophthalmology and Visual Science, 20,* 263–268.

Bedell, H. E., & Flom, M. C. (1983). Normal and abnormal space perception. *American Journal of Optometry and Physiological Optics, 60,* 425–435.

Bedell, H. E., Flom, M. C., & Barbeito, R. (1985). Spatial aberrations and acuity in strabismus and amblyopia. *Investigative Ophthalmology and Visual Science, 26,* 909–916.

Boring, E. G. (1942). *Sensation and perception in the history of experimental psychology.* New York: Appleton-Century.

Bridgeman, B., & Delgado, D. (1984). Sensory effects of eyepress are due to efference. *Perception and Psychophysics, 36,* 482–484.

Bridgeman, B., & Fisher, B. (1990). Saccadic suppression of displacement is strongest in central vision. *Perception, 19,* 103–111.

Bridgeman, B., Hendry, D., & Stark, L. (1975). Failure to detect displacement of the visual world during saccadic eye movements. *Vision Research, 15,* 719–722.

Bridgeman, B., Lewis, S., Heit, G., & Nagle, M. (1979). Relation between cognitive and motor-oriented systems of visual position perception. *Journal of Experimental Psychology: Human Perception and Performance, 5,* 692–700.

Bronson, G. W. (1982). The scanning patterns of human infants: Implications for visual learning. In L. P. Lipsitt (Ed.), *Monographs on infancy* (pp. 1–102). Norwood, NJ: Ablex.

Burr, D. C., Ross, J., & Morrone, M. C. (1986). Smooth and sampled motion. *Vision Research, 26,* 643–652.

Burt, P., & Sperling, G. (1981). Time, distance, and feature trade-offs in visual apparent motion. *Psychological Review, 88,* 171–195.

Clarkson, M. G., Clifton, R. K., & Morrongiello, B. A. (1985). The effects of sound duration on newborns' head orientation. *Journal of Experimental Child Psychology, 39,* 20–36.

Gibson, J. J. (1950). *The perception of the visual world.* Boston: Houghton Mifflin.

Hainline, L., Turkel, J., Abramov, I., Lemerise, E., & Harris, C. M. (1984). Characteristics of saccades in human infants. *Vision Research, 24,* 1771–1780.

Haith, M. M. (1980). *Rules that babies look by.* Hillsdale, NJ: Lawrence Erlbaum Associates.

Harris, P., & MacFarlane, A. (1974). The growth of the effective visual field from birth to seven weeks. *Journal of Experimental Child Psychology, 18,* 340–348.

Hein, A., Vital-Durand, F., Salinger, W., & Diamond, R. (1979). Eye movements initiate visual-motor developments in the cat. *Science, 204,* 1321–1322.

Helmholtz, H. von (1925). *Treatise on physiological optics* (Vol. 3.; J. P. C. Southall, Trans.). New York: Optical Society of America.

Hering, E. (1942). *Spatial sense and movements of the eye* (C. A. Raade, Trans.). Baltimore: American Academy of Optometry. (Original work published 1880)

Hofsten, C. von (1982). Eye-hand coordination in newborns. *Developmental Psychology, 18,* 450–461.

Ilg, U. J., Bridgeman, B., & Hoffmann, K. P. (1989). Influence of mechanical disturbance on oculomotor behavior. *Vision Research, 29,* 545–551.

Larsen, J. S. (1971a). The sagittal growth of the eye: I. Ultrasonic measurement of the depth of the anterior chamber from birth to puberty. *Acta Ophthalmologica, 49,* 239–262.

Larsen, J. S. (1971b). The sagittal growth of the eye: II. Ultrasonic measurement of the axial diameter of the lens and the anterior segment from birth to puberty. *Acta Ophthalmologica, 49,* 427–440.

Larsen, J. S. (1971c). The sagittal growth of the eye: III. Ultrasonic measurement of the posterior segment (axial length of the vitreous) from birth to puberty. *Acta Ophthalmologica, 49,* 441–453.

Larsen, J. S. (1971d). The sagittal growth of the eye: IV. Ultrasonic measurement of the axial length of the eye from birth to puberty. *Acta Ophthalmologica, 49,* 873–886.

Lee, D. N. (1974). Visual information during locomotion. In R. B. MacLeod & H. Pick (Eds.), *Perception: Essays in honor of J. J. Gibson* (pp. 250–267). Ithaca, NY: Cornell University Press.

Lewis, T. L., Maurer, D., & Kay, D. (1978). Newborns' central vision: Whole or hole? *Journal of Experimental Child Psychology, 26,* 193–203.

Lotze, R. H. (1852). *Medicinische Psychologie oder Physiologie per Seele* [Medical psychology or the physiology of the soul]. Leipzig: Weidmann'sche Buchhandlung.

MacFarlane, A., Harris, P., & Barnes, I. (1976). Central and peripheral vision in early infancy. *Journal of Experimental Child Psychology, 21,* 532–538.

Marr, D. (1982). *Vision.* San Francisco: W. H. Freeman.

Matin, L. (1986). Visual localization and eye movements. In K. R. Boff, L. Kaufman, & J. P. Thomas (Eds.), *Handbook of perception and human performance: Vol. I. Sensory processes and perception* (Chap. 20, pp. 1–45). New York: Wiley.

Matin, L., Matin, E., & Pearce, D. (1969). Visual perception of direction when voluntary saccades occur: I. Relation of visual direction of a fixation target extinguished before a saccade to a flash presented during the saccade. *Perception and Psychophysics, 5,* 65–80.

Matin, L., Picoult, E., Stevens, J. K., Edwards, M. W., Young, D., & MacArthur, R. (1982). Oculoparalytic illusion: Visual field dependent spatial mislocalization by humans with experimentally paralyzed extraocular muscles. *Science, 216,* 198–201.

McLaughlin, S. C. (1967). Parametric adjustment in saccadic eye movements. *Perception and Psychophysics, 2,* 359–362.

Miller, J. M., Anstis, T., & Templeton, W. B. (1981). Saccadic plasticity: Parametric adaptive control by retinal feedback. *Journal of Experimental Psychology: Human Perception and Performance, 7,* 356–366.

Moidell, B. G., & Bedell, H. E. (1988). Changes in oculocentric visual direction induced by the recalibration of saccades. *Vision Research, 28,* 329–336.

Muir, D., & Field, J. (1979). Newborn infants orient to sounds. *Child Development, 50,* 431–436.

Nakayama, K. (1985). Biological image motion processing: A review. *Vision Research, 25,* 625–660.

O'Regan, J. K. (1984). Retinal versus extraretinal influences in flash localization during saccadic eye movements in the presence of a visible background. *Perception and Psychophysics, 36,* 1–14.

Reichardt, W. (1961). Autocorrelation: A principle for the evaluation of sensory information by the central nervous system. In W. Rosenblith (Ed.), *Sensory communication* (pp. 303–317). Cambridge, MA: MIT Press.

Rieser, J., Yonas, A., & Wikner, K. (1976). Radial localization of odors by human newborns. *Child Development, 47,* 856–859.

Robinson, D. A. (1989). Integrating with neurons. *Annual Review of Neuroscience, 12,* 33–45.

Santen, J. P. H. van, & Sperling, G. (1985). Elaborated Reichardt detectors. *Journal of the Optical Society of America A, 2,* 300–321.

Schlodtmann, W. (1902). Ein Beitrag zur Lehre von der optischen Localisation bei Blindgeborenen [A contribution to the understanding of visual localization by persons born blind]. *Archives fur Ophthalmologie, 54,* 256–267.

Senden, M. von (1960). *Space and sight: The perception of space and shape in the congenitally blind before and after operations.* (P. Heath, Trans.). London: Methuen.

Shioiri, S., & Cavanagh, P. (1989). Saccadic suppression of low-level motion. *Vision Research, 29,* 915–928.

Stark, L., & Bridgeman, B. (1983). Role of the corollary discharge in space constancy. *Perception and Psychophysics, 34,* 371–380.

Stark, L., Kong, R., Schwartz, S., Hendry, D., & Bridgeman, B. (1976). Saccadic suppression of image displacement. *Vision Research, 16,* 1185–1187.

Steinbach, M. J. (1987). Proprioceptive knowledge of eye position. *Vision Research, 27,* 1737–1744.

Walls, G. L. (1951a). The problem of visual direction: Part I. The history to 1900. *American Journal of Optometry and Archives of American Academy of Optometry, 28,* 55–83.

Walls, G. L. (1951b). The problem of visual direction: Part II. The tangible basis for nativism. *American Journal of Optometry and Archives of American Academy of Optometry, 28,* 115–146.

Walls, G. L. (1951c). The problem of visual direction: Part III. Experimental attacks and their results. *American Journal of Optometry and Archives of American Academy of Optometry, 28,* 173–212.

Welch, R. B. (1986). Adaptation of space perception. In K. R. Boff, L. Kaufman, & J. P. Thomas (Eds.), *Handbook of perception and human performance: Vol. I. Sensory processes and perception* (Chap. 24, pp. 1–45). New York: Wiley.

Yuodelis, C., & Hendrickson, A. (1986). A qualitative and quantitative analysis of the human fovea during development. *Vision Research, 26,* 847–855.

5

Kinematic Foundations
of Infant Visual Perception

Philip J. Kellman
Swarthmore College

> *If asked what aspect of vision means most to them, a watchmaker may answer "acuity," a night flier "sensitivity," and an artist "color." But to animals which invented the vertebrate eye, and hold the patents on most of the features of the human model, the visual registration of motion was of the greatest importance.*
>
> —Walls, 1942, p. 342

Only mobile organisms have elaborate perceptual systems, and their functions are tied to motion in multiple ways. The most obvious importance of registering motion involves the detection of moving things, which may pose danger, offer nutrition, and so on. No less important is the registration of self-motion: the use of optical information to guide locomotion and other activities. In recent years, another central role of motion has been recognized and elaborated, most clearly in visual perception: The motions of objects and observers furnish information about persisting properties of the environment, such as objects and spatial layout (J. J. Gibson, 1966, 1979; Johansson, 1970; Johansson, von Hofsten, & Jansson, 1980). Information given by spatiotemporal changes or *kinematic* information has been argued to be central in mature perception because of its greater accuracy in specifying properties of the environment, and because perceivers seem specially equipped to utilize it (Braunstein, 1976; J. J. Gibson, 1966, 1979; Johansson et al., 1980). In this chapter, I connect these notions of the primacy of kinematic information about objects and events with a conjecture about the development of visual perception: Kinematic information may be fundamental to the earliest perceptual capacities. The initial abilities of human

121

infants to perceive objects, spatial layout, and events may depend predominantly on information carried by spatiotemporal patterns. After elaborating this thesis, I evaluate it by examining research in three areas: perception of the unity and boundaries of objects, perception of three-dimensional form, and perception of motion and stability by moving observers.

Traditionally, students of visual perception have pondered how knowledge of the world might be obtained from momentary images projected to the eyes. Changes in stimulation given by motion and events were often considered as complexities compounding the already difficult problem of interpreting images. The past two decades have witnessed something of a reversal in this characterization in perceptual theory. Some theorists, especially J. J. Gibson (1966, 1979) and Johansson (1970), have gone so far as to suggest that temporal and spatiotemporal variation in the optic array is most fundamental to perception. From this characterization of perception as *event perception,* information in static optic arrays (purely spatial variation) is considered a limiting or degenerate case.

Two related ideas are central to an event perception perspective. One is that information carried by motion has, in principle, greater power to specify properties of objects, space, and events than purely spatial (static) information. The second is that perceptual systems are specially adapted to utilize such information. Regarding the first claim, mathematical analyses have indicated the richness of optical change information about spatial layout, object structure, and particular events (Koenderink, 1986; Lee, 1974; Longuet-Higgins & Prazdny, 1980; Nakayama & Loomis, 1974). Optical transformations can specify unequivocally the rigidity or non-rigidity of a scene, the three-dimensional (3-D) layout of surfaces and the forms of objects. Events, such as the motion of an observer through an environment or the approach of an object, are also specified by information available in transforming optic arrays. Although the linkages between available information and aspects of spatial layout and events depend in every analysis upon certain assumptions, these assumptions are often satisfied in ordinary perception and, moreover, can in some cases be verified by other available optic flow information (e.g., Lee, 1974; Longuet-Higgins & Prazdny, 1980). Brunswik (1956) used the phrase *ecological validity* to refer to the accuracy, in ordinary circumstances, of the relation between perceptual information and facts about the environment. In terms of ecological validity, a strong case has been made that spatiotemporal information is generally superior to information available in momentary projections (Braunstein, 1976; J. J. Gibson, 1966; Hochberg, 1974). J. J. Gibson's use of the term *ecological* (1966, 1979), as in *ecological optics,* is both different and related. It refers to the ways in which the physical world structures energy; such structured energy (e.g., the optic array) carries information specific to the environment producing it. Brunswik's notion, a grading of the value of various information sources, is more neutral with regard to the origins of information. Much of the importance claimed for kinematic information in perception depends on the connection between Gibson's and Brunswik's notions of ecology. If spatiotemporal patterning in the optic array carries information specific to the structure of the environment, this information is part of ecological optics in Gibson's sense and has high ecological validity in Brunswik's sense.

Evidence that kinematic information about the environment is not only available in principle but actually utilized in ordinary perception has also accumulated rapidly, both in psychophysical and psychobiological investigations. The study of perception of structure from motion (SFM) has become a central area of research in visual perception (Braunstein, 1976; Johansson, 1970; Rogers & Graham, 1982; Ullman, 1979). Kinematic information comprises some of the most effective bases for structural properties of the environment, such as relative depth and surface layout (Braunstein, 1976; J. J. Gibson, Kaplan, Reynolds, & Wheeler, 1969; Rogers & Graham, 1982) and perception of 3-D form (e.g., Todd, 1982; Wallach & O'Connell, 1953). Information in optic flow has also been shown to be effective and precise in specifying events, such as an observer's motion through the environment (Warren, 1976) and the time to contact between an observer and an object (Lee, 1974).

Evidence for physiological specialization has also emerged. The possibility of neural circuits specifically designed to detect properties of optical change has been suggested by both psychophysical experiments in humans and receptive field mapping in other species (Regan & Beverly, 1978; Regan & Cynader, 1979). Results reported by Allman, Miezin, and McGuinness (1985) raise the possibility that a large number of cortical cells previously thought to have classical (local) receptive fields actually respond better to relative motions involving both local and more remote regions of the retina. Such findings may ultimately lead to the positing of certain optical transformations, as opposed to static dots, edges, and corners, as the basic neurological "vocabulary" of visual perception.

Event Perception and Early Perceptual Competence

A number of theorists have suggested a relation between spatiotemporal information and the evolution of perceptual systems (E. J. Gibson, 1984; J. J. Gibson, 1966; Johansson, 1970; Marr, 1982; Shepard, 1984). The linkages between objects, spatial layout, and events in the world on one hand, and spatiotemporal changes in optic array on the other, depend on the basic geometry of space and time. For example, the projective changes given by a rigid, rotating 3-D object are determined by projective geometry, along with some basic physical constraints (e.g., light moves in straight lines; objects tend to be opaque). The specificity of this relationship is such that, given a few ecologically plausible constraints, the 3-D form of an object is recoverable from the information in optical transformations (Ullman, 1979). Because such relationships are rooted in basic aspects of the ecology, it is plausible that they have been exploited in the evolution of perceptual systems. For example, Johansson (1970) suggested that the visual system might have evolved to be a "perspective decoder," detecting objects from optical transformations by the rules of projective geometry.

Compatible with such evolutionary hypotheses is a developmental one. Kinematic information—information given over time by motion—may be fundamental in perceptual development. An evolutionary origin already suggests that such perceptual abilities, subserved by specialized perceptual mechanisms, might operate without learning. The developmental hypothesis intended here goes further in suggesting that kinematically based abilities appear earliest in development and constitute the primary source of meaningful contact with the environment in the early months of life. An evolutionary origin need not imply developmental primacy; mechanisms sensitive to kinematic information might arise by maturation after others already operate. The developmental hypothesis that kinematic information is fundamental requires an additional rationale.

Ecological Validity and Risk Aversion

Adult perceivers use information from a variety of sources, each having different informational validity. As Berkeley (1709/1963) made clear, information about 3-D space that is present in a single, momentary image is ambiguous. Yet it can hardly be denied that monocular spatial information plays some role in perception. Pictorial cues, such as the depth indicated by two converging lines (linear perspective), might sometimes be misleading (as when the lines are not really parallel in 3-D space) but can be shown to operate in the absence of other information. The Ames room and Ames window (Ames, 1951) are dramatic examples. Wallach (1985) has argued that any stimulus variable that correlates to some degree with depth will come to function as a depth cue, and he has documented some surprising examples of this hypothesis.

These cues, which generally have lesser ecological validity, are in most cases readily overridden by kinematic or stereoscopic information (Braunstein, 1976; J. J. Gibson, 1966; Wallach & O'Connell, 1953). The existence of multiple information sources in adult perception differing in their conditions of availability and their ecological validity might be viewed in terms of optimization. When the most reliable information is not available, it is better to have information of some validity than no information at all. This would be especially true in situations demanding prompt responses; obtaining the best possible description of the environment under a given set of perceptual circumstances may be preferable to perceiving an indeterminate reality.

For perceivers in the early months of life, the situation may differ radically. Relative to adult perceivers, infants' perception might serve best by being *risk-averse*. This conjecture would make sense if the functional role(s) of perception in early development differ from that later in life. During the earliest months of life, an infant's perceptual capacities may serve mostly to underwrite his or her cognitive development. Learning about the properties of the environment, about the objects and people it contains, developing conceptual categories, and so forth, may be primary (cf., Mandler, 1988). Perceptual abilities initially serve at most a modest role in helping a person avert danger, acquire nutrition, and move safely through the environment, because early locomotor abilities are minimal. To use a somewhat non-ecological example, compare an infant lying in a crib and an adult driving a car. When something moves in the visual periphery, it is less important for the infant's perceptual system to deliver a plausible description of it than it is for the adult's, because there is little the infant can do to react. For the adult, the need for rapid reaction or further exploration may be urgent. Moreover, errors would have different significance. The momentary classification by an adult of a moving blur in the periphery as an oncoming car rather than a fly, may be relatively insignificant (and easily corrected). Correcting an error may be easier for adults because further perceptual-motor activity can reveal (or repeal) a misperception. Infants are less mobile, have shorter attention spans, have inferior sensory resolution, and are capable of using only a subset of the information sources available to adults. As a result, infants' errors may often go uncorrected. Even in cases where additional information becomes available, an error might be relatively more consequential for an infant, who may not know whether or not cars ever turn into houseflies. Misperceptions might have deeper implications in infancy.

This line of reasoning suggests that the basic perceptual capacities of infants should be those with the least possibility to mislead, that is, those with the highest ecological validity. The fact that much of the world may appear indeterminate or ambiguous early in life is not of primary importance. More crucial is that those aspects of the world that *are* perceived be perceived with high accuracy. It is in this sense that infant perception may be risk-averse.

As noted earlier, information defined by spatiotemporal changes is in general a more valid indicator of environmental circumstances than information in static arrays. Thus, risk aversion in early perception leads to the hypothesis that kinematic information might underlie the earliest perception of objects and spatial layout.

Although plausible, there are reasons why this hypothesis could be false. First, very young infants do not move through environments as much as adults, and they do not produce coordinated, self-initiated movements in the earliest months. Perceptual systems dependent on kinematics might lie dormant during too many of an infant's waking hours. Second, although the importance of kinematic information in adult perception has been amply demonstrated, the relevant perceptual abilities might be due to learning. Helmholtz (1909/1962), for example, was well aware of the importance of motion parallax in mature perception, and of differing consequences of observer motion and object motion. Yet, his view was that the use of optical changes to specify properties of the world required extensive learning, probably the connecting of visual experience with tactile experience. Piaget (1954) argued that the interpretation of visual stimulation depends on associating visual changes with self-initiated movement or action (cf. Held & Hein, 1963). The existence of basic physical and geometric regularities that could have been exploited by evolution does not guarantee that they are, in fact, built into perceptual systems.

The question of kinematic foundations of visual perception is, then, an empirical one. But it is one about which we are learning a great deal. Research over the past two decades suggests that kinematic information may underlie much of perceptual development. In this chapter I describe some of this research in several areas of object and space perception. Beyond describing these kinematic foundations of perception, there are several more specific goals. First, the role of kinematic information appears to differ in various perceptual domains. It is useful to consider these differences (e.g., the equivalence or non-equivalence of object and observer motion) in understanding particular perceptual abilities. Second, we show that the category of kinematic information may itself include information sources of differing ecological validity. Considerations of validity may help us to understand developmental patterns even within this category of information. Finally, these varieties of kinematic information have important consequences for perceptual theory. Some, but not all, cases are compatible with the idea from direct theories of perception that optical information is directly linked to perceptual outcomes, without mediation by inference or intermediate levels of representation.

PERCEPTION OF OBJECTS: UNITY AND BOUNDARIES

One of the most crucial aspects of the descriptions of our environment delivered by perceptual processes is the division of the perceived world into objects. The most basic, even defining, aspect of object perception is determining object unity and boundaries. The world perceived visually is neither an unbroken canvas of sensory qualities nor a 2-D array of millions of separate points at minimally distinguishable locations. It is instead a world of objects and surfaces. Within any one such object or surface, there is internal connectedness. Each is also bounded or separated from other objects and surfaces. Segmentation of the visual world is successful insofar as perceived units correspond to functional units in the world; that is, areas seen as unified tend to persist as physical units, to move together, and to maintain their shape, size, and other properties.

A basic problem in determining object unity and boundaries in the 3-D world is the problem of occlusion. In ordinary environments, most objects are partly hidden behind other objects. How can the visual system determine in occluded arrays which visible areas are connected?

Principles of organization, proposed by the Gestalt psychologists, have long been considered to be an approximate answer to this question (Kellman & Spelke, 1983; Michotte, Thines, & Crabbe, 1964; Wertheimer, 1912). Objects may be perceived in accordance with similarity, continuity, and overall symmetry or "good form." A principle of *common fate*, or common motion, holds that visible areas that move in the same ways are connected (Wertheimer, 1912). Although these principles are vague, probably redundant, and may to some extent confuse outcomes with causes (see Kellman & Shipley, 1991), they have pointed to important aspects of stimulus relations that underlie object perception. Further on I consider some recent efforts to obtain a more precise account of unit formation.

Even in advance of refinement of these principles, however, it is obvious that their ecological validities differ. A principle of common fate appears to be the strongest. When visible areas share identical motions in space (or rigid motions in general), it is highly likely that they are connected. The sensitivity of this principle is nearly perfect: The parts of connected entities will almost invariably move in connected ways. Specificity is also high. Connected motion will rarely occur for separate entities. Even separate objects falling under the influence of gravity, or flocks of birds headed in the same direction will ordinarily be detectably inconsistent with a rigid unity (although such cases may occasionally appear non-rigidly connected). The ecological root of a common fate principle is that object motions ordinarily result from the application of forces. The likelihood of forces being applied by chance to separate objects so that their motion paths are rigidly related must be vanishingly small. Not only would the direction of force have to be identical, but the magnitudes of forces applied to objects of differing mass would have to be exactly adjusted to result in the same velocity and acceleration patterns. (Those who have attempted to arrange common motion of visible objects by hidden mechanical means, e.g., in perception laboratories, can attest that it is a painstaking process.) Of course, this assessment of the validity of a common fate principle rests on the assumption that the visible parts actually move in space. Common fate in optical projections may also arise from observer motion through a stationary environment. During translation perpendicular to the line of sight, for example, many visible areas at roughly the same distance from the observer will undergo the same optical changes. Such areas may have little likelihood of being connected, beyond the basic probability that nearby areas are more often connected than are areas far apart. This difference between object and observer motion turns out to have important consequences, as we will see.

The situation is different for principles pertaining to spatial variables in stationary arrays. A principle of good form depends on the regularity that objects are regular or symmetrical. A principle of good continuation depends on the smoothness of object boundaries. A principle of similarity depends on the homogeneity of an object's surface qualities. In all of these cases, the regularity is a probabilistic one; objects in normal environments may fit these descriptions to varying degrees. There are obviously cases in which objects are not symmetrical, edges are jagged, and surfaces are varied in quality. The actual levels of ecological validity of such principles are not known. Brunswik (1956) proposed a program of ecological surveys to assess such principles, but such a program has never been carried out. As a preliminary assessment, however, one might expect that principles based on object regularities are somewhat less secure than those rooted in physical dynamics and kinematics (J. J. Gibson, 1966; Shepard, 1984; Spelke, 1985). We will return to this issue.

A number of years ago, my colleagues and I began to study the perception of partly occluded objects in early infancy, using Gestalt descriptive principles as a guide (Kellman & Spelke, 1983). The general method in each experiment was to habituate 16-week-old infants to an occlusion display in which the center of an object was hidden behind a nearer object. After habituation to such a display, we recorded looking times to two types of unoccluded displays. The complete test display contained a single, connected object joining the previously visible parts. The broken test display contained only the two separate pieces visible in habituation. Figure 5.1 shows the general scheme of the experiment. Generalization of habituation to the complete test display and dishabituation to the broken test display were taken to indicate perception of the original display as containing a unified, partly occluded object. This general method was used to test a variety of relationships between the two visible parts. These included a number of relationships available in stationary arrays, such as the alignment of edges on either side of an occluding object, the possibility of a symmetrically shaped object uniting the visible parts, similarity of color and lightness, and so on. Additional studies by Schmidt and Spelke (1984) addressed these static variables using a wider range of objects and including subjects up to 24 weeks of age. In these and other studies (Kellman & Spelke, 1983; Kellman, Spelke, & Short, 1986), a variety of motion relationships were tested, including common lateral translation of visible parts, translation in other dimensions (vertical and in-depth), and rotation (Kellman & Short, 1985).

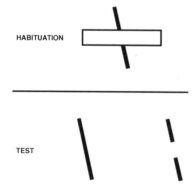

FIG. 5.1. Schematic of habituation method used to test perceived unity. The upper portion of the figure depicts the partly occluded object shown during habituation; the lower portion depicts the complete and broken test displays shown on alternating trials after habituation.

The results of these studies have been remarkably consistent in supporting two generalizations about early object perception. First, kinematic information, specifically, common translation in space of an object's visible parts, supports perception of object unity. Second, information available in static optic arrays does not support unit formation under occlusion in the first 6 months of life. Each of these conclusions is elaborated in turn.

Kinematic Information for Object Unity

In his classic paper, "Laws of Organization in Perceptual Forms," Wertheimer (1912) devoted a mere two paragraphs to the principle of common fate. A version of this principle, however, has turned out to be fundamental to early object perception. In occlusion cases, certain motion relationships of separate visible areas result in their being perceived as a single, unitary object. Data from one such condition, involving 16-week-old infants, are shown in Fig. 5.2. After habituation to a display in which the visible parts undergo the same translation, infants dishabituate markedly to an unoccluded broken display, but generalize

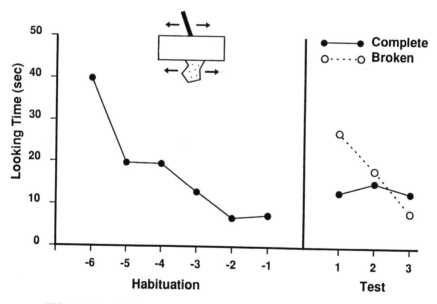

FIG. 5.2. Results of an experiment testing unity perception from common motion of visible areas. Infants were habituated to two dissimilar, misaligned visible areas that shared a common lateral translation (pictured at top). Looking times are shown for the last six habituation trials (with the final one labeled −1) and the test trials. Test trials consisted of successive presentations of unoccluded, complete and broken displays, with half of the subjects seeing the complete test display first. From Kellman and Spelke (1983).

habituation to an unoccluded complete display. A control group shown the two test displays without prior habituation to an occluded display shows no such difference in visual attention to the two test displays. This type of result occurs for translations in the plane, both lateral and vertical (Kellman & Spelke, 1983; Kellman et al., 1986). The results for vertical translation suggest that common fate relates to rigid translation of visible areas rather than to similar optical changes shared by visible areas, because in vertical translation one visible area is progressively revealed while the other is concealed. Perception of unity also occurs from translation in depth (Kellman et al., 1986). The latter result is interesting because the information for translatory motion in depth is considerably different from that specifying planar translation. Translation in depth may be specified by optical expansion/contraction, changes in convergence or disparity, or some combination. Planar translation is based on image displacement. These results suggest that common translatory motion in three-dimensional space underlies perceived unity, regardless of how that motion is specified.

A limitation on the role of kinematic information in unity perception was found by Kellman and Short (1985). When the visible parts of a partly occluded object were related by a rigid rotation (around a stationary center) or by a combination of rotation and translation (see Fig. 5.3), 16-week-old infants did not, in general, perceive the unity of the object. The difficulty in these cases appears to be the

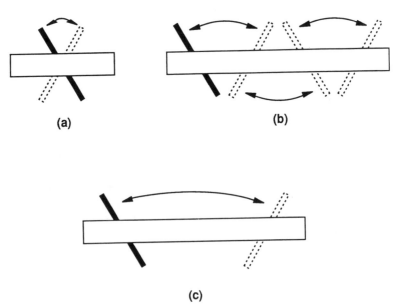

FIG. 5.3. Occlusion display with visible areas of partly occluded object related by (a) rotation, (b) rotation and translation with 3 cycles of rotary oscillation per cycle of translation, and (c) rotation and translation with 1 cycle of rotary oscillation per cycle of translation.

simultaneous motion of visible parts in opposite directions. When translation was combined with a rotary motion of the same period and phase (Fig. 5.3c), infants did respond as if they perceived a unified object. In this case, which looks something like a windshield wiper, the visible parts of the object always move in the same direction, although the velocity of the two visible areas differs. Other combinations of rotation and translation, all of which contained clear opposite directions of motion by the visible areas, produced no evidence of complete object perception.

These results suggest that the kinematic basis of early unity perception does not include the complete class of rigid motions: translations, rotations, and their combinations. Rather, a more restricted principle, based primarily on common translation, applies. One possibility is that accurate registration of rotation, or combinations of rotation and translation, present difficulties. Such combinations are known to pose problems in adult perception (e.g., Todd, 1982).

Object and Observer Motion in Perception of Object Unity

The findings reviewed so far, showing that certain motion relationships can indicate the unity of partly occluded objects, may be subject to two very different interpretations. The common motion of object parts in our experiments produces common changes in the optical projections of those parts (e.g., common retinal displacements). Does infant perception of unity depend on the real motions of objects in space or on commonalities in optical change? The latter can occur without the former when optical changes are produced by an observer moving through a stationary environment. The two possible characterizations of the relevant information—real motion vs. common projective change—require a test in which optical changes from the two sources are compared. Such a comparison raises two important issues.

First, the two possibilities would seem to differ in ecological validity. I have already noted that the common fate principle has perhaps the strongest validity of any information about unity under occlusion, when the principle is defined in terms of real object motion. The possibility of visible areas moving in certain related ways without being unitary is remote. By comparison, a common fate principle defined over optical changes would dilute ecological validity considerably. When an observer moves, common optical displacements can occur for visible areas that are not connected but happen to be at roughly the same distance from the observer. Thus, from the standpoint of ecological validity, one might predict that a common fate principle, especially one operating early in life, would be based on relationships in real motion rather than optical change. On the other hand, a principle defined over real motion in space might be more difficult to implement. It is straightforward to imagine mechanisms that respond to spatiotemporal relationships at the retina. Perceived motion, however, arises from a variety of stimulus conditions; if perceived unity depended on relation-

ships in real motion, it would suggest a somewhat intricate computation where-
by the motions of visible areas were first detected and then used to determine
unity.

Second, the question of whether real or optical displacements govern unity
perception raises another, somewhat prior, set of questions. Can infants tell
the difference between optical consequences of their own motion and those
produced by moving objects? If so, do they perceive object motion only in the
latter case? In other words, do they have *position constancy,* the ability to detect the stationary position of objects whose optical projections are undergoing
change due to observer movement?

Kellman, Gleitman, and Spelke (1987) explored both questions. There were
two groups in their experiment, diagrammed in Fig. 5.4. Seated in a movable
chair, infants were moved back and forth in an arc while viewing arrays of objects. In both groups, infants were habituated to a partly occluded rod, whose
center was hidden by a nearer rectangular object. After habituation, they were
tested for generalization/dishabituation to alternating presentations of an unoccluded complete rod and an unoccluded display with two separated rod pieces,
as in earlier studies (Kellman & Spelke, 1983; Kellman et al., 1986).

The difference between groups involved the motion characteristics of the
rods. In the observer motion group, the rod displays were stationary throughout the entire experiment (see Fig. 5.4a). However, the occluding block, the
rod, and the background were separated in depth so that during the observer's
motion, the visible parts of the rod underwent a unique optical displacement.
The difference in optical displacement between the rod and the occluder, and
also between the rod and the background, were designed to be the same as
in earlier studies when stationary observers viewed a moving rod. Thus, if specification of object unity depends on differences between the optical displacement
of the object's visible parts and other visible surfaces, unity should be specified
in this case. If, however, perceived unity depends on real motion of the occluded object in space, and infants can accurately perceive the object as stationary,
unity would not be perceived.

The other group (the conjoint motion group) was designed to be the logical
converse of the first, having real motion of the occluded object in space, but
no subject-relative movement. This was achieved by linking the moving infant
chair and the partly occluded rod mechanically, out of sight beneath the chair
and display (see Fig. 5.4b). The observer and object were rigidly connected,
moving around a fixed pivot point in between. (When the infant's chair moved
to the left, the object moved to the right, and vice versa.) Because the pivot
point was close to the front of the block, there was little relative displacement
between the occluded object and the occluder.

Perceived unity and perceived motion were assessed in different ways. As
in previous studies, dishabituation patterns to unoccluded complete and broken
rod displays were used to determine perception of unity. Motion perception was

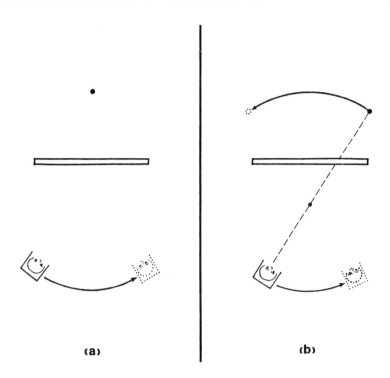

FIG. 5.4. Conditions in the experiment of Kellman, Gleitman, and Spelke (1987). Top views are shown, with solid and dotted figures indicating endpoints of motion: (a) observer motion condition, (b) conjoint motion condition.

assessed by comparing the absolute levels of looking time to those in previous studies in which stationary infants viewed moving or stationary displays. In those studies, looking times were consistently two to three times higher to moving displays than to stationary ones.

Results for the two conditions are shown in Fig. 5.5. There were three important findings. First, infants did distinguish optical changes given by their own motion from those given by moving objects. Looking times to stationary objects were on the same order as those in prior studies in which stationary observers viewed stationary displays. Second, moving infants showed evidence of motion detection. Looking times to the moving rods (conjoint motion group) were markedly higher than those in the observer motion group, and they were more similar to looking times shown in prior studies by stationary observers viewing moving objects. Finally, perception of unity depended on real motion. Infants in the conjoint motion group dishabituated to the broken test display while generalizing habituation to the complete test display. This result was remarkably strong and consistent across subjects; 15 of 16 subjects looked more than twice as long at the broken than the complete test display on the first test trial.

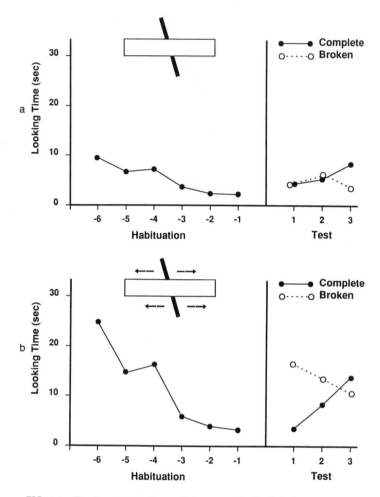

FIG. 5.5.   Results of the Kellman, Gleitman, and Spelke (1987) experiment: (a)
observer motion condition, (b) conjoint motion condition.

(As is typical in these studies, the effect diminished after the first set of test
trials, although it was also reliable for the three test trials taken together.) In
contrast, the observer motion condition showed no reliable differences in looking time to the complete and broken test displays, indicating that the subjects
had not previously detected the unity of the partly occluded rod.

These findings have several interesting implications for perception of motion
and stability. First, it appears that young infants have position constancy under
at least some circumstances. Infants did not respond to optical displacements
produced solely by their own motion as they respond to moving objects. Second, it appears that infants were able to detect the moving object in the con-

joint condition during their own motion. This is noteworthy given the absence of subject-relative motion by the object.

Most important for object perception, the common fate principle in infant perception appears to be defined over real motions of objects' visible areas. Commonalities in optical change that were not based on real motion did not produce perceived unity. This outcome has implications for our hypothesis about ecological validity in perceptual development and also for accounts of the process of perception. Regarding the former, it appears that the more valid principle, defined over actual motions of objects, guides infant perception. Common optical displacement, produced solely by observer motion, does not specify a unitary object to infants. The common fate principle, as we find it in infancy, ensures high accuracy in early perception of connectedness, and accordingly furnishes a sound basis for learning about objects' properties.

From the standpoint of general theories of perception, these results have diverse implications. The findings confirm several tenets of ecological theories of perception (J. J. Gibson, 1979) and their application to perceptual development (E. J. Gibson, 1969, 1984). The primacy of kinematic information and the possibility that perceptual systems detect properties of objects and events from such information without learning are consistent with the data.[1] The evidence suggests, however, that the *process* involved is not readily explicable from the standpoint of direct perception. The dependence of perceived unity upon perceived motion appears to be an example of dependent variable coupling in perception (Epstein, 1982; Hochberg, 1974). That is, perceived unity cannot be directly ascribed to stimulus relationships (independent variables) but depends in part on another perceptual variable: perceived motion. Rather, it appears to depend on registration of visible areas undergoing certain motions in space. From our current vantage point, the process of unity detection appears most compatible with computational views of perception involving multiple levels of representation (Hochberg, 1974; Marr, 1982; Rock, 1977).

Static Spatial Information for Unity

I noted earlier that spatial relationships alone (and relations based on surface quality, such as similarity) do not seem to specify unity to infants. This leads

---

[1]A recent paper by Slater et al. (1990) suggests that common motion does not specify unity to newborn infants, but begins to do so some time between birth and 16 weeks. Although the investigators carefully considered (and ruled out) some alternative explanations, lack of competence is not the only plausible way to account for their results. Until these issues are studied further, the origins of the "primitive process" are clouded somewhat. If the primitive process turns out not to be strictly innate, from the ecological perspective advanced here, maturation would be its likely origin. At minimum, an alternative account in terms of learning would have to differ from classical ones based on correlations of visual sensations with touch and action, because these are disconfirmed by results from 16-week-olds. For discussion, see Kellman and Spelke (1983).

to an interesting question. In the absence of object motion, what do infants see when objects are occluded? Kellman and Spelke (1983) argued that such displays are perceived as containing occlusion, but the occluded areas are seen as indeterminate. This argument was based on evidence that occlusion boundaries (e.g., where a rod is interrupted by a block) are not responded to in the same way as non-occlusion boundaries (e.g., where the end of a rod is visible). In an habituation paradigm, the test trial response pattern to the former is dishabituation to a complete object, indicating that the initial display was perceived as containing unconnected pieces (Kellman and Spelke, 1983, Experiments 2, 3, and 4). In the case of occlusion boundaries, however, test trial responses indicate roughly equal looking times to complete and broken test displays (Kellman & Short, 1985; Kellman & Spelke, 1983), ordinarily with modest, but reliable dishabituation to both. Thus, occlusion boundaries do not seem to be mistaken for object boundaries; if such a perceptual error did exist, it would be a considerable handicap for early perceptual knowledge.

It is not known at what age nonkinematic information becomes able to specify object unity. Studies by Schmidt and Spelke (1984) indicate that static variables do not specify object unity even at 6 months of age. On other grounds, there is reason to expect that these abilities might arise at around 7 to 9 months of age. During this period, infants appear to begin to utilize pictorial depth cues (Yonas & Granrud, 1984), including interposition. Moreover, at least one study has found evidence of illusory contour perception at about 7 months of age, but not earlier (Bertenthal, Campos, & Haith, 1980). Recent work in adult perception (Kellman & Shipley, in press) suggests a close relationship between perception of partly occluded objects, perception of illusory figures, and the depth cue of interposition. In fact, it has been proposed that a single boundary interpolation process underlies perception of partly occluded objects and perception of illusory or subjective figures (Kellman & Shipley, 1991; Shipley & Kellman, 1990). This emerging understanding of interpolation processes in adult perception may shed some light on the developmental patterns appearing in research over the past 10 years. Thus, a brief overview may be useful.

A Reformulation of Information for Unity:
The Primitive Process and the Rich Process

In studies of infant object perception, as in many previous studies with adults, the information available for perceiving object unity was considered in terms of Gestalt organizational principles, such as common fate, good form, good continuation, and so on. Although it was clear that these principles were vague and perhaps unduly numerous (Helson, 1933), they provided the only serviceable account at hand. Recently, a new account of perception of interpolative processes in object perception has been proposed (Kellman & Shipley, 1991). This account emphasizes local variables, such as the tangents of edges at points of occlusion. The theory provides a unified account of boundary interpolation processes in occlusion cases, illusory figures, and other unit formation phenomena, both static and kinematic, in which boundaries are perceived in the absence of local specification. Some of the Gestalt influences are held to be outcomes, not causes, of perceptual processes; the tendency to see simple, regular forms— good form—is one example.

Briefly, the theory posits that unit formation is initiated by first-derivative discontinuities (sharp corners) in projected edges. The usefulness of first-order discontinuities derives from the fact that all cases of occlusion will give rise to projected discontinuities. Interpolation occurs when edges leading into discontinuities are *relatable* to other edges leading into discontinuities in the optic array. Relatability is defined mathematically, but embodies the requirements that two surface edges may be connected by a surface boundary that is smooth (i.e., that contains no first-order discontinuities) and monotonic. More precisely, referring to the construction in Fig. 5.6, if $E1$ and $E2$ are the edges of surfaces, and R and r are perpendiculars to the tangents at the ends of the edges, with R assigned to the longer of the two, then $E1$ and $E2$ are relatable if $0 \leq R \cos \Phi \leq r$. It can be shown that whenever two edges meet the relatability criteria, they can be joined by a smooth, monotonic curve (Kellman & Shipley, 1991). Figure 5.7 gives some examples of edges that are and are not relatable. Figure 5.8 shows examples of unit formation in equivalent occlusion, illusory figure, and transparency cases, based on the same discontinuities and relatable physically specified edges in all cases.

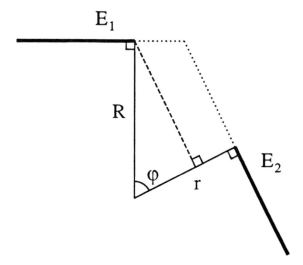

FIG. 5.6. Illustration of relatability criteria proposed by Kellman and Shipley (1991). $E1$ and $E2$ are edges of projected regions. R and r are perpendiculars to the tangents of $E1$ and $E2$, assigned so that R is the longer; Φ is the angle of intersection of R and r. Edges are relatable if $0 \leq R \cos \Phi \leq r$.

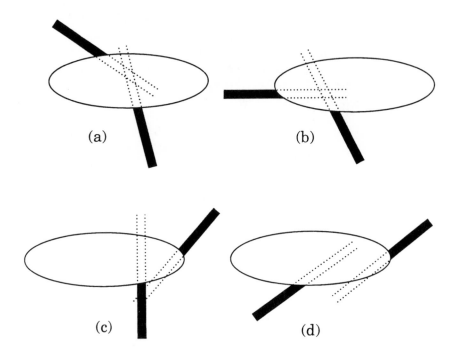

FIG. 5.7.   Examples of relatable and nonrelatable edges. The visible rod parts
in (a) and (b) are relatable; those in (c) and (d) are not. After Kellman and Shipley
(1991).

The theory embodies the central notion of the Gestalt idea of good continuation, while giving it a more precise form. Other Gestalt notions, such as good
form and closure, do not figure in the computations required by the theory, but
characterize the outcomes of the process to some extent. The effect of the relatability criteria is that some projected discontinuities end up being classified as
due to occlusion rather than as due to sharp corners in object boundaries. Thus,
the overall smoothness and simplicity of perceived objects derives in this theory from more local, computationally tractable processes.

Most important for the present discussion is the separation of unit formation
under occlusion into two putative processes what Kellman and Shipley (1991)
label the *primitive process* and the *rich process*. The primitive process refers to
the perception of unity from certain motion relations of visible parts of objects,
that is, the Gestalt idea of common fate. It might also be called the *edge-insensitive
process*, because projected orientations and arrangements of edges are incon-
sequential to it. The process is labeled *primitive* because, when acting alone,
it leads to perception of unity, but not specific form. That is, two very different-
looking visible parts, whose edges cannot be connected in a smooth manner,
can still be seen as unified if they share a common motion in space.

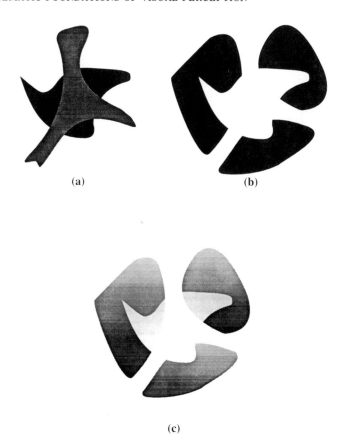

(a)   (b)

(c)

FIG. 5.8.   Examples of equivalent unit formation cases: (a) partly occluded object, (b) illusory figure, (c) transparent figure.

The rich process, however, leads to both unity and form perception. It might equally well be termed the *edge-sensitive* process, because it is crucially dependent on the spatial and temporal relations of physically specified parts of objects. In the Kellman and Shipley account (see also Kellman & Loukides, 1987), the rich process is characterized in a way that accounts for both interpolation of object edges under occlusion and subjective or illusory contours. A series of experiments with adults by Shipley and Kellman (1990) provides confirming evidence that a single underlying process is at work in both types of unit formation.

The rich process may involve either kinematic information or information in static arrays. One crucial difference between motion information in the two processes is that the rich process works equally well from real motion of the partially specified object or relative motions, that is, of occluding and occluded objects.

The characterization of a rich, or edge-sensitive, process and a primitive, or edge-insensitive, process allows some useful reconsideration of findings in infant perception. Specifically, the division (between abilities present early and those achieved later) is not strictly between kinematic and static information. Infants seem to lack the edge-sensitive process during at least the first half year of life. Thus, unit formation that involves motion but does not depend on relations of edge orientations appears early. In such cases unity is perceived without specific form being determined. Other unit formation phenomena depend on both motion and edge relations; two such (related) phenomena are shown schematically in Fig. 5.9. In both kinetic occlusion and kinetic illusory figures, optical changes given sequentially over time carry information about both unity and edge relations. There is some evidence that young infants do not perceive specific form from kinetic illusory figure displays (Kaufmann-Hayoz, Kaufmann, & Walther, 1988). From the foregoing analysis, we would expect that the perception of stationary illusory figures, of stationary, partly occluded objects from edge relations and form (as opposed to amorphous unity) in kinetic illusory figures should appear at the same time in perceptual development. Systematic studies to test this prediction would be extremely useful.

How does the breakdown of unit formation into the rich and primitive processes fit with our earlier conjectures about the superior ecological validity of kinematic information? At a superficial level, our generalization requires some qualification. Not all information carried by motion appears early in life; moreover,

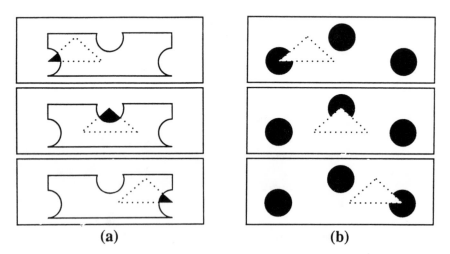

(a)   (b)

FIG. 5.9.   Examples of the rich (edge-sensitive) process involving motion. Equivalent kinetic subjective figure and kinetic occlusion cases are shown: (a) Kinetic occlusion: The object moves behind the occluder projecting parts sequentially as shown in the three views; (b) Kinetic subjective figure: Background (inducing) elements are sequentially occluded by a moving form of the same color as the background.

the relevant divisions between early- and late-appearing abilities may depend on other factors. On closer examination, however, our guiding conjectures still serve well. The primitive process provides a good example of the ecological validity of kinematic information. It requires actual motion of objects, not simply sameness of optical change as might be given by observer motion. Accordingly, false-alarms—mistaken assignments of unity—are minimized, because forces acting on separate objects so as to give them common translations in space are improbable.

Compared to the primitive process, the rich or edge-sensitive process is less fundamental. Our (adult) perception and effective functioning with objects would scarcely be possible without edge interpolation given by the rich process, but its roots in ecological optics are nevertheless not as secure as the primitive process. The validity of the rich process ultimately depends on the ecological constraint that objects tend to be smooth (Hoffman & Richards, 1984; Kellman & Shipley, 1991; Marr, 1982). Certain relations between pairs of edges support visual interpolation, whereas others do not; the simplest characterization of those in the former class is that they can be connected by smooth (first-order continuous) monotonic curves. Smoothness, however, is at best only a rough, probabilistic characterization of objects (Spelke, 1985). When objects or parts of objects are not smooth, the rich process may fail to unite visible parts of an occluded object; there may also be cases (probably rare) in which parts of separate objects spuriously meet the criteria for interpolation.

Returning to the case of kinetic occlusion and kinetic illusory figures, these phenomena involve motion but also involve edge relations necessary to the rich process. The specification over time of spatial edge relations really has no greater ecological validity than simultaneous specification of such edge relations. The information about objects in kinetic occlusion and kinetic illusory figures depends as fully on a smoothness constraint as do stationary cases of the rich process.

Perception of object unity under occlusion, then, rests initially on information given exclusively by motion relationships. Of the information sources usable by adults, it is this information that appears to have the most secure roots in the physics and geometry of objects and their projections to observers. Perception based on further constraints, such as relations in edge orientations, appear to be secondary from a developmental standpoint.

PERCEPTION OF THREE-DIMENSIONAL FORM

Next to unity, the property of objects perhaps most important to our transactions with them is 3-D form. As in the case of unity, 3-D form may be given perceptually to adults by a variety of sources of information, including both static and kinematic sources.

One account of 3-D form perception—that objects are constructed out of more elementary sensory experience—has a long tradition of supporters, including British empiricist philosophers (Berkeley, 1709/1910; Mill, 1865/1965), the structuralist psychologists who dominated early experimental psychology (Titchener, 1924), as well as more contemporary advocates (Harris, 1983; Piaget, 1954). On this general account, 3-D form, perceived visually, is a construction from momentary 2-D images of an object, associated together in memory along with other sensory experiences, such as the feel of an object or the actions one performs on it. Mill's (1865/1965) formulation is perhaps most elegant: An object ject is "the permanent possibilities of sensation." Taking sensations to be the only directly given data, what a 3-D object must logically be is the set of possible sensory images one might obtain by seeing or otherwise sensing the object from various vantage points.

A more general and abstract notion of form perception was proposed by the Gestalt psychologists (Koffka, 1935). The 2-D projection of an object was claimed to activate dynamic forces in the nervous system that would cause perception of objects that were as simple and regular as possible. That objects are perceived in accordance with principles of regularity and simplicity was also suggested by Brunswik (1956), although he suggested that such principles arise from learning about the probable characteristics of objects.

Kinematic information has a more recent history, often dated from Wallach and O'Connell's classic (1953) paper, *the kinetic depth effect*. Wallach and O'Connell cast shadows of 3-D wire figures onto a translucent screen, and observers viewed the shadows from the other side. When stationary views were projected, observers reported planar figures on the surface of the viewing screen. When the wire figures were made to rotate in depth, however, observers quickly and effortlessly perceived accurately the objects' 3-D forms. Later analyses placed this "effect" into a more systematic context: Three-dimensional form may be recovered by the laws of projective geometry from optical transformations given by object or observer motion (J. J. Gibson, 1966; Johansson, 1970; Ullman, 1979). Perception of "structure from motion" has subsequently become one of the most active areas in contemporary visual perception research.

Each of the various approaches to form perception implies or readily coexists with certain ideas about development. From the constructivist standpoint, 3-D form must be learned from accumulated 2-D views and associations with touch and/or action. From the Gestalt view, 3-D organization should occur without learning, whereas a Brunswikian would expect the same organizational principles to govern perception only after a long process of learning. Finally, from kinematic analyses comes the possibility that projective geometric information given by optical transformations might be utilized by perceptual mechanisms that are products of evolution (Fodor, 1983; J. J. Gibson, 1966; Shepard, 1984).

In the first two decades of active infant perception research, beginning in the late 1950s and early 1960s, most research related to form perception employed static, 2-D displays (for reviews, see Bond, 1972; Fantz, Fagan, & Miranda, 1975; Salapatek, 1975). Implicit in much of this early research was the empiricist assumption that the perception of stationary, 2-D arrays was logically or psychologically prior to the perception of 3-D form.

A different expectation derives from an event perception perspective. In terms of the validity of information, perspective transformations given by relative motion between an observer and an object offer the most accurate information about form. In static optic arrays, when a stationary observer views a 3-D object from a single vantage point, its whole form may be predicted on the basis of considerations of simplicity, symmetry, or similarity to previously viewed objects. The accuracy of such predictions rests on probabilistic facts about the sorts of objects that exist, the likelihood of vantage points that give misleading symmetry information, and so on. In contrast, under conditions easily satisfied when a moving observer views a 3-D object, the perspective transformations provably contain sufficient information to specify 3-D form (Ullman, 1979). Illusory specification of a given object is possible only if an object deforms or the optic array is otherwise manipulated to present misleading transformations. This sort of event, however, requires a high degree of skilled manipulation (or incredible coincidence). It is true that the separation of optic flow components due to observer motion and object change (i.e., motion, deformation) is a complex task with certain limitations (discussed further on). In general, however, when an observer moves and a viewed object also moves or deforms, the transformations will not be consistent with some other rigid object. This constraint does not derive from the particular types of objects that tend to be viewed, such as symmetrical or nonsymmetrical ones, although it is related to the facts that objects tend to be rigid, or nonrigid in characteristic ways.

The ecological validity of kinematic information about 3-D form leads naturally to the possibility that it may be primary in development. Assumptions about the symmetry of objects, or inferences from past experiences, might be less reliable and later-appearing. Interestingly, one of the major motivations for their study, according to Wallach and O'Connell (1953) was to shed light on the development of 3-D form perception. They reasoned that knowledge of 3-D form seems to be available to monocular observers; yet, in development, congenitally monocular observers would not have had access to stereoscopic information about 3-D form. It is clear that with adequate learning about objects, adults can perceive 3-D form even from pictorial information. But where might the initial notion of 3-D form come from? Wallach and O'Connell hypothesized that there might be an unlearned process of detecting 3-D form from optical changes given by motion.

Experiments by several investigators have given us a relatively clear picture of early 3-D form perception (Kellman, 1984; Kellman & Short, 1987; Owsley, 1983; Yonas, Arterberry, & Granrud, 1988), and it is consistent with the conjecture of Wallach and O'Connell (1953). The evidence suggests that the earliest competence for perceiving overall form appears to be based on kinematic information. To illustrate this claim and to understand further the nature of early 3-D form perception, we consider some of this evidence in detail.

Testing 3-D form perception is challenging. When we perceive a 3-D object, we ordinarily do so from a particular station point, or a changing sequence of station points. At these station points, particular projections of the object reach the eyes. To test perception of 3-D form, one must somehow exclude particular 2-D projections as an adequate basis of response. For example, suppose infants were habituated to a stationary 3-D object from a particular vantage point. Suppose also that after habituation, infants generalized habituation to continued presentations of the same display, but dishabituated to a novel 3-D object. This pattern of response might indicate that infants detected the 3-D form of the original object, and discriminated it from the novel 3-D form. However, the observed responses could instead be based on differences in the 2-D projections; 3-D form may not have been perceived at all.

The method we developed to counter this problem is based on the geometry of the kinetic depth effect. Information about a given 3-D form can be provided by rotation around various axes, provided there is some component of rotation in depth. If objects are chosen that are not too symmetrical, one can test for recognition of an object with rotation sequences that have not been shown before.

The earliest experiment of this type (Kellman, 1984) used two objects of the sort shown in Fig. 5.10. Kinematic information for form was tested by habituating infants to videotaped displays of a single object rotating in depth. Two different axes of rotation in depth were used in habituation on alternate trials, so that the only constant from trial to trial was the 3-D form of the object—if

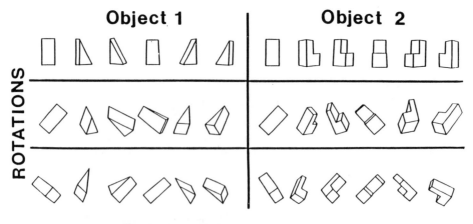

FIG. 5.10. Schematic views of objects and axes of rotation used in an experiment on 3-D form perception (Kellman, 1984). Successive views 60° apart are shown. All views in the same column are of a single 3-D object; views in the same row are from a single axis of rotation.

it could be recovered from the transforming projections. After habituation, subjects were tested on alternating trials with presentations of the same object, now moving around a new (third) axis of rotation and the different object, also rotating around the same new axis. The change to a new axis of rotation in the test period ensured that the particular proximal views and transforming patterns were novel for both the object shown previously and the new object. Thus, generalization of habituation to the same object could not be based on matching the particular views shown in the test period with particular views seen earlier.

Besides the kinematic condition, two groups viewed sequential stationary views (photographic slides) taken from the rotation sequences. The two groups differed in the number and spacing of the views (see Kellman, 1984); successive views were taken from the rotation sequences at 60° intervals for one group and at 15° intervals in the other. There were two reasons for testing infants' perception from stationary views. First, it was possible that infants could detect the 3-D forms of these objects from single views, or sequences of views. Adults can certainly do this; even the line drawings in Fig. 5.10 allow overall form to be perceived from most of the views. The slides used allowed adults to perceive overall form even more readily; besides contour information, the images contained shading information. If infants detected overall form from single views or sequences of static views, successful performance in the kinematic condition might not indicate use of optical change information; rather, it might indicate that transforming arrays are processed as sequences of static views.

The second reason for testing performance from static views was to obtain a check on the method. Although the changes of rotation axis introduced large changes in the proximal stimuli, it remained possible that views of a given object from different axes of rotation bore enough similarities to each other to allow them to be distinguished from views of the other object. In such a case, infants might show dishabituation to views of a new object without having any perception of 3-D form.

The results were unequivocal. Infants in the kinematic condition (Fig. 5.11a) generalized habituation to the same object in a new rotation, and dishabituated robustly to the new object. This result held regardless of the object and the particular axes of rotation used in the habituation and test trials. In contrast, infants habituated to sequential static views of one object showed no reliable difference in response to new views of that object versus views of a new object. Data from one of the two static conditions (successive views 15° apart, shown for 1 sec each) are shown in Fig. 5.11b.

The results suggested that young infants have the ability to perceive 3-D form, but only from continuous optical transformations. This conclusion is consistent with the work of other investigators (Owsley, 1983; Yonas et al., 1987). These results are compatible with an ecological view of the perception of structure from motion (J. J. Gibson, 1966, 1979; Shepard, 1984). Evolution of perceptual mechanisms may reflect the basic geometry of space and time, allowing

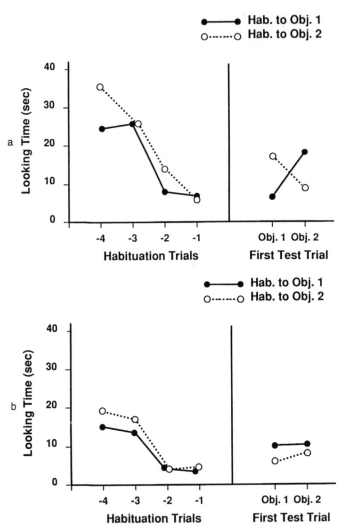

FIG. 5.11. Results from 3-D form perception experiment. Looking times are shown for the last four habituation trials and the test trials. Solid and dotted lines show data for subgroups who viewed different objects during the habituation period: (a) kinematic condition, (b) static condition (successive views spaced 15° apart).

recovery of object structure from optical transformations. Although studies with younger infants would be desirable, to determine whether such mechanisms operate from birth, existing data suggest that kinematically based 3-D form perception depends on mechanisms that are innate or early-maturing. Those learning accounts of 3-D form perception that have been proposed seem implausible given the developmental order in which kinematic and static information sources become useful. The reason parallels the question posed by Wallach and O'Connell (1953). Where might information about 3-D form come from initially? Suppose young infants were able to encode optical transformations, but that these initially did not specify 3-D form. The meanings of particular optical changes would have to be supplied from other information. J. J. Gibson and E. J. Gibson (1955) termed this general type of account of perceptual development *enrichment*. Yet it is currently hard to see how enrichment might operate. Because 3-D form is apparently not apprehended from single or multiple static views of objects, and because infants even at 16 weeks are not skilled haptic explorers, it is unclear how the "meanings" of optical transformations might be found out.

Motion Perspective in Perception of 3-D Form

The idea that initial perception of 3-D form depends on mechanisms sensitive to kinematic information leads to an interesting prediction. In considering the ecological validity of kinematic information for object unity, I noted that optical changes produced by observer motion were not equivalent to those given by object motion; only the latter specify object unity. The ecological basis of 3-D form perception is different. Optical transformations that specify a particular form may be given in principle by either object or observer motion. The specificity of the motion patterns, insofar as 3-D form is concerned, is the same in both cases. Thus, an observer walking in an arc around a stationary object receives the same optical transformations, relevant to that object's form, as if the object rotated while the observer was stationary. The kinematic information about form and spatial layout given to a moving observer has been termed *motion perspective* (J. J. Gibson, 1966).

Kellman and Short (1987) tested whether motion perspective could specify the 3-D forms of stationary objects. A sketch of that apparatus is shown in Fig. 5.12. The experiment served an additional purpose as well. Suppose the superiority of kinematic information arises not from the nature of the information available but from the fact that moving displays attract more attention. Perhaps with enhanced attention, or with a certain critical amount of fixation time, infants can detect 3-D form from static views. Kellman (1984) offered several arguments and some data against this view. However, assessing 3-D form perception from motion perspective information provides a more direct test. If the presence of object motion, rather than certain optical changes, is crucial, 3-D form perception should not occur when a moving infant observer views a stationary object.

The procedure in this study was the same as in Kellman (1984), except that the different axes of rotation used in the habituation and test periods were given by attaching a vertical axis into the display objects at different places. A stationary control group was also tested in which successive static views of the ob-

FIG. 5.12.   Apparatus used in testing form perception from motion perspective.
Observers were passively moved in an arc while viewing 3-D objects. From
Kellman and Short (1987).

jects were presented. This was achieved by covering the display object on any
trial momentarily during movement of the subject. Thus, the subject saw the
stationary object from numerous vantage points, but continuous transformations
of the object's projection were not available.

The results (shown in Fig. 5.13) indicated that 16-week-old infants did perceive objects' 3-D forms from motion perspective. They generalized habituation to the same object presented in a new rotation, but not to a novel object.
As in the previous study with moving objects, continuous transformations are
crucial to the effect. A comparison group, shown multiple, successive, static
views of the objects from the same rotation sequences, showed no evidence
of 3-D form perception. Those data are discussed further on.

Perspective Transformations and Early Form Perception

So far the findings I have discussed indicate an early ability to perceive 3-D form
from kinematic information, but I have not specified more explicitly the nature
of the information that makes form perception possible. Most analyses of adult
perception of structure from motion have emphasized perspective transformations of object edges (J. J. Gibson, 1979; Ullman, 1979; Wallach & O'Connell,
1953). However, the transforming optical projection of a rotating (solid) object

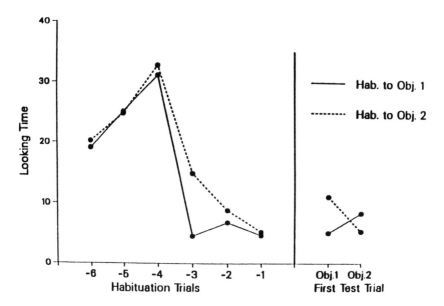

FIG. 5.13. Looking times during habituation and test trials in the motion perspective experiment.

also contains changes in brightness and texture gradients. Recently, Pentland (1990) has emphasized the potential usefulness of this sort of information about form. Regarding infant 3-D form perception, Shaw, Roder, and Bushnell (1986) argued that changes in brightness and texture are necessary for infants younger than 24 weeks of age to detect form. In the experiments described earlier, by Kellman (1984) and Kellman and Short (1987), solid objects were illuminated primarily from one direction. Thus, brightness changes were available along with transformations involving projected edges.

To disentangle the contributions of perspective transformations from brightness changes during motion, we carried out a study using wire figures similar to those introduced by Wallach and O'Connell (1953). Such figures contain thin edges but no surfaces connecting them; when such figures rotate, they provide the same geometric transformations of surface boundaries as do solid objects, but unlike solid objects, transformations of surface brightness and texture are virtually absent. In our experiment, the lighting was directionally balanced to eliminate detachable shading changes even along the thin edges of the figures. The figures used in the study are shown in Fig. 5.14.

Both figures resembled the ''parallelogram'' figure used by Wallach and O'Connell (1953). Each consisted of two triangles, in different planes, that shared a common edge. In one figure, the triangles were oriented at 95° to each other, whereas in the other figure, the triangles formed an angle of 165°.

Besides eliminating transformational shading information, these figures were

95° Object   165° Object

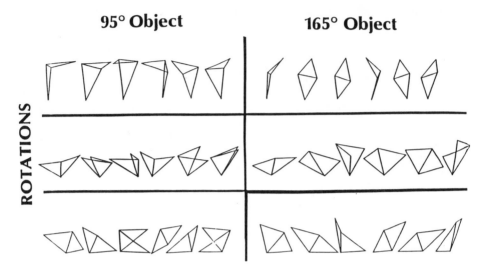

ROTATIONS

FIG. 5.14.   Objects and rotations used to test 3-D form perception from perspective transformations alone. Successive views 60° apart are shown.

designed to accomplish another purpose. The method used in our prior studies
of form assessed perception of 3-D form, apart from 2-D projections, by changing the rotation axes between habituation and test periods. Thus, generalization of habituation to the same 3-D form always required infants to remain
habituated despite being shown particular transforming projections that had not
previously been seen. Despite these changes, it was possible that varying rotations of a given object bore some similarities to one another. Data from control
groups were reassuring in this respect, indicating that stationary views taken
from the rotation sequences did not support 3-D form perception.

The experiment with wire figures, however, allowed an additional way of
ruling out contributions from 2-D similarities across axes of rotation. Not only
were the two test objects designed to be very similar to each other, but their
structure added an even greater safeguard. A theorem of projective geometry
states that all triangles are projectively equivalent; that is, any 2-D projection
of one triangle could be the projection of any other triangle in some 3-D orientation and distance. By constructing each 3-D figure in our experiment from two
triangles, the overall structure of the object was minimized. As a check on this
manipulation, we tested adults' ability to sort static, 2-D views of the two objects, taken from the three rotation axes used for each, into two separate groups.
Accuracy of sorting views of the two 3-D objects did not differ from chance
(Kellman & Short, 1987, Experiment 3b).

When continuous optical transformations were shown (on videotape), however, adults readily discriminated the two objects from each other, and effortlessly perceived the identity of each object across the three axes of rotation

used in the experiment. If our interpretation of earlier experiments was correct, and if perspective transformations alone are sufficient, 3-D form perception by infant subjects (16-week-olds) was expected as well.

This expectation was confirmed. Infants showed robust evidence of 3-D form perception, generalizing habituation to the same object in a new axis of rotation, and dishabituating to a new 3-D object, shown in the same, new rotation. Figure 5.15a shows the data from this group. Infants in a static control group, who viewed successive stationary views of the objects, showed no evidence of discrimination based on 3-D form. As shown in Fig. 5.15b, viewing of one object or the other during the habituation period did not differentially affect subsequent looking at the two test objects.

This experiment shows that perspective transformations of the bounding con-

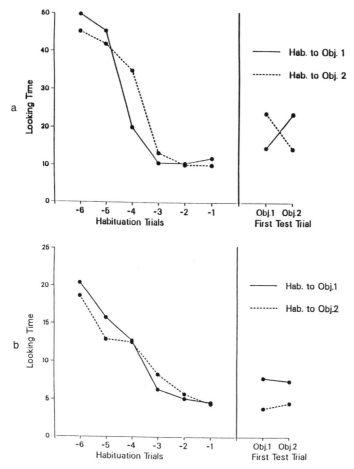

FIG. 5.15. Looking times during habituation and test trials in perspective transformation experiment: (a) kinematic condition, (b) static condition.

tours of objects contain sufficient information to specify 3-D form perception to young perceivers. The results with these stimuli, which provided little in the way of shading or brightness change information, were as robust as those in prior work with solid objects (Kellman, 1984). Although these findings do not rule out the possible informativeness of transformations of shading and texture, these are clearly not necessary for early 3-D form perception.

Static 3-D Form Perception

Adults perceive the 3-D forms of objects not only from kinematic information but from single or multiple static views of objects. For example, in Fig. 5.10, the overall shapes of the objects are evident from most of the individual views. In the course of our research on 3-D form, my colleagues and I have accumulated a good deal of evidence that these abilities arise relatively late in development. In Kellman (1984), subjects in two static conditions viewed multiple, sequential static views taken from the rotation sequences used in the kinematic condition. One group viewed six 2-sec views per rotation, spaced 60° apart. The other group viewed twenty-four 1-sec views from each rotation sequence, spaced 15° apart. Neither group showed any differential responding in the test period as a function of the habituation object presented previously. This initial failure of static views was interpreted with caution, because the views were given as photographic slides. Perceiving 3-D form from static views may be more difficult when using photographs, which may present depth cue conflicts, than from real scenes.

The failure of static information, however, is not unique to 2-D stimuli. Ruff (1978) found that 6-month-old infants failed to apprehend 3-D forms from stationary views of 3-D objects. The objects used were rather complex, however. Kellman and Short (1987, Exp. 2) tested multiple, stationary views of the objects pictured in Fig. 5.10 with infants aged 4 and 6 months. The general method was the same as in earlier form studies, except for the mode of presentation. On a given trial, multiple, stationary views of a 3-D object were presented, but the movements of the object through successive positions was blocked from the subjects' view by an occluder that hid the object momentarily during each position change. During test trials, again with sequences of static views, neither group dishabituated differentially to views of the two objects based on the object presented in habituation. Figure 5.16 shows the results of this experiment.

The difficulty of deriving 3-D form perception from static information is not limited to 16-week-olds. In recent experiments, we have obtained the same results at 24 and 32 weeks. At both of these later ages, infants still show no reliable differential responding to static views of the two test objects as a function of the object whose views were given in the habituation period.

Because adults perceive 3-D form so readily even from single views of ob-

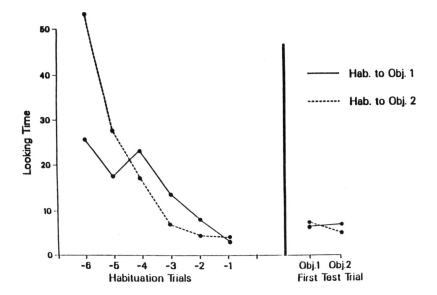

FIG. 5.16.   Looking times during habituation and test trials by 16-week-olds in experiment with static views of 3-D objects.

jects, it is surprising that even at 8 months of age, there is no evidence that infants do. The unexpectedness of this result led us to consider whether some aspect of our method was obscuring infants' competence. We entertained several possibilities. First, in our method successive static views were given by hiding the object momentarily; while occluded, the object was moved to a new position. Despite the fact that each shift in position was only 15°, it was possible that infants have some ability to perceive 3-D form from multiple static views but that the changing of the object's position in space while occluded disrupts integration of the views into a coherent representation. A second possibility is that attentional factors limit static form perception. Only a subtle version of an attentional explanation would fit the data, however. Attention, to the successive static views in these studies, as indexed by fixation times at least, is not low. Initial trial looking times on the order of 40 or 50 seconds were not uncommon, as can be seen in Fig. 5.16. Many infant perception experiments have demonstrated habituation and novelty responses to aspects of static patterns with per-trial looking times of one fifth or even one tenth of these levels. Nevertheless, any inference about the inability of infants to perceive 3-D form from static information rests on negative results and leaves open the possible roles of attentional or other extraneous factors.

To pursue these issues further, we modified our approach. Concerning the first problem—that unseen movements of the object may have been disruptive—we altered the situation so that the position of the observer, not the object, changed. During each trial, successive static views were presented by displaying the object, occluding it momentarily, and moving the observer to a new position (15° around an arc). The display situation contained ample stationary references, potentially allowing the observer to detect the constant position of the object. To check for some attentional problem in the test trials, we followed the normal test trials with an additional test. In the additional test, we changed a characteristic of the habituation object that we are certain infants are capable of detecting: the color of the object. Whereas the normal display objects were red-orange, the final test object was yellow. If attention has dwindled by the time infants reached the test trials, we might expect infants to fail to respond to any change, including color. On the other hand, if infants' difficulty is not attentional, but has to do with the inability to detect the invariant 3-D form from multiple static views, then we might expect to find a novelty response to a color change, despite the absence of such a response to form change.

Figure 5.17 shows the results of this experiment at 16 weeks of age. The final habituation trial, the first test trial with each test object, and the final (yellow) trial are shown. Two aspects of the data are salient. First, as in the earlier studies at 4, 6, and 8 months of age, there is no differential responding to the test objects as a function of habituation exposure. Second, there is a reliable novelty preference to the yellow object, presented at the very end of the experiment, indicating that subjects had not suffered some overall attentional lapse.

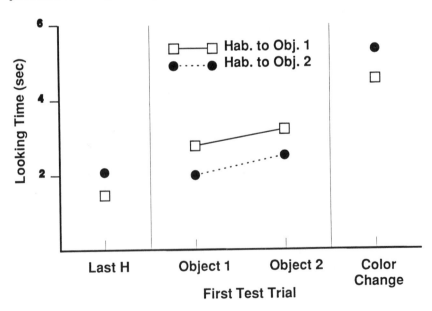

FIG. 5.17. Results in the modified static-view experiment. Looking times on the final trial of habituation, the first test trial with each test object, and the attentional probe trial (color change) are shown.

These results give further indication that static information does not furnish infants with 3-D form information.

There is some evidence that binocular, static views of objects can allow recognition of 3-D forms that have previously been perceived from kinematic information (Owsley, 1983; Yonas et al., 1987). This suggests that some aspects of 3-D structure can be apprehended from stationary, binocular viewing and compared to an overall representation of form given by motion information. There is no evidence that the overall form of the object can be given initially from static views, even multiple and sequential ones.

What is the limitation on 3-D form perception from static information? An abundance of evidence indicates that infants from the earliest months of life can detect and distinguish 2-D patterns, colors, and orientations (e.g., Cohen, DeLoache, & Strauss, 1979). By 6 months of age, virtually all infants have stereoscopic depth perception, which should accurately indicate the slants of surfaces in the studies using real objects. The problem seems to be extrapolating beyond the information in a single view to the whole form. The process is not well understood in adult perception, either, but such extrapolations seem to invoke considerations of symmetry or simplicity (Buffart, Leeuwenberg, & Restle, 1981). Such assumptions may be products of learning. Whether they arise from learning or maturation, the late appearance of such heuristic processes fits our general view about ecological validity in perceptual development. The conformity of unseen parts of objects with predictions made from symmetry or simplicity may be likely but is nowhere near certain. Such extrapolations may form part of the adult perceiver's optimization in perceiving, but they are poor candidates for the repertoire of the risk-averse infant perceiver.

Summary: Perception of 3-D Form

In sum, 3-D form appears to be first perceived visually from perspective transformations given over time. This ability is unlikely to be dependent on learning, because no other source of information about 3-D form is readily available in the early months of life. As one might predict from an ecological analysis of the information, perception of 3-D form occurs from optical changes given by both object and observer motion. In many respects, perception of 3-D form provides developmental evidence for Johansson's (1970) description of the visual system as a *perspective decoder,* using the rules of projective geometry to extract spatial arrangement from optical change. Our studies of form perception are also consistent with an event perception perspective in that static sources of information about form seem to be inoperative through much of the first year of life. Their later appearance parallels their lesser validity from an ecological perspective. It is likely that the 3-D forms of stationary objects viewed from a stationary position are, to a young infant, indeterminate. The overall picture of early 3-D form perception fits closely our portrait of the risk-averse perceiver: The information usable earliest is also the soundest.

PERCEPTION OF MOTION AND STABILITY
BY MOVING OBSERVERS

Perceptual theorists have long pondered the fact that motion is signaled by changes in the optical projection, but that such changes can also be produced by an observer moving in a stationary environment. Helmholtz (1909/1962) speculated that early in life, the optical changes produced by self-motion and by object motion were indistinguishable; an active perceiver might learn, however, that certain transformations of the world, such as those caused by moving one's head, can be reversed or undone, while others cannot. In Helmholtz's view, the perception of a stationary world during one's own movement develops from learning about such reversible transformations.

A contrasting view of object and observer motion perception was proposed by J. J. Gibson (1966, 1979). Gibson argued that the visual information specifying motion of objects differs from that specifying motion of the observer. For example, when only a single object moves, optical changes are confined to relatively local regions of the optic array. When the observer moves, global transformations of the optic array result. Given the availability of information distinguishing object and observer motion, and given the fundamental importance of observer motion in perception, such information might be usable by perceivers without learning.

Despite its theoretical centrality, there has not been much research on the development of perception of motion and stability during observer motion in early infancy. Besides its theoretical interest, it would appear to have important practical interest. The Helmholtzian infant would live in a dramatic kaleidoscopic world in which every head or eye movement would set the world into motion. Developing an understanding of both the physical and social worlds would be far more challenging from this starting point than from a more stable representation of the environment. Consider, for example, the task of comprehending the principles governing moving bodies, under conditions in which many, perhaps most, cases of perceived object motion are spurious.

Understanding early abilities for perceiving motion and stability is, thus, a high priority in the study of cognitive development. Although a detailed consideration of the various types of active and passive movements, eye and head movements around various axes, and so forth, is beyond the scope of this chapter (see Kellman & Hofsten, in press), I describe here some initial research into the perception of motion and stability by moving observers.

Motion and Distance Perception

This work focuses on cases in which perceiving motion and stability is related to distance perception. When an observer translates orthogonally to the line of sight, perceived objects undergo optical changes that depend on their distances from the observer. Figure 5.18 depicts this situation. Specifically, if D is the (perpendicular) distance from the observer's motion path to the object and M is the extent of motion, the optical change, Θ, in visual angle is given by:

$$\Theta = 2 \arctan (M/2D) \tag{1}$$

For small Θ, this can be approximated by the simpler expression:

$$\Theta = M/D, \tag{2}$$

where Θ is expressed in radians. The same optical change can be given by a moving object at distance $D + d$, if it moves parallel to the observer's motion. The extent of motion x that gives this optical change at distance $D + d$ is given by:

$$x = -dM/D \tag{3}$$

Note that when d is negative, that is, the moving object is closer than D, x is positive, and the object motion is in the same direction as the observer's.[2] Without referring to a stationary reference point D and an additional increment of distance d, the motion of the target can be determined from the total distance T (equal to $D + d$), the observer's motion (M) and the angular change (Θ) by:

$$x = M - \Theta T \tag{4}$$

A more revealing form of equation 4 is:

$$x = M - (M/D)(D + d) \tag{5}$$

in which M/D has been substituted for Θ, and $D + d$ has been substituted for T. In the case in which there is no target movement ($x = 0$), $d = 0$ and $T = D$. Thus, D in general gives the position at which a *stationary* object would give rise to a particular optical displacement given a particular extent of observer motion (the "pivot point" in Gogel's, 1980, terminology). All other combinations of target motion and distance giving the same optical change are pairs (x, d) such that $-x/d = M/D = \Theta$. Perceptually, discriminating a stationary object from one moving parallel to the observer presents a difficult perceptual task because of the ambiguity of optical change alone. Additional information

---

[2]For simplicity, this analysis is presented for the case in which the stationary target is straight ahead, that is, the line of sight is perpendicular to the direction of motion. The more general analysis would include a correction for the eccentricity of the target; the more eccentric the target (at a given distance from the observer) the smaller the angular change produced by a given observer motion.

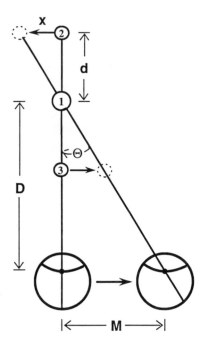

FIG. 5.18.   Geometry of parallel object and observer motions. M is the extent
of lateral observer motion; D is the initial distance from the object of the nodal
point of the eye; Θ is the angular change for an object at position 1 given by motion M. For an object at distance $D + d$ (labeled 2), object motion x gives the
same optical change.

(e.g., distance information) is needed to determine whether a given optical change
arises from observer or object motion.

Gogel (1980, 1982) has shown that this geometry of distance and motion is
utilized in adult perception. That is, perceived movement depends in some circumstances upon perceived distance. Can infants also detect the moving and
stationary parts of their environment based on these relations?

To explore these questions, we developed a new method (Kellman, Hofsten,
Condry, & O'Halloran, 1991). Infants are passively moved laterally back and
forth in a moving chair while viewing arrays of objects. On each trial, one object
in the array also moves, parallel to the infant's path of motion. The motions
of object and observer are always either in-phase or in opposite-phase (180°
out of phase); moments of acceleration/deceleration always coincide. These connections are achieved by mechanically linking the infant's chair and the moving
object in a way not visible to the subjects (Fig. 5.19). On each trial, an object
moved, either on the right or left side of the array. To control for the particular
optical displacement, a stationary object at a different distance is always placed
on the other side of the display to give the same extent of optical displacement

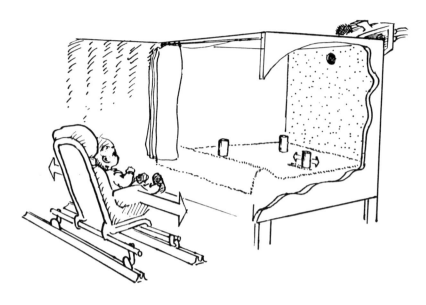

FIG. 5.19.   The object-observer motion apparatus.

as the moving object. For in-phase motion, the control object was placed further away; in the opposite-phase condition, the control object is nearer. Examples are given in Figs. 5.20a and b. Additional stationary objects in the displays controlled for possible tendencies of subjects to fixate preferentially the nearest object in the array, the largest object, and so on.

We assumed that if the infants detected one moving object in an array of stationary ones, they would tend to fixate that object preferentially. Infants ordinarily devote greater visual attention to moving objects (Carpenter, 1974; Volkmann & Dobson, 1976). Preferential looking in the direction of the moving object was thus taken to indicate motion detection.

We excluded information about the relation of the objects to the ground surface at their points of tangency by placing a hump at the near edge of the surface, which occluded the bottoms of all objects. Object visual angle was also not a clue to distance: It varied in the arrays between 2.7° diameter × 5.5° height to 4° diameter × 8° height in a way that was uncorrelated with distance.

There were several additional controls for response tendencies that might have biased the results. For example, infants might always prefer to fixate the closest object in an array. This possibility was controlled in opposite-phase conditions because the stationary object with equivalent optical change was always nearer than the moving object. When motion was in-phase, an additional stationary object, closer than the moving one and on the opposite side, was always present. A second possibility is that subjects might attend to the locus of maximum optic flow. In its simplest form, this possibility was controlled for by the

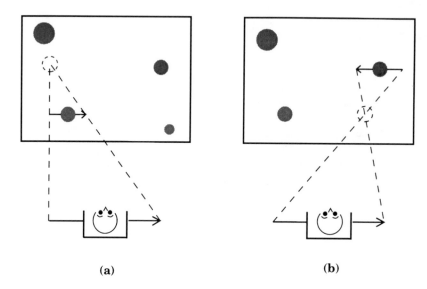

(a)   (b)

FIG. 5.20.   Examples of arrays used in object–observer motion experiments. Top views are shown. Solid circles are cylindrical objects; arrows indicate motion. The dotted object represents the position a stationary object must occupy to produce an optical change identical to the moving object. Such a stationary object is placed in the corresponding position on the other side of the display: (a) in-phase condition, (b) opposite-phase condition. From Kellman, Hofsten, Condry, and O'Halloran (1991).

front edge of the hump, which always had the fastest optical velocity in all conditions. However, a more complex version of this concern is that subjects might attend to the locus of greatest optical shear, that is discontinuities in the optic flow (cf., Nakayama & Loomis, 1974). The hump, which obscured the bottoms of objects, ensured that the shear relations between the moving object and other surfaces were equivalent for the moving and stationary control objects.

Under these conditions, determination of the motion or stability of objects required the combining of distance information with registered optical change. Information given by optical (angular) change and registered extent of self-motion is not sufficient because of the geometric relations already described. In the absence of distance information, an object in this array could be located at one particular position and be stationary, or it could be located at some other distance and moving.

The dependent variable in the experiments was looking time to the left or right halves of the array, as a function of the presence of the moving object on the left or right. With the moving object presented half of the time on the left and half on the right, subjects were presented with a series of 15-sec trials. A session continued until the subject became fussy or a maximum of 25 trials was reached. Certain criteria were established in advance for including subjects and trials in the analyses. A trial was considered valid if the infant looked at least 1.5 sec at an object. This criterion was used to weed out random, nonattentive glances. Subjects were disqualified if they did not have at least one valid trial of looking to the right and one to the left during the experiment (without regard to the position of the moving object). This criterion eliminated infants whose position bias was so strong that they never looked to one side. To assess motion perception, we compared looking times to the left and right sides of the display as a function of the placement of the moving object. To control for side preferences, the following comparison was used: For all trials, the measure L – R (looking time to the left minus looking time to the right) was calculated. Then, for each subject, mean L – R was calculated separately for trials with the moving object on the left $(L-R)_L$ and right $(L-R)_R$ sides of the display. Finally, $(L-R)_R$ was subtracted from $(L-R)_L$. This gave a single number for each subject, thus ensuring that each subject counted equally in the overall analysis, regardless of differences across subjects in the number of valid trials. This measure—$(L-R)_L$ minus $(L-R)_R$—was then tested against the null hypothesis of 0. That is, if looking times are the same regardless of the position of the moving object, then this derived measure will not differ from 0. The measure will be more positive the more looking time differs with the position of the moving object.

In our first experiments, 16-week-olds viewed the arrays binocularly. Separate groups were tested with in-phase and opposite-phase motion. Results are shown in Figs. 5.21a and b.

Overall looking times in this paradigm are not high. Infants' fixation tendencies, however, were reliably influenced by the position of the moving object. Subjects fixated more to the left when the moving object was on the left, and vice versa. No differences in this pattern were found between the in-phase and opposite-phase conditions. The effect of position of the moving object on the patterns of looking was highly reliable ($p < .01$).

Moving infants can apparently distinguish optical changes resulting from their own motion from those resulting from object motion. Infants seemed both to detect real motion and to attend preferentially to it. Because perceiving position constancy and motion in this situation required distance information apart from optic flow, the results indicate an early ability to combine optical change information with non-flow distance information.

What distance information could this be? Distance and depth information are commonly viewed as falling into four classes: Kinematic, stereoscopic, oculomotor, and pictorial information (e.g., Kaufman, 1974). Pictorial cues do not seem to operate in the first half year of life (Yonas & Granrud, 1984). Many sources of depth information, including stereopsis and most pictorial cues, provide only relative depth information (i.e., depth order). Metrical information about distance would be needed to determine motion or stability. A number of cues were intentionally excluded from the situation. Among cues with the potential

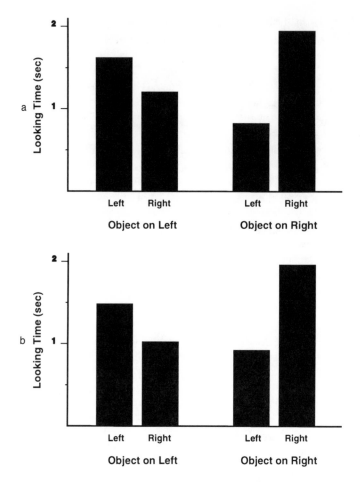

FIG. 5.21.   Results of object–observer motion experiment with 16-week-olds,
viewing the arrays binocularly. Looking times are shown to the left and right sides
of the array when the moving object was on the left or right: (a) in-phase condition, (b) opposite-phase condition. From Kellman, Hofsten, Condry, and O'Halloran (1991).

to indicate absolute distance, a number were explicitly excluded from providing
useful information in our set-up. Relative size was excluded by approximately
equating the visual angle of relevant objects in the array and randomizing others
(i.e., there was no correlation between visual angle and distance). I noted earlier that certain kinematic variables (e.g., optical shear) between the object and
support surface at points of object tangency, were eliminated by occluding the
bottoms of all objects. Another kinematic information source is motion perspective. When a moving observer views a stationary object, if the extent of observer motion is known, the absolute distance of the object is potentially re-

coverable. In our arrangement, however, motion perspective information could not determine object motion or stability. When both the motion/stability and the depth of an object is in question, the optical change cannot be used to specify both.

The remaining two classes of information offer better prospects. Oculomotor cues—accommodation and convergence—involve information from the eye muscle adjustments needed to focus or converge the eyes. The other remaining information source is *stereopsis,* or binocular disparity. Stereopsis is perhaps the only static information source whose ecological validity and precision equals or approaches that of kinematic information. In recent years, a clear picture of the emergence of stereoscopic depth perception has emerged from a number of investigations (Braddick, Wattam-Bell, Day, & Atkinson, 1983; Fox, Aslin, Shea, & Dumais, 1980; Held, Birch, & Gwiazda, 1980). Stereoacuity seems virtually non-existent from birth to about 12 to 14 weeks, after which it reaches near-adult levels fairly rapidly. By 16 weeks, estimates are that about half of infants have stereoscopic function (Held et al., 1980). The relatively abrupt onset and increase in acuity, along with certain electrophysiological findings, suggest that stereoscopic depth perception arises from maturation of the nervous system (Braddick & Atkinson, 1988; Held et al., 1980).

Stereoscopic and oculomotor function are closely related. For instance, proper convergence of the eyes is a prerequisite for obtaining meaningful disparity information. Oculomotor information may also be used to calibrate binocular disparity (Wallach & Zuckerman, 1963). The advantage of this combination is that disparity alone provides only relative depth information, but with very high sensitivity. The oculomotor cues (especially convergence) can provide *absolute* distance information, but only in very near space (approximately 2 meters) and with modest precision.

There has been little study of convergence as a source of distance information early in life. Several studies have assessed the accuracy of convergence (Aslin, 1977; Slater & Findlay, 1975), showing vergence changes appropriate in direction, if not highly precise, from birth. One study attempted to assess perception of distance based on convergence. Hofsten (1977) altered 20-week-olds' convergence using optical devices. He found appropriate changes in the lengths of subjects' reaches for objects. Whether convergence provides useful distance information earlier than 20 weeks is unknown. Convergence appears, however, to be the best candidate for the distance information underlying motion detection in our experiments with 16-week-olds. It is also possible that a combination of convergence and binocular disparity provide the needed distance information. Convergence has also been suggested to be the distance information underlying size perception by neonates (see Granrud, this volume).

To test the hypothesis that convergence provided necessary information in our experiments, we carried out experiments under monocular viewing. Subjects were fitted with a patch over one eye. If motion detection depended on

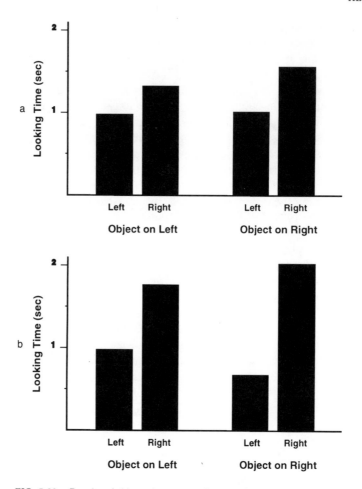

FIG. 5.22.   Results of object–observer motion experiment with 16-week-olds, viewing the arrays monocularly: (a) in-phase condition, (b) opposite-phase condition. From Kellman, Hofsten, Condry, and O'Halloran (1991).

convergence or convergence plus disparity, it should have been eliminated under monocular viewing.[3] Figure 5.22 shows the results from these studies for in-phase and opposite-phase object-observer motions. As predicted, monocular viewing eliminated motion detection: Infants' looking patterns were not reliably influenced by the position of the moving object.

The results described so far suggest that moving infants detect motion and stability by using binocular distance information. There is an alternative inter-

---

[3]This excludes the possibility of accommodatively triggered vergence. The results disconfirm this possibility, however.

pretation, however. The eyepatch used in the monocular condition might have caused some general distress or inattention rather than reducing the ability to detect motion. An experiment carried out by Kirsten Condry tested this possibility (Condry, 1988; Kellman, Hofsten, Condry, & O'Halloran, 1991). Infants wore an eyepatch but were stationary throughout the experiment. The moving objects appeared just as in previous studies, half of the time on the left and half on the right. Detecting motion in this case requires no binocular information, because the observer is stationary. If the negative results in the previous monocular conditions resulted from general inattention or distress caused by the eyepatch (rather than from an inability to detect motion), then these infants were predicted to fail to look preferentially at the moving object. If distress or inattention was not the reason for monocular infants' difficulty in the earlier study, infants would be expected to show motion detection in this case.

Figure 5.23 shows the data from this experiment. Stationary, monocular infants clearly detected the moving objects. Fixation was greater toward the side of the array on which the moving object appeared. The eyepatch did not cause distraction sufficient to keep the infants from attending to motion. From this outcome, it appears unlikely that the failure of moving, monocular infants to detect object motion was due to general distress or inattention caused by the eyepatch. It appears that moving, monocular infants did not detect motion because they require binocular distance information to do so.

As noted already, if binocular distance information underlies infants' motion detection, this binocular information could be supplied by convergence or by a combination of convergence and binocular disparity. Can we specify further which information is at work?

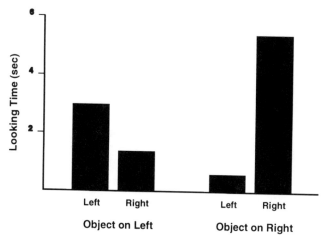

FIG. 5.23. Results of experiment with stationary viewing by monocular subjects. From Kellman, Hofsten, Condry, and O'Halloran (1991).

In our studies of 16-week-old infants, we did not pretest for stereoscopic ability. It is thus possible that some combination of binocular disparity and convergence furnished the relevant information about distance. Binocular disparity cannot specify absolute distance; however, it can provide precise absolute depth intervals in combination with a source of absolute distance information, such as convergence, that can specify the distance of at least one visible point (Wallach, Moore, & Davidson, 1963).

To assess the roles of convergence and disparity, we conducted experiments in the object–observer motion paradigm with 8-week-old infants (Kellman, Hofsten, Van de Walle, & Condry, 1991). Infants of this age, in general, show no stereoscopic depth perception, but they do show convergence. There is little or no data, however, indicating whether convergence provides usable distance information at this age.

The experiments were carried out in the same way as those with older infants. Object motion of the same phase and of opposite phase were tested in separate studies. Only binocular conditions were run; we assumed that since monocular 16-week-olds had been unable to detect motion, younger infants would be also.

Results are shown in Fig. 5.24. In contrast to earlier studies, there was a difference between the data obtained from in-phase and opposite-phase motion. When the object moved in opposite phase to the observer (Fig. 5.24a), 8-week-olds showed clear evidence of motion detection, but when the object moved in phase (Fig. 5.24b), motion detection was not observed.

From the results in the opposite-phase condition, it appears that motion detection is possible from convergence information alone. The motion preference in this condition was as strong as that of 16-week-olds in either phase condition. Such a pattern was not evident, however, in the in-phase condition. This outcome may reflect certain sensory limitations of 8-week-olds, along with finer discriminations demanded by the in-phase motion condition (in which the stationary control object was positioned further away than the moving object; for discussion, see Kellman & Hofsten, in press).

These studies suggest that at 8 weeks convergence alone can furnish the absolute distance information that underlies motion detection. Subjects' difficulty with in-phase motion indicates that these younger infants are not as well-equipped to use distance-motion relations as their older counterparts; nevertheless, the basic perceptual capacity appears to be present. Stereoscopic depth perception, which 8-week-olds lack, does not appear to be a prerequisite. Still, it is likely that the later onset of depth perception from disparity increases the specificity of detection of motion and stability.

The possibility that convergence is a primary source of distance information is consistent with recent studies of size constancy in newborns (Granrud, 1987; Slater, Mattock, & Brown, 1990). Evidence from these studies suggests that newborns are sensitive to the real sizes of objects across changes in their project-

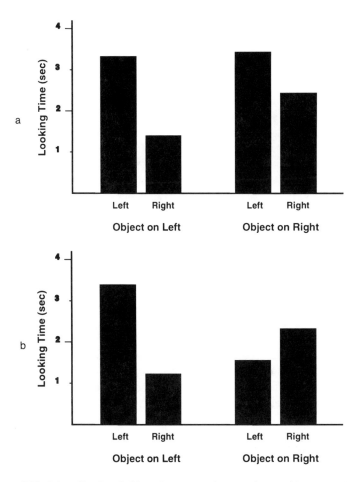

FIG. 5.24.   Results of object–observer motion experiment with 8-week-olds, viewing the arrays binocularly: (a) in-phase condition, (b) opposite-phase condition. From Kellman, Hofsten, Van de Walle, and Condry (1991).

ed size and distance. Although size constancy may sometimes be achieved in other ways, such as in connection with optical texture gradients (J. J. Gibson, 1950, 1979), Granrud's situation is one in which distance information, implicit or explicit, appears to be required. Hence, his experiments suggest that some form of absolute distance perception is innate.

Motion and the "Blooming, Buzzing Confusion"

In discussing perception of object unity and 3-D form, we were concerned with persisting properties of the environment. In this section, I have considered some of the kinematic foundations of perceiving *events* or changes in the environment, such as the motions of objects and observers. Our findings suggest an early capacity for perceiving a coherent environment, in which stationary objects remain perceptually at rest when the observer moves, and moving objects may be detected. The basis of these early abilities seems to be a combination of optic flow information with nonflow distance information. This combination successfully grapples with the geometry of object–observer motion, in which an optical change alone may be produced in more than one way.

Taken at face value, the present results constitute another example of linkages in perception among dependent variables. Perceived motion is not strictly a function of some optical change, but results from a computation involving distance as well (Gogel, 1982). This characterization, however accurate, may have limited generality. Recall that we have restricted our test conditions intentionally to cases in which detection of motion required distance information. Although these cases form an important subset of naturally occurring cases, in many, perhaps most, ordinary circumstances additional information is available. Perception of the moving and stationary parts of the environment may often be accomplished directly from optic flow variables, such as optical shearing or relations between optical velocity and occlusion (Lee, 1974). Thus, it would be incorrect to claim from our results to date that moving infants' motion detection generally requires distance information. What can be said is that infants display such dependent variable coupling in cases that require it.

The role of kinematic information in motion detection fits our general view of ecological validity and risk aversion. Information in spatiotemporal change is crucial, but its specific status depends on its ecological roots. In some cases when objects and observers move, the geometry of the situation requires information in addition to optic flow; when information sources are combined, the movements and positions of parts of the environment are well-specified. Perhaps because of its ecological validity, perceptual systems capable of utilizing this spacetime geometry are present early in life.

CONCLUSION

Perception of persisting properties, such as object unity and form, and events, such as object or observer motion, comprise some of the most fundamental tasks of development. I have argued that spatiotemporal information, because of its ecological status and the evolution of perceptual systems, plays a preeminent role in the achievement of these tasks. As a closing example, we might contrast this perspective with a different one on the initial perception of motion. The notion that optical changes due to observer and object motion are not distinguishable early in life has a long history (Helmholtz, 1909/1962; James, 1890; cf., Piaget, 1954). On such a view, the world would appear to move whenever objects or observers do. The resulting chaos would surely contribute greatly to the "blooming, buzzing confusion," as James (1890, p. 173) characterized the world of the newborn.

Such a view could hardly be at greater variance with our conjecture of risk aversion in perceptual development. To a newborn, the mistaken assignment of motion to objects in the world would be a severe handicap to learning about the physical world. The learning process suggested by Helmholtz—that perceivers come to notice and discount observer-contingent motions—might be of little consolation. Infants might just as well learn that when they move, some objects also move, instead of learning that the world remains at rest during observer motion. Although imaginable, misassignment of motion to external objects would require an unlearning process of considerable sophistication.

The results we have considered, in motion as well as object perception, are consistent with a wholly different view: Perceptual systems have evolved to furnish useful descriptions of the environment. At no time in human development is the soundness of information of greater import than during infancy; consequently, infant perception may be risk-averse. Risk aversion is best served by early perceptual capacities that utilize the most ecologically secure information. From such a perspective, it is not surprising that the geometry of observer and object motion seems to be appropriately utilized to perceive motion and stability in the early weeks of life.

We have seen that the particulars of kinematic information differ in different domains. The motions of objects through the environment are crucial to the primitive process of unity perception. For 3-D form perception, on the other hand, either object or observer motion alone can furnish the crucial information. Where perception of motion is itself the issue, the geometry of distance and motion requires combining kinematic information with other sources of spatial information. The invariant theme is not that early perceptual competence is tied to one sort of motion or optical change, but that in each domain it appears to be tied to the kinematic information possessing the highest ecological validity.

The conjecture that kinematic information dominates early perception because of its superior ecological validity is consistent with the evidence I have discussed about early perception of objects, space, and motion. It is, however, a broad characterization not subject to a single empirical test. My examples and arguments have been selective. At least, however, the conjecture is heuristically useful for summarizing current knowledge about early perceptual development. At most, it may be much more. The young perceiver seems to be able to extract meaningful information about objects, the spatial layout, and events. The means to achieve these feats do not comprise the full complement of adult abilities, but a clear subset. That subset seems to be dominated by spatiotemporal information sources that not only are usable by the perceptual systems of inexperienced perceivers, but are apparently the very sources of information most securely rooted in the basic physics and geometry of space and time.

ACKNOWLEDGMENTS

Portions of this work were presented at meetings of the Society for Research in Child Development, the International Conference on Event Perception and Action, and the International Conference on Infant Studies between 1985 and 1989.

I gratefully acknowledge support from National Science Foundation Research Grants 82-10110, 85-19851 and 89-13707, and several Swarthmore College Faculty Research Grants.

I thank Martha Arterberry, Martin Banks, Kirsten Condry, Carl Granrud, Claes von Hofsten, Sandra Shea, Thomas Shipley, and Gretchen Van de Walle for helpful discussions related to this chapter. I thank Donald R. Reynolds for expertise and persistence in building nearly impossible apparatus; and Ramona O'Halloran, Kirsten Condry, Gretchen Van de Walle, and Peter Vishton for able laboratory assistance.

REFERENCES

Allman, J., Miezin, F., & McGuinness, E. (1985). Direction- and velocity-specific responses from beyond the classical receptive field in the middle temporal visual area. *Perception, 14,* 105–126.

Ames, A. (1951). Visual perception and the rotating trapezoidal window. *Psychological Monographs, 67* (7, Whole No. 324).

Aslin, R. N. (1977). Development of binocular fixation in human infants. *Journal of Experimental Child Psychology, 23,* 133–150.

Aslin, R. N. (1988). Anatomical constraints on oculomotor development: Implications for infant perception. In A. Yonas (Ed.), *The Minnesota symposia on child psychology: Vol. 20. Perceptual development in infancy* (pp. 67–104). Hillsdale, NJ: Lawrence Erlbaum Associates.

Berkeley, G. (1910). *Essay toward a new theory of vision.* London: Dutton. (Original work published 1709)

Bertenthal, B. I., Campos, J. J., & Haith, M. M. (1980). Development of visual organization: The perception of subjective contours. *Child Development, 51,* 1072–1080.

Bond, E. (1972). Perception of form by the human infant. *Psychological Bulletin, 77,* 225–245.

Braddick, O., & Atkinson, J. (1988). Sensory selectivity, attentional control, and cross-channel integration in early visual development. In A. Yonas (Ed.), *The Minnesota symposia on child psychology: Vol. 20. Perceptual development in infancy* (pp. 105–144). Hillsdale, NJ: Lawrence Erlbaum Associates.

Braddick, O., Wattam-Bell, J., Day, J., & Atkinson, J. (1983). The onset of binocular function in human infants. *Human Neurobiology, 2,* 65–69.

Braunstein, M. (1976). *Depth perception through motion.* New York: Academic Press.

Brunswik, E. (1956). *Perception and the representative design of psychological experiments.* Berkeley: University of California Press.

Buffart, H., Leeuwenberg, E., & Restle, F. (1981). Coding theory of visual pattern completion. *Journal of Experimental Psychology, 7,* 241–274.

Carpenter, G. C. (1974). Visual regard of moving and stationary faces in early infancy. *Merrill-Palmer Quarterly, 11,* 182–193.

Cohen, L., DeLoache, J., & Strauss, M. (1979). Infant visual perception. In J. Osofsky (Ed.), *Handbook of infant development* (pp. 393–438). New York: Wiley.

Condry, K. (1988). *Four-month-old infants' perception of moving objects during observer motion.* Unpublished manuscript.

Epstein, W. (1982). Percept-percept couplings. *Perception, 11,* 75–83.

Fantz, R. L., Fagan, J. F., III, & Miranda, S. B. (1975). Early visual selectivity as a function of pattern variables, previous exposure, age from birth and conception, and expected cognitive deficit. In L. B. Cohen & P. Salapatek (Eds.), *Infant perception: From sensation to cognition* (Vol. 1, pp. 241–345). New York: Academic Press.

Fodor, J. (1983). *The modularity of mind.* Cambridge, MA: MIT Press.

Fox, R., Aslin, R., Shea, S., & Dumais, S. (1980). Stereopsis in human infants. *Science, 207,* 323–324.

Gibson, E. J. (1969). *Principles of perceptual learning and development.* New York: Appleton-Century-Crofts.

Gibson, E. J. (1984). Perceptual development from the ecological approach. In M. Lamb, A. Brown, & B. Rogoff (Eds.), *Advances in developmental psychology* (Vol. 3, pp. 243–285). Hillsdale, NJ: Lawrence Erlbaum Associates.

Gibson, J. J. (1950). *The perception of the visual world.* Boston: Houghton-Mifflin.

Gibson, J. J. (1966). *The senses considered as perceptual systems.* Boston: Houghton-Mifflin.

Gibson, J. J. (1979). *The ecological approach to visual perception.* Boston: Houghton-Mifflin.

Gibson, J. J., & Gibson, E. J. (1955). Perceptual learning: Differentiation or enrichment? *Psychological Review, 62,* 32–41.

Gibson, J. J., Kaplan, G., Reynolds, H. N., & Wheeler, K. (1969). The change from visible to invisible: A study of optical transitions. *Perception and Psychophysics, 5,* 113–116.

Gogel, W. (1980). The sensing of retinal motion. *Perception & Psychophysics, 28*(2), 155–163.

Gogel, W. (1982). Analysis of the perception of motion concomitant with a lateral motion of the head. *Perception & Psychophysics, 32*(3), 241–250.

Granrud, C. E. (1987). Size constancy in newborn human infants. *Investigative Ophthalmology and Visual Science, 28,* (Supplement), 5.

Harris, P. (1983). Infant cognition. In M. M. Haith & J. J. Campos (Eds.), *Cognitive development* (pp. 689–782). New York: Wiley.

Held, R., Birch, E. E., & Gwiazda, J. (1980). Stereoacuity of human infants. *Proceedings of the National Academy of Sciences (USA), 77,* 5572–5574.

Held, R., & Hein, A. (1963). Movement-produced stimulation in the development of visually-guided behavior. *Journal of Comparative and Physiological Psychology, 56,* 872–876.

Helmholtz, H. von (1962). *Treatise on physiological optics* (3rd ed.; J. P. C. Southall, Ed.). New York: Dover. (Original work published 1909)

Helson, H. (1933). The fundamental propositions of Gestalt psychology. *Psychological Review, 40,* 13–32.

Hering, E. (1861). *Beitrage zur Physiologie* (Heft 1) [Introduction to physiology, Vol. 1]. Leipzig: Englemann.

Hochberg, J. (1974). Higher-order stimuli and inter-response coupling in the perception of the visual world. In R. B. McLeod & H. L. Pick, Jr. (Eds.), *Perception: Essays in honor of J. J. Gibson* (pp. 17–39). Ithaca, NY: Cornell University Press.

Hoffman, D. D., & Richards, W. A. (1984). Parts of recognition. *Cognition, 18,* 65–96.

Hofsten, C. von (1977). Binocular convergence as a determinant of reaching behavior in infancy. *Perception, 6,* 139–144.

James, W. (1890). *The principles of psychology* (Vol. 2). New York: Holt.

Johansson, G. (1970). On theories for visual space perception. *Scandinavian Journal of Psychology, 11,* 67–74.

Johansson, G., Hofsten, C. von, & Jansson, G. (1980). Event perception. *Annual Review of Psychology, 31,* 27–63.

Kaufman, L. (1974). *Sight and mind.* New York: Oxford University Press.

Kaufmann-Hayoz, R., Kaufmann, F., & Walther, D. (1988, April). *Perception of kinetic subjective contours at 5 and 8 months.* Paper presented at the Sixth International Conference on Infant Studies, Washington, DC.

Kellman, P. J. (1984). Perception of three-dimensional form in infancy. *Perception and Psychophysics, 36,* 353–358.

Kellman, P. J., Gleitman, H., & Spelke, E. S. (1987). Object and observer motion in the perception of objects by infants. *Journal of Experimental Psychology: Perception and Performance, 13*(4), 586–593.

Kellman, P. J., & Hofsten, C. von (in press). The world of the moving infant: Perception of objects, motion and space. In C. Rovee-Collier & L. Lipsitt (Eds.), *Advances in infancy research.* Norwood, NJ: Ablex.

Kellman, P. J., Hofsten, C. von, Condry, K., & O'Halloran, R. (1991). *Motion and stability in the world of the (moving) infant.* Unpublished manuscript.

Kellman, P. J., Hofsten, C. von, Van de Walle, G., & Condry, K. (1991). *Perception of motion and stability during observer motion by pre-stereoscopic infants.* Unpublished manuscript.

Kellman, P. J., & Loukides, M. G. (1987). An object perception approach to static and kinetic subjective contours. In G. Meyer & G. Petry (Eds.), *The perception of illusory contours* (pp. 151–164). New York: Springer-Verlag.

Kellman, P. J., & Shipley, T. F. (1991). A theory of visual interpolation in object perception. *Cognitive Psychology, 23,* 141–221.

Kellman, P. J., & Short, K. R. (1985, April). *Infant form perception from perspective transformations.* Paper presented at the meeting of the Society for Research in Child Development, Toronto, Canada.

Kellman, P. J., & Short, K. R. (1987, June). *Infant perception of partly occluded objects: The problem of rotation.* Paper presented at the Third International Conference on Event Perception and Action, Uppsala, Sweden.

Kellman, P. J., & Spelke, E. (1983). Perception of partly occluded objects in infancy. *Cognitive Psychology, 15,* 483–524.

Kellman, P. J., Spelke, E., & Short, K. R. (1986). Infant perception of object unity from translatory motion in depth and vertical translation. *Child Development, 57,* 72–76.

Koenderink, J. J. (1986). Optic flow. *Vision Research, 26,* 161–180.

Koffka, K. (1935). *Principles of Gestalt psychology.* New York: Harcourt Brace Jovanovich.

Lee, D. N. (1974). Visual information during locomotion. In R. B. McLeod & H. L. Pick (Eds.), *Perception: Essays in honor of J. J. Gibson* (pp. 239–252). Ithaca, NY: Cornell University Press.

Longuet-Higgins, H. C., & Prazdny, K. (1980). The interpretation of moving retinal images. *Proceedings of the Royal Society, London B, 208,* 385–397.

Mandler, J. (1988). How to build a baby: On the development of an accessible representational system. *Cognitive Development, 3,* 113–136.

Marr, D. (1982). *Vision.* San Francisco: W. H. Freeman.

Michotte, A., Thines, G., & Crabbe, G. (1964). Les complements amodaux des structures perceptives. *Studia Psycologica.* Louvain: Publications Universitaires de Louvain.

Mill, J. S. (1965). Examination of Sir William Hamilton's philosophy. In R. Herrnstein & E. G. Boring (Eds.), *A source book in the history of psychology* (pp. 182–188). Cambridge, MA: Harvard University Press. (Original work published 1865)

Nakayama, K., & Loomis, J. M. (1974). Optical velocity patterns, velocity-sensitive neurons, and space perception: A hypothesis. *Perception, 3,* 63–80.

Owsley, C. (1983). The role of motion in infants' perception of solid shape. *Perception, 12,* 707–718.

Pentland, A. (1990). Photometric motion. *Investigative Ophthalmology and Visual Science Supplements, 31,* 172.

Piaget, J. (1954). *The construction of reality in the child.* New York: Basic Books.

Regan, D., & Beverly, K. I. (1978). Looming detectors in the human visual pathway. *Vision Research, 18,* 415–421.

Regan, D., & Cynader, M. (1979). Neurons in area 18 of cat visual cortex selectively sensitive to changing size: Non-linear interactions between responses to two edges. *Vision Research, 19,* 699–711.

Rock, I. (1977). In defense of unconscious inference. In W. Epstein (Ed.), *Stability and constancy in visual perception* (pp. 321–373). New York: Wiley.

Rogers, B., & Graham, M. (1979). Motion parallax as an independent cue for depth perception. *Perception, 8,* 125–134.

Ruff, H. A. (1978). Infant recognition of the invariant form of objects. *Child Development, 49,* 293–306.

Salapatek, P. (1975). Pattern perception in early infancy. In L. B. Cohen & P. Salapatek (Eds.), *Infant perception: From sensation to cognition* (pp. 133–248). New York: Academic Press.

Schmidt, H., & Spelke, E. S. (1984, April). *Gestalt relations and object perception in infancy.* Paper presented at the International Conference on Infant Studies, New York.

Shaw, L., Roder, B., & Bushnell, E. (1986). Infants' identification of three-dimensional form from transformations of linear perspective. *Perception and Psychophysics, 40,* 301–310.

Shepard, R. N. (1984). Ecological constraints on internal representation: Resonant kinematics of perceiving imaging, thinking, and dreaming. *Psychological Review, 91,* 417–447.

Shipley, T. F., & Kellman, P. J. (1990). Perception of partly occluded objects and subjective figures: Evidence for a common process. *Investigative Ophthalmology and Visual Science Supplements, 31,* 106.

Slater, A. M., & Findlay, J. M. (1975). Binocular fixation in the newborn baby. *Journal of Experimental Child Psychology, 20,* 248–273.

Slater, A., Mattock, A., & Brown, E. (1990). Size constancy at birth: Newborn infants' responses to retinal and real size. *Journal of Experimental Child Psychology, 49,* 314–322.

Slater, A., Morison, V., Somers, M., Mattock, A., Brown, E., & Taylor, D. (1990). Newborn and older infants' perception of partly occluded objects. *Infant Behavior and Development, 13,* 33–49.

Spelke, E. S. (1985). Perception of unity, persistence and identity: Thoughts on infants' conceptions of objects. In J. Mehler & R. Fox (Eds.), *Neonate cognition* (pp. 89–113). Hillsdale, NJ: Lawrence Erlbaum Associates.

Titchener, E. B. (1924). *A textbook of psychology.* New York: Macmillan.

Todd, J. T. (1982). Visual information about rigid and nonrigid motion: A geometric analysis. *Journal of Experimental Psychology: Human Perception and Performance, 8,* 238–252.

Ullman, S. (1979). *The interpretation of visual motion.* Cambridge, MA: MIT Press.

Volkmann, F. C., & Dobson, M. V. (1976). Infants responses of ocular fixation to moving visual stimuli. *Journal of Experimental Child Psychology, 22,* 86–89.

Wallach, H. (1985). Learned stimulation in space and motion perception. *American Psychologist, 40,* 399–404.

Wallach, H., & O'Connell, D. N. (1953). The kinetic depth effect. *Journal of Experimental Psychology, 45,* 205–217.

Wallach, H., & Zuckerman, C. (1963). The constancy of stereoscopic depth. *American Journal of Psychology, 76,* 404–412.

Walls, G. (1942). *The vertebrate eye and its adaptive radiation.* New York: Hafner.

Warren, R. (1976). The perception of egomotion. *Journal of Experimental Psychology: Human Perception and Perfeormance, 2,* 448–456.

Wertheimer, M. (1912). Experimentelle studien uber das sehen von bewengung. *Zeitschrift fur Psychologie, 61,* 161–265.

Yonas, A., Arterberry, M., & Granrud, C. (1987). Four-month-old infants' sensitivity to binocular and kinetic information for three-dimensional object shape. *Child Development, 58,* 910–917.

Yonas, A., & Granrud, C. (1984). The development of sensitivity to kinetic, binocular, and pictorial depth information in human infants. In D. Ingle, D. Lee, & M. Jeannerod (Eds.), *Brain mechanisms and spatial vision.* Amsterdam: Martines Nijoff.

6

Infants' Perception of Biomechanical Motions: Intrinsic Image and Knowledge-Based Constraints

Bennett I. Bertenthal
University of Virginia

One of the most notable contributions of the infant research literature over the past decade has been its revolutionary impact on our thinking about perceptual and cognitive development (J. M. Mandler, 1990). No longer can we assume that *basic concepts* about number, people, causality, and so forth must await the development of concrete operational thinking (Piaget, 1970), or, for that matter, even preoperational thinking. Much of the recent research points to the conclusion that the infant comes into the world with a set of fundamental constraints on, or processing heuristics relating to, how information can be organized or extracted (Keil, 1981; Rozin, 1976).

The presence of constraints on information extraction is nowhere better demonstrated than in recent studies on infants' sensitivity to motion-carried information. During the past few years, my colleagues and I have been centrally concerned with this issue while studying infants' sensitivity to biomechanical motions. These are the motions that correspond to the movements of a person, and are typically depicted by an array of point-lights moving as if attached to the major joints and head of a person walking.

Biomechanical displays provide a unique opportunity for studying the development of structure from motion. In contrast to most displays shown to infants, these displays depict objects that are functionally important and frequently seen. Moreover, the jointed motions that are depicted in these displays are morphologically equivalent to some of the same motions that are produced by infants. Thus, there is the rather unusual opportunity for "knowledge by acquaintance" in the perception of biomechanical motions by infants.

In spite of the importance of these displays, we are only just beginning to understand what constraints govern the perception of biomechanical displays by either infants or adults. In this chapter, I review some of the recent research by myself and others that is designed to identify which constraints are used in the perception of biomechanical motions and whether these constraints are available to infants.

LOGICAL NECESSITY
FOR PROCESSING CONSTRAINTS

The *raison d'etre* for investigating the presence of processing heuristics in the visual system rests on the contention that constraints represent an important component in the perceptual process. Therefore, I begin with a discussion of why perceptual constraints are necessary for explaining the perception of a unique structure from an optical display.

From a mathematical perspective, any two-dimensional (2-D) image is indefinitely ambiguous when construed as a projection of a 3-D object. Yet, except for the well-known set of ambiguous figures (Necker cube, Schroder stairs, etc.), most 2-D images are seen by adults as having a unique interpretation. These images are disambiguated because additional *processing constraints*, such as pictorial depth cues, familiarity with the objects depicted, and knowledge of representational conventions, are implemented by observers. Even when the image is continuously transformed by the proximal information, the same problem exists: There are an indefinite number of possible moving 3-D objects that, when projected onto a surface, produce the same 2-D pattern of optical flow. The finding that these transforming images are also perceived uniquely implies that the visual system implements additional processing constraints for organizing motion-carried information.

One of the most striking examples of this perceptual accomplishment is the Kinetic Depth Effect (KDE), in which adults veridically perceive 3-D objects from 2-D patterns of optical flow without any of the aforementioned picture perception cues. In the KDE, a 2-D shadow of an unfamiliar 3-D form is cast onto a screen. When viewed statically, the shadow appears as an ambiguous 2-D shape; conversely, as soon as the shadow begins to rotate, a rigid, 3-D form is perceived (Wallach & O'Connell, 1953). The same effect is also produced with an array of revolving point-lights (Braunstein, 1976; Green, 1961). Interestingly, infants as young as 4 months of age perceive 3-D forms from transforming 2-D projections of point-lights (Arterberry & Yonas, 1988) or shadows (Kellman, 1984).

Although these findings are impressive, it is important to emphasize that demonstrating that observers extract a 3-D structure from a moving 2-D pattern does not provide any specific explanation as to how a unique interpretation is achieved. In contrast to the traditional approach emphasizing the phenomenology of the event, computational approaches (e.g., Marr, 1982) seek to isolate processing constraints, which serve to delimit the possible structures that correspond to the geometry of the 2-D image. Ullman (1979), for example, proposed that the visual system implements a rigidity assumption for delimiting the possible interpretations that are consistent with a transforming 2-D projection. If the object is globally rigid and consists of at least four non-coplanar points in three orthographic views, then this processing assumption or constraint is sufficient for rendering a unique interpretation (up to an absolute distance, and a mirror reflection about the image plane) of the viewed image transformations. Although this constraint is generally successful when applied to moving rigid objects, it fails when we try to account for the perception of jointed or nonrigid objects, because these displays do not necessarily include four non-coplanar points that are rigidly connected.

One of the best examples of a moving jointed object is seen in a display of biomechanical motions. These are the stereotypical motions that correspond to the movements of a person. Typically, they are produced by filming a person in the dark with small lights attached to the major joints and head (Johansson, 1973). These same motions can be synthesized by a computer (Bertenthal & Kramer, 1984; Cutting, 1978b), which mimic many but not all of the kinematic properties present in more natural displays. Johansson (1977) reported that adult observers perceive the human form and identify its action (push-ups, jumping jacks, etc.) in displays with durations of only 200 msec, corresponding to about five frames of a film sequence. This finding is impressive, because observers rarely recognize the human form in a static frame. Later research revealed that observers are capable of recognizing friends, the gender of a person, and even certain dispositional characteristics of a person from biomechanical motions (Cutting & Proffitt, 1981; MacArthur & Baron, 1983).

PROCESSING CONSTRAINTS IMPLEMENTED IN THE PERCEPTION OF BIOMECHANICAL MOTIONS

A point-light display of a person walking is typically composed of 10 to 13 points of light corresponding to the major joints (e.g., wrists, elbows, etc.) of the human body. These displays are devoid of all featural information, such as clothing, hair color, and so on; thus, recognition depends entirely on the extraction of structure from the motion-carried information. It is quite easy to demonstrate that a tranforming 2-D image of a biomechanical display is not sufficient to specify a unique interpretation. Consider the motion vectors associated with the point-light walker display depicted in Fig. 6.1. Each of these vectors follows a complex trajectory that bears little relation to the form of a person walking; moreover, these vectors can be grouped collectively into one or more objects that appear

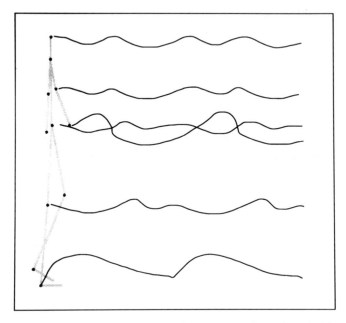

FIG. 6.1.   Trajectories of individual point-lights corresponding to the major joints
on the right side of a person walking along a path parallel to the image plane.

in the same or multiple depth planes. In searching for processing heuristics that
would delimit the possible interpretations of a biomechanical display, investigators have proposed informational, geometric, dynamic, and knowledge-based
constraints. These constraints exploit different properties associated with the
dynamic structure of a person locomoting.

   The most pervasive of these properties derive from the anatomical structure
of a person, and are best described as a hierarchical nesting of limbs that move
in pendular fashion. The limbs are symmetrically aligned along a vertical axis,
and they move in dynamic symmetry. This latter property is especially useful
for preserving a stable center of gravity while moving around in a variety of different terrains. At a more local level, the individual joints are rigidly connected,
and those located on the same limb share a common temporal phase of oscillation. These singular properties of human gait suggest the availability of multiple
constraints for perceiving a unique structure in a point-light walker display.[1]

----

[1]It is interesting to note that Gould (1983), among others, argues that the diverse tasks con-
fronting humans significantly constrained the possible range of viable structures available for locomotion. As an illustration of this point, he considered the consequences of designing a locomotor
organism with wheels. Such an organism would find it extremely difficult to move along any terrain
involving more than minor discontinuities in its surface. Moreover, it would be virtually impossible
to design a circulatory system to deliver sufficient nutrients to the wheels given their physical separation from the axle.

In the remainder of this chapter, I review five specific constraints or processing heuristics that have been proposed for explaining the perception of biomechanical motions. These proposals include: (a) perceptual vector analysis, (b) coding theory, (c) geometric constraints, (d) temporal phase relations, and (e) knowledge-based constraints. For each proposal, I discuss the logic of the constraint, and evaluate the extant evidence relevant to whether or not infants implement the constraint in their perception of biomechanical motions.

PERCEPTUAL VECTOR ANALYSIS

Johansson (1973) was the first to systematically investigate the perception of biomechanical motions. He proposed that the perception of a unique structure from continuously transforming point-lights was accomplished by the visual system according to the principles of perceptual vector analysis. This model was originally formulated to explain the perception of simple mechanical motions (Johansson, 1950), which comprise the components of a more complex biomechanical display. The fundamental principle of this model is that the perceptual system parses the proximal information (*absolute motions*) into two separate components. *Common motions* correspond to those motion vectors that are equal and simultaneous; all point-lights sharing these vectors are perceived as a perceptual grouping. This component of motion specifies the common movement of the group of point-lights relative to the observer. *Relative motions* correspond to the specific relations between the movements of one point-light and another. These motions specify the pattern or configuration of the display.

Logic of the Model

The process of perceptual vector analysis can be best illustrated using Fig. 6.2. In this figure, two point-lights are shown moving as if attached to the rim and center of a wheel moving along a flat surface. When shown this display, most observers do not perceive the absolute trajectories of these point-lights; instead they report perceiving one point-light rotating around the other while the entire configuration undergoes a horizontal translation. A vector analysis of this event reveals why this percept occurs. The point-light corresponding to the center of the wheel follows a horizontal linear path, whereas the point-light corresponding to the rim follows a cycloidal path. This latter path represents a compound vector that can be analyzed into two component vectors, a translatory component corresponding to a horizontal linear path, and a rotational component corresponding to a circular path. The two point-lights share the same horizontal linear path of motion, and thus, this component is perceived as the common motion of the event. The residual of the cycloidal path of motion is seen rotating around

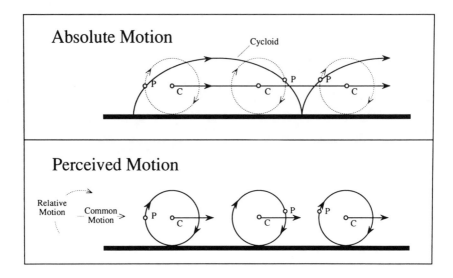

FIG. 6.2. The upper panel shows the absolute motions of two point-lights moving as if attached to the center (C) and periphery (P) of a rolling wheel. Point P follows a path corresponding to a cycloidal curve; point C follows a horizontal linear path. The lower panel shows the translatory and rotational components of motion.

the center point-light. This residual constitutes the relative motion of the event and describes a wheel-shaped configuration.

A second example concerns the perception of pendular motions, which correspond to many of the component motions in a biomechanical display. Figure 6.3 depicts the endpoints of a rod moving in pendular fashion. In Panel A, the relative motions of the two point-lights are perceived as a pendulum moving in the fronto-parallel plane. In Panel B, the same motions correspond to a pendulum that is perceived as moving in a plane that is tilted away from the fronto-parallel plane. Neither of the preceding examples includes a common motion vector. In Panel C, both a common and a relative motion vector are present, resulting in the perception of a pendular motion in which the axis is linearly translating to the right. Note, however, that the perception of a pendular motion is not available directly from the absolute motion paths of the point-lights depicted in panel C.

According to Johansson (1973), these and similar examples show how the movements of point-lights can be thought of as the results of vector addition, and the perception of these point-light displays as vector analysis. It is proposed that the perceptual system subtracts the common motion component first, and the residual motion forms the relative translatory, rotary, or pendular motion (but see Proffitt & Cutting, 1979, for a different sequence of analysis).

The motion vectors in a biomechanical display can be analyzed in an analo-

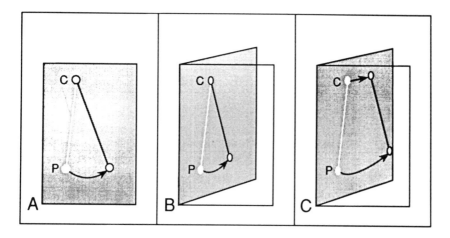

FIG. 6.3.   Two point-lights producing three different pendular motions. A: This pair is perceived as a pendular motion in the fronto-parallel plane. B: This pair is perceived as a pendular motion tilted away from the fronto-parallel plane. C: This last pair corresponds to the same pendular motion seen in B except that the axis is translating during the cycle.

gous fashion. All the point-lights include a common translatory component with an additional undulation produced by the changing height of the hips during the gait cycle. The motions of the knees and elbows correspond to rigid pendulum motions relative to the common motion reference frame. A similar logic applies to the ankle and wrist point-lights except that these pendulum motions occur relative to the movement of the joints located at the next level within the hierarchy (i.e., the knee and wrist). Thus, for example, the ankle describes a pendular motion relative to the knee, and the knee describes a pendular motion relative to the hip; the hip describes a translatory motion relative to the ground plane.

A specific prediction from this analysis is that the recognition of the form of a person should be independent of the common translatory component. This prediction was tested by Johansson (1973), and subsequently by Cutting (1981), who presented observers with a biomechanical display that remained in the center of the viewing monitor. Both investigators reported that this display is easily recognized as a person appearing to walk on a treadmill.

Empirical Findings

Our initial research on infants' sensitivity to biomechanical motions was guided by this model. The first series of experiments was designed to test whether infants perceived the absolute motions in a biomechanical display, or alternatively, parsed the display into its respective relative and common motions. More specifically, we wanted to know whether infants were sensitive to any of the configural information specified by the relative motions in the display. Our operationalization of this question involved holding the common motions constant in Experiment 1, and the absolute motions constant in Experiment 2. If infants discriminated the displays in both experiments, we could then conclude that they were sensitive to the relative motion information in the display.

In the first experiment, 3- and 5-month-old infants were tested for discrimination of a translating point-light walker display and an inverted mirror-image of this display (see Fig. 6.4, panels A and B). The common motions in these two displays were virtually identical; thus, discrimination would imply the detection of either the individual absolute motions or the relative motions of the display. An habituation paradigm with a partial lag design (Bertenthal, Haith, & Campos, 1983) was used to test discrimination in this and all subsequent experiments. Figure 6.5 (left panel) presents the findings from this experiment showing that both 3- and 5-month-old infants discriminated the moving point-light displays. Additional groups of infants were tested with static versions of

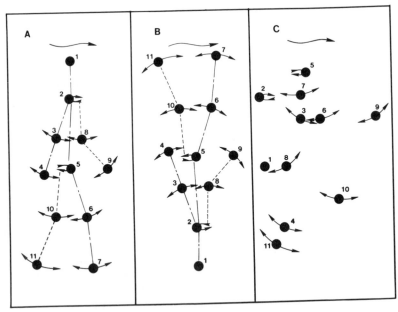

FIG. 6.4.   Depicted in panel A is an array of 11 point-lights corresponding to the head and joints of a person walking. The motion vectors drawn through each point-light represent the perceived relative motions within the figure, and that drawn above the walker depicts its perceived observer-relative displacement. Panel B depicts an inverted, mirror image version of the stimulus in A. The point-light display shown in panel C is identical to that shown in A, except that the relative locations of the point-lights are scrambled. Correspondingly numbered point-lights have the same absolute motions.

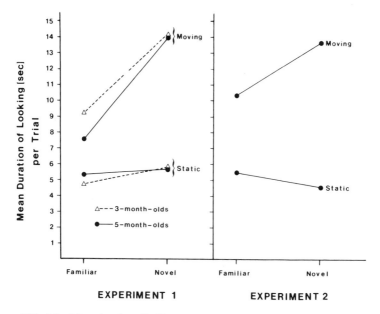

FIG. 6.5.   Mean duration of looking at the novel stimulus on the two test trials and at the familiar stimulus on the preceding two trials as a function of age and condition.

the upright and inverted display to assess whether differences in the spatial relations, per se, were responsible for the discrimination. As shown in Fig. 6.5, the evidence was negative.

The second experiment tested whether 5-month-old infants were sensitive to the relative or absolute motions in the display. Two displays were computer synthesized using the same base algorithm (Cutting, 1978b). One display corresponded to the canonical walker display used in the previous experiment (see Fig. 6.4, panel A), except that the common motion was removed. Thus, this point-light walker always remained in the center of the screen. The second (Fig. 6.4, panel C) was a scrambled version of the first, consisting of the same number of point-lights moving with exactly the same absolute motions. In contrast to the canonical version, the spatial locations of the point-lights were scrambled such that the perception of this event to an adult suggests little more than a cyclically moving swarm of bees (Cutting, 1981). Although the relative motions of these two displays were quite different, their absolute motions were identical. Thus, sensitivity to only the absolute motions in the display would prove insufficient for discrimination. The results (Fig. 6.5, right panel) revealed that infants discriminated between the moving canonical and anomalous (or scrambled) point-light displays, suggesting that they are sensitive to differences in the relative motions between the two displays. Additional groups of infants were tested for sensitivity to differences in the global distribution of the point-lights (anomalous vs. inverted anomalous displays), as well as differences presented by static cues, but neither of these possible confounding factors was detected.

The results from this initial investigation were encouraging for a number of reasons. First, infants were responsive to more than just the absolute motions in the display. They showed sensitivity to relative motion information even though these motions necessitate a decomposition of the absolute motion vectors in the display. Second, these results were consistent with the principles of perceptual vector analysis, suggesting that this processing heuristic is available prior to extensive visual experience. Finally, and most importantly, these results challenged the conventional wisdom that a straightforward quantification of the amount of motion in a stimulus display is sufficient for predicting infants' performance. Rather, the perceived organization of a display depends on the specific processing heuristics that are implemented. Thus, predictions concerning infants' perception of different displays depends on knowledge of the specific processing constraints available to the infant as well as knowledge concerning the organization of the stimulus. This complementarity between stimulus information and perceptual competencies represents a fundamental relation that continues to figure prominently in all of our research on infants' perception of biomechanical motions.

Further inquiry into what infants perceive when viewing biomechanical motions has been instructive, because new questions highlighted the limitations of perceptual vector analysis for predicting infants' performance. In particular, the results from the preceding investigation confirmed that infants were sensitive to the relative motions in the display, but perceptual vector analysis is not precise enough to either confirm or refute that the relative motions correspond to the configuration of the human form. Indeed, any perceived grouping of elements would suffice to produce the same pattern of results, including triads of point-lights corresponding to a single limb, pairs of wrist point-lights rotating around an axis, or any other configuration consistent with the morphology of the human form that does not capture its global character.

CODING THEORY

One solution to making the perceptual analysis of biomechanical motions more rigorous was proposed by Cutting (1981), who introduced an information constraint to explain the processing of biomechanical motions. Cutting recognized that the extraction of relative motions from a hierarchically organized display, such as a biomechanical display, requires a principled set of rules to organize the sequence of information extraction. If observers adhere to these rules, then their perceptual performance could be predicted using a metric adapted from Restle's (1979) coding theory.

Restle's version of coding theory is one of a general class of theories that seeks to explain perceptual performance as a set of heuristics designed to *minimize* the processing of stimulus information (Cutting & Proffitt, 1982; Hatfield & Epstein, 1985). According to this theory, the absolute motions of rotating or oscillating point-lights are specified by the following five parameters of rotary motion: amplitude, tilt, phase, orientation, and wavelength. The central tenet of this theory is that the processing of motion information is minimized when the number of shared parameters is maximized. Perceived coherence is measured by the number of parameters shared among the point-lights.

Logic of the Model

In Cutting's adaptation of coding theory, each parameter is defined as a complex motion vector corresponding to the motion of a given point-light. *Coherence* is defined as the total number of motion vectors divided by the number of uniquely specified motion vectors in the display. The sharing of motion vectors depends on how the structure is analyzed. Consider the point-light walker display depicted in Fig. 6.6, left panel. Previous findings from Cutting and Proffitt (1981) suggested that observers use a single abstract point, the *center of moment,* in the geometric space of the object as a reference point for the movements of all other points. In a biomechanical display, all motion vectors are then hierarchically organized around this common motion vector located between the shoulders and hips. The path of this common vector is defined by the translation and undulation (up and down movement attributed to changing height of the hips) of a person walking along a flat surface. All point-lights corresponding to the joints of the person share this common motion, but also include a pendular motion that makes their paths much more complex. The complexity of these paths increases with the distance of the joint from the *center of moment,* but their hierarchical relation to each other reduces the number of unique motion vectors necessary to specify their trajectories.

For example, the movement of the shoulder is composed of two motion vectors (the common motion vector and the shoulder vector), and the movement of the elbow is composed of three motion vectors (the common motion vector, the shoulder vector, and the elbow vector), but two are shared with the shoulder. As such, the perceived trajectory of the elbow requires the processing of only one new motion vector, not three. The measured coherence of these two motion vectors is obtained by dividing the total number of motion vectors (which in this example is five) by the total number of unique motion vectors (which is three) to yield a value of 1.67. This same logic is applied to all the point-lights in the display to calculate a coherence rating for the entire display.

Cutting (1981) created two pairs of point-light walker displays to evaluate the usefulness of this metric for predicting perceptual performance. One pair

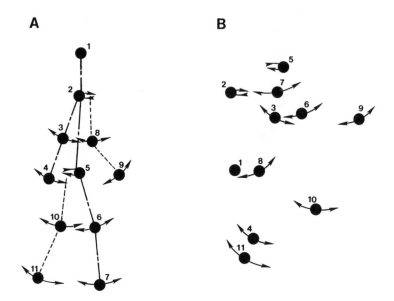

FIG. 6.6. Panel A shows the canonical display of 11 point-lights moving as if
attached to the head and major joints of a person walking. The motion vectors
drawn through each point represent the perceived motions of the display. Panel
B depicts the scrambled walker display, which is identical to the canonical display
except that the relative locations of the point-lights are scrambled. Correspondingly numbered points in the two displays undergo identical motions.

consisted of the canonical and scrambled displays (see Fig. 6.6) that were
described in the previous section. For both canonical and scrambled displays,
the coherence rating could range between 1 and 19, with 19 representing the
most coherent display (all point-lights specified completely by the common motion vector), and 1 the least coherent (each point-light a composite of a different set of motion vectors). According to Cutting's analysis, the coherence rating
for the canonical display was 2.71, whereas the coherence rating for the scrambled display was 1.46; thus, the canonical display was expected to appear more
coherent. The other pair consisted of 7 point-lights moving as if mounted on
the head, shoulder, hip, wrists, and ankles of a person walking (on-joint; Fig.
6.7) or moving as if mounted between the major joints of a person walking (off-
joint; Fig. 6.7). For these displays, the coherence rating could range between
1 and 15. The coherence rating for the on-joint display was 1.86, and the rating
for the off-joint display was 1.36; thus, the on-joint display was expected to appear more coherent.[2]

---

[2]One problem with these ratings is that they are not normalized, but are based upon the specific
number of point-lights in the display. Accordingly, these ratings provide only a relative, and not
an absolute, measure of coherence.

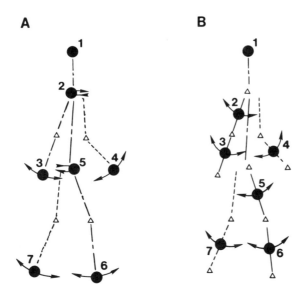

FIG. 6.7. Panel A shows the on-joint walker display of seven point-lights moving as if attached to the head, shoulder, hip, two wrists, and two ankles of a person walking. Motion vectors are drawn through each point to represent the perceived motions of the displays. The triangular elements represent the location of those major joints not depicted by a moving point-light. Panel B depicts the off-joint walker display of seven point-lights moving as if attached between the major joints of a person walking. Correspondingly numbered points in the two displays do not undergo identical motions.

The perceived coherence of the first pair was assessed by asking observers to describe what they saw when viewing these displays. Observers did not perceive the scrambled point-light display as depicting a person walking; the most common responses were an abstract machine and a swarm of bees. In contrast, almost all observers perceived a canonical point-light display as depicting a person (see also Proffitt, Bertenthal, & Roberts, 1986). The perceived coherence of the second pair was assessed using a different procedure, because observers recognized both displays as depicting a person walking. For this pair, observers were asked to identify whether the display depicted a male or female walker. Previous research by Cutting (1978a) showed that variations in the *center of moment* were systematically related to whether the biomechanical display emulated the gait of a male or female. In the current study, observers were significantly better at identifying the gender of the on-joint than the off-joint point-light walker display. Cutting interpreted these results as preliminary support for the logic of the proposed information extraction process captured by the coherence ratings.

ED: 1 LINE SHORT

Empirical Findings

The quantification of figural coherence in point-light walker displays by Cutting (1981) enabled us to assess whether infants were perceptually organizing bio-mechanical motions in a manner similar to adults. In general, more coherent displays are encoded faster, remembered better, and described more simply than are less coherent displays (Garner, 1981). This generalization applies to infants as well as adults (Werner & Perlmutter, 1979). If infants extract the information in a biomechanical display according to the model proposed by Cutting, then they should encode the displays with the higher coherence ratings more rapidly than those with the lower coherence ratings. This prediction was put to the test in two experiments by Bertenthal, Proffitt, Kramer, and Spetner (1987).

In the first experiment, 3-month-old infants were shown either the canonical or scrambled point-light walker display during the familiarization phase of an habit-uation procedure; they were shown the other display for two trials following a criterion determined by an infant control procedure (Bertenthal et al., 1983). In this procedure, the criterion is defined as the total looking time on three con-secutive familiarization trials that sums to no more than 50% of the total looking time on the first three familiarization trials. One group of infants was shown displays that included a common translatory component of motion (translating walker), and the other group was shown displays without this translatory com-ponent; these displays showed a point-light walker moving as if on a treadmill

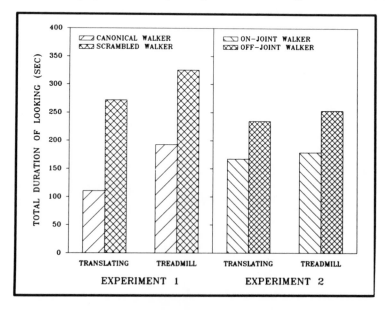

FIG. 6.8.   Results from two experiments showing total duration of looking (in seconds) on habituation trials as a function of stimulus coherence and form of move-ment (treadmill vs. translating).

(treadmill walker). It was predicted that the less coherent display, the scrambled point-light walker, would require more looking time before criterion was reached. The results clearly supported this prediction. Infants looked significantly longer at the scrambled than at the canonical point-light walker, regardless of whether the displays included a translatory component (Fig. 6.8). These two displays were also discriminated, suggesting that infants not only encoded the displays at different rates, but that they organized them differently once they were encoded.

In the second experiment, another group of 3-month-old infants were shown both the on-joint and off-joint displays using the same habituation paradigm. These displays were also presented as either translating or not. Although the pattern of looking was in the predicted direction (see Fig. 6.8), infants in this experiment did not show differences in total duration of looking during the habituation phase; they did, however, show differences in the form of the habituation function. Infants viewing the on-joint displays showed a monotonically decreasing habituation function, whereas infants viewing the off-joint displays showed a much more variable rate of habituation (see Table 6.1). This variability was operationalized as two or more trials on which looking times increased 20% or more relative to the preceding trial. Interestingly, these two displays were not discriminated, suggesting that the process of encoding was different, but that the perceived organization following encoding was not.

TABLE 6.1
Number of Infants Showing Continuously Decreasing Versus
Fluctuating Habituation Curves

	Habituation Curves	
Stimulus Conditions (n = 6)	Continuously Decreasing	Fluctuating
Experiment 1		
Translating		
Canonical	5	1
Scrambled	2	4
Treadmill		
Canonical	4	2
Scrambled	2	4
Experiment 2		
Translating		
On-joint	5	1
Off-joint	2	4
Treadmill		
On-joint	6	0
Off-joint	1	5

This latter finding is one of the most intriguing results of the entire study. It suggests that infants took more time to organize the global relations in the off-joint than in the on-joint display, but once organized, the percept was similar. If infants were responding simply to pairwise relations, such as the two point-lights on the arm, then the task of extracting the relevant information would have been identical up to a scaling factor in the two displays. In particular, the two point-lights on the arm depict the same piston-like rotation in both displays. It is unlikely that the size of the apparent piston would be sufficient to require additional encoding time. As an alternative to the extraction of local relations, it is possible that a global form corresponding to a stick figure of a person walking was extracted in both displays. Clearly, adult observers extract this form in both displays because they describe both as a person walking (Cutting, 1981). From the standpoint of information extraction, the off-joint display should require more encoding time because fewer joints are specified. Webb and Aggarwal (1982) suggested that an additional interpolation step is required to locate the unmarked joints. This additional step in the computational process could explain the encoding differences shown by infants to the two displays, assuming that they were encoding more than local relations.

In sum, the results from this series of experiments provided additional support for our earlier conclusion that infants extract information specified by the relative motions and not the absolute motions of the display. Recall that the absolute motions in the canonical versus scrambled pair are identical, and are also very similar in the on-joint/off-joint pair. More importantly, the results from this research were predicted by a formal model of information extraction based on a minimization principle. Although the results do not provide definitive support for the implementation of this processing heuristic by infants, this possibility has considerable face validity and is consistent with many other theories proposing that the visual system is intrinsically organized to appreciate figural coherence (Bertenthal, Proffitt, Kramer, et al., 1987).

LOCAL RIGIDITY

In the preceding section, the evidence for perceiving a specific form depicted by a point-light display was somewhat indirect. The model proposed by Cutting (1981) made explicit predictions about the sequence of information extraction, but ignored the problem of how the visual system assigns connections between point-lights. Logically, this step precedes the extraction process, and is by no means trivial. The geometry of the point-light configuration suggests that there are a large number of possible connectivity patterns consistent with a point-light display of a person walking. A number of possible constraints for detecting the appropriate connectivity pattern have been proposed and found wanting. For example, one model (Rashid, 1980) uses a closest neighbor algorithm for specifying the appropriate connections, but some of these point-lights are not always the closest neighbors. For example, the two wrist and the two ankle lights are closer to each other during portions of the gait cycle than they are to their corresponding elbow and knee lights.

Logic of the Model

A more successful constraint for extracting the appropriate connectivity pattern in a point-light display is based upon the property of local rigidity. Hoffman and Flinchbaugh (1982) observed that the appropriate connectivity pattern for specifying the form of a person in a point-light display is provided by a specific anatomical constraint. As is the case for all animals with a skeleton, each joint is connected to an adjacent joint by a bone that corresponds to a rigid rod of fixed length. Accordingly, as one joint, such as the wrist, rotates in a pendular fashion around another joint (the elbow in this case), the distance between the joints remains constant. This distance invariance is true for all appropriate connections, and is violated for all other possible connections. For example, the distance between the wrist joint and the knee joint changes continuously.

Hoffman and Flinchbaugh devised a computational algorithm, dubbed the *planarity assumption,* to exploit this constraint for perceiving biomechanical motions. A more general version of this algorithm is the fixed-axis assumption proposed by Webb and Aggarwal (1982). In essence, both algorithms are designed to test for local rigidity (or invariant distances between points in 3-D space) from the 2-D projection of pairs of points rotating or translating in depth. The model operates by testing the local relations between all pairs of points in an iterative fashion. All pairs that are projectively equivalent to a rigid translation or rotation around a fixed axis in depth are interpreted as connected, whereas all other pairs are interpreted as unconnected. After all possible pairs of points are tested, the model proceeds to connect pairs with one point in common. Consider an example from a point-light walker display. In examining all possible pairings of point-lights, the algorithm assigns a connectivity status to those joints showing pairwise rigidity. For example, the knee is connected to the ankle as well as to the hip, the shoulder is connected to the elbow, the elbow is connected to the wrist, and so forth.

Computational experiments in which one or the other of these algorithms were used revealed that local rigidity is a successful constraint for recovering the appropriate connectivity pattern of the human form, as long as the moving point-lights conform to a fixed-axis of rotation for short periods of time. The only displays for which the algorithm was not successful were those in which the human form was twirling, as occurs during figure skating or swinging a baseball bat. Psychophysical studies also show that judgments of rigidity and connectivity among moving point-lights are more frequent when the point-lights rotate around a fixed-axis as opposed to a rotating axis (Green, 1961; Proffitt & Bertenthal, 1988). The latter transformation corresponds to a tumbling motion.

Empirical Findings

A few years ago, we conducted an experiment that was designed to test whether infants are sensitive to locally rigid relations in the perception of biomechanical displays (Bertenthal, Proffitt, & Kramer, 1987). Because these relations are present only for appropriately connected point-lights, positive evidence for this sensitivity by infants would provide more definitive evidence of their perceiving a structure consistent with a "stick-figure" representation of the human form. Three different stimulus displays were created. The first corresponded to a lo-cally rigid point-light walker display in which the distal path of motion was nor-mal to the line of sight. In this case, the analysis of local rigidity is especially easy, because the fixed distances between the joints project onto the image plane as constant distances between the point-lights. A "foil" was created by perturbing the fixed distances between the joints (see Fig. 6.9). Adult observ-ers viewing this display report that the connections between the joints appear elastic.

One problem with this foil is that the temporal phase relations between pairs of lights were also perturbed. In other words, the triad of point-lights correspond-ing to each limb no longer moved in the same direction at all times during the

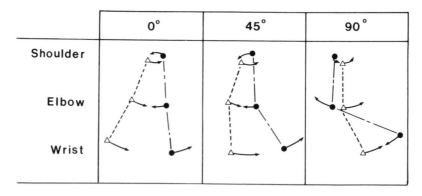

Δ: **Rigid**

●: **Nonrigid**

FIG. 6.9.   Algorithm used for perturbing local rigidity between joints is illustrat-ed using the relative positions of the shoulder, elbow, and wrist lights at 0°, 45°, and 90° of the gait cycle. The filled circles represent the visible point-lights in a nonrigid display. The open triangles represent the positions of the point-lights in a locally rigid display. Note that for the nonrigid display, the distances between point-lights are different in each frame.

gait cycle. Conversely, these triads of lights are directionally coupled through-out the gait cycle of the canonical display. In order to control for this additional variable, we created a second display with a different set of perturbed phase relations. An algorithm was used to ensure that the total phase difference be-tween the two perturbed displays was the same as the total difference between each of these displays and the canonical display.

The availability of two different perturbed displays allowed us to assess sensi-tivity to differences in phase relations independent of variations in local rigidity. Procedurally, discrimination of the three stimuli was tested using an habituation paradigm in which one of the two perturbed displays was presented as the familiar stimulus, and then the locally rigid display and the other foil were presented alter-nately for two trials each (in counterbalanced order) after criterion was reached.

Both 3- and 5-month-old infants were tested. The results from this experi-ment are shown in Fig. 6.10. Five-month-old infants discriminated the locally rigid display from the familiar nonrigid display, but did not discriminate the two nonrigid displays. This finding appeared to provide evidence that these infants were sensitive to a local rigidity constraint in their perception of biomechanical motions. In contrast, 3-month-old infants discriminated not only the locally rigid

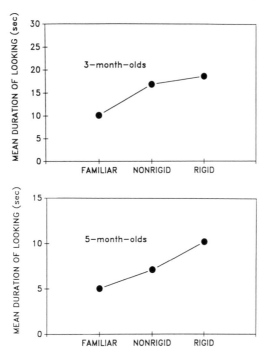

FIG. 6.10. Mean duration of looking at the two novel stimuli (rigid and nonrigid) on the four test trials and at the familiar stimulus on the preceding two trials as a function of age.

from the familiar nonrigid display, but also discriminated the two nonrigid displays that varied with regard to the temporal phase relations of the point-lights. This latter finding was not predicted by any of the current models for explaining the perception of structure from motion, and thus gave us reason to reevaluate the contribution of temporal phase relations to the perception of structure from motion, and biomechanical motions, in particular.

This unexpected result prompted us to test independently infants' sensitivity to local rigidity and to temporal phase relations. Two experiments were conducted. The first experiment tested 3- and 5-month-old infants' discrimination of a canonical and phase-shifted display; the point-lights in the latter display were temporally phase-shifted, but their projective distances remained invariant (see Fig. 6.11 for an illustration of this perturbation). Results from this experiment revealed that infants at both ages were sensitive to the perturbation in the phase relations (see Fig. 6.12). The second experiment tested 3- and 5-month-old in-

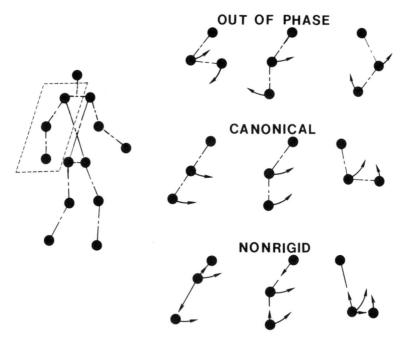

FIG. 6.11.   The left side depicts 13 point-lights moving as if attached to the major joints and head of a person walking on a treadmill. The three right panels depict the relations of the right shoulder, elbow, and wrist lights, enclosed by the dashed lines in the left hand panel, during three successive stages of the gait cycle. Upper panel (out-of-phase): The point-lights remain at fixed distances, but differ as to when they reverse direction. Middle panel (canonical): The point-lights remain at fixed distances and all reverse direction simultaneously. Lower panel (nonrigid): The point-lights do not remain at fixed distances relative to each other, but do change direction simultaneously.

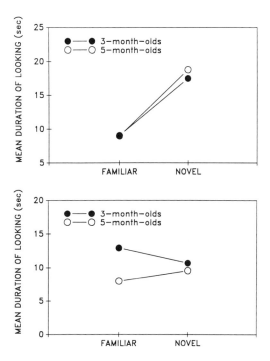

FIG. 6.12. Mean duration of looking at the novel stimuli on the two test trials and at the familiar stimulus on the preceding two trials as a function of age. Top panel shows results from comparison of canonical and phase-shifted displays; bottom panel shows results from comparison of canonical and nonrigid displays.

fants' discrimination of a canonical and logically nonrigid point-light display; the point-light distances of this latter display were continuously changing according to a stochastic process while the phase relations remained consistent with those of the canonical display (Fig. 6.11). Results from this experiment revealed no evidence of discrimination at either age (Fig. 6.12).

Collectively, the results from these last two studies cast the earlier findings investigating the usefulness of the fixed-axis assumption in a somewhat different light. Contrary to our initial expectation, infants appeared sensitive to the temporal phase differences that exist between a canonical and phase-shifted point-light walker display. One interpretation for this result is that the temporal phase relations associated with the canonical display provide a more coherent structure than do the phase relations associated with the perturbed displays. Indeed, this possibility is consistent with a simple demonstration experiment (Bertenthal & Davis, 1988) conducted with 286 adult observers. These observers were shown a canonical point-light display for 10 sec; 98% of the observers recognized the display as depicting a person walking. Prior to this display, these same observers were shown a phase-shifted display for 10 sec, and only 62% of the observers recognized this display as depicting a person. Apparently, the temporal phase relations of the canonical display are useful for perceiving the point-light display as a person walking.

The second finding suggesting that infants are not sensitive to perturbations in local rigidity is somewhat more difficult to interpret. One possibility is simply that infants are not sensitive to this property, but a second possibility is that infants actually exploit this property whenever possible using a more broadly tuned filter than tested. For example, local rigidity might be defined as some statistical distribution, with only the mean corresponding to the precise distance measured between the point-lights. If this latter hypothesis is correct, then infants could have perceived the canonical and perturbed displays as equivalent because the stretchings of the limbs in the perturbed display were not large enough to go beyond the range of a broadly tuned local rigidity analyzer. Interestingly, this interpretation is consistent with additional data collected in the adult demonstration experiment just described. When these observers were shown a point-light walker display violating local rigidity, almost all (95%) reported that the display depicted a person walking, even though this display was also shown prior to the canonical display. Many of these observers reported that the depicted figure appeared to "swagger," which is actually the best approximate description of this display when perceived as locally rigid in 3-D space. In sum, the current (albeit limited) evidence suggests that local rigidity is such a pervasive constraint that the visual system will tolerate significant distortions of the perceived form, such as the depiction of a very large swagger, rather than ignore locally rigid relations that are organized in depth. Although this conclusion is certainly true for adult observers, the status of a local rigidity constraint operating during infancy remains somewhat more questionable.

TEMPORAL PHASE RELATIONS

Our findings on the importance of temporal phase relations for perceiving the structure of the human form were anticipated in a brief reference to the importance of phase by Cutting (1981), but the logic for this prediction was never elaborated. Aside from this one reference to phase relations, the field has virtually ignored the relevance of temporal patterning to the perception of biomechanical motions. Nevertheless, some of the research discussed in the preceding section raises the intriguing possibility that temporal phase relations constitute another constraint in the perception of point-light walker displays.

Logic of the Model

The precedent for this proposal dates back to the Gestalt notion of common fate. According to Wertheimer (1938), elements moving together are seen as corresponding to a single unitary form. More recently, Ramachandran and his colleagues (Ramachandran & Anstis, 1986; Ramachandran, Inada, & Kiama, 1986) showed the operation of global field effects over time using ambiguous apparent motion displays. Although such displays need not be perceived in a coherent fashion, they are almost always perceived as a uniform field of motion. For example, Ramachandran et al. (1986) presented observers with a display that consisted of a number of spatially separated pairs of dots that blinked in alternation. One additional dot was paired with an occluder (a gray patch on the screen), and was programmed to simply blink on and off. This latter dot was ambiguous because it could be perceived as merely blinking without moving, or it could be seen as moving behind the occluder. In almost every case, however, this unpaired blinking is entrained by the apparent motion of its neighbors, and observers report that the dot appears to pass behind the occluder.

For the purpose of the present discussion, it is important to note that the entrainment of the unpaired dot depends on its temporal phase relation to the other pairs of dots (Gilden, Bertenthal, & Othman, 1991). As the temporal modulation of the unpaired dot is phase-shifted relative to the other paired dots, observers report a decline in the perception of illusory occlusion. These results suggest that temporal synchrony is used by the visual system for the perceptual grouping of elements. In more complex groupings, the specific configuration of the figure is specified by the simultaneous organization of the discrete motion paths (Gilden et al., 1991). This latter proposal is similar to Johannson's concept of relative motions, but is not restricted to an organization derived exclusively by vector analysis; instead other principles, such as symmetry and similarity, are acknowledged as operating in the pattern formation process.

In essence, the preceding discussion suggests that the perceived structure of a moving stimulus display is the product of an emergent process mediated by the temporal organization of the display. This view of the pattern formation process is formally very similar to the abstract patterns that correspond to the organization of human movements (Bertenthal & Pinto, in press; Kelso & Pandya, 1991). Stable and repetitive human movements, such as gait, are temporally organized relative to their cycles of activity. As such, the change in a specific parameter, such as frequency, does not affect the topography of the movement. This pattern invariance across different frequencies is analogous to the pattern invariance shown by the visual system when it is presented with projections of the same object that vary in size, distance, or orientation.

The temporal organization of human movement is best understood using a phase plane diagram (see Fig. 6.13). These diagrams are unfamiliar to most readers, so a brief digression describing this graphical tool will be useful. Human movements are most accurately modeled by nonlinear differential equations of motion. The solution to these equations corresponds to a periodic set of values, which can be represented as a specific orbit within the phase plane diagram. The phase plane is the space of all possible states of the system, in which the first derivative or the velocity of movement ($\dot{x}$) is plotted against its

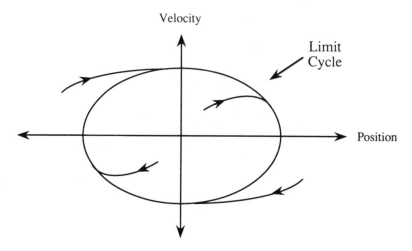

FIG. 6.13.   Examples of phase plane trajectories converging on a limit cycle or
stable orbit.

position (x). As time varies, the point P(x, ẋ) describing the motion of the system converges toward a certain trajectory (i.e., limit cycle) on the phase plane.
This trajectory is periodic because the velocity and position of the moving point
return repeatedly to the same values. *The shape of the phase plane trajectory
is an abstract representation of the underlying dynamic organization* (Abraham
& Shaw, 1982). These trajectories, when produced by a well-organized and highly
stable process, such as a human movement, exhibit a tendency to maintain a
fixed orbital shape (or limit cycle) across a range of perturbations. During brief
transition periods produced by perturbations to the movement, the shape of
the trajectory will vary, but it will quickly return to its more stable form. The
changing shape of the trajectory corresponds to a different organization of the
movement, which is perceptually distinct from its more stable organization.

Phase plane diagrams illustrate how the perturbation of temporal organization disrupts the perceived pattern invariance of a movement. In a canonical
point-light walker display, the joint motions correspond to those observed during a stable period of gait, whereas the joint motions in a phase-shifted display
correspond to those observed during an unstable period of gait, where movements conform to a different temporal organization. A comparison of the phase
plane trajectories for corresponding joints in the canonical and phase-shifted displays reveals that their orbital shapes are consistently different. Figure 6.14
shows this graphical analysis for the trajectories corresponding to the right knee.
These differences in the trajectories of individual joints are predictive of the
perceived identification by adults and discrimination by infants of the two point-
light displays. Interestingly, the phase plane trajectories for a locally nonrigid
point-light walker display are identical to those generated for the canonical point-

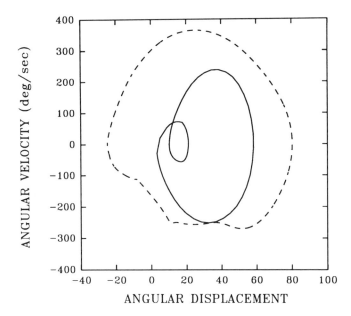

FIG. 6.14. Phase plane diagram for right knee. Solid line trajectory was produced from the joint motions of a canonical display; dashed line trajectory was produced from the joint motions of a phase-shifted display.

light walker display, because perturbing local rigidity does not affect the dynamical organization (temporal patterning) of the display. This result is consistent with the performance shown by infants and adults to this perturbation. Recall that this perturbation did not affect the identification of a point-light display by adults, nor produce discrimination by infants. Thus, perceptual performance is predicted by the phase plane trajectories corresponding to the two displays.

These comparisons of phase plane trajectories in canonical and perturbed displays of biomechanical motions led my colleagues and me (Bertenthal & Davis, 1988; Bertenthal & Pinto, in press) to conjecture that the temporally ordered information represented by a phase plane trajectory is the same abstract pattern information that perceivers use to identify, discriminate, and classify such patterns (also see Kelso & Pandya, 1991, for a related position). If this conjecture is correct, then some of the constraints necessary for perceiving and recognizing the temporal patterns observed in biomechanical motions, may be carried in the low-dimensional dynamical laws that also govern the generation of the pattern.

Empirical Findings

Although the proposal for a complementarity between production and perception constraints is somewhat speculative, the evidence for the implementation of temporal constraints for perceiving biomechanical motions is quite convincing. In addition to those studies already described in the previous section. I briefly review here two additional experiments that point to the role of temporal constraints in organizing point-light displays.

The first is a recent investigation by Cutting, Moore, and Morrison (1988), in which they investigated the perception of biomechanical motions under conditions of simultaneous masking by additional moving point-lights. Adult observers were shown a canonical point-light walker display consisting of 11 point-lights that was masked by the superposition of 22 to 55 additional moving point-lights (see Fig. 6.15). The positions of the masking elements were generated randomly, and their movements varied as a function of condition. In general, the conditions involved masking elements moving in linear, circular, or pendular paths. The pendular paths were generated by scrambling the spatial locations of the absolute motions of the point-lights in the canonical display. Observers were requested to judge the apparent direction of the gait. The most relevant results of this investigation are quite easy to summarize: Stimuli that were masked by elements that did not share the absolute motions of the point-lights in the canonical display were generally easier to judge than stimuli masked by the absolute motions of the walker. The differences are quite striking in that the canonical point-light walker display is perceptually distinct from the masking elements that do not share the same absolute motions. In contrast, the canonical display is more difficult to segregate from masking elements sharing the same absolute motions. The finding that the absolute motions are more effective distractors than the motions in any of the other masking conditions suggests that spatial factors, such as density or proximity, are not sufficient for explaining the results. Rather, it is the *shared* temporal patterning of the elements

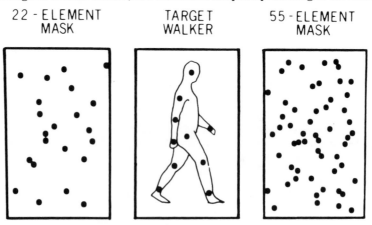

22 - ELEMENT MASK   TARGET WALKER   55 - ELEMENT MASK

FIG. 6.15. Middle panel depicts the organization of the 11 point-lights corresponding to the point-light walker. Left and right panels depict relative locations of masking elements in 22- and 55-element masks, respectively. From Cutting, Moore, and Morrison (1988).

A **B**

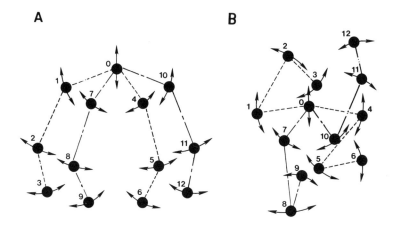

FIG. 6.16. Panel A shows a point-light display designed to resemble a four-legged spider. The 12 point-lights are positioned as if they are located on the body and major joints of this spider. The motion vectors drawn through the point-lights correspond to their relative motions. Panel B shows the same point-light display, except that the orientation of the individual limb segments were perturbed. Correspondingly numbered point-light pairs in the two displays undergo the same relative motions.

that is most effective in disrupting performance. Specifically, it appears that the sinusoidal velocity patterns of the elements determine the effectiveness of the mask. This result thus suggests that the temporal patterning of the point-light motions contributes to the perceptual organization of the display.

A converging line of evidence derives from an unpublished study conducted in our lab (Bertenthal, Proffitt, & Kramer, 1986). This experiment was originally designed to test infants' discrimination of an unfamiliar point-light display and its foil (see Fig. 6.16). In essence, the unfamiliar display resembled a four-legged spider. It is important to emphasize, however, that although the configuration of the display was unfamiliar, it shared many of the structural and kinematic properties of the point-light walker display. This display corresponded to a nested hierarchy of pendular motions moving in dynamic symmetry relative to a common center of motion, pair-wise connections were locally rigid, and the display contained bilateral symmetry. The foil was created by shifting the orientation of the individual joints, such that the configuration of the display was significantly altered. In fact, adult observers in another study judged the point-light spider and its foil as configurally more dissimilar than any other pair of point-light displays that were shown except for a pair involving a canonical versus a scrambled display (see Table 6.2). Also note that a canonical point-light display and a phase-shifted version, which were reported previously as discriminable, are rated as much more similar than are the two point-light spider displays. Nevertheless, 3- and 5-month-old infants showed no evidence of discriminating the two point-light spider displays (Fig. 6.17).

TABLE 6.2
Ratings of Perceived Similarity Between Point-Light Displays

Stimulus Pair	Block 1	Block 2	M
Canonical versus Scrambled Walker	4.8	5.9	5.3
Spider versus Scrambled Spider	4.1	4.4	4.3
Canonical versus Out-of-Phase Walker	2.5	3.3	2.9
Rigid versus Nonrigid Walker	2.3	3.0	2.7
Nonrigid-1 versus Nonrigid-2 Walker	2.0	2.4	2.2

Note: 1 = most similar; 7 = most different

Initially, this finding was quite perplexing because infants were apparently not responding to the rather dramatic configural differences between the two point-light displays. It was only after recognizing that temporal phase plays such a significant role in the perception of biomechanical displays that I was able to reconcile this finding with others from our lab. In contrast to the canonical and phase-shifted point-light walker displays, the point-light spider display and its perturbed version share the same temporal patterning. Specifically, all point-lights are phase-locked to simultaneously change direction every 0° and 180° of the gait cycle. We recently completed an experiment testing 3- and 5-month-old infants to investigate whether or not they are sensitive to phase-shifting in the point-light spider display. Preliminary findings suggest that 3- but not 5-month-olds discriminate these two displays. Although this finding does not appear entirely consistent with our prediction that infants are sensitive to the

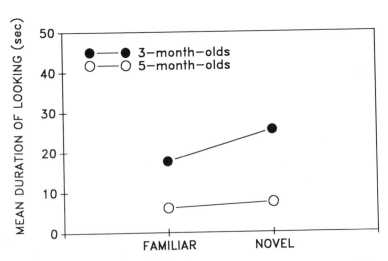

FIG. 6.17. Mean duration of looking at the novel stimulus (canonical or perturbed point-light spider displays) on the two test trials and at the familiar stimulus on the preceding two trials as a function of age.

temporal phase coherence in a biomechanical display, related evidence suggests that the familiarity of a biomechanical display interacts with the perceptual performance of 5-month-olds, but not with the performance of 3-month-olds (see the next section for more details).

In sum, the temporal patterning in a biomechanical display appears essential for perceiving a coherent organization. This organizational constraint is so embedded within the dynamic symmetry of a point-light walker display that it was ignored by most investigators interested in this phenomenon. Recent findings from our lab suggest that the perceived organization of a biomechanical display is significantly affected by phase-shifting the point-lights. Adult observers are less likely to perceive this perturbed display as depicting a person walking, and infants perceive this display as discriminable from a canonical point-light walker. From a teleological perspective, it is intriguing to speculate that temporal phase coherence constitutes a fundamental perceptual constraint because of its complementary status in constraining the organization of human movements.

KNOWLEDGE-BASED CONSTRAINTS

Knowledge plays an important role in the perception of biomechanical motions by adult observers (Cutting et al., 1988). Two findings are relevant to this conclusion. First, the entire point-light walker display is unnecessary for perceiving the gender of the walker if it is already known that the point-lights correspond to a person walking (Kozlowski & Cutting, 1977). Recall that the gender of the walker is specified by the relative location of the *center of moment*. Because the judgment of gender does not necessarily require the perceptual availability of this invariant information (if the depicted form of the point-light display is already known), it appears that retrieved information does contribute to constraining the interpretation of a point-light display. Second, point-light walker displays are not frequently recognized as depicting a person walking when presented upside-down (Sumi, 1984). In fact, the inverted display is often perceived as depicting the movement of multiple objects, whereas, the upright display is almost always perceived as depicting a unitary object. Apparently, information about human gait is stored with respect to the normal upright, and thus, an inverted display does not often make contact with this information. This finding provides convergent support for the conclusion that retrieved information about human gait constrains the interpretation of the point-light display further.

Logic of the Model

Operationally, little is known about how stored knowledge could constrain the possible interpretations of a point-light display. Moreover, the literature offers few suggestions as to the form of the specific information that is stored about biomechanical motions. Possibilities range from a stored image of the form of a person to a list of features (e.g., joint angles, step size, etc.) that correspond to the movements of a person walking to more abstract semantic knowledge about the gaits of people. Marr and Nishihara (1978) suggested that biological objects are represented as generalized cylinders that are hierarchically ordered within an object-centered frame of reference. Although portions of this model are quite parsimonious with the available data on the perception of biomechanical motions, the model loses some of its credibility by predicting that recognition of an object is independent of its orientation.

Given our current understanding of visual perception and stored knowledge, we must be content with a much more modest explication of how this constraint operates than was true for those previously described. In fact, I restrict my comments to a discussion of a few general distinctions that are important when discussing the contribution of stored knowledge to the perceptual process. The first is a distinction between recognition and identification (cf. G. Mandler, 1980). It is quite possible to recognize an object as familiar, but still not be able to place it within any specific context. For example, it is not at all uncommon to recognize the face of a person as familiar, but not remember anything else about that person. Conversely, the identification of an object necessarily assumes recognition, and moreover, it assumes that the object can be related to other stored information. As a network of relevant knowledge is acquired, infants begin to identify the perceived objects as associated with more general categories of knowledge. Accordingly, the identification of a point-light walker display as depicting a general category, such as animate objects, or biological motions, or even human gait, provides infants with the opportunity to discriminate these displays at a more conceptual level of processing than would be necessary for the discrimination of purely configural differences between two displays.

The other relevant distinction is between discrimination and recognition. This topic was recently discussed at length (Proffitt & Bertenthal, 1990) so I keep my comments here brief. Proffitt and Bertenthal suggested that it is especially difficult to interpret a failure to discriminate between two point-light displays because negative results could be attributable to a lack of interest between two unfamiliar displays rather than to a failure to detect a difference between them. Indeed, some of the recent findings from our lab suggest that 5-month-olds are less likely than 3-month-olds to discriminate simple configural differences between displays because the new displays are not sufficiently novel or interesting to recruit additional attention. We conjecture that the older infants are responding to the displays in terms of whether or not the stimuli are recognized or associated with different networks of stored knowledge. When neither display accesses some form of stored knowledge, attention to the novel display remains low, and the two displays are not discriminated.

The flip side to the preceding generalization is that when the displays are discriminated, neither is necessarily recognized. For example, it is possible for adults to discriminate among a large number of faces without recognizing any of them. Likewise, infants may discriminate different stimuli (e.g., point-light walker displays) without recognizing any of them as familiar. Stated simply, recognition implies discrimination, but discrimination does not always imply recognition. This principle provides a framework for interpreting much of the empirical data I now present.

Empirical Findings

The principal evidence for the operation of knowledge-based constraints is a series of experiments that are all convergent with a developmental shift (between 3 and 5 months of age) in the perception of biomechanical motions. The first experiment (Bertenthal & Davis, 1988) is analogous to the one testing infants' sensitivity to canonical versus phase-shifted displays, except that the two point-light displays were inverted. Recall that both 3- and 5-month-old infants showed significant discrimination of these two displays when they were presented in the canonical upright orientation. When these displays were inverted, 3-month-olds continued to discriminate them, but 5-month-olds showed no evidence of discrimination (see Fig. 6.18). In order to ensure that the inconsistent performance of the 5-month-olds reflected a reliable shift rather than a change in performance specific to only this age, we conducted an additional experiment with 7-month-old infants. In this experiment, the canonical and phase-perturbed displays were both presented in either an upright or inverted orientation. Consis-

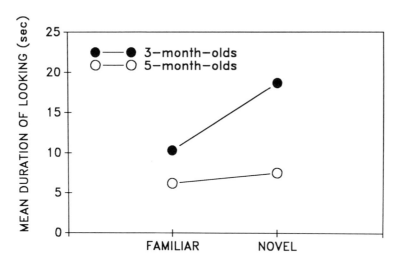

FIG. 6.18. Mean duration of looking at the novel stimulus (inverted canonical or inverted phase-shifted point-light displays) on the two test trials and at the familiar stimulus on the preceding two trials as a function of age.

tent with the performance of the 5-month-olds, the 7-month-olds showed discrimination of the upright but not of the inverted displays (see Fig. 6.19). Our interpretation for the failure of the 5- and 7-month-olds to discriminate the inverted displays is that by 5 months of age infants are responding to the perceived familiarity of the displays, and the inverted displays are not perceived as related to any stored knowledge about the human form. Thus, the two inverted displays are perceived equivalently because they are both unfamiliar.

Convergent evidence for this interpretation appears in a study by Fox and McDaniels (1982). In one of their experiments, infants' sensitivity to the movements of a pair of hands was investigated. A canonical point-light display of the two hands was contrasted with a perturbed version. The results revealed that 6-month-olds, but neither 2- nor 4-month-olds, discriminated these two displays. Interestingly, infants do not generally engage in visually guided reaching until around 5 months of age (Gesell, 1928). Thus, we conjecture that hand movements remain relatively unfamiliar until approximately 5 months of age, at which time the two point-light displays can be discriminated on the basis of familiarity. It should be noted that complete convergence between these latter findings and the previously proposed interpretation for a developmental shift in the perception of biomechanical motions also predicts that the younger infants should have discriminated these displays on the basis of more local configural differences. The finding that these displays were not discriminated is somewhat perplexing, but perhaps the phase relations were fairly constant in the two displays. Recall that infants did not detect the difference between the two point-light spider displays because the phase relations in these two displays were equivalent.

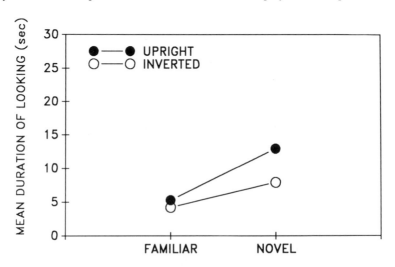

FIG. 6.19.   Mean duration of looking at the novel stimulus (canonical or phase-shifted point-light displays) on the two test trials and at the familiar stimulus on the preceding two trials as a function of orientation for 7-month-old infants.

Admittedly, the preceding conclusion that 5-month-old infants perceive the canonical point-light walker display as familiar is somewhat tentative; yet, it would receive further support if we could specify more precisely how stored knowledge affects the perceptual process. The literature suggests that infants are beginning to organize their knowledge into concepts by the second half of the first year (J. M. Mandler, 1990). In the case of especially familiar objects, such as those depicted in biomechanical displays, it is not unreasonable to predict that, by 5 months of age, these displays could be perceived as belonging to a general category, and that other displays not sharing the defining properties of this category would be discriminated.

In an effort to offer a preliminary test of this hypothesis, a study of perceptual categorization using point-light walker displays was conducted (Pinto & Davis, 1991). Three- and 5-month-old infants were shown three exemplars of a point-light display of a person walking. These exemplars were created by filming a person wearing LEDs on the major joints of the body while producing the following three sequences of movements: (a) walking back and forth along a circular path; (b) marching back and forth along a circular path; (c) walking back and forth along a circular path while waving her arms above her head. Each of these sequences was shown on successive trials, and repeated four times for a total of 12 trials. Following these familiarization trials, a computer-synthesized point-light walker display was presented in upright and inverted orientations alternately for 4 trials. The goal of this study was to show that infants were extracting some property that was not specific to any individual stimulus display, but was rather a more general property of human gait. If infants extract some property common to the global form of the three familiarization displays, then they should show generalization to the upright test display (which presumably shares this property) and discrimination of the inverted display (which does not share this property). Operationally, this prediction would be confirmed if infants showed significantly greater looking at the inverted than at the upright displays.

The results of this experiment are shown in Fig. 6.20. As predicted, 5-month-olds showed greater looking to the inverted than to the upright displays, whereas 3-month-olds did not.[3] This finding thus suggests that the older infants were extracting some general property of the display that was orientation-specific.

---

[3]Interestingly, neither age group looked, on average, significantly longer at either of the two test displays than at the last block of familiarization displays. Although this result is usually considered a necessary criterion for concluding discrimination in a standard habituation paradigm, it is confounded by additional factors in the current paradigm. In particular, the familiarization displays depicted somewhat unusual forms of gait and were created by filming lights attached to a person in the dark. The test displays, on the other hand, were computer synthesized and depicted a much simpler event of a person walking in place. Adult observers judged the familiarization displays as much more interesting than the two novel displays. Accordingly, it is not surprising that looking times to the test displays were depressed relative to the familiarization displays. Nevertheless, the relative amount of looking to the two test displays was different, and it is that difference that I find theoretically significant.

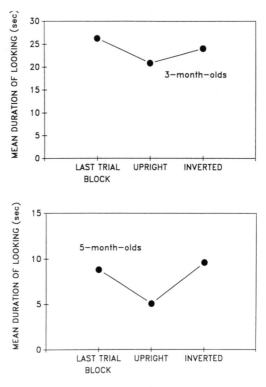

FIG. 6.20.   Mean duration of looking at the last block of familiarization displays
and at the two novel displays (upright and inverted point-light walkers) on the
four test trials as a function of age.

Given the design of the experiment, there are but two candidates that could
correspond to the general property extracted by the infants.

The first involves the orientation of the pendular motions. With few excep-
tions, the pendulum-like motions of point-light pairs were all oriented in the same
direction in the three familiarization displays as well as in the upright test display. The one stimulus not sharing this property was the inverted test display
where the pendulum motions are all rotated 180° relative to the upright display. Although the orientation of the pendulum in these displays is thus correlated with performance of the 5-month-old infants, it is nevertheless not
sufficient to explain all the results. In another experiment involving the point-
light spider displays, we tested 5-month-olds' discrimination of an upright versus an inverted display. These two displays, thus, differed from each other according to the same property (orientation of the pair-wise pendular motions)
that we are now considering. Nevertheless, there was no evidence of discrimination. Interestingly, we have previously shown (Bertenthal, Proffitt, & Cutting, 1984) that these same-age infants do discriminate the orientation of a

point-light walker display. Apparently, the familiarity of the display is a necessary component in eliciting discrimination by 5 months of age.

The second possibility relates more directly to the familiarity of the display.
As argued previously, the inverted display does not make contact with any stored
knowledge about human gait, and thus, this display is perceived as different from
those retrieving information about human gait. In contrast, all three of the familiarization displays as well as the upright test display are recognized as similar because they all make contact with stored knowledge about human gait. At the
very least, this interpretation suggests that infants categorize perceived point-
light displays into familiar versus unfamiliar objects. We are currently trying to
learn more about the boundary conditions of this general category that includes
biomechanical motions.

In sum, we are beginning to compile some fairly compelling evidence that
visual experience with human gait contributes to the perception of biomechanical motions by 5 months of age. The principal finding supporting this conclusion
is that the detection of differences in point-light walker displays undergoes a
shift between 3 and 5 months of age, and becomes orientation-specific by the
latter age. It is important that this shift in responsiveness not be confused with
a loss of sensitivity to lower-order differences between displays. When 5-month-
old infants fail to show discrimination of the same displays that are discriminated by 3-month-old infants, it is most likely attributable to the older infants'
responding to the displays at a different level of perceptual processing. More
specifically, we suggest that this higher level is one that interacts with prior
knowledge about the perceived object: They are beginning to respond to these
displays on the basis of their perceived *meaning* as opposed to their perceived
structure.

CONCLUDING REMARKS

If young infants are to perceive a biomechanical display as depicting a person
walking, then it is necessary for them to implement the same processing constraints as those used by adults. The data I have reviewed suggest that infants
are sensitive to these processing constraints, and, with the exception of
knowledge-based constraints, there is no clear lower-bound on the age at which
they are first implemented. It is therefore quite reasonable to propose that these
constraints are part of the intrinsic organization of the visual system. As such,
these processing constraints share many formal properties with other fundamental properties of the mind. They operate automatically, they are embedded deeply
within the information processing machinery, and they are neither easily accessible nor easily generalizable to other functions. In brief, these are special-
purpose processing heuristics akin to those present in the input modules
described by Fodor (1983) in his monograph, *The Modularity of the Mind.*

Knowledge-based constraints are the one exception to those just described. By definition, these constraints emerge with the acquisition of relevant information that is stored in an accessible fashion. Thus, it is not until 5 months of age that we begin to observe the operation of these constraints in the perception of biomechanical motions. Let me be clear, however, that there is no reason to think that this particular age possesses some unique status. Some percepts will not interact with stored knowledge until later ages, whereas others might be constrained at even earlier ages. The deciding factor is the relevance and accessibility of the stored knowledge. A case in point is seen in the perception of faces by infants. Even 3-month-old infants show orientation specificity in the perception of point-light displays depicting faces (Stucki, Kauffman-Hayoz, & Kauffman, 1987). According to the logic discussed in the preceding section, this particular finding provides prima facie evidence for the operation of knowledge-based constraints in the perception of faces by 3 months of age.

It is not clear whether any of the aforementioned intrinsic constraints show substantive changes with age, but certainly knowledge-based constraints change with age, experience, and the development of higher level conceptual functions. In the discussion of these specific constraints, I suggested that the development of conceptual knowledge will affect the infant's responsiveness to biomechanical motions. As we begin to examine more closely the effects of knowledge on perception, it will become necessary to develop more complex tasks that demand more elaborate forms of perceptual analysis and comparison. For example, identification tasks can be designed to draw on the accumulation and categorization of networks of knowledge that relate to human gait. Interestingly, recent research by Diamond and Carey (1987) suggests that as these networks attain the organization of an expert, adult observers become increasingly sensitive to second-order relational features, such as the distance between the eyes and the nose on the face, when differentiating displays that all share the same general configuration. One of the most important implications of this finding is that the acquisition and organization of specific knowledge about objects continues to influence perceptual processing well into adulthood.

Another age-related characteristic of knowledge-based constraints is that these processing heuristics will sometimes obscure differences that are specified by more intrinsic constraints. One example of this generalization is the finding that 5-month-olds presented with inverted point-light displays do not show increased visual attention to a phase-perturbed display, whereas 3-month-olds do show a recovery in looking times. The failure of the older infants to show recovery is clearly not attributable to a loss of sensitivity to the relevant property of temporal phase, but rather reflects a change in the level of organization at which the representation is made accessible to cognitive processing. My suspicion is that the perceived organization of a display becomes increasingly labile with age as knowledge-based constraints begin to exert greater influences on the perceptual process.

In addition to this type of interaction, it would be a disservice to the past research not to acknowledge that interactions occur among the other constraints as well. At the very least, the data suggest that all of these constraints are necessary for the perception of a structure consistent with the form of a person walking. In almost every case tested, a perturbation or omission of one constraint significantly affected the perceived organization of a point-light walker display. Although these constraints were discussed separately for expository purposes, the differences between them are more a matter of emphasis than of formal design. For example, perceptual vector analysis proposed by Johansson (1973) is a logical component of all the other intrinsic processing constraints. Likewise, the center of moment in coding theory is formally equivalent to the fixed axis in the local-rigidity constraint. Thus, the perturbation of any one constraint will frequently result in some additional perturbation to one or more of the other constraints.

Operationally, it is often impossible to design a single experiment to test the contribution of a specific processing constraint. Our solution to this problem has been to use a conceptual bootstrapping approach, called *converging operations* (see Proffitt & Bertenthal, 1990, for an extended discussion of this approach). In this chapter, I summarized by example the mechanics of this experimental strategy. The principal conclusion emerging from this program of research is that infants as well as adults implement a delimited number of overlapping constraints in order to perceive a biomechanical display as a coherent representation of a person walking.

As a brief postscript to this discussion, it is fitting to remind readers that the 100th anniversary of the publication of *The Principles of Psychology* by William James (1890) has already passed. Included in this book is the oft-quoted description of the newborn's perceptual world as a "blooming, buzzing confusion" (p. 488). Although this characterization of the newborn's world has been effectively challenged by numerous findings (e.g., J. M. Mandler, 1990), a clear explication of how the young infant organizes perceptual information has been slow in coming. The recent research that my colleagues and I have conducted on the perception of biomechanical motions convince us that a good portion of this answer is linked to the availability of processing constraints that are present from the child's earliest interactions with the environment.

ACKNOWLEDGMENTS

The preparation of this chapter and the research reported herein were supported by NIH grants HD-16195 and HD-25066, NIH career development award HD-00678, and a sabbatical award from the James McKeen Cattell Fund. I am indebted to Steven Kramer, Jeannine Pinto, and Dennis Proffitt for many valuable discussions about the perception of biomechanical motions. I would also like to thank Jeannine Pinto and Philip Kellman for comments and suggestions on an earlier draft, and Robert Freedland and Adam Rubenstein for their assistance in creating some of the figures.

REFERENCES

Abraham, R. H., & Shaw, C. D. (1982). *Dynamics: The geometry of behavior*. Santa Cruz, CA: Aerial Press.

Arterberry, M. E., & Yonas, A. (1988). Infants' sensitivity to kinetic information for three-dimensional object shape. *Perception and Psychophysics, 44,* 1–6.

Bertenthal, B. I., & Davis, P. (1988, November). *Dynamical pattern analysis predicts recognition and discrimination of biomechanical motions*. Paper presented at the annual meeting of the Psychonomic Society, Chicago, IL.

Bertenthal, B. I., Haith, M. M., & Campos, J. J. (1983). The partial lag design: A method for controlling spontaneous regression in the infant-control habituation paradigm. *Infant Behavior and Development, 6,* 331–338.

Bertenthal, B. I., & Kramer, S. J. (1984). The TMS 9918A VDP: A new device for generating moving displays on a microcomputer. *Behavior Research Methods, Instruments, and Computers, 16,* 388–394.

Bertenthal, B. I., & Pinto, J. (in press). Complementary processes in the perception and production of human movements. In E. Thelen & L. Smith (Eds.), *Dynamical approaches to development: Vol. 2. Approaches.* Cambridge, MA: Bradford Books.

Bertenthal, B. I., Proffitt, D. R., & Cutting, J. E. (1984). Infant sensitivity to figural coherence in biomechanical motions. *Journal of Experimental Child Psychology, 37,* 213–230.

Bertenthal, B. I., Proffitt, D. R., & Kramer, S. J. (1986). *Orientation specificity in the perception of biomechanical motions.* Unpublished manuscript.

Bertenthal, B. I., Proffitt, D. R., & Kramer, S. J. (1987). The perception of biomechanical motions: Implementation of various processing constraints. *Journal of Experimental Psychology: Human Perception and Performance, 13,* 577–585.

Bertenthal, B. I., Proffitt, D. R., Kramer, S. J., & Spetner, N. B. (1987). Infants' encoding of kinetic displays varying in relative coherence. *Developmental Psychology, 23,* 171–178.

Braunstein, M. L. (1976). *Depth perception through motion.* New York: Academic Press.

Cutting, J. E. (1978a). Generation of synthetic male and female walkers through the manipulations of a biomechanical invariant. *Perception, 75,* 393–405.

Cutting, J. E. (1978b). A program to generate synthetic walkers as dynamic point-light displays. *Behavior Research Methods and Instrumentation, 10,* 91–94.

Cutting, J. E. (1981). Coding theory adapted to gait perception. *Journal of Experimental Psychology: Human Perception and Performance, 7,* 71–87.

Cutting, J. E., Moore, C., & Morrison, R. (1988). Masking the motions of human gait. *Perception and Psychophysics, 44,* 339–347.

Cutting, J. E., & Proffitt, D. R. (1981). Gait perception as an example of how we may perceive events. In H. Pick & R. Walk (Eds.), *Perception and perceptual development* (Vol. 2, pp. 249–273). New York: Plenum.

Cutting, J. E., & Proffitt, D. R. (1982). The minimum principle and the perception of absolute, common, and relative motions. *Cognitive Psychology, 14,* 211–246.

Diamond, R., & Carey, S. (1987). Why faces are and are not special: An effect of expertise. *Journal of Experimental Psychology: General, 115,* 107–117.

Fodor, J. (1983). *The modularity of mind.* Cambridge, MA: MIT Press.

Fox, R., & McDaniels, C. (1982). The perception of biological motion by human infants. *Science, 218,* 486–487.

Garner, W. R. (1981). The analysis of unanalyzed perceptions. In M. Kubovy & J. R. Pomerantz (Eds.), *Perceptual organization* (pp. 119–139). Hillsdale, NJ: Lawrence Erlbaum Associates.

Gesell, A. (1928). *Infancy and human growth.* New York: Macmillan.

Gilden, D. L., Bertenthal, B. I., & Othman, S. (1991). Image statistics and the perception of apparent motion. *Journal of Experimental Psychology: Human Perception and Performance, 16,* 693–705.

Gould, S. J. (1983). *Hens' teeth and horses' toes.* New York: Norton & Co.

Green, B. F. (1961). Figure coherence in the kinetic depth effect. *Journal of Experimental Psychology, 62,* 272–282.

Hatfield, G., & Epstein, W. (1985). The status of the minimum principle in the theoretical analysis of visual perception. *Psychological Bulletin, 97,* 155–186.

Hoffman, D. D., & Flinchbaugh, B. E. (1982). The interpretation of biological motion. *Biological Cybernetics, 42,* 195–204.

James, W. (1890). *The principles of psychology* (Vol. 1). New York: Dover.

Johansson, G. (1950). *Configuration in event perception.* Uppsala: Almquist & Wiksell.

Johansson, G. (1973). Visual perception of biological motion and a model for its analysis. *Perception and Psychophysics, 14,* 201–211.

Johansson, G. (1977). Studies on visual perception of locomotion. *Perception, 6,* 365–376.

Keil, F. C. (1981). Constraints on knowledge and cognitive development. *Psychological Review, 88,* 197–227.

Kellman, P. J. (1984). Perception of three-dimensional form by human infants. *Perception and Psychophysics, 36,* 353–358.

Kelso, J. A. S., & Pandya, A. S. (1991). Dynamic pattern generation and recognition. In D. Zeltzer, N. Badler, & B. Barsky (Eds.), *Making them move: Mechanics, control and animation of articulated figures* (pp. 332–358). San Mateo, CA: Morgan Kauffman.

Kozlowski, L. T., & Cutting, J. E. (1977). Recognizing the sex of a walker from a dynamic point-light display. *Perception and Psychophysics, 21,* 575–580.

MacArthur, L. Z., & Baron, R. M. (1983). Toward an ecological theory of social perception. *Psychological Review, 90,* 215–238.

Mandler, G. (1980). Recognizing: The judgment of previous occurrence. *Psychological Review, 87,* 252–271.

Mandler, J. M. (1990). A new perspective on cognitive development in infancy. *American Scientist, 78,* 236–243.

Marr, D. (1982). *Vision: A computational investigation into the human representation and processing of visual information.* San Francisco: Freeman.

Marr, D., & Nishihara, H. K. (1978). Representation and recognition of the spatial organization of three-dimensional shapes. *Proceedings of the Royal Society of London B, 200,* 269–294.

Piaget, J. (1970). Piaget's theory. In P. H. Mussen (Ed.), *Carmichael's manual of child psychology* (Vol. 1, pp. 703–732). New York: Wiley.

Pinto, J., & Davis, P. V. (1991, April). *The categorical perception of human gait in 3- and 5-month-old infants.* Paper presented at the meetings of the Society for Research in Child Development, Seattle, WA.

Proffitt, D. R., & Bertenthal, B. I. (1988). Recovering connectivity from moving point-light displays. In W. N. Martin & J. K. Aggarwal (Eds.), *Motion understanding: Robot and human vision* (pp. 297–328). Hingman, MA: Kluwer.

Proffitt, D. R., & Bertenthal, B. I. (1990). Converging operations revisited: Assessing what infants perceive using discrimination measures. *Perception and Psychophysics, 47,* 1–11.

Proffitt, D. R., Bertenthal, B. I., & Roberts, R. J. (1986). The role of occlusion in reducing multistability in moving point-light displays. *Perception and Psychophysics, 35,* 315–323.

Proffitt, D. R., & Cutting, J. E. (1979). Perceiving the centroid of configurations on a rolling wheel. *Perception and Psychophysics, 25,* 389–398.

Ramachandran, V. S., & Anstis, S. M. (1986). The perception of apparent motion. *Scientific American,* *254,* 102–109.

Ramachandran, V. S., Inada, V., & Kiama, G. (1986). Perception of illusory occlusion apparent motion. *Vision Research, 26,* 1741–1749.

Rashid, R. F. (1980). Towards a system for the interpretation of moving light displays. *IEEE PAMI 2, 6,* 574–581.

Restle, F. (1979). Coding theory of the perception of motion configurations. *Psychological Review, 86,* 1–24.

Rozin, P. (1976). The evolution of intelligence and access to the cognitive unconscious. In J. M. Sprague & A. A. Epstein (Eds.), *Progress in psychobiology and physiological psychology* (Vol. 6, pp. 245–280). New York: Academic Press.

Stucki, M., Kaufmann-Hayoz, R., & Kaufmann, F. (1987). Infants' recognition of a face revealed through motion: Contribution of internal facial movement and head movement. *Journal of Experimental Child Psychology, 44,* 80–91.

Sumi, S. (1984). Upside down presentation of the Johansson moving light spot pattern. *Perception, 13,* 283–286.

Ullman, S. (1979). *The interpretation of visual motion.* Cambridge, MA: MIT Press.

Wallach, H., & O'Connell, D. N. (1953). The kinetic depth effect. *Journal of Experimental Psychology, 45,* 205–217.

Webb, J. A., & Aggarwal, J. K. (1982). Structure from motion of rigid and jointed objects. *Artificial Intelligence, 19,* 107–130.

Werner, J. S., & Perlmutter, M. (1979). Development of visual memory in infants. In H. W. Reese & L. P. Lipsitt (Eds.), *Advances in child development and behavior* (Vol. 14, pp. 1–56). New York: Academic Press.

Wertheimer, M. (1938). Laws of organization in perceptual forms. In W. D. Ellis (Ed.), *A source book of Gestalt psychology* (pp. 71–88). London: Routledge & Kegan Paul. (Original work published 1923)

Infants' Sensitivity to Motion-Carried Information for Depth and Object Properties

Martha E. Arterberry
Gettysburg College

Lincoln G. Craton
Trinity University

Albert Yonas
University of Minnesota

Since the early 1980s, research on infants' sensitivity to motion-carried information has typically reported early competence. For example, Yonas and his colleagues (Yonas, Pettersen, & Lockman, 1979) and Nanez (1988) found that infants between 3 weeks and 3 months of age respond to optical expansion information specifying impending collision. Kellman and his colleagues (Kellman & Spelke, 1983; Kellman, Spelke, & Short, 1986) found that 4-month-old infants perceive the unity of a partially occluded object only when the visible ends of the object undergo a rigid translation. Moreover, several researchers have found evidence that 4-month-olds perceive the three-dimensional shape of moving objects (Arterberry & Yonas, 1988; Kellman, 1984; Kellman & Short, 1987; Owsley, 1983; Yonas, Arterberry, & Granrud, 1987a), but infants provide no evidence of perceiving the three-dimensional shape when presented with successive static views of a rotating object (Kellman, 1984).

These findings have led to a widespread view that motion-carried information is the primary information used by young infants. Sensitivity to some types of motion-carried information is present before sensitivity to binocular disparity (which emerges around 4 months of age) and pictorial depth cues (which emerge between 5 and 7 months of age). Thus, before 4 months it is likely that infants' spatial perception is based on motion cues (Yonas & Granrud, 1984; see Yonas, Arterberry, & Granrud, 1987b for a review). In addition, Kellman's work (Kellman, 1984; Kellman & Spelke, 1983) suggests that motion information provides for the perception of three-dimensional object shape and object unity before static cues. These findings are consistent with a Gibsonian (1950, 1966,

1979) view that perception is a process that occurs over time, that motion simplifies the perceiver's task, and that motion may be a primary, fundamental source of spatial information.

The apparent early development of sensitivity to motion-carried information may lead one to believe that there is no lower age limit on perceptual abilities based on motion. The research we present in this chapter suggests otherwise. Although infants are sensitive to motion-carried information early in life, there are interesting developmental changes that occur within the first year. This chapter describes and contrasts two programs of research investigating infants' sensitivity to motion-carried information for the perception of depth, segregation of figure from ground, and perception of object properties. One set of studies documents early sensitivity to motion-carried information for the perception of relative depth of two surfaces. In addition, we show that young infants can use this information to perceive figure–ground relations; that is, they know that a background surface continues behind an object in the foreground. The second set of studies addresses infants' ability to perceive object properties over time, such as the length of an object as it passes behind an aperture. Evidence from the second set of studies suggests that this ability develops late in the first year of life. Thus, it appears that the frequently reported sensitivity of infants to motion-carried information may not apply to all tasks involving motion.

PERCEPTION OF DEPTH AND SEGREGATION OF FIGURE FROM GROUND

At least three types of kinetic depth information can be used to determine the relative depth of two surfaces lying on either side of a depth edge. The first type is motion parallax. For an observer undergoing pure translation through an otherwise static scene, motion parallax is sufficient for the recovery of depth order. Because the magnitude of optical flow is inversely proportional to the distance of a surface point from the observer, the surface that has the larger magnitude of flow in the retinal projection is closer. Observer rotation, however, complicates this analysis considerably (Banks, 1988). In addition, if objects in the field of view move with respect to each other, there is no direct relationship between magnitude of flow and depth. Two other, perhaps more reliable, sources of kinetic information for the relative depth of two surfaces are the accretion and deletion of texture and boundary flow information.

Accretion and Deletion of Texture

When an observer moves about in the environment, some surfaces are revealed while others are hidden from view. Gibson, Kaplan, Reynolds, and Wheeler (1969) noted that whether texture elements in the optic array are accreted (i.e., appear) or are deleted (disappear) specifies that a particular surface is being uncovered or covered, respectively. Kaplan (1969) reported the first evidence that the adult visual system is sensitive to accretion and deletion information. Subjects viewing an animated film of random texture (depicted in Fig. 7.1) perceived an edge in the image at the locus of accretion and deletion of texture. In addition, these displays provided subjects with a vivid impression of relative depth at the edge, with the accreted and deleted texture appearing as part of a background surface that was being covered and uncovered.

Recent work suggests that young infants are also able to use accretion and deletion information to perceive edges and to determine the relative depth of adjacent surfaces. Using a habituation procedure, Kaufmann-Hayoz, Kaufmann, and Stucki (1986) found evidence that young infants perceive the two-dimensional outline of forms (e.g., a cross) specified by accretion and deletion of texture. Three-month-old infants were habituated to one of two moving forms defined solely by the common motion of a portion of the visual field relative to other parts and the associated accretion and deletion of texture on the "background" surface. Following habituation, infants viewed static displays of the same form and of a new form. Kaufmann-Hayoz et al. found that the 3-month-olds looked longer at the new form than at the original one. This result demonstrates that the infants detected enough information about the moving form during habituation to allow them to establish a correspondence between the moving form and the identical static form presented during the test phase. They may have accomplished this by simply perceiving aspects of the two-dimensional outline of the moving form and then recognizing the outline in the static test dis-

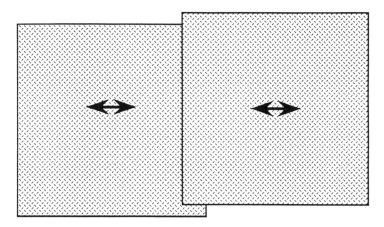

FIG. 7.1. Schematic drawing of one surface covering and uncovering a second surface. The texture on the left surface is accreted and deleted, specifying that it is background. In the texture on the right, the foreground surface is preserved. The interior vertical line indicates the location of subjective depth edge.

play. Thus, it is not possible to conclude from these data that the infants perceived the moving form as protruding in depth. However, at the very least, 3-month-olds can use accretion and deletion of texture to identify the edges of surfaces.

Other research does allow for the inference that young infants use motion-carried information to perceive the relative depth of surfaces. Granrud et al. (1984) have shown that 5- and 7-month-old infants perceive displays like those used by Kaplan (1969) as surfaces ordered in depth. Infants viewing computer-generated random-dot displays reached significantly more often for the "foreground" than for the "background." Because infants reach preferentially to the closer of two surfaces if a depth difference is perceived (Yonas & Granrud, 1985), Granrud et al. concluded that infants as young as 5 months of age are sensitive to accretion and deletion of texture as information for the depth order of surfaces.

Boundary Flow

An additional source of information for the ordering in depth of surfaces at occlusion boundaries has recently been described (Craton & Yonas, 1990a; Thompson, Mutch, & Berzins, 1985; Yonas, Craton, & Thompson, 1987). This new cue, called *boundary flow*, relies on the fact that when there are two surfaces at different depths, an edge exists between them. The relative depth order of the two surfaces is specified by the relationship between the motion of the depth edge, referred to here as an *image boundary*, and that of the texture elements from the two surfaces on either side of the edge. The principle underlying the boundary flow cue is that texture projected from the foreground surface moves with the image boundary. Because the boundary belongs to the foreground surface, the background surface, which is being covered, projects texture elements that move in a direction different from that of the image boundary. Thus, the "common" motion of boundary and texture specifies a foreground surface; the "uncommon" motion of boundary and texture specifies a background surface.

To explore sensitivity to the boundary flow cue isolated from accretion and deletion of texture, Yonas et al. (1987) presented adults with displays in which the texture on both sides of a vertical line was separated from the central boundary by a blank space (Fig. 7.2). This "gap" allowed for lateral motion of texture and boundary without providing accretion/deletion information for depth at an edge. Adults reported perceiving a clear depth separation in these boundary flow displays and reliably reported the surface with "common" motion as in front.

The discovery that adult subjects employ the boundary flow constraint in in-

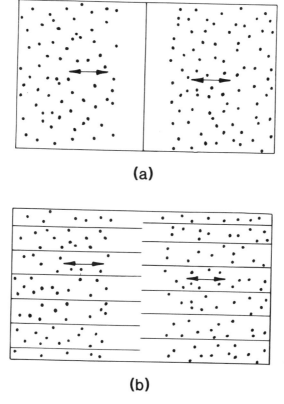

(a)

(b)

FIG. 7.2. Schematic drawing of displays to isolate boundary flow information. The relative motion of a boundary and texture on either side of the boundary specified relative depth. A line (a) or a vertical subjective contour, generated by end-stopped horizontal lines (b), served as a boundary. The "gap" between boundary and texture eliminated accretion and deletion information for depth.

terpreting two-dimensional kinetic displays (Craton & Yonas, 1988; Craton & Yonas, 1990a; Yonas, Craton, et al., 1987) has necessitated reinterpretation of earlier studies (Granrud et al., 1984; Kaplan, 1969). These studies demonstrated that subjects presented with random-dot accretion/deletion displays as depicted in Fig. 7.1 perceive two surfaces ordered in depth. Because the boundary flow constraint had not yet been described when these studies were conducted, these results were taken as evidence of sensitivity to accretion/deletion information. However, the analysis just presented reveals that these displays contain both accretion/deletion information and boundary flow information, so the obtained depth effect could have been based on either or both of these cues.

Craton and Yonas (1988) recently obtained evidence that 5-month-old infants are sensitive to boundary flow information when no accretion/deletion cues are present. Infants reached preferentially to the apparently nearer region of the displays depicted in Fig. 7.2. One implication of this result concerns the previous finding by Granrud et al. (1984) that 5-month-old infants reach preferentially to the apparently closer side of accretion/deletion displays (see Fig. 7.1). It is now apparent that this result could be based on infants' sensitivity to the boundary flow information in this display rather than on sensitivity to accretion/deletion information. There is as yet no incontrovertible evidence for human sensitivity to accretion/deletion information for the depth order of surfaces, because stimuli containing this cue have always contained boundary flow information as well.

Figure and Ground Segregation

An important aspect of how adults perceive accretion/deletion displays and boundary flow displays is that the apparent background surface is perceived as extending *behind* the boundary between the two adjacent surfaces. This indicates that kinetic information allows not only the recovery of the order of depth at an edge, but also the segregation of a scene into figure and ground regions. These two sorts of perceptual outcomes can be distinguished by the sorts of representation they imply. The former ability, in the absence of perceived figure–ground relations, suggests a viewer-centered representation of depth, in which the distance of regions relative to the observer is specified. This corresponds to the *2½-D sketch*, as described by Marr (1982). In Marr's computational theory, viewer-centered representation is contrasted with object-centered representation (the "3-D model"), which specifies the shape of objects and the position of objects relative to one another, but does not include near/far relationships with the observer. The perception of figure and ground constitutes an intermediate level of representation, in which viewer-centered depth is included and, in addition, the invisible ground is represented as continuing behind foreground surfaces or figures in a scene. Thompson, Craton, and Yonas (1988) have dubbed this the *2¾-D sketch*, in order to distinguish it from the other two levels of representation.

The research discussed in previous sections strongly argues that infants can perceive edges defined by kinetic information (Kaufmann-Hayoz et al., 1986), and that they can perceive the relative depth of surfaces in a scene on the basis of kinetic information (Craton & Yonas, 1988; Granrud et al., 1984). However, it was not known until recently whether infants can use kinetic information to segregate scenes into figure and ground regions in the sense we have described. On the one hand, the results of the Kaufmann-Hayoz et al. study can be attributed to 3-month-old infants' ability to detect the two-dimensional outline of moving figures from accretion and deletion information; it is not necessary to conclude that infants perceived the moving figures as protruding in depth. On the other hand, because the studies by Craton and Yonas (1988) and Granrud et al. (1984) used reaching as a dependent measure, they indicate only that 5-month-old infants perceive some parts of kinetic occlusion displays as closer than others. Infants this age may or may not represent the background surface as extending behind the foreground surface.

What would constitute convincing evidence for infants' perception of figure and ground from motion-carried information? In a recent study, Craton (1989) used the stimuli depicted in Fig. 7.3 to test young infants' ability to parse a scene into figure and ground regions. In Fig. 7.3a, if the jagged line in the center of the rectangle is taken as the edge of a surface, there are several ways in which the scene can be interpreted. Region A may be an object (shaped somewhat like the state of Minnesota) with a concave border in front of a continuous background surface, labeled B. Alternatively, the region labeled B may be an object (shaped somewhat like Wisconsin) with a convex edge in front of a continuous background surface, A. The crucial point is that, for adults, the boundary "shapes" whatever region is perceived as being closer, while the region that is perceived as being farther away is unshaped and appears to continue behind the foreground region.

In the static display shown in Fig. 7.3a, the spatial layout is ambiguous, and the perception of figure and ground is reversible. If kinetic information is introduced, however, adults use this information to perceive which region is figure and which is ground. Craton (1989) habituated 3½- and 5-month-old infants to computer-generated displays in which the accretion and deletion of texture and boundary flow information specified that either the concave or convex region of Fig. 7.3a was figure and that the other region was ground. Following habitu-

HABITUATION

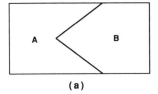

(a)

TEST

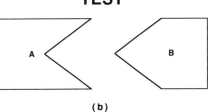

FIG. 7.3.   Habituation (a) and test (b) stimuli for the study of infants' use of kinetic information to segregate figure from ground.

(b)

ation infants viewed, on alternate trials, the convex or concave shape in the center of the screen (see Fig. 7.3b).

If infants can use kinetic information to parse a dynamic scene into figure and ground regions, then only the region specified as figure would be perceived as having a specific shape defined by the central boundary. The region specified as ground would be perceived as not having a distinctive shape and as extending behind the figure. Thus, after habituation, infants who can parse figure and ground would be expected to look longer at the test object that is different in shape from the region specified as figure during habituation. If infants use kinetic information to perceive the relative depth of the two regions, but do not perceive figure–ground relations (i.e., if they form a 2½-D sketch of the scene rather than a 2¾-D sketch), then they would perceive both the foreground and background regions as having distinctive shapes defined by the central boundary. As a result, they would be expected to look equally at the two test objects.

The results of the 3½- and 5-month-old infants are shown in Fig. 7.4. Five-month-olds who viewed the concave region as figure during the habituation phase looked longer at the convex object during the test phase; those in the convex habituation group showed an increase in looking at the concave object during the test phase. These results provide evidence of figure–ground segregation in 5-month-old infants. The 3½-month-old infants also showed a different pattern of looking at the two test objects, depending on which display they viewed during habituation (see Fig. 7.4). Unexpectedly, they looked longer at the test object that was the same as the region specified as figure during habituation.

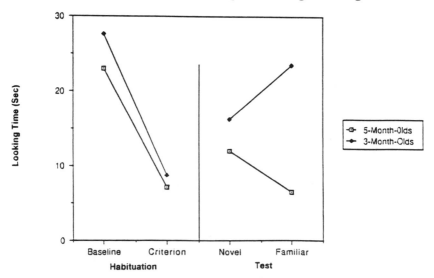

FIG. 7.4. Mean looking time during the habituation and test phase by 3½-month-old and 5-month-old infants. "Baseline" is the mean of the first three trials during the habituation phase; "criterion" is the mean of the last three trials during the habituation phase.

Although familiarity effects have been found in studies with young infants (for example, Meltzoff & Borton, 1982; Wagner & Sakovitz, 1986), we should note that we have been unable to replicate this finding with 3½-month-olds. Thus, at this point no conclusions can be drawn regarding the figure–ground segregation abilities of the younger age group.

In summary, infants as young as 3 months are sensitive to accretion and deletion of texture for the perception of two-dimensional shape. In addition, 5-month-olds perceive the ordering of surfaces in depth when that order is specified by motion-carried information. Moreover, by 5 months of age infants can use this type of information to segregate regions of figure and ground.

PERCEPTION OF OBJECT PROPERTIES OVER TIME

A common situation in which we are presented motion-carried information is when we view someone pass behind a door that is slightly ajar. At any particular instant, only a single "slice" of the person is available on our retina; yet, we do not experience these as separate slices. Instead, we perceive a whole person walking behind the opening. While we do not experience all the parts of the person as being visible simultaneously, we have little difficulty perceiving that a person is passing behind the opening.

One way researchers investigate the ability to perceive information available over time is in studies in which displays are presented behind an aperture. The perception of form, viewed through an aperture, has been demonstrated in the late 19th century by various investigators, including Helmholtz, Plateau, and Zollner (discussed in Rock, 1981). The phenomenon was rediscovered by Parks (1965). In his original study, he presented subjects with a line drawing of a camel moving behind a narrow stationary slit. Subjects were able to report the shape of the whole form as it moved behind the slit, even with slits as narrow as 1/64th of an inch and with figures more than 1 inch wide.

In order for infants to successfully perceive an object or its properties behind an aperture, they may need to know that when parts of objects are hidden from view they retain their physical and spatial properties. Baillargeon's work (see this volume, chap. 9) suggests that very young infants possess this ability. A second ability required when parts of an object are viewed successively is sensitivity to motion-carried information, including accretion and deletion of texture. The research presented in the previous section suggests that young infants use motion-carried information to perceive depth. Moreover, Kellman (see this volume, chap. 5) and Bertenthal (see this volume, chap. 6) provide evidence of sophisticated abilities for the perception of object shape and coherence specified by motion-carried information.

Arterberry (1989) investigated infants' ability to perceive the properties of objects behind an aperture over time. In the studies that follow, infants' perception of object properties (length and number), rather than object shape, was investigated. In studies in which an object of a particular shape passes behind an aperture, it is possible that within a single glimpse infants (or adults) may perceive an aspect of the object's contour that will differentiate it from all other objects. Thus, it would be unclear whether the discrimination of shape was based on the information available over time or the information obtained from one glimpse.

Perception of Object Length

The first object property investigated was length. Infants were tested for discrimination between a long and a short rectangle that were identical except for their length. The only information available to the infants for object length was the amount of time it took the rectangles to pass behind the aperture (the longer rectangle taking longer than the shorter). The rectangles were covered with random texture elements that provided information for the object's speed and direction of movement. In addition, accretion and deletion of texture and boundary flow provided information for the different depth planes of the object and the aperture.

The first group to be tested were 24-month-olds. In a verbal task, these children were presented with both long and short rectangles moving behind an aperture and were asked to identify whether they were seeing a long or a short object. Children at this age were able to discriminate the lengths of the objects as they moved behind the aperture.

Before testing younger infants' ability to perceive object length behind an aperture, 4- and 8-month-old infants were tested for discrimination of long and short objects when they were presented in full view. In an habituation procedure, infants were presented with a rectangle (long or short) translating left to right in a plane perpendicular to the line of sight. The rectangle was fully visible at all times. Following habituation, infants viewed both the long and short rectangles on alternate trials. Both 4- and 8-month-old infants looked significantly longer at the new object than at the habituation object (see Fig. 7.5). These results suggest that infants at this age can discriminate the length of objects when the whole object is present at all times.

Next, infants were tested for the ability to perceive the length of objects moving behind an aperture. Infants 8, 10, and 12 months old were habituated to either the long or short rectangle translating from left to right in full view. Prior to the habituation phase, infants were presented with two pretest trials, in which they viewed a panel that contained a narrow aperture. A stationary object (the long rectangle) completely filled the aperture with no edges visible. This pretest was designed to familiarize the infants with the aperture before it was introduced during the test phase. Following habituation, the panel with the aperture was reintroduced and the infants were presented with four test

4-MONTH-OLD INFANTS

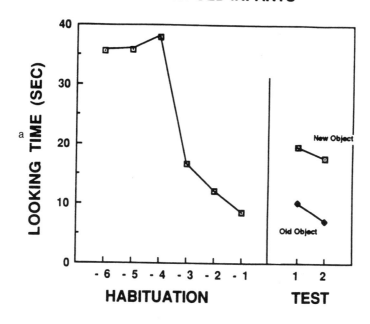

8-MONTH-OLD INFANTS

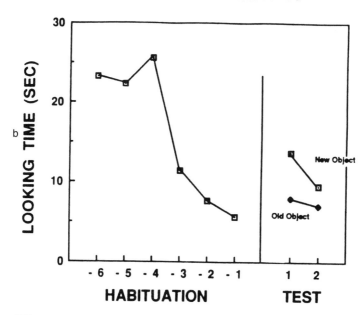

FIG. 7.5. Mean looking time during the habituation and test phase by (a) 4-month-old and (b) 8-month-old infants.

trials in which they viewed, on alternate trials, the long and the short rectangle moving behind the aperture. The results are shown in Fig. 7.6. Only the 12-month-old group provided any evidence of perceiving the length of the objects moving behind the aperture. Neither the 8- nor the 10-month-olds showed a significant increase in looking at the object of a novel length during the test phase.

Thus far, the results suggest that the ability to discriminate between a long and a short object passing behind an aperture is present in 12- and 24-month-olds. This apparently late appearance is surprising in light of other research, much of which is described elsewhere in this volume, that suggests mature perceptual and cognitive competency earlier in life. It is possible that object length is a difficult property for infants to perceive over time. Even though the displays were rich in information about the objects' speed and direction of movement, infants may have had difficulty using duration to determine object length. Rock (1981) suggested that even adults have difficulty using absolute time in perceiving the length of objects moving behind an aperture. In light of this possibility, Arterberry (1989) conducted a second series of studies designed to investigate infants' perception of a more qualitative property: the number of objects moving behind an aperture.

Perception of Object Number

The problem of perceiving a single object viewed through an aperture can be extended to perceiving multiple objects. For example, when two people pass by a slightly ajar door, we know in what direction they are traveling, how many people have passed, and their relative spatial positioning (i.e., which person was first and how much space was between them). This information is obtained from their speed of travel, the duration of the interval between the disappearance of the first person and the appearance of the second, and their direction of motion). For example, if one person passes by and then another (even identical) person is viewed moving in the same direction, most likely two people are present. In contrast, if one person passes by and then another identical person is viewed moving in the opposite direction, most likely only one person is present and has just been viewed twice. Although the studies by Arterberry (1989) provide little evidence that infants younger than 12 months of age are sensitive to the amount of time it takes for an object to pass behind an aperture, it is possible that younger infants are sensitive to the direction of motion of objects passing behind an aperture and that they may be able to use this information to determine the number of objects present.

Recently, a number of researchers have demonstrated that young infants are able to discriminate numerosities (Antell & Keating, 1983; Starkey & Cooper, 1980; Starkey, Gelman, & Spelke, 1985; Starkey, Spelke, & Gelman, 1983; see Strauss & Curtis, 1984 for a review). The following experiments utilized

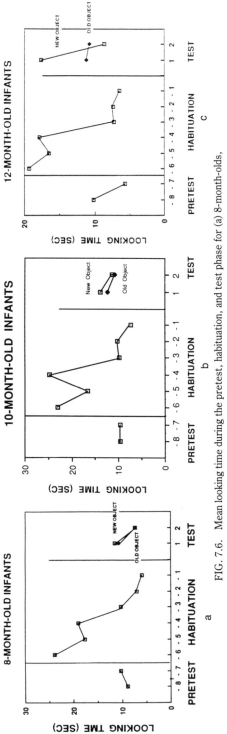

FIG. 7.6. Mean looking time during the pretest, habituation, and test phase for (a) 8-month-olds, (b) 10-month-olds, and (c) 12-month-olds.

this early numerical sensitivity to investigate the perception of object properties over time.

To investigate infants' perception of number over time, Baillargeon's (this volume, chap. 9) procedure for studying infant cognition was adapted. Her procedure capitalizes on the fact that infants look longer at an event that violates an expectation. When infants are shown a likely or expected event, they do not show much interest and exhibit short looking times. In contrast, when they are shown an unlikely or unexpected event, they show greater interest (and look longer).

Before testing infants' perception of object number over time, a control experiment tested 8-month-olds' ability to discriminate between one and two objects when information for the number of objects present was available in a single view. Infants were seated in front of two curtains. Behind the curtains, a stage moved on a track from left to right. Periodically, the curtains would open to reveal the whole stage; otherwise, the stage was only partially visible through a gap in the curtains. Initially, infants were familiarized to an empty stage moving behind the curtains. Following the familiarization phase, infants were presented with two test events (illustrated in Fig. 7.7). In the expected condition, two rabbits passed behind the curtains. The gap in the curtains was wide enough to permit viewing of parts of both objects at once. When the curtains opened, two rabbits were present on the stage. In the unexpected condition, again two rabbits passed by the small gap in the curtains and parts of both were visible at the same time, but when the curtains opened only one rabbit was on the stage (the other having been removed prior to the opening of the curtains). If the infants were able to determine that two rabbits passed behind the small gap, they should find the event in which only one rabbit was present after the curtains opened surprising and look at it longer.

The results are shown in Fig. 7.8 (see 8-Control). Eight-month-old infants looked longer at the unexpected event than the expected event, suggesting that when parts of both objects are available in a single glimpse (so that number need not be perceived over time) 8-month-old infants are able to perceive the number of objects present.

To test 8-, 10-, and 12-month-old infants' perception of object number over time, the same procedure was used except that the gap in the curtains was reduced such that only one rabbit could be seen at a time as the stage passed. The expected and unexpected test events are illustrated in Fig. 7.9. In order for the infants to know how many objects were present, they needed to take account of how many objects passed by the aperture and the direction in which the objects were traveling. The results are shown in Fig. 7.8. Only the 12-month-olds looked significantly longer at the unexpected event than at the expected event, suggesting that they were able to perceive the number of objects behind the aperture and found the event in which the number changed surprising.

In summary, Arterberry (1989) has found a similar pattern of results in two

Expected Test Event

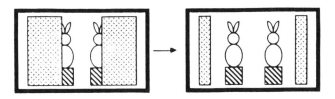

Unexpected Test Event

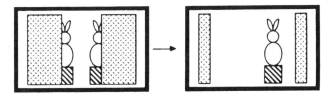

FIG. 7.7. Schematic representation of expected and unexpected test events presented to infants. Notice parts of both objects are visible at one time through the gap.

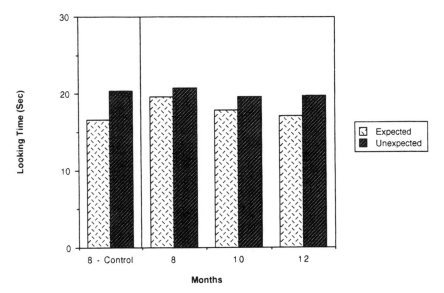

FIG. 7.8. Mean looking times to the unexpected and expected test events by 8-, 10-, and 12-month-old infants. Comparisons marked * indicate significant difference ($p < 0.05$).

Expected Test Event

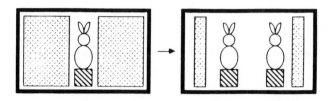

Unexpected Test Event

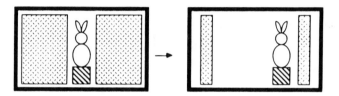

FIG. 7.9.   Schematic representation of the expected and unexpected test events presented to infants. Notice that only one object can be seen at a time through the gap.

sets of experiments investigating two different object properties. It appears that the ability to integrate information over time for the object properties of length and number may not be present until 12 months of age.

CONCLUSIONS

Two programs of research have investigated infants' ability to use motion-carried information for the perception of depth, segregation of figure and ground, and the perception of object properties. If age of appearance provides us with any information regarding underlying processes (and this is surely debatable), then spatial information provided by boundary flow and accretion and deletion of texture may be governed by the same processes. By 5 months, infants are able to use boundary flow information and perhaps accretion and deletion of texture to perceive depth and to segregate figure and ground. Whereas 3-month-olds can perceive the two-dimensional shape of an object specified by accretion and deletion of texture and boundary flow information (Kaufmann-Hayoz et al., 1986), it is unclear whether they possess the ability to segregate figure from ground. Further research is needed to explore the possibility that there is a developmental progression in infants' ability to use accretion and deletion of texture and boundary flow that proceeds from the perception of the relative depth of surfaces to the segregation of surfaces into figure and ground.

In an area where much of the research demonstrates early perceptual capabilities, the second series of studies suggests that the ability to perceive object properties over time develops in the second half of the first year of life. This apparent late development is surprising, given the fact that infants much younger in age appear to possess perceptual and cognitive abilities of the sort needed to complete this task. Several of these abilities are now discussed.

When viewing a moving object behind an aperture, infants (and adults) must be able to perceive the different depth planes of the object and the aperture. In the aperture viewing studies by Arterberry (1989), infants were provided with binocular information and kinetic information for the depth difference between object and aperture. Infants develop sensitivity to binocular disparity around 4 months of age (Fox, Aslin, Shea, & Dumais, 1980; Held, Birch, & Gwiazda, 1980; Petrig, Julesz, Kropfl, Baumgartner, & Anliker, 1981) and are able to use kinetic information to perceive the ordering of two surfaces in depth by at least 5 months of age, as previously discussed. Thus, it seems unlikely that the 8- and 10-month-olds' apparent inability to perceive object properties over time is due to their inability to discriminate the depth planes of the aperture and the objects.

Another ability infants need in order to perceive object properties over time is knowledge that hidden objects or partially hidden objects continue to exist. Baillargeon's work (this volume, chap. 9) suggests that by 5½ months, and maybe by 3½ months of age, infants can represent objects that are no longer in view. Her work suggests that infants also possess some understanding that hidden objects retain their physical and spatial properties. In addition, the research on figure-ground relations presented in this chapter indicates that young infants may be using motion-carried information to represent surfaces that are not in view. Thus, it appears that by 5 months of age infants should have little trouble understanding that the rectangle moving behind the aperture is of a constant size, and that the two rabbits should remain in their perceived positions on the stage.

An ability needed for the perception of the object properties in the present experiments that cannot be overlooked is memory. At a minimum, infants need to detect and remember how long it took for each rectangle to pass and how many objects passed by the aperture. Infants apparently possess memory skills that may be relevant. For example, Baillargeon, DeVos, and Graber (1989) suggested that 8-month-old infants remember the spatial location of a hidden object for up to 70 seconds. While infants appear to retain information about an object's location, there may be a limit on the amount of information they can store. In the aperture task, infants may need to quickly and efficiently store information obtained from the successive views through the aperture (as discussed by Rose, 1988).

It is possible that attentional capacities by themselves or in addition to memory limitations account for the apparent late onset of aperture viewing abilities. Infants until 12 months of age may not be able to maintain their attention for as long as was required in the aperture studies. This possibility can be tested in the future by reducing the amount of time the infant has to attend to the aperture. This can be accomplished by presenting shorter objects or by increasing the velocity of the displays.

At the present time, we cannot rule out the explanations based on infants' memory or attentional limitations. However, we would like to offer an alternative account. Perhaps infants younger than 12 months of age are simply unable to integrate successive views of an object into a single representation (for a related discussion, see Craton & Yonas, 1990b). It is precisely this sort of representational process, one that integrates successively presented information, that Gibson (1966) argued was *not* required for perceiving information over time. Gibson maintained that visual perception is a process that picks up invariant information available over time as easily as it picks up information that is available simultaneously on the retina. But if the perception of temporally extended information is no more complex a problem for the perceiver than the perception of simultaneous structure, then young infants should have no more difficulty perceiving the length of objects moving behind an aperture than they do perceiving the length of the objects when they are in full view. The results summarized in this chapter suggest otherwise and thus provide preliminary support for a non-Gibsonian view of infant perception, one that relies on representational skills.

Moreover, the final story may be more complex. New work (Craton & Baillargeon, 1991; Kaufmann-Hayoz, Kaufmann, & Walther, 1990) provides evidence for priming effects in tasks involving the integration of information presented over time. In Arterberry's (1989) work on object length, infants were required to *construct* a representation over time of the object. If they are presented with a full view of an object that then moves behind an opaque panel and subsequently is revealed over time through an aperture, 8- and 9-month-old infants provide some evidence of perceiving the object's shape. Thus, when infants are first presented with an object in full view, they appear to be able to *recognize* the object when it is subsequently presented over time behind an aperture. This new work suggests a developmental progression in infants' abilities to perceive object properties over time. The reasons for this intriguing asymmetry remain to be explored.

ACKNOWLEDGMENTS

Support for this research was provided by grant HD-16924 from the National Institute of Child Health and Human Development awarded to Albert Yonas and Dissertation Fellowships awarded by the University of Minnesota Graduate

School to Martha Arterberry and Lincoln Craton. We thank Carl Granrud for organizing the symposium and for his helpful comments on an earlier draft.

REFERENCES

Antell, S. H., & Keating, D. P. (1983). Perception of numerical invariance in infancy. *Child Development,* 54, 695–701.

Arterberry, M. E. (1989). *Development of the ability to integrate information over time.* Unpublished doctoral dissertation. University of Minnesota, Minneapolis.

Arterberry, M. E., & Yonas, A. (1988). Infants' sensitivity to kinetic information for three-dimensional object shape. *Perception and Psychophysics, 44,* 1–6.

Baillargeon, R., DeVos, J., & Graber, M. (1989). Location memory in 7- and 8-month-old infants in a nonsearch AB task: Further evidence. *Cognitive Development, 4,* 345–367.

Banks, M. S. (1988). Visual recalibration and the development of contrast and optical flow perception. In A. Yonas (Ed.), *Minnesota symposia in child psychology: Vol. 22. Perceptual development in infancy* (pp. 145–196). Hillsdale, NJ: Lawrence Erlbaum Associates.

Craton, L. G. (1989). *Infants' perception of figure and ground from kinetic stimulus information.* Unpublished doctoral dissertation. University of Minnesota, Minneapolis.

Craton, L. G., & Baillargeon, R. (1991). *Limitations in 13- and 9-month-old infants' temporal integration abilities.* Unpublished manuscript.

Craton, L. G., & Yonas, A. (1988). Infants' sensitivity to boundary flow information for depth at an edge. *Child Development, 59,* 1522–1529.

Craton, L. G., & Yonas, A. (1990a). Kinetic occlusion: Further studies of the boundary flow cue. *Perception and Psychophysics, 47,* 169–179.

Craton, L. G., & Yonas, A. (1990b). The role of motion in infants' perception of occlusion. In J. T. Enns (Ed.), *The development of attention: Research and theory* (pp. 21–46). Amsterdam: Elsevier North Holland.

Fox, R., Aslin, R. N., Shea, S. L., & Dumais, S. T. (1980). Stereopsis in human infants. *Science, 207,* 323–324.

Gibson, J. J. (1950). *Perception of the visual world.* Westport, CT: Greenwood Press.

Gibson, J. J. (1966). *The senses considered as perceptual systems.* Prospect Heights, IL: Waveland Press.

Gibson, J. J. (1979). *The ecological approach to visual perception.* Boston: Houghton Mifflin.

Gibson, J. J., Kaplan, G., Reynolds, H., & Wheeler, K. (1969). The change from visible to invisible: A study of optical transitions. *Perception and Psychophysics, 5,* 113–116.

Granrud, C. E., Yonas, A., Smith, I. M., Arterberry, M. E., Glicksman, M. L., & Sorknes, A. (1984). Infants' sensitivity to accretion and deletion of texture as information for depth at an edge. *Child Development, 55,* 1630–1636.

Held, R., Birch, E., & Gwiazda, J. (1980). Stereoacuity in human infants. *Proceedings of the National Academy of Sciences,* (USA), 77, 5572–5574.

Kaplan, G. (1969). Kinetic disruption of optical texture: The perception of depth at an edge. *Perception and Psychophysics, 6,* 193–198.

Kaufmann-Hayoz, R., Kaufmann, F., & Stucki, M. (1986). Kinetic contours in infants' visual perception. *Child Development, 57,* 353–358.

Kaufmann-Hayoz, R., Kaufmann, R., & Walther, D. (1990, April). *Moving figures seen through a narrow slit.* Paper presented at the International Conference on Infant Studies, Montreal.

Kellman, P. J. (1984). Perception of three-dimensional form by human infants. *Perception and Psychophysics, 36,* 353–358.

Kellman, P. J., & Short, K. (1987). Development of three-dimensional form perception. *Journal of Experimental Psychology: Human Perception and Performance, 13,* 545–557.

Kellman, P. J., & Spelke, E. S. (1983). Perception of partly occluded objects in infancy. *Cognitive Psychology, 15,* 483–524.

Kellman, P. J., Spelke, E. S., & Short, K. R. (1986). Infant perception of object unity from translatory motion in depth and vertical translation. *Cognitive Development, 57,* 72–86.

Marr, D. (1982). *Vision.* San Francisco: Freeman.

Meltzoff, A. N., & Borton, R. W. (1979). Intermodal matching by human neonates. *Science, 282,* 403–404.

Nanez, J., Sr. (1988). Perception of impending collision in 3- to 6-week-old infants. *Infant Behavior and Development, 11,* 447–463.

Owsley, C. (1983). The role of motion in infants' perception of solid shape. *Perception, 12,* 707–717.

Parks, T. (1965). Post-retinal visual storage. *American Journal of Psychology, 78,* 145–147.

Petrig, B., Julesz, B., Kropfl, W., Baumgartner, G., & Anliker, M. (1981). Development of stereopsis and cortical binocularity in human infants: Electrophysiological evidence. *Science, 213,* 1402–1405.

Rock, I. (1981). Anorthoscopic perception. *Scientific American, 244,* 145–153.

Rose, S. A. (1988). Shape recognition in infancy: Visual integration of sequential information. *Child Development, 59,* 1161–1176.

Starkey, P., & Cooper, R. (1980). Perception of numbers by human infants. *Science, 210,* 1033–1035.

Starkey, P., Gelman, R., & Spelke, E. (1985). Detection of number or numerousness by human infants. *Science, 228,* 1222.

Starkey, P., Spelke, E., & Gelman, R. (1983). Detection of intermodal numerical correspondences by human infants. *Science, 222,* 179–181.

Strauss, M. S., & Curtis, L. E. (1984). Development of numerical concepts in infancy. In C. Sophian (Ed.), *Origins of cognitive skills* (pp. 131–155). Hillsdale, NJ: Lawrence Erlbaum Associates.

Thompson, W. B., Craton, L. G., & Yonas, A. (1988, May). The 2¾-D sketch: Psychophysical and biological approaches to computer vision. *Proceedings of the AAAI workshop spring symposium series.* Palo Alto, CA.

Thompson, W. B., Mutch, K. B., & Berzins, V. A. (1985). Dynamic occlusion analysis in optical flow fields. *IEEE Transactions on Pattern Analysis and Machine Intelligence, PAM 1-7,* 374–383.

Wagner, S. H., & Sakovits, L. J. (1986). A process analysis of infant visual and cross-modal recognition memory: Implications for an amodal code. In L. P. Lipsitt & C. Rovee-Collier (Eds.), *Advances in infancy research* (pp. 196–217). Norwood, NJ: Ablex.

Yonas, A., Arterberry, M. E., & Granrud, C. E. (1987a). Four-month-old infants' sensitivity to binocular and kinetic information for three-dimensional object shape. *Child Development, 58,* 910–917.

Yonas, A., Arterberry, M. E., & Granrud, C. E. (1987b). Space perception in infancy. In R. Vasta (Ed.), *Annals of child development* (pp. 1–34). Greenwich, CT: JAI Press.

Yonas, A., Craton, L. G., & Thompson, W. B. (1987). Relative motion: Kinetic information for the order of depth at an edge. *Perception and Psychophysics, 41,* 53–59.

Yonas, A., & Granrud, C. E. (1984). The development of sensitivity to kinetic, binocular, and pictorial depth information in human infants. In D. Engle, D. Lee, & M. Jeannerod (Eds.), *Brain mechanisms and spatial vision* (pp. 113–145). Dordrecht: Martinus Nijhoff.

Yonas, A., & Granrud, C. E. (1985). Reaching as a measure of infants' spatial perception. In G. Gottlieb & N. Krasnegor (Eds.), *Measurement of audition and vision in the first year of life: A methodological overview* (pp. 301–322). Norwood, NJ: Ablex.

Yonas, A., Pettersen, L., & Lockman, J. (1979). Young infants' sensitivity to optical information for collision. *Canadian Journal of Psychology, 33,* 1285–1290.

Future-Oriented Processes in Infancy: The Case of Visual Expectations

Marshall M. Haith
University of Denver

I have been interested in a problem for almost 25 years, sparked by observations during a postdoctoral fellowship with William Kessen at Yale from 1964 to 1966. The problem concerns how babies organize their current activity around future events. This chapter summarizes progress that several collaborators and I have made on this problem in the past few years and describes some ancillary issues that have emerged from our work.

As several other chapters in this volume illustrate, researchers have made stunning progress in understanding infant visual perception and cognition since the 1960s. To a large extent, this understanding is based on infants' reactions to currently available input: for example, discrimination and preference to tell us about infants' pattern, shape, color, motion, and depth perception (see, for example, Banks & Salapatek, 1983). We have also learned a lot about processes that depend on past input: short- and long-term memory, retroactive interference, and memory generalization. So, we have done well with processes that focus on the present and the past.

However, our progress has been less satisfactory with processes that depend on the future. Such future-oriented processes include goal formation and motivation, intention, planning, expectation, and set. When one unpacks what is involved in a future-oriented process (FOP), the domain becomes especially interesting, because the exercise usually reveals that a FOP depends both on present conditions and how those conditions have unfolded in the past. As Wentworth (1988) observed, FOPs require a knitting together of the past and the present, so they can integrate perspectives of the past, the present, and the future.

FOPs are pervasive even in fairly low-level sensorimotor actions. For example, Aslin (1981) pointed out that even smooth eye tracking of a moving visual target requires moment-to-moment expectations about the trajectory of the target. If the target were repeatedly fixated on an ad hoc basis, tracking would be jerky, with approximately 300 msec fixations, separated by single or multiple saccades. In fact, infant eye tracking of smoothly moving visual targets is initially jerky and becomes increasingly smooth after about 2 months of age (Aslin, 1987); this shift may reflect, in part, the development of skill in forming visual expectations. Effective manual reaching for objects also seems to involve feed-forward components, a prospect that is supported by careful attempts to model this activity (Bullock & Grossberg, 1988). Evidence for feed-forward processes is also available for manual reaching in infants. For example, von Hofsten (1983) has demonstrated that infants make predictive reaches to a future location of a moving target rather than to its current location. By 9 months of age, as the baby reaches for an object, his or her hand adjusts for the object's size just before contact (von Hofsten & Ronnqvist, 1988). Reach and grasp adjustments may be made even earlier. Infants who are 5½ months old select one hand to reach for an object rotating clockwise and the other hand to reach for the same object when it is rotating counterclockwise (Wentworth, Benson, & Haith, 1989). In fact, it is hard to imagine that smooth actions could be accomplished in the absence of anticipatory elements, what von Hofsten and others have termed *prospective control.*

One important reason why FOPs are necessary for efficient action is that there is a significant delay in the body's ability to respond to signals. Both the inertia of body mass and the afferent and efferent delays in the nervous system contribute to this delay. In the absence of future perspective, people would bump into walls before reorienting their bodies, they would drive their cars into curbs and walls, step into puddles rather than over them, and have a devilish time trying to negotiate rocky beaches and even steps. Carnivorous predators would become extinct (Lee, 1989).

The implications of FOPs for behavior extend well beyond their role in the on-line execution of adept sensorimotor behavior. The "why" of action execution has become the next frontier for so-called *emergent* or *dynamic* accounts of action. Dynamic theories provide excellent accounts of the coordination and phase changes in motor behavior without appealing to higher level executive processes, but such theories provide little understanding of why actions occur in the first place and why they are directed toward some targets and not others. A complete account of actions must include provisions for goal selection and motivation, and this stipulation includes the reaching, crawling, and walking infant (Aslin, 1989; Benson, 1990; von Hofsten, 1988).

One need not limit discussion about FOPs to issues that involve observable actions. Concepts such as expectation, set, and priming occupy central status in every major current theory of cognition. The case is no clearer than in script and schema theories for which expectations fill default slots and guide memory, judgment, search, and perception (Biederman, Glass, & Stacy, 1973; Goodman, 1980; Schank & Abelson, 1977). Modern theories of learning give equal emphasis to the central role of expectations (Bolles, 1972; Holyoak, Kol, & Nisbett, 1989; Rescorla, 1975). The conclusion that FOPs are immanent in virtually everything we think or do seems inescapable. Thus, an understanding of how FOPs emerge in early development may tell us something about the cognitive and perceptual life of the infant.

As already mentioned, however, very little information exists in the general domain of FOPs in infancy. This claim holds for the one aspect of this larger domain to which this chapter is limited: the aspect of visual expectations. Some might challenge this statement, arguing that habituation studies often depend on infants' expectations for familiar events to display recovery of interest to a novel event (e.g., Kagan, 1970). However, habituation and recovery studies do not, in fact, demonstrate an expectation prior to exposure to a novel event; the event may itself activate a search process that produces a different outcome depending on whether it is recognized as familiar or novel.

Even if one grants the tenuous assumption that the infant's recovery of interest to a novel stimulus requires that he or she had formed an expectation for a familiar stimulus, the putative expectation plays a negative role. The role of expectation in habituation theory is to effect disregard of familiar inputs. In contrast, in the examples I mentioned earlier, expectations play a positive role in the guidance of smooth behavior, decision making, cognitive processing of dynamic events, and cognitive organization. My focus here is on the active role that expectations play in the processing of ongoing events and in the guidance of action.

It is useful to start with the example that triggered my interest in how expectations appeared to guide action and led to the research effort that is described here. In 1965, William Kessen, Doris Collins, and I were studying how 4-month-old infants respond to different levels of visual complexity (Haith, Kessen, & Collins, 1969). Complexity was defined in terms of the predictability in the sequence of onsets of red lights in a 3 × 3 array. The study focused on the effects of complexity on limb movement. Babies can be contrary, however, and they sometimes revealed more with their eyes than with their limbs. A very interesting event often occurred near the beginning of the experiment. One group of babies received a left-to-right sequence of three lights (no interstimulus interval) on the top row of the matrix (see Fig. 8.1). The offset of the rightmost light was followed by onset of the light just below it. Babies usually fixated each of the first three lights in turn but, surprisingly, many of them then fixated to the right of Light 3, where there was nothing, rather than to the illuminated light just below Light 3. Nothing had ever appeared in the location to the right

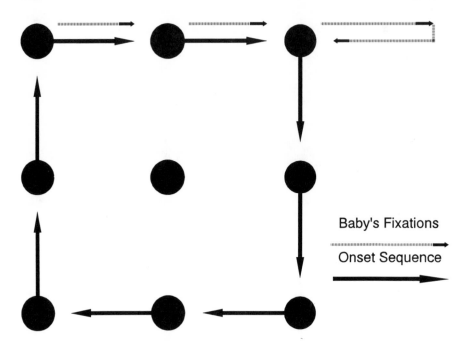

FIG. 8.1.   Diagram of 3 × 3 light matrix (circles), the sequence of light onsets
(solid lines), and the sequence of the first few visual fixations (dotted lines) for
one infant in Haith, Kessen, and Collins (1972).

of Light 3, and the baby's "errant" tendency seemed to disappear after the
early cycles of repetition of this sequence. Of course, there are several interpretations of this observation. Babies might simply have an inertial tendency to
continue moving their eyes in the same direction, a tendency that is suppressed
with repeated exposures to the actual visual sequence. Or, babies may rapidly
form a tendency to repeat a previously reinforced response; if an eye movement to the right had just produced fixation of an interesting stimulus fractions
of a second earlier, the likelihood of making another eye movement to the right
might increase. The most interesting interpretation is that babies abstracted
directionality and time in the sequence, formed an expectation that the direction of events would continue and executed an eye-movement command based
on that expectation at about the time that Light 3 went off; increasing exposure
to the actual sequence gradually produced a conflicting expectation that a light
below would go on rather than a light to the right, and the additional eye movement to the right ceased.

   If this latter interpretation were correct, the implications for addressing questions about how infants form expectations for future events and translate these
expectations into action would be substantial. Babies can control the movements
of their eyes much earlier than they are able to reach for, or effectively act on,

objects. In fact, the eye-movement system is more mature at birth than any other motor system the baby possesses, at least with respect to the adult state. Because eye movements are relatively fast, and visual signals are processed quickly, a paradigm might be developed that places minimal memory demands on the infant and that ties into his or her ongoing flow of activity. A crucial feature of this phenomenon is that it occurred naturally, with no explicit training at all. Thus, one might be able to capitalize on a natural tendency of the baby, as had Fantz (1961) and others in studying habituation. At the same time, positive rather than negative acquisition might be available for observation. There were, however, several limitations with the original setup: The simple colored lights did not hold the infants' interest for very long; it was necessary to present several light onsets before one could obtain a data point for a critical direction change; one light was always on, so the baby's tendency to generate an anticipatory fixation required suppression of a tendency to fixate an available stimulus; and the setup provided limited opportunity for simplifying or for complicating the cognitive demands of the task. Recently, we succeeded in developing a procedure that overcomes these limitations while also capitalizing on the control, speed, and limited memory-demand advantages afforded by the infant visual system. We refer to this new procedure as the *visual expectation paradigm*.

THE VISUAL EXPECTATION PARADIGM
AND THE FIRST STUDY

The visual expectation paradigm shares features with the light-matrix paradigm portrayed in Fig. 8.1, but it also differs in a number of respects. In both, discrete visual events appear, and one infers expectations from eye movement activity. In the visual expectation paradigm, however, the visual stimuli appear in only two locations; an interstimulus interval (ISI) separates the appearance of successive stimuli; and the stimuli vary, are multicolored, and move up and down. The interval between pictures provides a time window in which one can observe anticipatory fixations.

In the first study, babies saw a series of pictures, presented one at a time, centered 5.7° to the left or right of the center of their visual field. The pictures appeared for 700 msec, and moved down and back up again at a rate of 4.4 °/sec, completing one full cycle for each exposure. The pictures were images of multicolored bull's eyes, checkerboards, schematic faces, and diagonal lines. Between the appearances of successive pictures, an ISI occurred; this was a constant 1,100 msec for an alternating series (e.g., left, right, left, right, etc.) and varied among the values 900, 1,100, and 1,300 msec for an irregular series (e.g., left, left, right, left, etc.). The time scheme for three picture presentations for the alternating series is shown in Fig. 8.2. Babies saw 30 pictures in an alternating left–right (L–R) sequence and 30 pictures in an irregular spatial sequence in

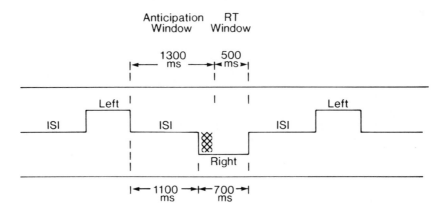

FIG. 8.2. Schematic diagram of the timing of three picture onsets and their associated ISIs for the alternating sequence in the first study of infant visual expectations. Time windows indicate when fixations were considered as anticipations or as reactions to picture onset.

which the ISI varied. Half the babies saw the sequences in an alternating–irregular sequence and half the babies saw them in an irregular–alternating sequence. The whole experiment lasted about 102 seconds (Haith, Hazan, & Goodman, 1988).

Before continuing, clarification of three key terms is called for. Discussions in the literature often use the terms *expectation* and *anticipation* interchangeably and fail to distinguish when a cognitive construct as opposed to an observable action is being referenced. Here, the term *expectation* has the status of a cognitive/perceptual or mental construct that refers to the forecasting of a future event. An expectation is inferred from the timing of fixations that fit the behavioral categories of anticipation or facilitation. *Anticipation* refers to an appropriate action that begins prior to an event. *Facilitation* refers to enhancement of behavior (e.g., faster reaction) after the event occurs (when, of course, there was no anticipation). Figure 8.2 displays the time windows we used to measure anticipation and facilitation. The baby was credited with an anticipation if he or she shifted fixation to the side opposite the prior picture side either during the ISI or within 200 msec after picture onset (200 msec is near the fastest time adults were able to respond to stimulus onset in our setup). If the baby did not anticipate the stimulus, his or her reaction time (RT) was calculated for that event. Faster RTs for the alternating series than for the irregular series would constitute facilitation, presumably reflecting the presence of an expectation.

Figure 8.3 illustrates the experimental arrangement. The baby saw slide-projected pictures, reflected in an overhead two-way mirror tilted at a 45° angle. (For later studies, the arrangement was converted to computer-animated images on a color monitor.) Behind the mirror, an infrared TV camera recorded

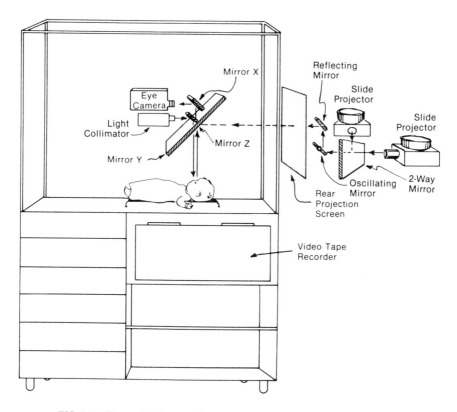

FIG. 8.3. Portrayal of the recording and stimulus-presentation arrangement used in the first expectancy study. Stimuli were presented by the two projectors through computer-controlled tachistoscopic shutters. The beam from one projector reflected from a two-way mirror, and the beam from the other was transmitted through the two-way mirror. Both beams reflected from an oscillating mirror and a first-surface reflecting mirror before forming an image on the projection screen. One projector presented stimuli positioned on the right, and the other presented stimuli positioned on the left. The infant viewed the stimuli by reflection from Mirror Y. An infrared collimator illuminated the baby's eye by reflection from Mirror Z and transmission through Mirror Y. The image of the baby's eye was recorded by the infrared TV camera after passing through Mirrors Y and Z and reflecting from Mirror X.

the image of the eye. A time/date record was superimposed on the image of the eye, one digit of which denoted onset of the left or right picture. The interval between stimulus onset and fixation shifts was measured by counting video frames with stop-frame and slow-motion analyses. Figure 8.4 displays a tracking sequence for one baby in the alternating condition.

Table 8.1 displays the results for the whole experiment. Baseline RTs were taken for the first five pictures, as a measure of raw RT without the influence of expectations. Note the relation between the baseline and the post-baseline

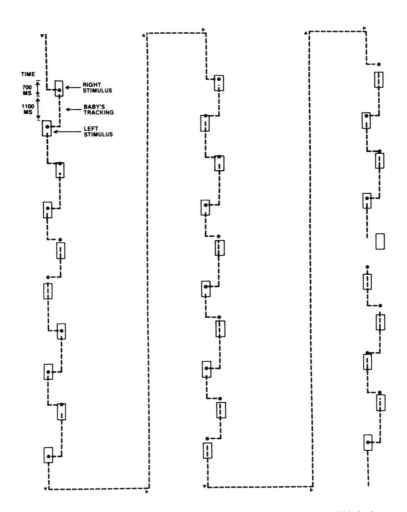

FIG. 8.4. Diagram of a fixation-tracking sequence for a 3½-month-old baby in the alternating condition. Time flows from top to bottom for each block of 10 pictures and from left to right for successive blocks. The outlined boxes represent picture onsets on the left and right sides, and the space between successive boxes represents the ISI. The dashed line represents the position of the baby's fixations. Fixation at the location of the impending picture during the ISI or within 200 msec of its onset were counted as anticipations; these are particularly frequent in the present diagram for the second and third blocks of trials (columns 2 and 3).

TABLE 8.1
Median RTs and Percent of Anticipations for the
First Infant Visual Expectation Study

	Sequence			
	Alternating Early		Alternating Late	
	Alternating	Irregular	Alternating	Irregular
Reaction Times:				
Baseline RT (median)	475	. . .	. . .	462
Median RT	409	445	373	478
Categories of RT (%):				
Fast (200–300 msec)	27.8	20.8	29.6	20.4
Intermed. (300–450 msec)	32.3	33.2	43.8	23.2
Slow (>450 msec)	39.9	46.0	26.6	56.4
Percent of Anticipation	10.4	7.4	33.7	14.8

median RTs for the irregular conditions. These values are 469 msec and 462 msec, respectively, for the two order (alternating early, alternating late) groups combined (not shown as combined medians in Table 8.1), or virtually no difference. Thus, there is no evidence of a practice effect; RTs were about the same for the first five pictures as for pictures presented unpredictably later in the series.

Apparently, babies did form expectations during the alternating series. Compared to the irregular series, the alternating series produced: (a) a reliably larger decline in RT from baseline; (b) a reliably higher percent of fast RTs (200 to 300 msec); and (c) a reliably lower percent of slow RTs (greater than 450 msec). Additionally, the percent of anticipations for the order groups combined (alternating or irregular series first), was twice as large for the alternating than for the irregular condition. The alternating sequence only lasted 51 sec, so expectations were formed quickly. A follow-up analysis revealed that babies who produced at least one anticipation in the alternating series produced their first anticipation, on average, on the 11th event. The 11th event occurred about 16 to 17 sec into the series, after only five onsets on that particular side.

An apparent anomaly in the data is a strikingly higher percent of anticipations when the alternating series occurred late (events 31 to 60) than when it occurred early, 33.7% versus 10.4%, respectively. We have replicated this finding and believe that it reflects a "dazzle" effect. The infants saw events that were novel, that appeared and disappeared, that changed color and form, and that moved up and down. They probably needed some time to adapt to these lower order physical changes before they could detect the higher order temporal and spatial regularities. Still, even in the early-alternation condition, RTs were significantly lower than both baseline and the irregular control condition.

The percent of anticipations during the alternating series may seem low, but there are several factors to consider in interpreting the absolute values. There was no extrinsic "payoff" for the baby to anticipate each picture; pictures appeared no matter what they did, and they could easily see each picture simply by waiting for it to appear and then fixating it. Thus, one might easily ask why infants made any anticipatory fixations at all. Additionally, the percent of anticipations represents all of the data, including both the pictures that appeared before the baby formed expectations as well as the pictures that appeared late in the series, when the baby's interest may have waned. Finally, one can report the anticipations in terms of how they were distributed across the alternating and irregular series, similar to how investigators typically report looking time distributions for habituation studies across the novel and familiar stimuli (i.e., percent of stimulus-looking time rather than total amount of time, because babies may look at the stimuli only 50% or less of the total time possible); this creates quite a different picture. For example, 68% of the anticipations were made in the regular series and 32% were made in the irregular series (actually side shifts during the anticipation window, which may or may not have coincided with a subsequent picture at that location). It is not unusual in habituation studies for a 53%/47% distribution of fixation time for novel and familiar stimuli to be significant.

These data suggest that babies as young as 3½ months of age rapidly detect spatial and temporal regularities that govern a spatial sequence. More importantly, they are able to form expectations for the impending events in a series and to support adaptive action based on those expectations. In the case of anticipation, the adaptive action (an accurate refixation) is triggered in the absence of visual input; in the case of facilitation, there is a coordination between the expectation and the sensory input that enhances adaptive action.

An exciting aspect of this paradigm is that it permits a peek at the infant's online processing of events in contrast to traditional approaches that depend on postprocessing. For example, consider the typical habituation paradigm used for studying discrimination of one stimulus from another. Investigators focus almost exclusively on postfamiliarization performance for evidence that the novel stimulus is discriminated from the familiar stimulus. However, many of the most interesting questions concern what is going on during the knowledge-acquisition process. There is an analogy here to research on reading. More traditional approaches typically question the reader after the text is completed. Eye movement recordings, however, permit indications of how the brain processes text on-line. In the latter instance, one's access to many of the processes of interest is considerably more direct.

Visual Expectation: A Multifaceted Phenomenon

These findings have spurred research in several different directions rather than a program of work that lies along a neatly defined path. Partly, this reflects the newness of the effort: a new paradigm, the relatively unexplored process of expectation, and new measures. To date, four themes have guided our thinking and research: expectancy formation as a process, a tool, a model, and a window on the baby's agenda.

Visual Expectation as a Process. There are important questions to ask about expectation as a process. These questions include whether the visual expectation paradigm really taps expectations or whether, instead, the findings reflect something unique to an alternating visual spatial series that has nothing to do with FOPs. If "true" expectations are involved, what sort of model will best describe what is going on? Can a conditioning model do the trick? What brain circuits support expectations? For example, might there be a correspondence between behavioral indices of expectation and the expectancy wave? The paradigm shares many features with the delayed-alternation paradigm that Goldman-Rakic (1989) has used to study the evolution of prefrontal lobe functioning in rhesus monkeys. That is, the subject performs in the absence of a stimulus, must remember a prior spatial location and responds to a current location on the basis of a rule of alternation. The brain circuits that support the rhesus monkey's performance of this task have been mapped as completely as the circuits for any other known cognitive function. Could the same circuits be involved in the visual expectation paradigm? What is the developmental course of the ability to form expectations? Do individual differences exist in this capacity?

Visual Expectation as a Tool. Joe Campos and I (Haith & Campos, 1977) have noted elsewhere that researchers in infancy have gone through similar stages in their thinking about generalized concepts such as learning and habituation. At first, the processes themselves capture interest and are thought of as unitary phenomena with a particular brain locus. Parametric studies explore such properties as their acquisition and decay, their stability, and their physiological underpinnings. Gradually, the spotlight shifts from the process, qua process, toward its value as a tool for studying other phenomena. For example, the process of habituation has served as a valuable tool for studying visual acuity, color vision, shape discrimination, and memory, to name only a few examples. The process of expectation and the paradigm that is being used to study it have similar potential for studying several phenomena and, perhaps, an unusual potential for exploring skills of a more dynamic nature than current tools. One example is the infant's capability for representing ongoing events. Does the baby construct a rule for the visual series it sees or can one appeal to a "simpler" conditioning explanation? If a rule is formed, how complicated are the rules that infants can represent? In forming an expectation, is the baby representing spatial location, time, stimulus content, or a mix of these possibilities? (The term *representation* will be used here to refer to stored information and not to symbols.)

Visual Expectation as a Model. The visual system is special. Other than touch, it is the only system that shares both motor and sensory capacities, and it far exceeds the parallel processing capacities of other sensory systems. As a motor system, it is unique in depending primarily on nonmodulated (ballistic) movements and in providing extremely limited proprioceptive feedback about its status. No other motor system is as fast nor controls so little mass. There is a question, then, about how much our understanding of expectation formation in the visual system will help us to create a general model of expectation formation for other action systems (like reaching or crawling, for example). Additionally, if FOPs constitute a sensible category, will our understanding of the process of forming visual expectations tell us anything that will help us model other FOPs (like goal orientation or planning)?

Visual Expectation as a Window on the Baby's Agenda. Inadequate attention has been directed to the question of why babies deploy their perceptual skills in the way they do. An adequate answer might tell us something about how the baby is put together to get what it needs and to make sense of its world (Haith, 1980). One can ask why the baby might form expectations for regularity and then act on those expectations rather than simply reacting to events. A solid answer may tell us something about what the baby is trying to accomplish and how it develops a knowledge base in the early months of life.

These are themes that run through the studies I now describe. Most of the studies touch several of these themes and, in fact, the themes overlap in important ways.

Studies of Visual Expectation

Can Babies Form Expectations for Event Sequences That are More Complex Than Alternation? Several issues arise in a strong interpretation of the data based on the symmetrical, alternating, series described in Study 1. An important issue is whether there might have been a natural rhythm or oscillation that became entrained to the alternating series. If so, one might argue that the entrained rhythm sped up with time, producing what looked like faster RTs and anticipations. A second issue relates to what kind of model can account for the data. Can a conditioning model account for the observations, a model that might consider the conditioned stimulus (CS) to be light-offset on one side, and the unconditional stimulus (UCS) light-onset on the other? Even if the baby was using a rule in Study 1 to govern the detection–expectation–action sequence, the rule was extraordinarily simple. Are babies able to represent more complicated rules than simple alternation? Rick Canfield and I carried out a study that addressed these questions by using asymmetrical series (Canfield, 1988; Canfield & Haith, 1991). The basic paradigm was modified to increase the number of times a picture remained on one of the sides for some babies. Figure 8.5 presents a schematic of the four groups of 2- and 3-month-old babies in this study: one group received the original 1/1 or alternating series; a second group received a 2/1 series: two events on one side, followed by one event on the

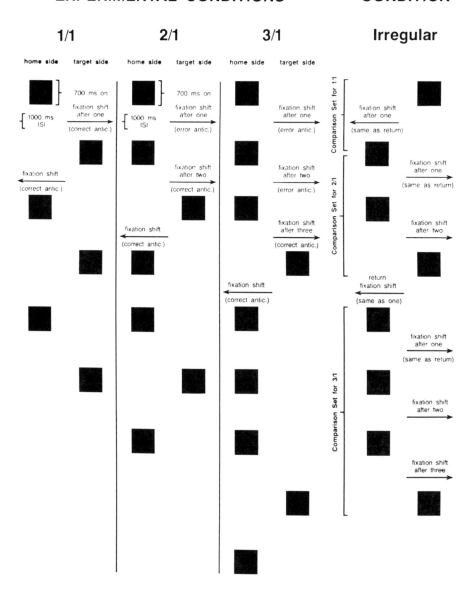

FIG. 8.5. Diagram of the locations of the series of pictures for the four groups in the Canfield (1988) study. Time flows from top to bottom and each column represents the series for a different group. The solid boxes represent the picture onsets for each group.

other (e.g., L, L, R, L, L, R, etc.); a third group received a 3/1 series (L, L, L, R, L, L, L, R, etc.); a fourth group received an irregular series, in which 1/1, 2/1, or 3/1 minisequences were embedded for comparison with the other groups.

The question was whether or not infants would adjust their fixation shifts appropriately for the 2/1 or 3/1 series. Notice that for these groups expectations for an event to appear on one side was based on a different number of pictures (or duration) than for the other side. For example, in the 3/1 condition an expectation for an event on the right side ("target" side) might follow three left ("home" side) events, whereas an expectation for the event on the left, home, side would follow only one right, target, event. Figure 8.6 shows a tracking sequence for one infant in the 2/1 condition.

Between-subject analyses were possible for all of the rule-based conditions compared to the irregular condition in which 1/1, 2/1, or 3/1 minisequences were embedded. Additionally, within-subject comparisons could be made for the 2/1 and 3/1 conditions for relative frequency of side shifts. Here, one simply compares the percent of appropriate shifts with inappropriate shifts (e.g., in the 3/1 condition comparing the percent of shifts to the opposite side after three home events with the percent after one or two home events).

These analyses revealed the following for the 3-month-olds:

1. Babies in the 2/1 condition made significantly more correct anticipations from both sides than did comparison groups (see Fig. 8.7). That is, their fixations were more likely to shift sides after two events on the home side than for the irregular (fourth) condition or than the babies in the 3/1 condition. Additionally, their fixations were more likely to shift back to the home side after one target fixation than for the irregular condition. Thus, the anticipation data provided evidence for expectations both on the target side and on the home side.

2. Babies in the same 2/1 condition produced lower RTs to the target (after two home events) than did their counterparts for comparable episodes in the irregular condition. Thus, the facilitation data provided further evidence for expectations for the target event.

3. Babies in the 3/1 condition did *not* produce more anticipatory shifts to the target side after 3 home events than did controls for comparable episodes, but they did show a higher likelihood of returning home after one target-side event. Further, the within-subject analysis revealed that they were significantly more likely to make a target-side shift after three home events than after one or two events.

Thus, the anticipation data provided mixed evidence for expectations of the target after three home events. A plot of the RT drop from baseline reveals the predicted monotonic function of a decreasing effect with increasing complexity of the task (i.e., 1/1, 2/1, 3/1, irregular; see Fig. 8.8).

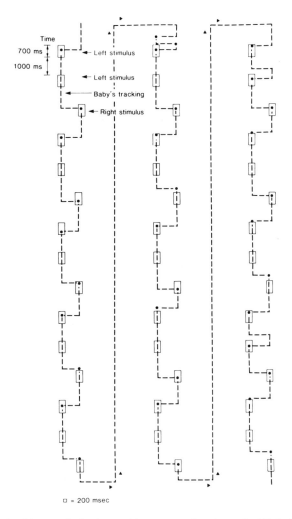

Time

700 ms

1000 ms

← Left stimulus

← Left stimulus

── Baby's tracking

← Right stimulus

□ = 200 msec

FIG. 8.6. Diagram of a fixation-tracking sequence for a 3-month-old baby in the 2/1 condition of the Canfield (1988) study. Time flows from top to bottom for each block of 15 pictures and from left to right for successive blocks. The outlined boxes represent picture onsets on the left and right sides, and the space between successive boxes represents the ISI. The dashed line represents the position of the baby's fixations. Fixation shifts from one side to the other during the ISI or within 200 msec of picture onset were counted as anticipations (sometimes incorrect). Correct anticipations occurred only on the target side in column 1, a single target-side anticipation accompanied three home-side anticipations in column 2, and two target-side pictures were anticipated in column 3, along with all five home-side opportunities.

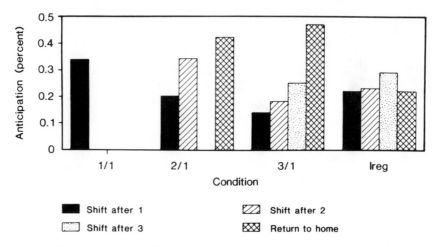

FIG. 8.7. Percent of shifts (anticipations when correct) for 3-month-olds during the anticipation window for each picture in a cycle for each of the four groups.

The 2-month-olds provided evidence for expectations in the 1/1 condition over the irregular condition but little evidence of expectations in the 2/1 or 3/1 conditions (see Fig. 8.9). What little evidence existed suggested that they suppressed shifting sides after one event on the home side in the 2/1 and 3/1 conditions. Perhaps they learned what not to do, but little else.

In summary, it appears that by 3 months of age, babies can develop simultaneous expectations for one number (or duration) of events in one place and another number (or duration) in another place. These data demonstrate that

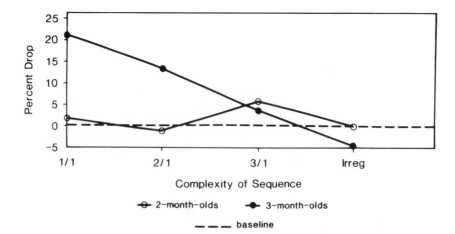

FIG. 8.8. Percent decline of RT for 3-month-olds from baseline for target events that were not anticipated.

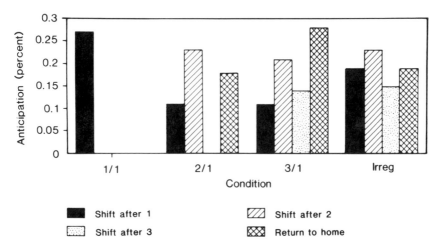

FIG. 8.9. Percent of shifts (anticipations when correct) for 2-month-olds during the anticipation window for each picture in a cycle for each of the four groups.

the expectation phenomenon is not limited to a simple alternating series. Therefore, these data pose serious problems for interpretations that depend on entrainment or oscillator models. Further, a simple conditioning model of the form $CS_{offset-left} \rightarrow UCS_{onset-right}$ is insufficient to account for the ability of infants to suppress eye movements when appropriate—for example, after one event on the home side in either the 2/1 or 3/1 conditions. On the positive side, the results suggest that by 3 months of age, babies can acquire one rule for one side, concurrent with a different rule for the other (or, perhaps, a single, more complex rule), and that babies seem to be able to represent something about number or time or the combination of the two. These capabilities appear to take shape between 2 and 3 months of age.

How Stable are Babies in Their Tendency to Form Expectations? If the visual expectation paradigm taps a cognitive capacity in infants, one might expect that capacity to be stable over at least short intervals. A second reason for asking about stability is more methodological. The RT measure seems applicable to a large number of questions; it would be useful to know if it is a measure that possesses any stability. Data on infant RT are very rare in the literature; we know of only one study of infant RT (Aslin & Salapatek, 1975) other than those employing a variant of the visual expectation paradigm. A typical way to test for behavioral stability on a task is to compare split-half performance. Because the visual expectation paradigm comprises a fairly large number of events (60), split-half comparisons are possible; however, the interpretation is not straightforward. The state and moods of babies fluctuate daily and, sometimes, minute to minute. Split-half stability might reflect more about state differences between babies than about cognitive differences. Therefore, it is important to observe babies on different days.

The study involved twenty-three 3-month-old babies in two sessions separated by 3 to 7 days (Haith & McCarty, 1990). In each session the babies saw 60 pictures in the alternating series taken from the basic paradigm. Split-half correlations were calculated for each session separately, and between-session correlations were calculated for both RTs and percent of anticipations. As shown in Table 8.2, the correlations were stable for several measures of RT for both split-half and between-session analyses. The correlation for anticipations was stable for both split-half session analyses and just missed significance for the between-session analysis (see Table 8.2).

Aside from providing the first evidence of stability of infant RTs, this study also provided leads for ways to look at RT. One problem is that babies seem to master the alternation rule at different times; afterward, they seem to become less interested in anticipating and making fast responses. When an infant's performance is averaged over all 60 events, a number of scores may be included that reflect this variable motivation. It would be desirable to obtain an index of how well a baby can do when it is performing its best. This logic led to the formulation of a measure of optimal performance. The optimal RT measure was the fastest median of a 10-trial block, presumably a time when the baby was maximally "tuned in." This optimal score correlated $r = .68$ between sessions—

TABLE 8.2
Median RTs and Percent Anticipations for the Infant Expectation Reliability Study

Variable	Means		Between-Session	Within-Session Correlations	
			Correlations	Split-Half	
	Visit 1	Visit 2		Visit 1	Visit 2
Anticipation Measure					
Percent Anticipation	17.4	19.4	$r = .34$†	$r = .51$**	$r = .52$**
Reaction Time Measures					
Baseline Median	534ms	490ms	$r = .52$**		
Postbaseline Median	480ms	445ms	$r = .48$*	$r = .47$*	$r = .69$***
Percent Fast (201–300 ms)	11.3	14.2	$r = .65$***	$r = .43$*	$r = .52$**
Percent Slow (>467 ms)	54.1	46.8	$r = .52$**	$r = .42$*	$r = .77$***
Median of Fastest Block	402ms	393ms	$r = .68$***		

†$p < .055$, one-tailed
*$p < .05$
**$p < = .01$
***$p < .001$

at this age, a very substantial correlation, indeed. However, one might question whether this correlation reflected anything at all about expectations; perhaps babies are simply wired differently, and when they are performing maximally, their wiring differences stand out most clearly. It would be useful to separate out the influence of raw RT, based primarily on the influence of neural wiring, from the effect of expectations on RT. The purest measure of raw RT in this study consisted of the baseline reactions taken for the first several RTs during each session. When the correlation between the baseline RTs and the optimal scores was partialed out, the correlation between optimal scores dropped only slightly to $r = .61$. Thus, despite the fact that raw RT (as measured by the baseline score) was stable across sessions ($r = .52$), there was also stability in the facilitating effect of expectations on optimal performance. Another indication that babies' tendencies to form expectations were playing a role in the stability of the RTs was revealed in an examination of where in the series their optimal performance block occurred. Presumably, the placement of this block reflected how quickly each baby mastered the rule; the cross-session correlation for this measure was stable ($r = .44$). The conclusion is that babies are stable in raw RT as well as in the speed and extent to which they form expectations.

The studies that have been described have all reached the publication stage. In order to provide examples of the potential for this line of work, I now discuss several studies that have not yet reached this level of finalization but are sufficiently far along to permit a progress report.

What Information do Infants Encode in Forming Expectations?   In forming expectations, the baby must somehow represent or map at least some aspects of the series it sees. There are three possible aspects that the baby might map: space, time, or content. Because the stimulus content changed from one picture onset to the next (bull's eyes, faces, stripes, checkerboards), content could not have supported the formation of expectations in those studies (but see further on). Apparently, babies can map spatial location to some extent; otherwise, anticipatory fixations to a location prior to stimulus appearance would be impossible. There is, however, no solid evidence that time predictability plays any role at all. Even for enhanced RTs, if the baby was able to predict the next location of a picture, that cue alone may have provided the basis for formation of an expectation and reduced the RT to picture onset. The following study was designed to explore the roles of space and time cues in the formation of visual expectations (McCarty, 1989).

Although the question of whether babies use time or space information is straightforward, finding a means to an answer can become complex, especially in varying the predictability of spatial location. In prior studies, babies saw pictures that appeared in only two locations; even for the irregular series, there was not a lot of uncertainty for the next picture location. Thus, it made sense to create some conditions for which pictures could appear in any of several locations to increase location uncertainty. However, there is then a problem in comparing one baby's RT for an eye movement to various locations with that of another baby who only moves his or her eyes to two locations, for example, the ±6° horizontal locations used in prior studies. Eye movements along the horizontal axis are typically made faster than those along the vertical or diagonal axes, and larger eye movements are typically initiated more slowly than smaller eye movements. It may also be the case that the time interval following offset of a prior picture affects the RT for the next picture. In order to be able to attribute potential RT differences only to differences in the formation of expectations, it was necessary to set up comparisons between babies for fixation shifts that had the same initial and terminal locations and the same ISIs, but which were predictable for one group and not for the other. This was accomplished by embedding identical minisequences (e.g., $+6°_{onset} \rightarrow 1000$ msec ISI $\rightarrow -6°_{onset}$ or vice versa) either in a context of identical events or in a context of unpredictable events. There was a cost; for most comparisons between groups, data were available for only the minisequences, one sixth of all the pictures.

Four groups of 3-month-old babies were used; all pictures appeared for 700 msec. The conditions were as follows:

Group 1. Time and location predictable: Pictures appeared in alternating locations (±6° on the horizontal axis) with a 1000 msec ISI.

Group 2. Only spatial location predictable: Pictures appeared in alternating locations (±6° on the horizontal axis) with ISIs that varied randomly among the values 700, 1,000, and 1,300 msec.

Group 3. Only time interval predictable: Pictures appeared in one of six locations (±12° or ±6° along the horizontal axis or ±6° on the vertical axis) in a constrained random series, but always with a 1,000 msec ISI.

Group 4. Neither time nor location predictable: Pictures appeared in the same constrained random series as for Group 3 but with ISIs that varied randomly as for Group 2.

For every group, multiples of the fifth and sixth events were identical and involved the ±6° horizontal locations: for example, onset of a picture at +6° followed by a 1000 msec ISI, and then onset of a picture at −6° (see Fig. 8.10).

This study is still in progress, but preliminary findings indicate that spatial predictability makes a difference for RTs (see Table 8.3). Groups 1 and 2 combined (both location predictable) had a significantly lower median RT than Groups 3 and 4 combined (both location unpredictable) and a smaller percent of slow RTs. The anticipation data were less revealing when target events alone were analyzed.

Although only minisequences could be analyzed in making comparisons across all groups, more powerful analyses were possible for some single-group comparisons that used all of the data. Babies in Groups 1 and 2 always saw pictures

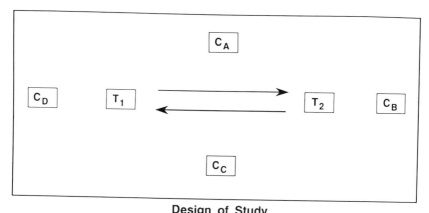

Design of Study

Groups	Predictable Dimension	Context Events	Context Timing	Test (every 5th – 6th event) Events	Test Timing
1	Time/Location	T_1 /T_2	Fixed	T_1 /T_2	Fixed
2	Location only	T_1 /T_2	Variable	T_1 /T_2	Fixed
3	Time only	All	Fixed	T_1 /T_2	Fixed
4	None	All	Variable	T_1 /T_2	Fixed

FIG. 8.10. Diagram of the spatial locations used in the Space/Time study. Arrows indicate the sequence that was used to test for whether infants were using location and/or time cues on every 5th and 6th event. The table below the diagram shows the four conditions that were used for different groups for nontest events that presumably established the background context of relative predictability.

TABLE 8.3
Median RTs and Percent Anticipations for Test Sequences in the Space/Time Study

Reaction Time Measures	Groups 1 (Space and Time)	2 (Space)	3 (Time)	4 (None)	Contrasts 1 versus 4	1 + 2 versus 3 + 4	1 + 3 versus 2 + 4
Median RT	503ms	488ms	545ms	541ms		*	
% Fast	11.7	5.8	5.7	5.0	*		
% Slow	52.8	51.5	65.5	69.4	*	**	
Anticipation Measure							
% Anticipations	20.6	17.3	19.5	12.8			

One-tail values
*$p < .05$
**$p < .01$

in only the $\pm 6°$ locations, so no problem arises about RTs being affected by fixations to different locations, and any chance likelihood of babies fixating to the opposite horizontal side during the anticipation window was equated. The only factor that differentiated these groups was the predictability of *when* the next picture would appear. This analysis revealed a reliably higher percent of anticipation for Group 1 (time and location predictable) than for Group 2 (location-only predictable) but no stable effect on RTs (Table 8.4). Thus, it appears that infants use both location and time cues in forming expectations. At least for the values of the dimensions we explored, location cues appeared to have a larger influence than time cues in the formation of expectations.

Our prototypic situation did not permit infants to use content information to support expectations, because the pictures changed unpredictably from one onset to the next. However, people typically form expectations not only for something to happen in a certain place at a certain time but, also, precisely for *what* that something will be. Perhaps the standard paradigm deprived the infant of an important cue for forming expectations for the onset of a particular event. Wentworth (1988) developed an ingeniously straightforward approach to this issue. She modified the original paradigm so that babies always saw the same picture on one side. As before, on the other side the picture changed from one appearance to the next.

If picture content plays no role in the formation of expectations, the prediction is for no difference in the percent of anticipations or in the speed of RTs to the two sides. A different possibility is that babies can store something about the pictures and that habituation operates to make the side with the unchanging picture less interesting. The result would be fewer anticipations and slower RTs to the side with the unchanging picture. The conclusion would be that the babies can form expectations for content but the effect is on motivation rather than on supporting the formation of expectations. The final possibility is that the side with the constant picture enjoys a higher percent of anticipations and

TABLE 8.4
Median RTs and Percent Anticipations for all Pictures for
Groups 1 and 2 in the Space/Time Study

	Groups	
	1 *(Space and Time)*	*2* *(Space)*
Reaction Time Measures:		
Median RT	525ms	498 ms
% Fast	8.4	6.4
% Slow	61.2	54.1
Anticipation Measure:		
% Anticipations	22.0	15.8 $p < .05$

faster RTs. This outcome would suggest that the opportunity to predict content supports the formation of expectations.

Three studies have employed this paradigm with 2- and 3-month-old babies. Table 8.5 summarizes the three studies. Babies had a significantly higher percent of fast RTs and significantly more anticipations for the constant side than for the changing side. The conclusion is that babies can represent the content of pictures in the visual expectation paradigm and that a predictable content facilitates the formation of expectations. The fact that babies are able to represent the contents of an absent picture and use those contents to guide action poses problems for the general assumption that out-of-sight is out-of-mind in the early sensorimotor ages. Baillergeon clearly echoes that suggestion in her chapter in this volume (chap. 9).

Can Babies Transfer Expectations to Different Motor Actions? An interesting question is whether or not babies' expectations can be generalized or utilized with different actions than the actions of acquisition. One might expect from a Piagetian perspective that expectations are not abstract and transferable at this early age; rather, they are embedded within the actions that express them. On the other hand, it is conceivable that the infant's expectations are based on a rule, for example, the rule of alternation. If so, the baby may be able to use this rule to enhance the formation of expectations that involve different actions.

To examine this possibility, we selected two action sets: horizontal eye movements, left and right, as before, and vertical eye movements, up and down (Arehart & Haith, 1990; McCarty & Haith, 1989). Horizontal and vertical eye movements call on different brain centers and involve quite different coordination of the eye-movement musculature. The logic of the experiment was first to engage one action set with one series of pictures and then to engage the second action set with another series. For the second action set, two groups of infants would see pictures that obeyed the rule of alternation. However, the prior action set of pictures would appear in regular alternation for one group but

TABLE 8.5
Median RTs and Percent Anticipations Summarized Across Three Studies
Which Compared Performance on Changing Versus Unchanging Pictures

	Location		Significance Test
	Constant Side	*Variable Side*	
Reaction Time Measures:			
% Fast	13.3	9.0	$p = < .05$
% Slow	55.4	57.3	$p = $ ns
Anticipation Measure			
% Anticipations	24.5	16.2	$p < .001$

TABLE 8.6
The Two Groups and Two Conditions for the Rule Study

Groups	Events	
	1–30	31–60
Rule$_V$–Rule$_H$	Alternate Vertical	Alternate Horizontal
Irregular$_V$–Rule$_H$	Irregular Vertical	Alternate Horizontal

irregularly for the other. The question was whether the first-set alternation experience would benefit that group in dealing with the second-set alternation.

All babies saw a regular, alternating, horizontal series of pictures (Rule$_H$ for horizontal rule-based series) for their second (i.e., test) series, which included pictures 31 through 60. The babies differed with respect to what they saw for the first 30 events. Half saw an alternating vertical series (Rule$_V$) and half saw an unpredictable vertical series (Irregular$_V$). Thus, the two groups were Rule$_V$–Rule$_H$ and Irregular$_V$–Rule$_H$ (see Table 8.6). Prior research indicated that both groups would form expectations for the Rule$_H$ series; however, if the baby learned an alternation rule from the first action set, to any degree that the rule transcended the specific actions, the baby might use that rule to enhance performance on the second action set. A similar line of reasoning predicts stronger correlations in performance between the two tasks for the Rule$_V$–Rule$_H$ group than for the Irregular$_V$–Rule$_H$ group.

It is reassuring that the basic expectancy findings replicated with the vertical alternating series. That is, the Rule$_V$ condition produced a reliably higher percent of anticipations and faster RTs than the Irregular$_V$ condition (Table 8.7).

Now to the transfer issue. The findings, so far, provide tantalizing but not overwhelming support for rule transfer. On the positive side, the between-action set correlations for the Rule$_V$–Rule$_H$ group were near .70 and were significant for all of the RT measures: overall median, the percent fast, the optimal score,

TABLE 8.7
Median RTs and Anticipations for the First Set of Vertical-Axis Pictures for the
Groups Receiving Either the Alternating or Irregular Sequence in the Rule Study

	Group		Significance Test
	Rule$_V$–Rule$_H$	Irregular$_V$–Rule$_H$	
Reaction Time Measures			
Median	495ms	525ms	
Optimal Median	420ms	495ms	$p < .01$
Anticipation Measure			
% Anticipation	20.4	14.2	$p < .05$

TABLE 8.8

Correlations of Median RTs and Anticipations Between the First and Second Series for
the Groups Receiving Either the Alternating or Irregular Sequence in the Rule Study

	Groups	
	$Rule_V-Rule_H$	$Irregular_V-Rule_H$
Reaction Time Measures:		
Overall Median	.70**	.39
Optimal Median	.72**	.39
Categories of Reaction Time:		
Percent Fast	.72**	.39
Percent Slow	.67**	.50†
Anticipation Measure:		
Percent Anticipations	.13	.41

$†p < .10$
$*p < .05$
$**p < .01$

and the percent slow. For the $Irregular_V-Rule_H$ group all but one correlation
hovered around .40, and none was significant (Table 8.8). Thus, it appears that
the $Rule_V-Rule_H$ group took something with them to the second condition that
the $Irregular_V-Rule_H$ group did not. Supporting this claim, the $Rule_V-Rule_H$
group demonstrated a significantly higher percent of anticipations in the second-
series condition than during baseline for every block of 10 events and performed
better than the $Irregular_V-Rule_H$ group on the first two blocks. The increase
in the percent of anticipations from baseline was not stable for any block for
the $Irregular_V-Rule_H$ group (Fig. 8.11). On the negative side, the differences
in RT correlations between the two groups were not significant, nor was the
interaction between trial block and groups for anticipations for the second series.

The direction of the findings suggests that infants do base expectations on
a rule and that this rule may be transferable, but the data are not definitive.
Additional subjects at this age may solidify the current trends and/or older infants may provide clearer support for the rule-transfer thesis. Presumably, older
infants will be more cognitively advanced and will display rule-based tendencies
even more strongly. If it can be demonstrated that rules can transcend specific
action sets in the early months of life, theories of early sensorimotor functioning would need to be modified.

DISCUSSION

With the findings of these experiments in hand as well as a discussion of potential avenues for further research, we now reconsider the themes that were raised
earlier.

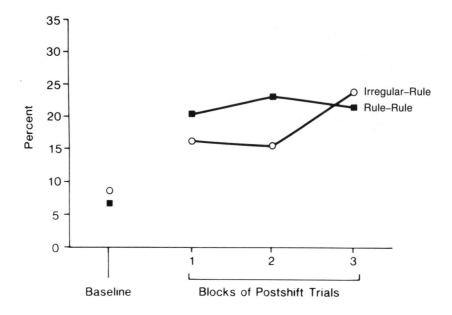

FIG. 8.11.   Percent of anticipations for the baseline trial and for the second series of pictures in the rule-transfer study for the two conditions.

Visual Expectation as a Process.   If there was a question about the validity of the expectation construct in 3-month-olds based only on results from
the original alternating series, it should be clear now that the phenomenon is
real. The findings that were obtained with the asymmetric series in the second
study eliminated a number of alternative interpretations of the original results.
Confidence in the validity of the process was bolstered by the findings that babies differ in their ability to form expectations and that this capacity is stable
at least over several days. Further support may be provided by studies of the
relations between performance in the visual expectation paradigm and brain activity; Naomi Wentworth is currently recording EEGs from infants while they
participate in this paradigm to address this question.

There is a host of questions to ask about how one might best model the
process. Current conditioning theory is quite open to concepts of expectations
and the mental models they imply. Although learning clearly occurs in this
paradigm, not all learning is conditioning; conditioning theory does not seem
adequate to account for this particular phenomenon. The evidence that babies
may be able to transfer rules, that babies can do even better with an alternating
series after exposure to a random series than with no preceding stimulus exposures at all, that asymmetric series are quickly mastered, and that a stable
stimulus content enhances expectations (presumably a stable UCS with a variable CS) strains straightforward conditioning models, even in their most current

form (Holyoak et al., 1989). An important task is to develop a useful alternative.

Visual Expectation as a Tool. The utility of the visual expectation paradigm as a tool seems clear enough from the new evidence it has provided with regard to infants' ability to map spatial, temporal, and stimulus-content information. Of course, there is other evidence in the literature that babies process each of these properties, typically in habituation studies. What has been demonstrated here is that these properties can be used positively for adaptive action. Note also that this information was garnered within the two minutes of the duration of the experiments, a far less time-consuming venture than is typical for learning and habituation approaches. Further, the paradigm seems applicable for understanding the baby's ability to acquire rules, and the asymmetric study provided a glimpse of how one might examine the development of rule processing in infancy. From a tool-use perspective, the reliability data are also encouraging. The fact that this paradigm provides so many RT measures so quickly makes for fairly stable averages and avoidance of the nasty and common problems of noise and variability in infant measures. From a different angle, the RT measure might provide a link to cognitive efforts and theory with older subjects, with whom RT has been used extensively. Comparable measures might help investigators bridge the "species gap" that seems to exist in cognitive theorizing for human infants and older humans.

Visual Expectation as a Model. The jury is out with regard to whether studies of the formation of expectations in the visual system can inform us about the formation of expectations in other action systems or about other future-oriented processes. As discussed in the opening section of this chapter, there is clear evidence that infants form expectations in using other action systems, for example, in reaching. Wentworth et al. (1989) recently reported adaptive anticipatory strategies that infants use in reaching for approaching and spinning targets. Benson and her colleagues are currently exploring infants' expectations in crawling (Benson, Arehart, Jennings, Boley, & Kearns, 1989). Babies appear to learn rules for how goals will change location while they are crawling, and preplanning strategies are apparent. One issue is whether there are interesting substages that occur in the formation of expectations (e.g., a sequence by which cues are used in a spatial, then time, then content, order, followed by the ability to use and transfer rules), which are replayed as each action system comes on line. A second issue is whether there is a repeating sequence in the evolution of FOPs within each action system (e.g., expectations for external events, and then for the interrelation between external and internal events, followed by goal-oriented action). Hopefully, additional research and thinking will reveal how well the visual system can serve as a model for other action systems and for various FOPs, or whether FOPs even form a meaningful conceptual set.

Visual Expectation as a Window on the Baby's Agenda. The observations on infants' formation of expectations add substance to the general claim that babies actively try to organize their world. At least one of the ways they do this is to map dynamic events going on around them, to form expectations for those events, and then to test the validity of their expectations by either manifest behavior (anticipations) or internal processes equivalent to perceptual set (RT facilitation). It is not clear at this time whether activity is essential to the infant's formation of expectations (as Piaget would suggest) or whether actions simply provide us a window on the baby's cognitive activity. Another important question is what motivates the baby to form expectations. In addition to the higher level answer that the baby is motivated to organize its world, there may also be a lower level answer. A baby without expectations is forced to react to each visual event as it occurs, a mode that is quite tiring, at least from the adult's point of view. Expectations permit the infant to acquire some degree of control over its own actions and, presumably, to trigger internal perceptual and cognitive sequences. One of the items on the baby's agenda may be to map and expect external dynamic events if for no other reason than that ad hoc processing is simply too slow, especially at this early age.

In any case, these studies provide evidence that babies deal positively with dynamic events that occur around them. Because so much emphasis has been placed on the infant's analysis of self–other contingencies and self–object contingencies for learning, it is important to remind ourselves that the baby had no control over the events they saw in these experiments. Nothing the baby did affected the timing, location, content, or anything else about the series. In fact, reflection on what an infant's life is like in the early months of motor immaturity reveals that the great majority of life events are not under self-control. Yet, babies seem to enter mid-infancy with a substantial knowledge base and significant understanding of what is going on around them. These experiments provide a glimpse of at least one process they engage in to create this knowledge base.

ACKNOWLEDGMENTS

This research was supported by research grant MH23412 from NIMH and HD20026 from NICHD to me, and was carried out while I was supported by NIMH Research Scientist Award MH00367. Portions of this manuscript were written while I was a fellow at the Center for Advanced Studies in the Behavioral Sciences, Palo Alto, CA; I am also grateful for financial support provided by the National Science Foundation #BNS87-00864.

Denise Arehart, Janette Benson, Rick Braaten, Rick Canfield, Roberta Hood, Michael McCarty, Nancy Robinson, and Naomi Wentworth provided helpful comments on earlier drafts of this paper and have provided continuing help in shaping my ideas. Denise Arehart, Rick Canfield, Michael McCarty, Nancy Robinson, and Naomi Wentworth have had a central role in the research described. I have also benefited from the input of other members of the future-oriented, goal-directed (FOGD) group.

REFERENCES

Arehart, D. M., & Haith, M. M. (1990, June). *Evidence for space–time rule transfer in 13-week-old infants*. Presented at the meeting of the Developmental Psychobiology Research Group, Estes Park, CO.

Aslin, R. N. (1981). Development of smooth pursuit in human infants. In D. F. Fisher, R. A. Monty, & E. J. Senders (Eds.), *Eye movements: Cognition and visual perception* (pp. 31–51). Hillsdale, NJ: Lawrence Erlbaum Associates.

Aslin, R. N. (1987). Visual and auditory development in infancy. In J. D. Osofsky (Ed.), *Handbook of infant development* (2nd ed., pp. 5–97). New York: Wiley.

Aslin, R. N. (1989, April). *Commentary*. National Institute of Child Health and Human Development Workshop on Dynamical Systems in Development, Kansas City, MO.

Aslin, R. N., & Salapatek, P. (1975). Saccadic localization of peripheral targets by the very young human infant. *Perception and Psychophysics, 17*, 293–302.

Banks, M. S., & Salapatek, P. (1983). Infant visual perception. In M. M. Haith & J. J. Campos (Eds.), *Infancy and developmental psychobiology* (pp. 435–572). New York: Wiley.

Benson, J. B. (1990). The significance and development of crawling in infancy. In J. E. Clark & J. H. Humphrey (Eds.), *Advances in motor development research* (Vol. 3, pp. 91–142). New York: AMS Press.

Benson, J. B., Arehart, D. M., Jennings, T., Boley, S., & Kearns, L. (1989, April). *Infant crawling: Expectations, action-plans and goals*. Presented at the meeting of the Society for Research in Child Development, Kansas City, MO.

Biederman, I., Glass, A. L., & Stacy, E. W., Jr. (1973). Searching for objects in real-world scenes. *Journal of Experimental Psychology, 97*, 22–27.

Bolles, R. C. (1972). Reinforcement, expectancy and learning. *Psychological Review, 79*, 394–407.

Bullock, D., & Grossberg, S. (1988). Neural dynamics of planned arm movements: Emerging invariants and speed-accuracy properties during trajectory formation. *Psychological Bulletin, 95*, 49–90.

Canfield, R. L. (1988). *Visual anticipation and number development in early infancy*. Unpublished doctoral dissertation, University of Denver, Denver, CO.

Canfield, R. L., & Haith, M. M. (1991). Young infants' visual expectations for symmetric and asymmetric stimulus sequences. *Developmental Psychology, 27*, 198–208.

Fantz, R. L. (1961). The origin of form perception. *Scientific American, 204*, 66–72.

Goldman-Rakic, P. S. (1987). Circuitry of primate prefrontal cortex and regulation of behavior by representational memory. In F. Plum (Ed.), *Handbook of physiology* (Vol. 5, pp. 373–417). Baltimore, MD: Williams & Wilkins.

Goodman, G. S. (1980). Picture memory: How the action schema affects retention. *Cognitive Psychology, 12*, 473–495.

Haith, M. M. (1980). *Rules that babies look by*. Hillsdale, NJ: Lawrence Erlbaum Associates.

Haith, M. M., & Campos, J. J. (1977). Human infancy. *Annual Review of Psychology, 28*, 251–293.

Haith, M. M., Hazan, C., & Goodman, G. S. (1988). Expectation and anticipation of dynamic visual events by 3.5-month-old babies. *Child Development, 59*, 467–479.

Haith, M. M., Kessen, W., & Collins, D. (1969). Response of the human infant to level of complexity of intermittent visual movement. *Journal of Experimental Child Psychology, 7*, 52–69.

Haith, M. M., & McCarty, M. (1990). Stability of visual expectations at 3.0 months of age. *Developmental Psychology, 26,* 68–74.

Hofsten, C. von (1983). Catching skills in infancy. *Journal of Experimental Psychology: Human Perception and Performance, 9,* 75–85.

Hofsten, C. von (1988, June). *A perception–action perspective on the development of manual movements.* Presented at Attention and Performance meeting, Saline Royale, France.

Hofsten, C. von, & Ronnqvist, L. (1988). Preparation for grasping an object: A developmental study. *Journal of Experimental Psychology: Human Perception and Performance, 14,* 610–621.

Holyoak, K. J., Kol, K., & Nisbett, R. E. (1989). A theory of conditioning: Inductive learning within rule-based default hierarchies. *Psychological Review, 96,* 315–340.

Kagan, J. (1970). Attention and psychological change in the young child. *Science, 170,* 826–832.

Lee, D. (1989, April). *The use of dynamic information for the perception of direction.* Presentation at the Center for Advanced Studies in the Behavioral Sciences, Palo Alto, CA.

McCarty, M. E. (1989, April). *Predictability and its effect on infant visual expectations.* Presented at the meeting of the Society for Research in Child Development, Kansas City, MO.

McCarty, M. E., & Haith, M. M. (1989, April). *Rule transfer in the infant visual expectation paradigm.* Presented at the meeting of the Society for Research in Child Development, Kansas City, MO.

Rescorla, R. (1975). Pavlovian excitatory and inhibitory conditioning. In W. K. Estes (Ed.), *Handbook of learning and cognitive processes: Vol. 2. Conditioning and behavior therapy* (pp. 7–35). Hillsdale, NJ: Lawrence Erlbaum Associates.

Schank, R. C., & Abelson, K. P. (1977). *Scripts, plans, goals, and understanding: An inquiry into human knowledge structures.* Hillsdale, NJ: Lawrence Erlbaum Associates.

Wentworth, N. (1988, April). *Infants' expectations: What, where, when?* Presented at the meeting of the International Conference for Infant Studies, Washington, DC.

Wentworth, N., Benson, J., & Haith, M. M. (1989, April). *The development of reaching for stationary and moving targets in infancy.* Presented at the meeting of the Society for Research in Child Development, Kansas City, MO.

9

The Object Concept Revisited: New Directions in the Investigation of Infants' Physical Knowledge

Renée Baillargeon
University of Illinois

An important concern of cognitive psychology in recent years has been the description of children's and adults' physical knowledge. This research has focused on three important questions. First, investigators have sought to describe the *content* of children's and adults' knowledge. Physical domains that have been examined include astronomy (Vosniadou & Brewer, 1989), biology (Carey, 1985), and physics (Clement, 1982; D. Gentner & D. R. Gentner, 1983; Karmiloff-Smith & Inhelder, 1975; McCloskey, 1983; Siegler, 1978). Second, researchers have attempted to elucidate the *structure* of children's and adults' physical knowledge. Different models have been proposed, ranging from lists of local rules to naive models or "theories" organized around causal principles (Carey, 1985; Gelman, 1990; D. Gentner & Stevens, 1983; Keil, 1990; Siegler, 1978, 1983; Vosniadou & Brewer, 1989; Wellman, in press). Finally, investigators have been concerned with the *development* of children's and adults' physical knowledge. Of particular interest has been the comparison of novices' and experts' representations of physical domains (Chi, Feltovitch, & Glaser, 1981; Larkin, 1983; Wiser & Carey, 1983).

In the realm of infancy research, investigators have also sought to characterize infants' physical world. Most of this research has focused on issues of content, and more specifically, on infants' understanding of occlusion events. When adults see an object occlude another object, they typically make three assumptions. The first is that the occluded object continues to exist behind the occluding object. The second is that the occluded object retains the spatial and physical properties it possessed prior to occlusion. The third is that the occluded

265

object is still subject to physical laws; its displacements, transformations, and interactions with other objects do not become capricious or arbitrary but remain regular and predictable. Collectively, these assumptions are generally referred to in the developmental literature as a concept of *object permanence* or, more broadly, as an *object concept.*

Piaget (1954) was the first to investigate whether infants share adults' assumptions about occluded objects—or, in other words, whether infants possess a notion of object permanence. Detailed analyses of infants' performances on manual search tasks led him to conclude that the development of infants' beliefs about occluded objects progresses through six stages and is not complete until 2 years of age.

Piaget's theory of the development of infants' beliefs about occluded objects has occupied a central position in the field of infant cognition (e.g., Flavell, 1985; Harris, 1983). The acquisition of a notion of object permanence is often considered to be the cornerstone of cognitive development in infancy, and indeed, what could be more basic than the object concept? The realization that visible and occluded objects exist in the same objective space and obey the same physical laws constitutes one of the fundamental tenets on which our representation of the physical world is built. It is not surprising, therefore, that considerable effort has been expended since the publication of Piaget's theory to confirm and extend his conclusions (see Bremner, 1985; Gratch, 1975, 1976; Harris, 1987, 1989; Schuberth, 1983; Sophian, 1984; Spelke, 1988; and Wellman, Cross, & Bartsch, 1987, for reviews).

Since the early 1980s, my collaborators and I have conducted an extensive series of experiments on young infants' understanding of occlusion events. In these experiments, we have used visual tasks rather than the manual search tasks used by Piaget and his followers. The selection of visual tasks stemmed from a concern that infants might perform poorly in manual search tasks, not because their concept of object permanence was underdeveloped, but because their ability to plan search action sequences was limited. Some of the experiments we carried out were designed expressly as tests of Piaget's theory; others focused on hitherto unexplored aspects of infants' understanding of occlusion events. In general, the results of these experiments paint a radically different picture of infants' ability to represent and to reason about occluded objects than that bequeathed by Piaget and, until recently, adopted by most developmental psychologists. Indeed, the results suggest that young infants' understanding of occlusion events is strikingly similar to that of adults.

This chapter is divided into four sections. The first section presents Piaget's description of the sequence of changes in infants' beliefs about occluded objects, and the evidence on which this description was based. The second section reviews the experiments we have conducted to test Piaget's theory and to pursue new directions suggested by the results of these initial tests. The third section considers possible explanations for the marked discrepancy between search and non-search assessments of infants' understanding of occlusion events. Finally, the last section examines the implications of the present research for descriptions of the content, structure, and development of infants' physical knowledge.

PIAGET'S THEORY

Piaget (1954) proposed that infants' beliefs about occluded objects develop through six stages. During the first three stages (0 to 9 months), infants do not realize that objects continue to exist when occluded: They assume that objects cease to exist when they cease to be visible and begin to exist anew when they come back into view. According to Piaget, the object at this stage is "a mere image which reenters the void as soon as it vanishes, and emerges from it for no objective reason" (1954, p. 11). During the fourth stage (9 to 12 months), infants begin to view objects as permanent entities that continue to exist when masked by other objects. However, this permanence is still limited. Infants do not yet conceive of occluded objects as occupying objective locations in space. It is not until the fifth stage (12 to 18 months), Piaget maintained, that infants begin to systematically attend to visible displacements and to assume that occluded objects reside in whatever locations they occupied immediately prior to occlusion. The sixth stage (18 to 24 months), which is signaled by the emergence of symbolic representation, constitutes the final advance in the development of infants' beliefs about occluded objects. Because of their new representational capacity, infants become able to imagine invisible displacements and hence to infer, as opposed to merely represent, occluded objects' locations. According to Piaget, objects' appearances and disappearances are then no longer mysterious but follow known, predictable patterns. By the end of the sixth stage, the world of the infant is thus radically different from what it was in the beginning stages. It is a world that contains both visible and occluded objects, existing in a unitary, objective space, and obeying the same physical laws.

As was mentioned earlier, the main evidence for Piaget's description of the sequence of changes in infants' beliefs about occluded objects came from studies of the development of manual search behavior. Thus, Piaget's first claim, that is not until about 9 months of age that infants begin to endow objects with permanence, was based on the finding that manual search does not emerge until this age. Piaget noted that, prior to Stage 4, infants do not search for objects they have observed being hidden. If a toy is covered with a cloth, for example, they make no attempt to lift the cloth and grasp the toy, even though they are capable of performing each of these actions. Beginning in Stage 4, however, infants do remove obstacles to retrieve hidden objects.

Why did Piaget select infants' willingness to search for hidden objects as marking the beginning of object permanence? This question is important because

Piaget observed several behaviors prior to Stage 4 that are suggestive of object permanence. For example, he noted that, as early as Stage 1 (0 to 1 month), infants may look at an object, look away from it, and then return to it several seconds later, without any external cue having signaled the object's continued presence. In addition, Piaget observed that,beginning in Stage 3 (4 to 9 months), infants anticipate the future positions of moving objects. If they are tracking an object and temporarily lose sight of it, they look for it further along its trajectory; similarly, if they are holding an object out of sight and accidentally let go of it, they stretch their arm to recapture it.

Piaget held that although these and other behaviors seem to reveal a notion of object permanence, closer analysis indicates "how superficial this interpretation would be and how phenomenalistic the primitive universe remains" (1954, p. 11). Prior to Stage 4, Piaget maintained, infants lack a concept of physical causality and regard all of reality as being dependent on their activity. When acting on an object, infants view the object not as an independent entity but as the extension or the product of their action. If the object disappears from view, infants reproduce or extend their action because they expect that this action will again produce the object. Proof for Piaget that infants regard the object as being "at the disposal" of their action is that if their action fails to bring back the object, they do not perform alternative actions to recover it. Beginning in Stage 4, however, infants act very differently. For example, if a ball rolls behind a cushion and they cannot recapture it by extending their reach, they try alternative means for recovering it: They lift the cushion, pull it aside, or grope behind it. According to Piaget, such activities indicate that infants conceive of the object, not as a thing at the disposal of a specific action, but as a substantial entity that is located out of sight behind the cushion and that any of several actions may serve to reveal.

Piaget's second claim, that it is not until about 12 months of age that infants begin to conceive of occluded objects as occupying objective locations in space, was suggested by the finding that perseverative search errors do not disappear until this age. Piaget noted that when Stage 4 infants search for hidden objects, they often search in the wrong location. Specifically, if an object is hidden in a location A and, after infants have retrieved it, the same object is hidden in a new location B, infants tend to search for the object in A, where they first found it. Piaget took these errors to indicate that, although infants endow the object with permanence, as evidenced by their willingness to search for it, this permanence is not yet complete. Infants still regard the object as the extension of their action: When the object disappears at B, they search for it at A because they expect that by reproducing their action at A they will again produce the object. According to Piaget, "in all the observations in which the child searches in A for what he as seen disappear in B, the explanation should be sought in the fact that the object is not yet sufficiently individualized to be dissociated from the global behavior related to position A" (1954, p. 63). Beginning in Stage

5, however, infants do search for objects where they were last seen, rather than where they were first found. According to Piaget, infants are becoming aware that objects reside not in special positions linked to their own actions, but in objective locations resulting from the objects' displacements within the visual field.

Finally, Piaget's third claim, that it is not until about 18 months of age that infants begin to infer the location of occluded objects, was based on the discovery that it is not until this age that infants succeed at search tasks involving invisible displacements. In these tasks, an object is hidden, in full view of the infant, in a small container, which is then moved behind each of several screens. The object is surreptitiously left behind one of the screens, usually the last. Piaget found that when asked to find the object, Stage 5 infants typically search the container, the location where they last saw the object. Failing to find the object there, they make no attempt to search behind the screens. Beginning in Stage 6, however, infants do search behind the screens. Piaget speculated that because of their new-found representational abilities, infants are able to imagine or to infer the object's probable displacements. Piaget described the transition from Stage 5 to Stage 6 in these terms:

> A world [such as the world of the fifth stage infant] in which only perceived movements are regulated is neither stable nor dissociated from the self; it is a world of still chaotic potentialities whose organization begins only in the subject's presence . . . [The] representation and deduction characteristic of the sixth stage result in extending the process of solidification to regions . . . which are dissociated from action and perception; displacements, even invisible ones, are henceforth envisaged as subservient to laws, and objects in motion become real objects independent of the self and persisting in their substantial identity. (Piaget, 1954, p. 86)

TEST OF PIAGET'S THEORY

Since the early 1980s, my collaborators and I have conducted an extensive series of experiments on young infants' understanding of occlusion events. This section summarizes the results of these experiments. The section is organized into three parts. The first reports experiments on young infants' ability to represent the existence of occluded objects; the second reviews experiments on young infants' ability to represent the spatial and physical properties of occluded objects; and the third presents preliminary experiments on young infants' ability to make inferences about the existence and properties of occluded objects.

Representing the Existence of Occluded Objects

During the 1960s and 1970s, Piaget's (1954) observation that young infants do not search for hidden objects was confirmed by many investigators (see Gratch, 1975, 1976, for reviews of this early work). Nevertheless, Piaget's interpretation of this observation was questioned. It was proposed that young infants might fail to search for hidden objects, not because of a lack of object permanence, but because of difficulties associated with manual search (e.g., Bower, 1974).

This analysis suggested that young infants might show evidence of object permanence if given tests that did not require manual search. Bower (1967, 1972, 1974; Bower, Broughton, & Moore, 1971; Bower & Wishart, 1972) devised several such tests and obtained three results that seemed indicative of object permanence in young infants. First, 7-week-old infants were found to discriminate between disappearances that signaled the continued existence of an object (e.g., gradual occlusions), and disappearances that did not (e.g., gradual dissolutions or sudden implosions; Bower, 1967). Second, 2-month-old infants were found to anticipate the reappearance of an object that stopped behind a screen, "looking to that half of the movement path the object would have reached had it not stopped" (Bower et al., 1971, p. 183). Finally, 5-month-old infants were found to show disruptions in their tracking when an object was altered while passing behind a screen: They tended to look back at the screen, as though in search of the original object (Bower, 1974; Bower et al., 1971).

Although suggestive, Bower's three results did not provide conclusive evidence of object permanence in young infants. First, methodological problems cast doubts on the validity of the results (e.g., Baillargeon, 1986, 1987b; Baillargeon, Spelke, & Wasserman, 1985; Goldberg, 1976; Gratch, 1975, 1976, 1982; Harris, 1987; Hood & Willatts, 1986; Meicler & Gratch, 1980; Muller & Aslin, 1978). Second, the results were open to alternative interpretations that did not implicate object permanence. In particular, the last two results could be explained by Piagetian theory in terms of the extension of an ongoing action or the reproduction of a previous action. When anticipating the reappearance of the object, the infants could simply have been extending a tracking motion begun prior to the object's disappearance. Furthermore, when looking back at the screen, after the novel object had emerged from behind it, the infants could have been repeating their prior action of looking in that direction, with the expectation that this action would again produce the original object.

The first of Bower's (1967) results could not be explained in terms of the extension or the reproduction of an action, but it, too, was open to alternative interpretations. One such interpretation was that the infants discriminated between the test disappearances on the basis of superficial expectations about the way objects typically disappear, rather than on the basis of a belief in object permanence. In their daily environment, infants often see objects occlude one another but they rarely, if ever, see objects implode or dissolve into the air. Hence, the infants could have responded differently to the occlusions than to the implosions or the dissolutions simply because the occlusions represented the only type of disappearance that was familiar to them.

Because of the difficulties associated with Piaget's and Bower's tasks, my colleagues and I sought a new means of testing object permanence in young infants (Baillargeon et al., 1985). Like Bower, we chose not to rely on manual search as an index of object permanence. However, we tried to find an index that did not depend on (a) the extension or reproduction of an action or (b) knowledge about superficial properties of object disappearances.

The method we devised focused on infants' understanding of the principle that a solid object cannot move through the space occupied by another solid object. We reasoned that if infants were surprised when a visible object appeared to move through the space occupied by another, occluded object, it would suggest that they took account of the existence of the occluded object.

In a series of experiments, 5½-month-olds (Baillargeon et al., 1985) and 4½-month-olds (Baillargeon, 1987a) were habituated to a screen that rotated back and forth through a 180° arc, in the manner of a drawbridge (see Fig. 9.1). Following habituation, a box was placed behind the screen and the infants saw a possible and an impossible test event. In the possible event, the screen stopped when it reached the occluded box; in the impossible event, the screen rotated through a full 180° arc, as though the box were no longer behind it. Both the 5½- and the 4½-month-old infants looked reliably longer at the impossible than at the possible event, suggesting that they (a) represented the existence of the box behind the screen; (b) understood that the screen could not rotate through the space occupied by the box; and hence (c) expected the screen to stop and were surprised in the impossible event that it did not.

There was, however, an alternative interpretation for the results. The infants could have looked longer at the impossible than at the possible event simply because they found the 180° screen rotation more interesting that the shorter rotation used in the possible event. To check this interpretation, we tested additional groups of infants in a control condition that was identical to the experimental condition except that no box was placed behind the screen. The infants now looked equally at the two screen rotations. This finding provided evidence that the infants in the experimental condition looked longer at the impossible event, not because they preferred the 180° screen rotation, but because they expected the screen to stop and were surprised that it did not.

In other experiments also reported in Baillargeon (1987a), 3½-month-old infants were examined using the same paradigm. The results indicated that the infants who were fast habituators[1] looked reliably longer at the impossible

---

[1] In this experiment, an infant received habituation trials until (a) the infant reached a criterion of habituation of a 50% or higher decrease in looking time on three consecutive trials relative to his or her looking time on the first three trials, or (b) the infant completed nine trials without satisfying the habituation criterion. Therefore, the minimum number of habituation trials an infant could receive was six, and the maximum number was nine. Infants who took six or seven trials to reach the habituation criterion were classified as *fast* habituators; infants who required eight or nine trials to reach the criterion or who failed to reach the criterion within nine trials were classified as *slow* habituators.

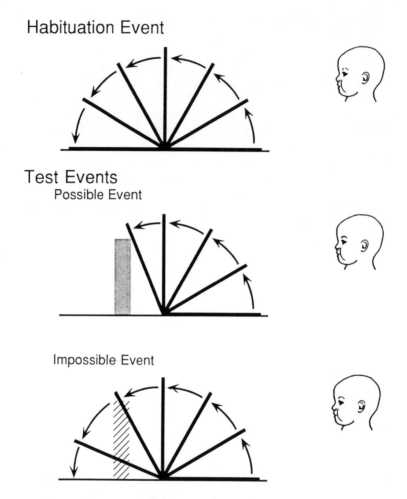

FIG. 9.1. Schematic drawing of the events shown to the infants in Baillargeon
et al. (1985) and in Baillargeon (1987a).

than at the possible event, whereas the infants who were slow habituators
looked equally at the two events. These findings suggested that, like the
5½- and the 4½-month-old infants in the initial experiments, the 3½-month-
old infants who were fast habituators expected the screen to stop and were
surprised in the impossible event that it did not. A control condition conducted without the box supported this interpretation. The results of these
experiments thus indicated that, contrary to what Piaget had claimed, infants as young as 3½ months of age represent the existence of occluded objects.

Representing the Properties of Occluded Objects

Location. The results presented in the last section indicated that infants represent the existence of occluded objects long before 9 months of age. Such a finding raised the possibility that infants represent the location of occluded objects—the next step in Piaget's (1954) developmental sequence—before the age of 12 months. To examine this possibility, 6½- and 8-month-old infants were tested using a novel paradigm (Baillargeon, 1986). The infants sat in front of a screen; to the left of the screen was a long inclined ramp (see Fig. 9.2). The infants were habituated to the following event: The screen was raised (to show the infants that there was nothing behind it) and then lowered; a toy car then rolled down the ramp, passed behind the screen, and exited the apparatus to the right. Following habituation, the infants saw a possible and an impossible test event. These events were identical to the habituation event except that a box was placed behind the screen. In the possible event, the box stood in back of the car's tracks; in the impossible event, the box stood on top of the tracks, blocking the car's path.

The results indicated that the infants looked reliably longer at the impossible than at the possible event. A second experiment in which the box was placed in front (possible event) or on top (impossible event) of the car's tracks yielded similar results. Together, these results indicated that the infants (a) represented the location of the box behind the screen; (b) assumed that the car pursued

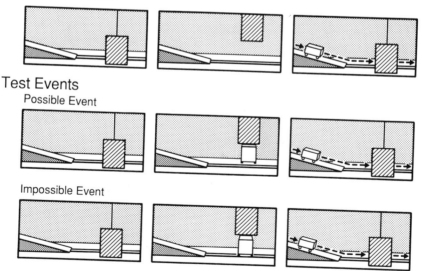

Habituation Event

Test Events
Possible Event

Impossible Event

FIG. 9.2. Schematic drawing of the events shown to the infants in Baillargeon (1986) and in Baillargeon and DeVos (1991, Exp. 3).

its trajectory behind the screen; (c) understood that the car could not roll through the space occupied by the box; and hence (d) were surprised in the impossible event to see the car roll past the screen.

In subsequent experiments, 4-month-old infants were tested using a similar procedure, except that the box was replaced by a toy mouse (Baillargeon & DeVos, 1991). The results showed that the *male* infants tended to look equally at the test events; in contrast, the *female* infants looked reliably longer when the toy mouse stood on top of the car's tracks than when it stood either in back or in front of the tracks. (This is no doubt the first evidence of female superiority in reasoning about cars! See Baillargeon & DeVos, 1991, for interpretations of this unexpected sex difference.) The results obtained with the female infants indicated that, like the 6½- and the 8-month-old infants in the original experiments, these younger infants were surprised to see the car reappear from behind the screen when the mouse stood in its path.

The results of these experiments thus indicated that, contrary to what Piaget had claimed, infants as young as 4 months of age assume that objects retain their locations when occluded.

Additional Properties.   The experiments described in this section asked whether infants could represent not only the location but also the height and the compressibility of occluded objects.

The first experiment in this series examined 7½-month-old infants' ability to represent the height and the location of a hidden object (Baillargeon, 1987b). The infants were habituated to a screen that rotated back and forth through a 180° arc (see Fig. 9.3). Following habituation, the infants saw a possible and an impossible test event. In both events, a box was placed behind the screen, which rotated back and forth through a 165° arc. The only difference between the events was in the orientation and location of the box behind the screen. In the possible event, the box lay flat 10 cm behind the screen and was 4 cm high; in the impossible event, the box stood upright 25 cm behind the screen and was 20 cm high. The 165° rotation of the screen was consistent with the horizontal orientation of the box (the screen stopped rotating when it reached the box), but not with its vertical orientation (the screen rotated through the space occupied by the top 14 cm or 70% of the box).

The infants looked reliably longer at the impossible than at the possible event, suggesting that they (a) represented the height and location of the box behind the screen; (b) used this information to estimate at what point the screen would reach the box; (c) understood that the screen could not rotate through the space occupied by the box; and therefore (d) were surprised when the screen continued to rotate after it reached the box. This interpretation was supported by a control condition in which the screen underwent a different motion (see Fig. 9.3). In the habituation event, the screen rotated upward 90° and then, remaining vertical, slid backward 30 cm. In the test events, the screen again rotated 90°

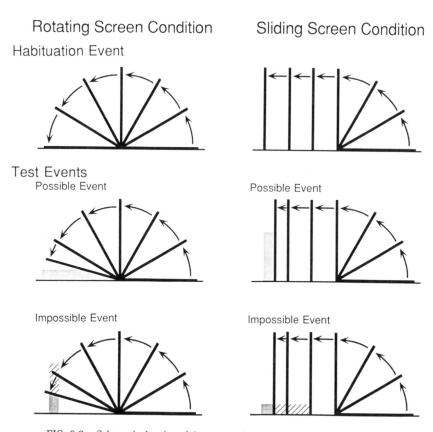

FIG. 9.3. Schematic drawing of the events shown to the infants in Baillargeon (1987b, Exp. 1).

but slid back 25 cm instead of 30 cm. As in the rotating screen condition, the box either stood upright 25 cm behind the screen (possible event), or lay flat 10 cm behind the screen (impossible event). The infants again looked reliably longer at the impossible than at the possible event. This result provided evidence that the infants in the rotating screen condition looked longer at the impossible event, not because they preferred the box in its vertical orientation, but because they were surprised that the screen continued rotating after it reached the box.

The next experiment (Baillargeon, 1987b) examined whether 7½-month-old infants could represent the compressibility as well as the height and location of a hidden object. The infants saw a possible and an impossible test event in which a screen rotated back and forth through a 157° arc (see Fig. 9.4). In the possible event, a soft, compressible object (an irregular ball of gauze) stood behind the screen, and in the impossible event, a hard, non-compressible ob-

Habituation Events
Soft Object (Fluff) Event

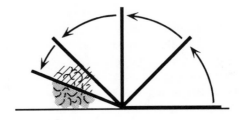

Soft Object (Plastic) Event

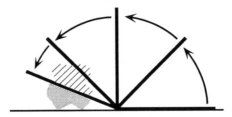

Test Events
Possible Event

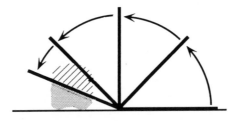

Impossible Event

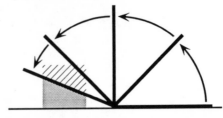

FIG. 9.4. Schematic drawing of the events shown to the infants in Baillargeon (1987b, Exp. 2).

ject (a wooden box) stood behind the screen (the infants were allowed to manipulate the test objects for a few seconds before the experiment began). The two objects were approximately the same color and size and they were placed at the same location behind the screen. The 157° rotation was consistent with the presence of the soft object (the screen could compress the object), but not with the presence of the hard object (the screen appeared to rotate through the space occupied by the top portion of the object). Prior to seeing the test events, the infants watched two habituation events that were identical to the possible event except that other soft objects were used (these were two irregular balls, one made of polyester stuffing and the other of plastic bags).

The infants looked reliably longer at the impossible than at the possible event, suggesting that they (a) represented the height and location of the object behind the screen, and used this information to decide at what point the screen would reach the object; (b) represented the compressibility of the object behind the screen, and understood that the screen could compress the soft but not the hard object; and hence (c) were surprised when the screen continued to rotate after it reached the hard object. This interpretation was supported by a control condition in which the screen rotated 112° instead of 157° and thus stopped before it reached the hard or soft object behind it. The infants in this condition tended to look equally at the test events. This finding provided evidence that the infants in the experimental condition looked longer at the impossible than at the possible event, not because they preferred the hard to the soft object, but because they were surprised that the screen continued to rotate after it reached the incompressible hard object.

Together, the results of these experiments suggested two conclusions. The first was that, by 7½ months of age, infants can represent the physical (e.g., height, compressibility) as well as the spatial (e.g., location) properties of occluded objects. The second was that infants this age can make both qualitative and quantitative predictions about occluded objects. The infants in the experiments not only realized *that* the screen should stop when an object blocked its path (qualitative prediction): They also were able to judge *at what point* the screen should stop, depending on the object's height, compressibility, and location (quantitative prediction). Following the terminology used in computational models of everyday physical reasoning (e.g., Forbus, 1984), the second prediction is said to be quantitative because it required the infants to compute a quantitative estimate of the screen's stopping point. Specifically, the infants had to determine how high above the apparatus floor the screen would be when it came to a stop. In contrast, the first prediction is referred to as qualitative because it embodied no quantitative judgments.

Developmental evidence. The next experiments asked two questions (Baillargeon, 1991). First, would younger infants, 6½- and 4½-month-olds, also be able to represent and to reason quantitatively about the height and location of an occluded object? Second, how precise was infants' quantitative reasoning? In Baillargeon's (1987b) experiment (shown in Fig. 9.3), the screen rotated through the top 70% of the space occupied by the occluded box—to adults, an obvious violation. Would infants still detect that the screen rotated farther than it should if it rotated through a smaller portion of the occluded box? The experiments compared infants' performances with 80% and 50% violations.

In the first experiment, 6½-month-old infants were habituated to a screen that rotated back and forth through a 180° arc (see Fig. 9.5). Following habituation, a box 25 cm tall was placed 12.5 cm behind the screen (as in Baillargeon, 1987a), and the infants saw a possible and an impossible test event. In the possible event, the screen stopped rotating before it reached the occluded box (112° arc); in the impossible event, the screen rotated through either the top 80% (157° arc) or the top 50% (135° arc) of the space occupied by the box.

The results indicated that the infants in the 80% rotation condition looked reliably longer at the impossible than at the possible event, whereas those in

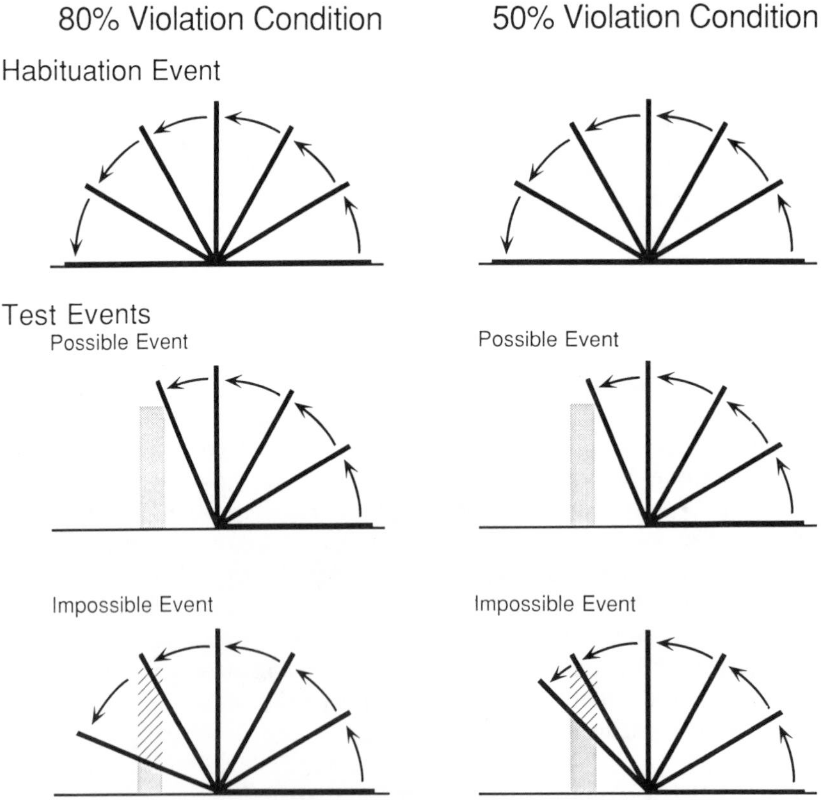

80% Violation Condition   50% Violation Condition

Habituation Event

Test Events
Possible Event   Possible Event

Impossible Event   Impossible Event

FIG. 9.5. Schematic drawing of the events shown to the infants in Baillargeon (1991, Exp. 1).

the 50% violation condition tended to look equally at the two test events. These results suggested that the infants were able to detect the 80% but not the 50% violation. A control condition conducted without a box behind the screen provided evidence that the infants in the 80% violation condition looked longer at the impossible event, not because they preferred the 157° rotation to the 112° rotation, but because they detected that the screen rotated farther than it should have given the box's height and location.

In a subsequent experiment, 4½-month-old infants were tested in the 80% violation condition. The infants failed to show a reliable preference for the impossible over the possible event, suggesting that, in contrast to the 6½-month-old infants, they were unable to detect the 80% violation.

The next experiments investigated whether infants would form more precise expectations about the screen's stopping point under different conditions. These experiments were identical to the last series with one exception: A second, identical box was placed 10 cm to the right of and in the same fronto-parallel plane as the box behind the screen (see Fig. 9.6). This second box stood out of the screen's path and so remained visible throughout the test trials.

With this second box present, (a) the 6½-month-old infants now looked reliably longer when the screen rotated through the top 50% of the occluded box, and (b) the 4½-month-old infants now looked reliably longer when the screen rotated through either the top 80% or the top 50% of the occluded box. These results suggested that the infants spontaneously made use of the second box to predict the screen's stopping point: They were able to detect with this box violations that they failed to detect without it. This interpretation was supported by control conditions in which the box behind the screen was removed, leaving only the box to the side of the screen. The infants in these control conditions tended to look equally at the different screen rotations. These findings provided evidence that the infants in the experimental conditions looked longer at the impossible events, not because they preferred the 157° or the 135° to the 112° screen rotation, but because they were surprised that the screen continued to rotate after it reached the occluded box.

How did the infants make use of the visible box to predict the screen's stopping point? At least two answers were possible. One was that the visible box facilitated the infants' *quantitative* reasoning by providing them with an exact reminder of the occluded box's height and distance from the screen. The other answer was that the visible box made it possible for the infants to offer a *qualitative* prediction about the screen's stopping point. That is, rather than computing the screen's approximate height at its stopping point, the infants could simply reason that the screen would stop when it was aligned with the top of the visible box. This prediction is said to be qualitative because it required no quantitative estimate of the screen's stopping point; the top of the visible box provided the infants with a direct reference point.

Did the infants in the experiments use the visible box to offer a quantitative or a qualitative prediction about the screen's stopping point? To decide between

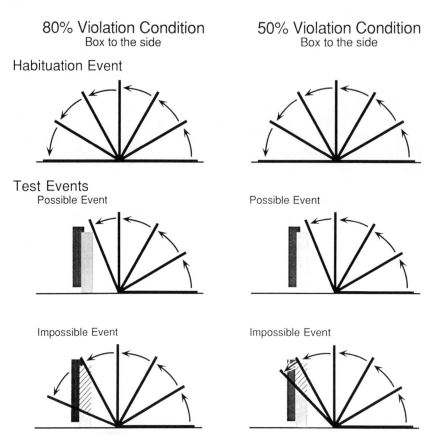

80% Violation Condition
Box to the side

50% Violation Condition
Box to the side

Habituation Event

Test Events
Possible Event

Possible Event

Impossible Event

Impossible Event

FIG. 9.6.   Schematic drawing of the events shown to the infants in Baillargeon (1991, Exp. 4).

these two possibilities, experiments were conducted that were identical to the two-box experiments just described except that the visible box was no longer in the same fronto-parallel plane as the box behind the screen. The visible box now stood 10 cm to the right and 8.5 cm in front of the box behind the screen. Under these conditions, the infants still had a reminder of the occluded box's height and approximate distance from the screen, but they could no longer use an alignment strategy: The screen rotated past the top of the visible box in both the possible and the impossible events. The results indicated that (a) the 6½-month-old infants were no longer able to detect the 50% screen violation, and (b) the 4½-month-old infants were no longer able to detect the 80% and the 50% screen violations.

Together, the results of the experiments reported in this section revealed an interesting developmental sequence. At 6½ months of age, the infants were able to predict both quantitatively and qualitatively at what point the screen would reach the occluded box and stop. Quantitative predictions were produced when only the box behind the screen was present; qualitative predictions were produced when the second box was placed to the right of and in the same plane as the box behind the screen. Not surprisingly, the infants' quantitative predictions were less precise than their qualitative counterparts: The infants could detect 80% violations when reasoning quantitatively, and smaller, 50% violations when reasoning qualitatively.

At 4½ months of age, however, the infants were unable to predict quantitatively at what point the screen would stop. When only the box behind the screen was present, the infants detected 100% violations (Baillargeon, 1987a) but not 80% or 50% violations. They could reason *that* the screen should stop, and were surprised if it completed its 180° rotation without doing so; but they were unable to predict *at what point* the screen should stop.[2] The 112°, 135°, and 157° stopping points were all judged to be consistent with the box's height and location. When the second box was placed to the right of and in the same plane as the occluded box, however, the infants had no difficulty predicting qualitatively at what point the screen would stop, and now viewed both the 135° and the 157° stopping points as unacceptable.

Further Developmental Evidence. The experiments described in the last section pointed to important developments in infants' quantitative reasoning. Additional experiments indicated that there might be differences in infants' qualitative reasoning as well. These experiments tested whether 4½- and 6½-month-old infants would still be able to make use of the second box to detect 50% violations if it differed in appearance from the box behind the screen (Baillargeon, 1992). Technically, the superficial similarity of the two boxes is, of course, irrelevant: As long as the boxes are of the same height and are placed in the same plane, one can be used as a reference point for the other.

The infants were assigned to one of three conditions (see Fig. 9.7). The infants in the high-similarity condition saw two red boxes, one decorated with green dots and the other with white dots; the infants in the moderate-similarity

---

[2]An alternative interpretation might be that, like the 6½-month-old infants, the 4½-month-old infants could predict both quantitatively and qualitatively at what point the screen should stop, but that their quantitative reasoning was so poor that it enabled them to detect only the 100% violation. Recall that the screen rotated through all 25 cm of the box in the 100% violation, and through the top 20 cm and 12.5 cm of the box in the 80% and the 50% violation, respectively. Thus, one might propose that infants can initially detect only extreme (25 cm or greater) violations, and gradually improve with age. However, some additional data are inconsistent with this view. In an unpublished experiment, 4½-month-old infants were found to detect a 100% violation in which a box only 12.5 cm high stood behind the screen. Similar results were obtained with 3½-month-old fast habituators (Baillargeon, 1987a). Such findings suggest that young infants use a qualitative strategy to detect 100% violations. Specifically, infants take as their point of reference the apparatus floor and reason that if the screen rotates until it lies flat against the floor, then it rotates farther than it should, given the presence of the box in its path.

High Similarity

Moderate Similarity

Low Similarity

FIG. 9.7.   Schematic drawing of the boxes shown to the infants in Baillargeon (1992).

condition saw a yellow box with green dots and a red box with white dots; the infants in the low-similarity condition saw a yellow box decorated with a brightly-colored clown face and a red box with white dots (boxes decorated with clown faces were used in all of the rotating screen experiments mentioned in the previous section). The results indicated that (a) the 6½-month-old infants detected the 50% violation in the high- and the moderate- but not the low-similarity condition and (b) the 4½-month-old infants detected the 50% violation in the high- but not the moderate- or the low-similarity conditions.

One possible interpretation for these findings was simply that, as the differences between the boxes increased, the infants became absorbed in the task of comparing the two boxes and as a result paid little or no attention to the screen's motion. To address this possibility, an additional group of 6½-month-old infants was tested using the low-similarity condition procedure. For these infants, however, the two boxes stood on either side of the screen throughout the habituation trials. The reasoning was that this prolonged exposure (the infants received a minimum of six and a maximum of nine habituation trials) would give the infants ample opportunity to peruse the two boxes. However, the results of the experiment were again negative: Despite their increased familiarity with the two boxes, the infants still failed to detect the 50% violation.

Two conclusions followed from the results of these experiments. One was that whether the infants used the visible box to predict when the screen would reach the occluded box depended on the perceptual similarity of the two boxes. The other conclusion was that the older the infants the less similarity they needed to make spontaneous use of the visible box. Whereas the 4½-month-old infants used the visible box to predict the screen's stopping point only when it was identical or highly similar to the occluded box, the 6½-month-old infants used the visible box even when it was only moderately similar to the occluded box. These results suggested that, with age, infants become better at dismissing irrelevant differences in objects they use as reference points in solving physical problems. One noteworthy aspect of these results is that they mirror findings from the analogical reasoning literature: Investigators have shown that children and adults are most likely to realize that the solution to a familiar problem may be of help in solving a novel problem when the superficial similarity between the two problems is high (Brown, 1989; D. Gentner & Toupin, 1986; Gick & Holyoak, 1980; Holyoak, Junn, & Billman, 1984; Ross, 1984).

Converging Evidence. The last set of experiments described in this section used a different paradigm than the rotating screen paradigm to gather converging evidence of young infants' ability to represent and to reason about the properties of occluded objects.

The experiments examined the ability of 5½-month-olds (Baillargeon & Graber, 1987) and 3½-month-olds (Baillargeon & DeVos, 1991) to represent and to reason about the height and trajectory of occluded objects. The infants were habituated to an object, such as a toy rabbit, that slid back and forth along a horizontal track whose center was hidden by a screen (see Fig. 9.8). On alternate trials, the infants saw a short or a tall rabbit slide along the track. Following habituation, the midsection of the screen's upper half was removed, creating a large window. The infants saw a possible and an impossible test event. In the possible event, the short rabbit moved back and forth along the track; this rabbit was shorter than the window's lower edge and thus did not appear in the window when passing behind the screen. In the impossible event, the tall rabbit moved back and forth along the track; this rabbit was taller than the window's lower edge and hence should have appeared in the window but did not in fact do so.

The infants looked equally at the short and the tall rabbit habituation events but looked reliably longer at the impossible than at the possible test event, sug-

Familiarization Events
Short Rabbit Event

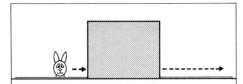

Tall Rabbit Event

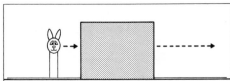

Test Events
Possible Event

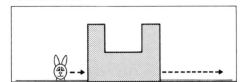

Impossible Event

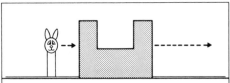

FIG. 9.8. Schematic drawing of the events shown to the infants in Baillargeon and Graber (1987).

gesting that they (a) represented the height of each rabbit behind the screen; (b) assumed that each rabbit pursued its trajectory behind the screen; and hence (c) expected the tall rabbit to appear in the screen window and were surprised that it did not. This interpretation was supported by the results of another condition that was identical to the experimental condition with one important exception: Prior to the habituation trials, the infants received two pretest trials in which they saw two short or two tall rabbits standing motionless, one on each side of the windowless habituation screen. Half of the infants saw the two short rabbits in the first trial and the two tall rabbits in the second trial; the other infants saw the rabbits in the opposite order. Unlike the infants in the experimental condition, the infants in this pretest condition looked equally at the impossible and the possible events. One explanation for these results was that the infants were able to use the information presented in the pretest trials to make sense of the impossible event. Specifically, the infants understood that the tall rabbit did not appear in the screen window because it did not in fact travel the distance behind the screen: Instead, one rabbit traveled from the left end of the track to the left edge of the screen and stopped just inside this edge; a second, identical rabbit then emerged from the right edge of the screen and traveled to the right end of the track (see Baillargeon & DeVos, 1991, for a fuller discussion of these results).

How did the infants in the experimental condition determine whether the tall or the short rabbit should appear in the screen window? The most likely answer, we believed, was that the infants visually compared the height of each rabbit, as it approached the screen, to that of the window. Such a direct visual comparison process was of course qualitative, because it did not require the infants to compute estimates of how high each rabbit would extend above the window's lower edge. This account is analogous to that offered in the last section to explain infants' performances in the two-box experiments.

Three conclusions followed from the present results. First, they confirmed the finding, reported earlier, that 3½-month-old infants represent the existence of occluded objects (Baillargeon, 1987a). Second, the results indicated that infants this age are also able to represent and to reason about some of the physical (height) and spatial (trajectory, location) properties of occluded objects. This finding provided evidence against the hypothesis that the object concept develops in stages, with infants representing first the existence and only later the properties of occluded objects. Finally, the absence of significant differences (Baillargeon & DeVos, 1991) between the responses of the 3½-month-old fast and slow habituators in the experimental condition indicated that both groups of habituators believed that objects continue to exist when out of sight. This finding ruled out one interpretation of the differences obtained in Baillargeon's (1987a) rotating screen experiment, namely, that only the fast habituators preferred the impossible event because only they had attained a notion of object permanence.

Inferring the Existence and Properties of Occluded Objects

The results reported in the last section indicated that infants represent the properties of occluded objects long before the age of 12 months. This finding suggested that infants might be able to make inferences about occluded objects—the last step in Piaget's (1954) developmental sequence—before 18 months of age. The experiments presented in this section examined infants' ability to infer the existence and the properties of occluded objects.

Existence. The first experiment in this series tested 6- and 9-month-old infants' ability to infer the presence of a hidden object from the presence of a protuberance in a soft cloth cover (Baillargeon & DeVos, 1992). The infants were shown a possible and an impossible event (see Fig. 9.9). At the start of each event, the infants saw two covers made of soft pink fabric; one lay flat on the table, and the other showed a large protuberance. Next, two screens were pushed in front of the covers, hiding them from view. A hand then reached behind the right screen and reappeared first with the cover and then with a toy bear of the same height as the protuberance seen earlier. The only difference between the two test events was in the location of the two covers at the start

Possible Event

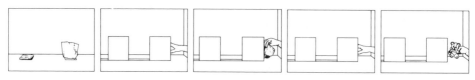

Impossible Event

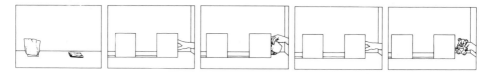

FIG. 9.9. Schematic drawing of the events shown to the infants in Baillargeon and DeVos (1992, Exp. 1).

of the trials. In the possible event, the flat cover was behind the left screen and the cover with the protuberance was behind the right screen; in the impossible event, the position of the two covers was reversed.

The results indicated that the 9-month-old infants looked reliably longer at the impossible event, suggesting that they (a) represented the appearance and location of the two covers behind the screens and (b) understood that an object could be retrieved from under the cover with a protuberance but not the flat cover. This interpretation was supported by a control condition in which the hand reached behind the left rather than the right screen so that the bear's position in the impossible and the possible events was reversed.[3]

In contrast to the 9-month-old infants, the 6-month-old infants looked equally at the impossible and the possible events, suggesting that they found it equally plausible for the bear to have been hidden under the cover with a protuberance or the flat cover. This negative result was replicated in another experiment conducted with a simpler procedure. In this experiment, the infants saw a single cover in each test event: the flat cover in the impossible event, and the cover with a protuberance in the possible event. After a few seconds, the cover was hidden by a screen. Next, the hand reached behind the screen and retrieved first the cover and then the toy bear. The infants again looked equally at the impossible and the possible events, suggesting that they believed that the bear could have been hidden under either the flat cover or the cover with a protuberance.

---

[3]These results have implications for explaining infants' perseverative search errors. Piaget (1954), Bower (1974), and others have noted that infants will return to a location, A, for an object they have seen disappear in a location B, *even when* the object creates a large protuberance or emits a sound under the B cover. The present results suggest that by 9 months of age infants have the cognitive ability to use such information to infer where the object is hidden. Why infants do not make this inference is addressed further on.

These negative results seemed inconsistent with the results of the first rotating screen task described earlier (Baillargeon, 1987a). In this task, 5½-, 4½-, and even 3½-month-old infants were surprised to see the screen lay flat against the apparatus floor when the box stood behind it. In the present task, 6-month-old infants were *not* surprised to see the bear retrieved from under a cover that lay flat against the apparatus floor. Both tasks called upon the same general physical knowledge: In each case, the infants had to appreciate that objects continue to exist when hidden, and that objects cannot occupy the same space as other objects. Nevertheless, there was one important difference between the two tasks. In the rotating screen task, the infants saw the box and then were asked to predict its effect on the screen. In the present task, however, the infants did not see the bear but had to infer its presence from its effect on the cover. What this analysis suggests is that infants are able to reason about known objects several months before they are able to make inferences about unknown objects. Having formed a representation of an object, infants can use this representation to reason about the object after it has become hidden from view. However, infants cannot make inferences about an unknown object, even when the cues that point to the existence of the object call upon precisely the same knowledge infants would use to reason about a known object. We return to this issue at the end of the next section.

Size. The results described in the last section indicated that, by 9 months of age, infants could use the presence of a protuberance in a soft cloth cover to infer the existence of an object beneath the cover. Our next experiment investigated whether infants could also use the size of a protuberance in a cloth cover to infer the size of the object beneath the cover (Baillargeon & DeVos, 1992).

In this experiment, 12½- and 13½-month-old infants watched two test events (see Fig. 9.10). At the start of each event, the infants saw a purple cloth cover with a protuberance approximately equal in size to that in the last experiment. Next, a screen was raised in front of the cover, hiding it from view. A hand then reached behind the screen twice in succession, reappearing first with the cover and then with either a small dog of the same size as the protuberance (possible event), or a large dog more than twice as large as the protuberance (impossible event).

The 13½-month-old infants looked reliably longer at the impossible than at the possible event, suggesting that they (a) used the size of the protuberance in the cover to infer the size of the object under the cover, and hence (b) were surprised to see the hand reappear holding the large dog. Support for this interpretation came from a control condition in which a cover with a protuberance as large as the large dog was shown at the beginning of the test events. The infants in this condition looked about equally when the large and the small dogs were retrieved from behind the screen. This finding showed that the infants in the experimental condition looked reliably longer at the impossible event, not

Possible Event

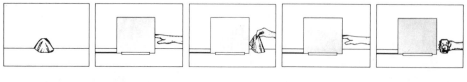

Impossible Event

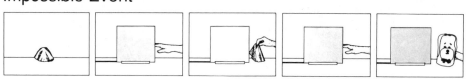

FIG. 9.10. Schematic drawing of the events shown to the infants in Baillargeon and DeVos (1992, Exp. 4).

because they preferred the large dog, but because they realized that its size was inconsistent with the size of the protuberance shown at the start of the event.

Why did the infants in the control condition look equally when the small and the large dogs were retrieved from under the cover? The most likely explanation, we believed, was that the infants realized that neither event was impossible: Either dog could have been hidden under the cover. Something in addition to the small dog could have been hidden under the cover, such as a doghouse, to give the cover its large protuberance.

In contrast to the 13½-month-old infants, the 12½-month-old infants (in the experimental condition) tended to look equally at the impossible and the possible events, suggesting that they believed that the large or the small dog could have been hidden under the cover. Our next experiment examined whether infants would perform better when provided, as in the two-box rotating screen experiments described earlier (Baillargeon, 1991), with a second, identical cover that remained visible throughout the experiment (see Figure 9.11). Subjects in the experiment were 12½- and 9½-month-old infants.

The 9½-month-old infants tended to look equally at the two test events. In contrast, the 12½-month-old infants looked reliably longer at the impossible than at the possible event, suggesting that they made use of the visible cover to judge that the small but not the large dog could have been hidden under the cover behind the screen. A control condition supported this interpretation. The infants in this condition were simply shown the hand holding the small or the large dog next to the visible cover, as in the right panels in Fig. 9.11. The infants in this condition looked about equally at the large and the small dog displays. This result provided evidence that the infants in the experimental condition looked longer at the impossible event, not because they preferred seeing the large dog next to the visible cover, but because they detected that this dog was too large to have been hidden under the cover behind the screen.

Possible Event

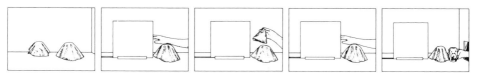

Impossible Event

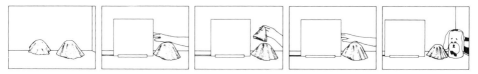

FIG. 9.11.   Schematic drawing of the events shown to the infants in Baillargeon and DeVos (1992, Exp. 5).

The 12½-month-old infants in this last experiment clearly made use of the visible cover to determine which dog could have been hidden under the cover behind the screen: They were able to detect, with the help of this second cover, a violation that they failed to detect without it. How did the second cover help the infants' performance? As in the two-box experiments described earlier (Baillargeon, 1991), two answers were possible. One was that the second cover enhanced the infants' quantitative reasoning by providing them with an exact reminder of the size of the hidden cover's protuberance. Armed with this reminder, the infants were then in a better position to compute a quantitative estimate of the size of the object hidden under the cover. The other possibility was that the visible cover enabled the infants to use a qualitative approach to judging which dog could have been hidden under the cover behind the screen, by comparing each dog to the visible cover.

To decide between these two possibilities, an additional group of 12½-month-old infants was tested in a control condition in which the visible cover was placed to the left rather than to the right of the screen. In this condition, the infants still had a reminder of the hidden cover's exact size, but because the dog was retrieved to the right of the screen they could no longer compare in a single glance the visible cover and the small or the large dog. The infants in this condition looked about equally at the two events. This finding provided evidence that the infants in the experimental condition detected that the large dog could not have been hidden under the cover behind the screen by directly comparing the size of the visible cover to that of the small and the large dogs.

The results of these experiments were in many ways strikingly similar to those of the rotating screen experiments discussed earlier (Baillargeon, 1991). Recall that the 6½-month-old infants could predict quantitatively, but the 4½-month-old infants only qualitatively, at what point the screen would reach the occluded box and stop. Similarly, in the present experiments, the 13½-month-old infants could reason quantitatively, but the 12½-month-old infants only qualitatively, about the size of the dog hidden beneath the cover behind the screen.

One explanation for these results is that, as infants become aware of specific variables affecting events' outcomes (e.g., the height and location of the box in the rotating screen task, or the size of the protuberance in the soft cover task), they are able to reason at first qualitatively and only later quantitatively about the effect of these variables. Why development should proceed in this manner is as yet unclear. However, the answer is unlikely to involve infants' memory for quantitative information. Recall that the infants in the rotating screen experiments failed to detect the 50% violation when the visible box was moved slightly forward of the hidden box, just as the 12½-month-old infants in the present experiments failed to realize that the large dog could not have been under the hidden cover when the visible cover was placed to the left of the screen. Providing the infants with a reminder of the hidden object's size and location thus did not improve their performance, suggesting that a faulty memory was not the primary source of their difficulty.

Despite their similarity, the results of the experiments reported in this section differ from the results of the rotating screen experiments in one crucial respect: They involve much older infants. The décalages revealed by these experiments parallel the one discussed in the last section. Recall that infants were found to be able to reason about the existence of a known, hidden object several months before they were able to infer the existence of an unknown hidden object. The present results suggest that infants are also able to reason (qualitatively and quantitatively) about the properties of a known hidden object long before they can infer (qualitatively and quantitatively) the properties of an unknown hidden object. Why are infants very good, from an early age, at reasoning about what they know, but very poor, until late in the first year, at inferring what they don't know? We return to this question in the Conclusion.

Location. Piaget (1954) held that infants less than 18 months of age are unable to infer the location of hidden objects because they are unable to infer displacements that occur behind occluders. We have recently begun experiments to examine this claim with infants aged 11½ to 13½ months. These experiments are too preliminary to be described here. The initial results we have obtained, however, tentatively suggest that by the end of the first year infants are already able to infer a hidden object's location. If valid, these results would indicate that Piaget underestimated the age at which infants begin to show evidence of this ability. In addition, the results would again point to a marked décalage between infants' ability to reason about locations and trajectories they have directly witnessed, even after these are hidden from view, and to infer novel locations and trajectories. Recall that in the rolling car experiments reported earlier, 8-, 6½-, and even 4-month-old infants were able to reason about the location of the box and the trajectory of the car behind the screen (Baillargeon,

1986; Baillargeon & DeVos, 1991). Similarly, in the sliding rabbits experiments, 5½- and 3½-month-old infants were able to reason about each rabbit's trajectory behind the screen (Baillargeon & Graber, 1987; Baillargeon & DeVos, 1991).

Piaget assumed that because young infants could not infer invisible displacements, they did not appreciate that occluded objects obey the same physical laws as visible objects. Although Piaget may have been right in claiming that young infants cannot infer hidden trajectories, there is reason to doubt that young infants do not understand that occluded objects follow the same predictable patterns as visible objects. The infants in the car and the sliding rabbits experiments clearly perceived the car's and the rabbits' displacements behind the screen to be constrained by the same laws that apply to visible displacements. In particular, the infants believed that the car and the rabbits moved along continuous paths behind the screen just as they did on either side of the screen; they understood that the car could not roll through the box in its path; and they assumed that each rabbit retained its height while traveling behind the screen. Such data support the notion that young infants' inability to make inferences about hidden objects stems not from a belief that hidden objects' displacements and interactions with other objects are arbitrary and unpredictable, but from an incapacity to reason without concrete representations of objects and their properties.

WHY THE DISCREPANCY BETWEEN SEARCH AND NON-SEARCH ASSESSMENTS OF OBJECT PERMANENCE?

The experiments reported earlier indicated that infants represent the existence and the location of hidden objects at a very early age. Why, then, do infants fail to search for hidden objects until 7½ to 9 months of age? And why do they search perseveratively when they begin to search for objects? These two questions are considered in turn.

Why do Young Infants Fail to Search for Hidden Objects?

If infants realize, at 3½ months of age, that objects continue to exist when hidden, why do they fail to search for objects until 7½ to 9 months of age (e.g., Diamond, 1985; Willatts, 1984)? It is not surprising that 3½-month-old infants, whose motor abilities are very limited, do not engage in search activities, but what of older infants? Why do they fail to search for hidden objects?

One possibility is suggested by observations on the development of action in infancy. Researchers (e.g., Diamond, 1988; Piaget, 1952; Willatts, 1989) have noted that it is not until infants are 7½ to 9 months of age that they begin to coordinate actions directed at separate objects into means–end sequences. In these sequences, infants apply one action to one object so as to create conditions under which they can apply another action to another object. Examples of such sequences include pulling the near end of a cloth to bring within reach a toy placed on the far end of the cloth, pushing aside a cushion to get a toy visible on the other side of the cushion, or reaching around to the opening of a transparent box to get a toy placed inside the box. Thus, young infants might fail to search for hidden objects simply because this task typically requires them to coordinate separate actions on separate objects (e.g., lifting a cloth to get a toy hidden under the cloth).

Support for this hypothesis comes from reports that infants *do* search for hidden objects when they can find the objects by performing direct, as opposed to means–end, actions. First, a number of authors (e.g., Bower & Wishart, 1972; Clifton, Rochat, Litovsky, & Perris, 1991; Hood & Willatts, 1986) have found that young infants readily search for objects "hidden" by darkening the room. For example, Hood and Willatts (1986) presented 5-month-old infants with an object on the left or the right side within reaching distance; the infants were restrained from reaching for the object. Next, the room lights were turned off, the object was removed, and the infants' hands were released. Infrared recordings indicated that the infants reached more often to the side where they had seen the object than to the opposite side.

Second, recall Piaget's observation that when young infants hold an object out of sight and accidentally let go of it, they often stretch their arm to recapture it. One of Piaget's protocols involved his son Laurent: "As early as 0;4(6) Laurent searches with his hand for a doll he has just let go. He does not look at what he is doing but extends his arm in the direction toward which it was oriented when the object fell" (Piaget, 1954, p. 23).

Finally, young infants search visually for objects, as when they anticipate objects' reappearance from behind occluders (e.g., Moore, Borton, & Darby, 1978; Piaget, 1954). In a similar vein, we have observed that infants who are shown impossible events involving an object hidden behind a screen sometimes lean to the side and attempt to look behind the screen, as if to verify for themselves the continued presence of the object.

Thus, it appears that young infants do search for hidden objects when they can search without producing means–end sequences, by groping for objects "hidden" by the dark or dropped out of sight, or by peering past or around screens that block their line of vision.

On the strength of this evidence, let us assume that young infants perform poorly on most search tasks because these tasks typically require them to produce means–end sequences. The next question we must address is: Why do infants less than 7½ to 9 months of age have difficulty producing means–end sequences? Two general hypotheses come to mind. One is that infants are unable to *perform* such sequences because of poor motor control; the other is that infants are unable to *plan* such sequences because of limited problem solving ability.

Studies of young infants' actions provide little support for the first hypothesis. The actions involved in the examples of means–end sequences I have listed (reaching for, grasping, pulling, pushing, lifting, and releasing objects) fall well within the behavioral repertoire of 4- to 7-month-old infants (Bushnell, 1985; Granrud, 1986; von Hofsten, 1980; Newell, Scully, McDonald, & Baillargeon, 1989; Piaget, 1952, 1954). Furthermore, infants this age seem to have little difficulty performing series of actions in rapid succession. Piaget (1952) described in meticulous and delightful detail how his children, beginning at 3½ months of age, would repeatedly kick, pull, swing, shake, or strike objects suspended from their bassinet hoods, at times systematically varying the speed and vigor of their actions, and at other times playfully intermingling bouts of different actions, such as pulling and shaking or striking and shaking. Such observations are inconsistent with the hypothesis that young infants' failure to produce means–end sequences stems from inadequate motor skills.

The second hypothesis was that young infants are unable to plan means–end sequences because of problem solving difficulties. Before discussing the potential source of these difficulties, let us define a few terms.

Problem solving is frequently described in cognitive psychology in terms of searching a *problem space*, which consists of various states of a problem. The goal pursued by the problem solver is referred to as the *goal state* and the initial situation that faces the problem solver as the *initial state; operators* are actions carried out by the problem solver to generate each successive *intermediate state* on the way to the goal (e.g., Anderson, 1985; Mayer, 1983; Newell & Simon, 1972).

Having established this terminology, we can now consider a typical search problem situation: A young infant watches an experimenter hide an attractive toy under a cover. To what should we attribute the infant's failure to search for the toy? A first possibility is that the infant's goal in the situation differs from what the experimenter has in mind. Instead of seeking to retrieve the toy, the infant may be pursuing a different, unrelated goal. A second possibility is that the infant's representation of the situations' initial state is inaccurate or incomplete, making it impossible for the infant to find a sequence of operators to retrieve the toy. For example, the infant may represent the existence but not the location of the hidden toy.

Neither of these two possibilities is likely, however. With respect to the first possibility, there is ample evidence that young infants reach readily for objects that are "hidden" by the dark (Clifton et al., 1991; Hood & Willatts, 1986), as well as for objects that are only partially visible (Piaget, 1954). Furthermore, young infants are sometimes distressed when desired objects are hidden before them and attempt to grasp the objects as soon as they are even partially uncovered, either by the experimenter's or by their own chance actions (Piaget,

1954). Such observations are inconsistent with the hypothesis that young infants do not search for hidden objects because they have no wish to possess them. With respect to the second possibility, it is difficult, given the results of the experiments I have summarized (e.g., Baillargeon, 1986, 1987a, 1991; Baillargeon & DeVos, 1991; Baillargeon et al., 1985; Hood & Willatts, 1986), to believe that young infants' representation of the initial conditions of search situations could be seriously flawed. The results of these experiments suggest that young infants are able to represent the existence and the location of hidden objects and to reason about these objects in sophisticated, adult-like ways. Such findings are not easily reconciled with the proposal that young infants fail to retrieve objects hidden behind obstacles because their representation of the objects, the obstacles, or the relations between them is deficient.

Young infants' representation of the goal state and initial state of means–end problem situations thus seems unlikely to be responsible for their lack of success in these situations. Another, more likely possibility is that this lack of success reflects difficulties in reasoning about operators—about the actions that are applied to transform the initial state into the goal state. Two general hypotheses can be distinguished. First, it may be that infants perform poorly in means–end situations because their knowledge of the relevant operators is lacking or incomplete. Infants may not be fully aware of the preconditions necessary for the application of an operator, or of the effects of an operator. For example, infants may realize that grasping an object will result in their possession of the object, but not that it will *also* alter the location of the object relative to other objects in the situation. Infants would thus be unable to appreciate why grasping the cover placed over a toy would bring them closer to achieving their goal of recovering the toy; to their minds, grasping the cover would result only in their holding the cover, not in their gaining access to the toy. Second, it may be that infants are unable to select or chain appropriate sequences of operators to achieve their goals, even when the relevant operators and their preconditions and effects are well-known to them.

Experiments were conducted to examine the first of the two hypotheses just mentioned, namely, that young infants are unable to plan means–end search sequences because they lack sufficient knowledge about the operators or actions involved in the sequences (Baillargeon, Graber, DeVos, & Black, 1990). In these experiments, 5½-month-old infants were shown events in which a toy was placed in front of, behind, or under an obstacle. The experiments tested whether the infants could distinguish between actions (performed by an experimenter's hand) that *could* result in the toy's retrieval and actions that could *not*. We reasoned that evidence that the infants could identify correct and incorrect actions for the toy's retrieval would argue against the hypothesis that young infants cannot plan search sequences because their knowledge of the relevant actions is lacking or incomplete.

Our first experiment examined whether 5½-month-old infants are aware that a direct reaching action is sufficient to retrieve a toy placed in front of an obstacle, but is not sufficient to retrieve a toy placed behind (barrier condition) or under (cover condition) an obstacle.

The infants in the barrier condition were shown a possible and an impossible test event (see Fig. 9.12). At the start of each event, the infants saw a toy bird and a barrier standing side by side at the center of a display box. After a few seconds, a screen was pushed in front of the objects, hiding them from view. Next, a hand reached behind the screen's right edge and reappeared holding the bird. The only difference between the two events was in the relative positions of the bird and the barrier at the start of the events. In the possible event, the barrier was on the left and the bird was on the right, directly accessible to the hand; in the impossible event, the bird was on the left and the barrier was on the right, blocking the hand's access to the bird. Prior to the test events, the infants saw familiarization events designed to acquaint them with various facets of the events (see Fig. 9.12).

The events shown to the infants in the cover condition were similar to those

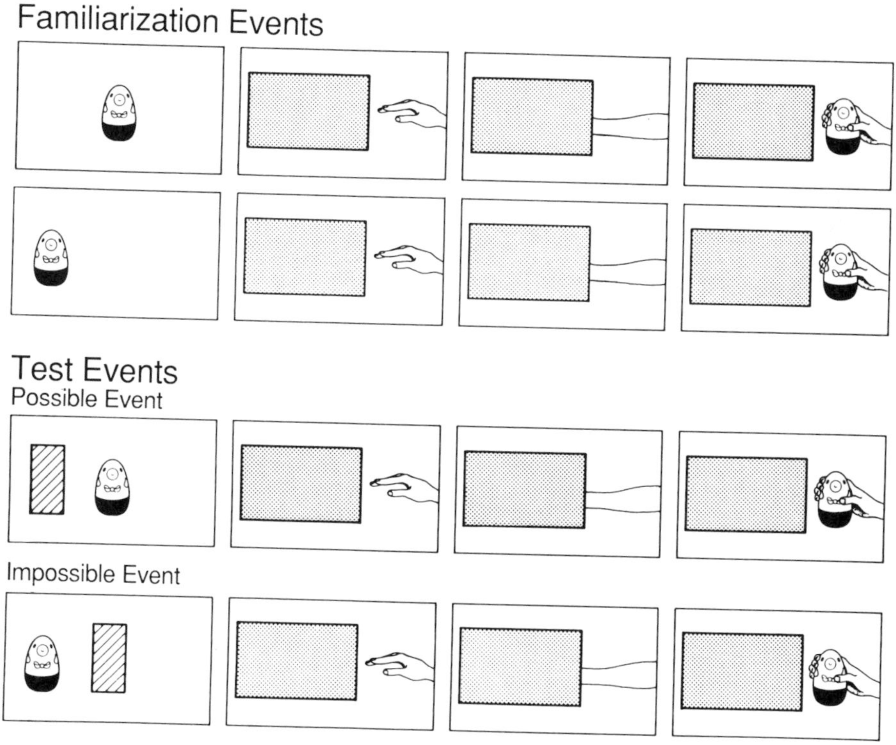

Familiarization Events

Test Events
Possible Event

Impossible Event

FIG. 9.12. Schematic drawing of the events shown to the infants in the barrier condition in Baillargeon et al. (1990, Exp. 1).

in the barrier condition except that the bird and the barrier were replaced by a bear and a clear rigid cover (see Fig. 9.13). In the possible event, the cover was on the left and the bear was on the right, where it could be retrieved by the hand; in the impossible event, the bear was under the cover and should therefore have been inaccessible to the hand.

The results indicated that the infants in the two conditions looked reliably longer at the impossible than at the possible event, suggesting that they (a) represented the existence and the location of the toy (bird, bear) and the obstacle (barrier, cover) behind the screen; (b) realized that the direct reaching action of the hand could result in the retrieval of the toy when it stood in front of, but not behind (barrier condition) or under (cover condition), the obstacle; and therefore (c) were surprised in the impossible event to see the hand reappear from behind the screen holding the toy. Support for this interpretation was provided by pretest trials which showed that the infants in the barrier condition did not prefer seeing the bird behind rather than in front of the barrier, and that the infants in the cover condition did not prefer seeing the bear under as opposed to in front of the cover.

The results of this experiment suggested that, by 5½ months of age, infants are aware that a direct reaching action is insufficient to retrieve an object placed behind or under an obstacle. Our next experiment examined whether

Familiarization Event

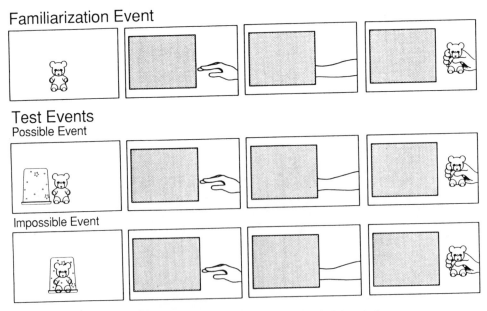

Test Events
Possible Event

Impossible Event

FIG. 9.13. Schematic drawing of the events shown to the infants in the cover condition in Baillargeon et al. (1990, Exp. 1).

Familiarization Events
Cage Familiarization Event

Right Familiarization Event

Left Familiarization Event

Test Events
Possible Event

Impossible Event

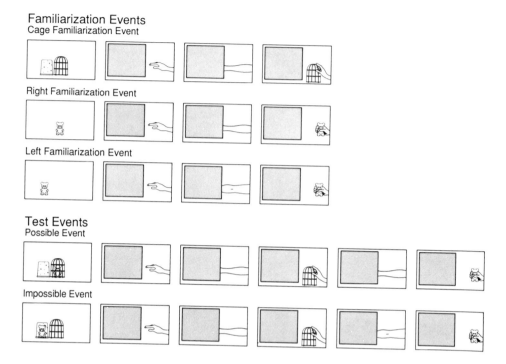

FIG. 9.14. Schematic drawing of the events shown to the infants in the experimental condition in Baillargeon et al. (1990, Exp. 2).

infants this age know what actions *are* sufficient to retrieve an object placed under an obstacle.

The infants again saw a possible and an impossible test event (see Fig. 9.14). At the start of each event, the infants saw two covers placed side by side: On the left was the clear cover used in the first experiment and on the right was a small cage. The toy bear used in the first experiment stood under one of the two covers. After a few seconds, a screen was pushed in front of the objects, hiding them from view. Next, a hand reached behind the screen's right edge and reappeared holding the cage. After depositing the cage on the floor of the apparatus, the hand again reached behind the screen and reappeared holding the bear. The only difference between the two test events was in the location of the bear at the start of the events. In the possible event, the bear was under the cage and hence could be retrieved after the cage was removed. In the impossible event, the bear was under the clear cover and hence should still have been inaccessible to the hand after the cage was removed. Prior to the test events, the infants saw familiarization events designed to acquaint them with different facets of the test situation.

A second group of 5½-month-old infants was tested in a control condition identical to the experimental condition except that the clear cover was replaced by a shallow, clear container. The bear's head and upper body protruded above the rim of the container (see Fig. 9.15). In this condition, the bear was always accessible to the hand after the cage was removed.

The infants in the experimental condition looked reliably longer in the impossible than at the possible event, whereas the infants in the control condition tended to look equally at the bear-in-container and the bear-in-cage events. These results indicated that the infants (a) represented the existence and the location of the bear, the cage, and the clear cover or container behind the screen; (b) understood that the hand's sequence of actions was sufficient to retrieve the bear when it stood under the cage or in the container but not when it was placed under the clear cover; and hence (c) were surprised in the impossible event when the hand reappeared holding the bear.

The results of these initial experiments indicated that young infants can readily identify what actions are and what actions are not sufficient to retrieve objects whose access is blocked by obstacles. Would young infants be as successful at reasoning about other means–end problems? To explore this question, we

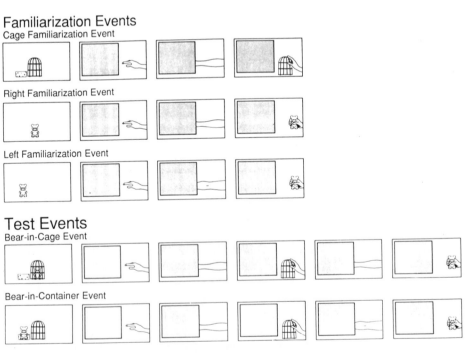

FIG. 9.15. Schematic drawing of the events shown to the infants in the control condition in Baillargeon et al. (1990, Exp. 2).

have begun experiments on another means–end sequence infants have been found not to produce until 7½ to 9 months of age, namely, pulling one end of a support to bring within reach an object placed on the opposite end of the support (e.g., Piaget, 1952; Willatts, 1989).

Only one experiment has been completed to date. This experiment tested whether 6½-month-old infants realize that pulling the near end of a support is sufficient to bring within reach an object placed on the far end of the support, but not an object placed next to the support (Baillargeon, DeVos, & Black, 1992). The infants watched a possible and an impossible test event (see Fig. 9.16). At the start of each event, the infants saw a rigid support (a long, narrow platform covered with brightly colored paper) lying across the floor of the apparatus, and a small toy bear. After a few seconds, a screen was pushed in front of the objects, hiding them from view. The upper right corner of this screen was missing, creating a small window. Next, a hand reached behind the screen's right edge, took hold of the support's right end, and pulled it until the bear's head became visible in the screen window. The hand then reached behind the screen, grasped the bear, and brought it out from behind the screen. The only difference between the two test events was in the location of the bear at the start of the event. In the possible event, the bear was placed on the left end of the support; in the impossible event, the bear was placed on the floor of the apparatus, to the left of the support.

The infants looked reliably longer at the impossible than at the possible event, suggesting that they (a) represented the existence and the location of the bear

Possible Event

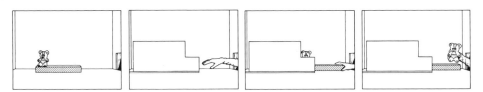

Impossible Event

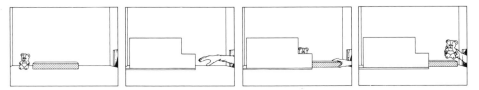

FIG. 9.16.   Schematic drawing of the events shown to the infants in Baillargeon, DeVos, & Black (1992).

and the support behind the screen; (b) understood that pulling the support was sufficient to bring the bear to the window when the bear stood on, but not off, the support; and thus (c) were surprised in the impossible event to see the bear appear in the window. Support for this interpretation was provided by pretest trials that indicated that the infants had no reliable preference for seeing the bear off as opposed to on the support.

The findings of the experiments presented in this section indicate that infants aged 5½ to 6½ months have little difficulty (in some situations, at least) determining what actions can and what actions cannot result in the retrieval of an object placed out of reach beneath a cover or at the far end of a support. Evidence that young infants can readily identify valid means–end sequences argues against the hypothesis that infants fail to plan such sequences because their knowledge of the operators involved in the sequences is inaccurate or incomplete.

To what, then, should one attribute young infants' inability to plan means–end sequences? One possibility, already alluded to, is that young infants are unable to select or chain appropriate operators, even when these are well-known to them. At least two explanations could be advanced for this inability. One is that young infants lack a subgoaling ability—an ability to form sequences of operators such that each operator satisfies a subgoal that brings infants one step closer to their goal. This explanation seems unlikely given that young infants routinely perform what appear to be intentional series of actions directed at single objects. An example of such a goal-directed action sequence might be infants' reaching for and grasping a bottle, bringing it to their mouths, and sucking its nipple. Piaget (1952) described many sequences of this type. Several of his observations involve his children's responses to chains suspended from rattles attached to their bassinet hood. For example, Piaget noted the following: "At 0;3(14) Laurent looks at the rattle at the moment I hang up the chain. He remains immobile for a second. Then he tries to grasp the chain (without looking at it), brushes it with the back of his hand, grasps it but continues to look at the rattle without moving his arms. Then he shakes the chain gently while studying the effect. Afterward he shakes it more and more vigorously. A smile and expression of delight" (p. 163). It is very difficult to imagine how an infant might be capable of such clearly intentional actions and yet lack a subgoaling ability. Laurent's reaching for, grasping, and shaking the chain are all actions performed in the service of his goal, experienced from the start, of shaking the rattle.

A second explanation for young infants' inability to chain operators in means–end sequences is that young infants possess a subgoaling ability but have difficulty with situations in which the performance of the means would put them in apparent conflict with the achievement of their goal. That is, if infants want to grasp a toy placed under a cover, or at the far end of a cover, then grasping the cover puts them in apparent conflict with their goal of grasping the toy. Similarly, reaching around a screen to retrieve an object placed behind the screen may be difficult for infants because it puts them in the position of having to reach away from where they know the object to be.

Exactly why infants have difficulty with these conflict situations is unclear. However, it should be noted that adults often show similar difficulties. Klahr (personal communication, April 16, 1990) has found that naive adults who are given the Tower of Hanoi problem will avoid performing moves that are in apparent conflict with their goal, even though these counterintuitive moves are, in fact, the correct ones. According to this second explanation, then, infants would be in the same position as adults who, when faced with physical problems whose solutions require counterintuitive actions, find themselves able to *identify* but not to *generate* correct solutions to the problems.

Why do Infants Search in the Wrong Location for Hidden Objects?

Piaget (1954) attributed infants' perseverative errors in the AB search task to limitations of their object concept. Infants, Piaget maintained, do not conceive of the hidden object as a separate entity whose displacements are regulated by physical laws, but as a thing "at the disposal" of their action: They return to A after watching the experimenter hide the object at B because they believe that by repeating their action at A they will again produce the object.

The results reported in the previous sections argued against Piaget's interpretation of infants' AB errors. These results indicated that infants aged 4 months and older are able to represent and to reason about the location of one or more hidden objects. Further evidence against Piaget's interpretation came from reports that AB errors rarely occur when infants are allowed to search immediately after the object is hidden at B; errors occur only when infants are forced to wait before they search (e.g., Diamond, 1985; Wellman et al., 1987). Furthermore, the older the infants, the longer the delay necessary to produce errors (e.g., Diamond, 1985; Fox, Kagan, & Weiskopf, 1979; Gratch, Appel, Evans, LeCompte, & Wright, 1974; Harris, 1973; Miller, Cohen, & Hill, 1970; Wellman et al., 1987). Thus, according to Diamond's (1985) longitudinal study, the delay needed to elicit AB errors increases at a mean rate of 2 seconds per month, from less than 2 seconds at 7½ months to over 10 seconds by 12 months. There is no obvious way in which Piaget's theory can explain these findings.

In recent years, several interpretations have been proposed for infants' search errors (e.g., Bjork & Cummings, 1984; Diamond, 1985; Harris, 1987, 1989; Kagan, 1974; Schacter, Moscovitch, Tulving, McLachlan, & Freedman, 1986; Sophian & Wellman, 1983; Wellman et al., 1987). One hypothesis is that these errors reflect the limits of infants' recall memory, with increases in the delay infants tolerate without producing errors corresponding to increases in their retention capacity (e.g., Kagan, 1974). There is a long-standing assumption within the field of infant memory (e.g., Bruner, Olver, & Greenfield, 1966; Piaget, 1951, 1952) that recognition memory is present during the first weeks of life, whereas recall memory does not become operative until late in infancy. Investigations of recognition memory using habituation and preferential-looking paradigms have shown that by 5 months of age infants can recognize stimuli after delays of several hours, days, and even weeks (e.g., Fagan, 1970, 1973; Martin, 1975). These data contrast sharply with those obtained with the AB search task and, it would seem, give credence to the notion that recall memory emerges long after recognition memory and is at first exceedingly fragile, lasting at most a few seconds.

There are serious grounds, however, to doubt explanations of infants' search errors in terms of a late-emerging and easily disrupted recall capacity. Meltzoff (1988) recently reported experimental evidence that young infants can recall information after intervals considerably longer than those used in the AB search task. In Meltzoff's study, 9-month-old infants watched an experimenter perform three actions on novel objects; 24 hours later, they were given the same objects to manipulate. The results indicated that half of the infants spontaneously imitated two or more of the actions they had observed on the previous day. This finding (which was supported by findings from control conditions) suggested that by 9 months of age, if not before, infants can recall information after a 24-hour delay.

The hypothesis that infants' perseverative and random search errors reflect the general limits of their recall memory is thus unlikely (because infants perform successfully in different circumstances with longer delays), but perhaps this hypothesis could be revised to render it more plausible. One could propose that infants' search errors stem from the absence or the immaturity of a *specific* recall mechanism that is critical for success on the AB task but not on Meltzoff's (1988) delayed imitation task. Comparison of the two tasks suggests several candidate mechanisms. For instance, the AB task requires infants to update the information they have in memory as the object's location is changed; no such updating is needed in Meltzoff's task. A difficulty with this particular candidate, however, is that infants perform well on the AB task with short delays, indicating that they have no trouble updating information.

A more likely candidate for the specific recall mechanism implicated in infants' search errors is an inability to hold updated information in memory. We have just seen that infants have little difficulty updating information, and we know from Meltzoff's data that they can hold information for long delays. Infants' search errors, it might be hypothesized, stem from an inability to correctly perform both of these tasks at once.

In recent years, several versions of this hypothesis have been put forth (e.g., Diamond, 1985; Harris, 1973, 1989; Schacter & Moscovitch, 1983; Sophian & Wellman, 1983; Wellman et al., 1987). For example, one account of infants' AB errors assumes that infants can update information about the object's hiding place but can retain this information only for brief delays because of an extreme sensitivity to proactive interference (e.g., Harris, 1973; Schacter & Moscovitch, 1983). According to this view, as infants grow older, they become able to withstand longer and longer delays before the B representation becomes supplanted by the A representation formed on the previous trial. Another account maintains that both the A and B representations remain available in memory. However, infants rapidly forget or dismiss the fact that the B representation represents the object's *current* location. When deciding whether the object is hidden at A or at B, before engaging in search, infants tend to choose the prior A location because of an inadequate selectivity rule (e.g., Sophian & Wellman, 1983), of a mistaken attempt to infer the object's current location from its prior location (e.g., Wellman et al., 1987), or of an undue reliance on long-term spatial information (e.g., Harris, 1989). In each case it is assumed that infants are more likely to choose the correct B location when there is no delay between hiding and search, and that with increasing age, infants choose correctly over increasingly long delays.

Do infants' search errors stem from some deficient recall memory mechanism? A series of experiments were carried out to examine this hypothesis (Baillargeon & Graber, 1988; Baillargeon, DeVos, & Graber, 1989). We reasoned that if infants are unable to update, hold, and selectively attend to information about an object's current location, they should perform poorly in *any* task requiring them to keep track of trial-to-trial changes in an object's location. The task we devised was a nonsearch task (see Fig. 9.17). In this task, 8-month-old infants watched a possible and an impossible test event. At the start of each event, the infants saw an object standing on one of two identical placemats located on either side of the infants' midline. After a few seconds, identical screens were slid in front of the placemats, hiding the object from the infants' view. Next, a human hand, wearing a long silver glove and a bracelet of jingle bells, entered the apparatus through an opening in the right wall and "tiptoed" back and forth in the area between the right wall and the right screen. After frolicking in this fashion for 15 seconds, the hand reached behind the *right* screen and came out holding the object, shaking it gently until the end of the trial. The only difference between the two test events was in the location of the object at the start of the trial. In the possible event, the object stood on the right placemat; in the impossible event, the object stood on the left placemat, and thus should not have been able to be retrieved from behind the right screen. The infants saw the possible and the impossible events on alternate trials (order was, as always, counterbalanced) until they had completed three pairs of test trials.

The results indicated that the infants looked reliably longer at the impossible than at the possible event. Furthermore, the infants showed the same pattern of looking on all three pairs of test trials. In a second experiment, the hand reached behind the *left* screen for the object; the position of the object during the possible (left screen) and the impossible (right screen) events was thus reversed. The infants again looked reliably longer at the impossible than at the

Possible Event   Impossible Event

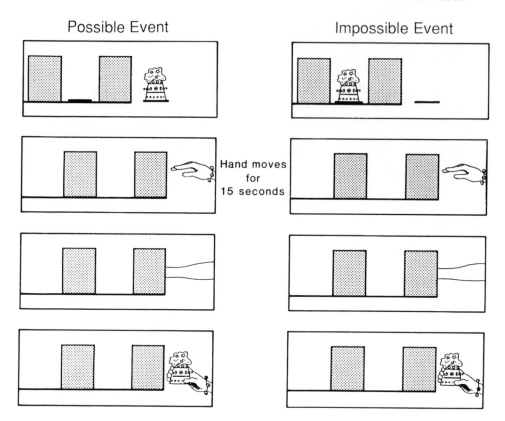

FIG. 9.17. Schematic drawing of the events shown to the infants in Baillargeon and Graber (1988).

possible event, and did so on all three test pairs. Together, the results of these two experiments suggested that the infants (a) registered the object's location at the start of each trial; (b) remembered this location during the 15 seconds the hand tiptoed back and forth; and (c) were surprised to see the object retrieved from behind one screen when they remembered it to be behind the opposite screen.

In our next experiments, we tested 8-month-old infants with delays of 30 and 70 seconds (Baillargeon, DeVos, & Graber, 1989). The infants again looked reliably longer at the impossible than at the possible event, indicating that they remembered the object's location during even the 70-second delay.

The results of these experiments revealed that 8-month-old infants have no difficulty remembering trial-to-trial changes in an object's hiding place after delays of 15, 30, and even 70 seconds. These results contrasted sharply with those obtained with the standard AB task: Investigators have found that 8-month-old infants typically search perseveratively after a 3-second delay (e.g., Butterworth,

1977; Diamond, 1985; Fox et al., 1979; Gratch & Landers, 1971; Wellman et al., 1987). The present results thus cast serious doubts on attempts to explain infants' search errors in terms of a deficient memory mechanism.

To what, then, should one attribute infants' search errors? One possibility (suggested by my husband, Jerry DeJong) is that these errors reflect problem solving difficulties caused by the demands of planning search actions. In order to describe this hypothesis, we must first distinguish between two types of problem solving, which may actually constitute opposite ends of a single continuum. One, *reactive* type corresponds to situations in which solutions are produced immediately, without conscious reasoning. Operators stored in memory and whose conditions of application are satisfied are simply "run off" or executed. An example of such problem solving might be reaching for an object whose location is known or driving home along a familiar route. The second, *planful* type of problem solving corresponds to situations in which solutions are generated through an active reasoning or computation process. An example of this second type of problem solving might be finding an object whose location can be deduced from available cues or planning a trip to a novel location. It is assumed that because the second type of problem solving is effortful, individuals use it only when no other avenues are available, preferring, whenever possible, to rely on previously computed solutions rather than generate new ones. Hence, when a problem situation is perceived to be similar to a previously experienced situation, individuals will attempt to apply the solution computed in the initial situation, thus engaging in reactive as opposed to planful problem solving (see Logan, 1988; Suchman, 1987, for interesting discussions of similar concepts).

To account for infants' performance in the AB search task, we must make two assumptions. The first is that, with *short* delays, infants engage in reactive problem solving: they "run off" an already existing operator to retrieve the object on both the A and the B trials. The second assumption is that, with *long* delays, for reasons that are still unclear, infants cannot use the short-delay operator. This leads them to perform differently on the A and the B trials. On the A trial, infants engage in planful problem solving: They compute a solution (i.e., determine where and how to find the object) and store this solution in memory. On the subsequent B trial, instead of recomputing a solution, infants engage in reactive problem solving and simply execute the solution they have just stored in memory, leading to perseverative errors. It is plausible that the overall similarity of the task context in the A and B trials lures infants into thinking "Aha, I know just what to do here!", and into blindly applying what is no longer an appropriate solution.

Two pieces of evidence are consistent with the hypothesis that infants' search errors reflect not memory limitations but deficiencies in problem solving. One such piece is that infants produce perseverative errors in the AB search task even when the object is visible at B instead of being hidden at B (e.g., Bremner

& Knowles, 1984; Butterworth, 1977; Nielson, 1982; see Wellman et al., 1987 for review and discussion). This finding creates serious difficulties for memory accounts but is easily explained by the notion that infants, instead of performing a close analysis of the task situation and computing the correct solution, are simply repeating a previously successful solution.

The other piece of evidence concerns data collected with tasks where no demands are made on infants' memory and yet perseverative errors very similar to those obtained in the AB task are found. Two such tasks are the locomotor detour tasks designed by Rieser, Doxsey, McCarrell, and Brooks (1982) and by Lockman and Pick (1984). Rieser et al. (1982) tested 9-month-old infants' ability to use auditory information to select an open as opposed to a blocked route to get to their mothers. Each infant and his or her mother sat on opposite sides of an opaque barrier; a side barrier stood perpendicular to the front barrier on the mother's left or right (the position of the side barrier on each trial was randomly determined). The front barrier was sufficiently high so as to hide both the mother and the side barrier from the infant. At the start of each trial, the mother asked the infant to join her behind the front barrier. The mother's calls were differentially reflected on her left and right sides because one side was open and the other side closed. The results indicated that on the initial trial the infants crawled or walked to the open side to find their mothers, suggesting that they detected the auditory cues that specified the location of the side barrier; on subsequent trials, however, the infants merely repeated the left or right direction of their first response. Lockman and Pick (1984) examined 12-month-old infants' ability to go around a barrier by the shortest route to get to their mothers. Each infant and his or her mother were positioned on opposite sides of one end of an opaque barrier (the left and right ends of the barrier were used on alternate trials). The infant could not step over the barrier but could see the mother above it. Lockman and Pick found that on the initial trial the infants chose the shortest route to go to their mothers; on subsequent trials, however, the infants tended to repeat their first response, going to their mothers via the same side across trials.

The results of these two detour tasks are very similar to those obtained in the AB search task with longer delays. On the initial trial, infants analyze the task situation and compute the correct solution (i.e., determine where to find the object hidden or visible at A, use auditory cues to decide which path to their mother is open and which path is blocked, and select the barrier end that constitutes the shortest route to their mother). On the subsequent B trial, however, instead of reanalyzing the situation and computing a novel solution, infants simply repeat the solution they performed successfully on the previous trial.

The account of infants' perseverative errors in terms of problem solving deficiencies possesses two additional advantages over alternative hypotheses. One is that it contradicts the view that these errors are peculiar responses characteristic of infancy but quite distinct from anything that occurs later in development. On the contrary, it leads us to view infants' perseverative errors on a continuum with or in the same light as errors produced by older subjects in other tasks. A number of tasks have been found in which adults perseverate by using in one context a solution devised or learned in another, superficially similar context. A well-known example of this phenomenon is the Luchins' water jar problem (A. S. Luchins, 1942; A. S. Luchins & E. H. Luchins, 1950; cited in Mayer, 1983). Another example is the "Moses illusion." Adult subjects who are asked, "How many animals of each type did Moses bring on the ark?" usually answer, "Two, a male and a female," without realizing that Moses was mentioned rather than Noah (e.g., Reder & Kusbit, 1991); Ross (1984) provided related evidence.

Children, too, can be lulled by context similarity into producing perseverative responses. An anecdote involving my son Antoine, aged 28 months, illustrates this point well. One morning I asked Antoine to play a guessing game with me; I would describe various objects and he would guess what they were. I said I was thinking of an animal with a very, very long neck, and Antoine correctly guessed a giraffe. I then said I was thinking of something he put on his feet to go outside to keep his toes warm, and Antoine correctly guessed boots. Later that day, I asked Antoine to play our guessing game a second time. I first said I was thinking of an animal with a very, very long neck, and Antoine again correctly guessed a giraffe. My next question was, "I am thinking of something you put on hour head when you go outside to keep your ears warm," and Antoine quickly responded "Boots." Because my son knew the difference between boots and hats and was familiar with both words, I concluded that he had been lulled by the similarity in context to repeat a previously correct but now inappropriate solution. Examples of this type are probably extremely common.

Two points about this anecdote are worth nothing. One is that my son was much quicker, during our second game session, at answering my questions; this is, of course, exactly what one would expect (shorter latencies) if answers are retrieved from memory rather than being computed on the spot. The second is that Antoine did not spontaneously realize he had erred in his answer to the second question. He did not behave as someone who knew full well the correct answer was *hat* but could not inhibit his prior response *boots*. He seemed perfectly satisfied with his answer, and did not change it until I repeated the question to him with appropriate exclamations and emphasis.

In brief, what I am claiming is that infants, like older children and adults, can be lured by overall context similarity into retrieving previously computed responses that changes in the context have rendered inappropriate. The main difference between infants and older subjects, in this account, is that infants are less likely to notice changes, or to integrate changes in the planning of future responses, and so are more prone to perseveration errors. Additional research is needed to specify the conditions under which infants are likely to notice contextual changes and to explain how this set of conditions is modified with age.

The second advantage that the problem-solving deficiency explanation has over alternative accounts of infants' AB errors is that it can be integrated relatively easily with the explanation, discussed in the previous section, of young infants' failure to search for hidden objects. Briefly, it is assumed that infants fail to search because they are unable to plan means–end sequences of actions; and that they search perseveratively, once they begin to search, because they are overly inclined (for reasons that are still unspecified) to rely on previously computed means–end sequences, rather than recompute or replan new ones. Furthermore, in both cases, infants show themselves better able to identify than to generate correct action sequences: as shown earlier, infants identify sequences that can result in the recovery of objects placed under obstacles or at the far end of supports long before they produce these sequences themselves (Baillargeon et al., 1990, 1992); in addition, infants identify context-appropriate searches after delays of 15, 30, and even 70 seconds long before they search correctly with similar delays (Baillargeon & Graber, 1988; Baillargeon et al., 1989).

CONCLUSION

The research summarized in this chapter has implications for at least three areas of infant development: object permanence, physical reasoning, and search. They are discussed in turn.

Object Permanence

When adults see an object occlude another object, they typically assume that the occluded object (a) continues to exist behind the occluding object; (b) retains its physical and spatial properties; and (c) remains subject to physical laws. Piaget (1954) proposed that infants initially do not share adults' beliefs about occlusion events, and adopt these beliefs one by one over the first two years of life.

The findings reported in this chapter clearly contradict Piaget's proposal. Consider the many experiments that obtained positive results with infants aged 3½ to 5½ months: the rotating screen experiments (Baillargeon, 1987a, 1991, 1992; Baillargeon et al., 1985), the rolling car experiments (Baillargeon & DeVos, 1991), the sliding rabbit experiments (Baillargeon & Graber, 1987; Baillargeon & DeVos, 1991), and the searching hand experiments (Baillargeon et al., 1990). The infants in these experiments seemed to have no difficulty representing the existence of one, two, and even three hidden objects. Furthermore, the infants represented many of the properties of the objects, such as their height, location, and trajectory. Finally, the infants expected the objects to behave not in capricious and arbitrary ways but in the same regular and predictable ways as visible objects. In particular, the infants realized that hidden objects, like visible objects, cannot move through the space occupied by other objects and cannot appear at two separate points in space without having traveled from one point to the other.

Thus, it appears that, far from adopting adults' beliefs about occlusion events in a stage-like manner over a protracted period of time, infants possess these beliefs from a very early age. Another way of stating this conclusion is to say that infants' understanding of occlusion events is qualitatively similar to that of older children and adults. This is not to say, of course, that no development remains to take place. Indeed, we saw several instances in which older infants' performance was distinctly better than that of younger infants. However, these differences seem to reflect improvements in infants' physical reasoning abilities, rather than changes in infants' conception of occluded objects.

Physical Reasoning

The research reported in this chapter suggests three hypotheses about the development of infants' physical reasoning. One is that in their first pass at understanding physical events, infants construct general, all-or-none representations that capture the essence of the events but few of the details (e.g., a rotating screen will stop when an obstacle is placed in its path; the presence of a protuberance in a soft cloth cover signals the presence of an object beneath the cover). These initial, core representations are progressively elaborated as infants identify variables that are relevant to the events' outcomes (e.g., the location, height, and compressibility of the obstacles in the path of a rotating screen can be used to determine at what point the screen will stop; the size of the protuberance in a cloth cover can be used to judge the size of the object beneath the cover). Infants incorporate this accrued knowledge into their reasoning, resulting in increasingly accurate predictions over time.

The second hypothesis is that, in reasoning about variables, infants can reason first qualitatively and only after some time quantitatively about the effects of these variables. Recall that the 4½-month-old infants in the rotating screen experiments (Baillargeon, 1991) and the 12½-month-old infants in the soft-cover experiments (Baillargeon & DeVos, 1992) were able to solve the two-box or the two-cover tasks before they were able to detect violations in the one-box or the one-cover task. It does not seem unreasonable that development should proceed in this manner. Indeed, infants' success in generating qualitative solutions to physical problems may facilitate their production of quantitative solutions to the same problems. For example, having determined, by using the visible box, at what point the screen will encounter the occluded box, infants might be in a better position, when the visible box is removed, to compute a quantitative estimate of when the screen should stop.

The foregoing discussion presupposes that infants' approach to learning about physical events—the representation of core events and the progressive identification of pertinent variables—reflects the operation of innate, highly constrained learning mechanisms that direct infants' attention to particular observations and guide the quantitative and qualitative analyses of these observations. The third hypothesis suggested by the present research is that, although infants' approach to learning about the physical world remains the same throughout infancy, which events are understood at which ages depends on a host of developmental factors. These include infants' visual abilities (what cannot be seen cannot be understood) and motoric capacities (some knowledge may arise from manipulations that cannot occur until infants can reach successfully, sit with support, and so on). In addition, there are undoubtedly cognitive factors having to do with the development of infants' memory and representational abilities. With respect to the latter factor, the present research suggests that infants can reason about objects they have seen, even after these objects are hidden from view, long before they can make inferences about hidden objects. The fact that young infants appear limited to physical reasoning based on concrete representations clearly must restrict the range of physical problems they can solve.

The three hypotheses described in this section suggest new directions for research on the development of infants' physical reasoning. How do infants go about forming representations of core events? How do they identify variables that are relevant to these events? How do they devise qualitative and quantitative strategies for reasoning about the effects of these variables? Do infants integrate their representations of events? If yes, how should these networks of representations be described? Finally, what are the sensorimotor and cognitive factors that interact with infants' approach to learning about the physical world to yield the knowledge revealed in the present experiments?

Search

Researchers have identified two distinct stages in the early development of infants' search behavior: Prior to about 7½ months of age, infants do not search for objects they have observed being hidden, and prior to about 12 months of age, infants do search for hidden objects but their performance is fragile and easily disrupted by task factors, such as the introduction of a delay between hiding and retrieval. According to the arguments put forth in this chapter, both of these stages reflect limitations in problem solving. During the first stage, infants are unable to plan means–end sequences, such as search sequences, possibly because the performance of the means (e.g., grasping a cover) places them in an apparent conflict with the achievement of their goal (grasping the toy beneath the cover). During the second stage, infants become able to plan search sequences but are overly inclined, under certain conditions, to repeat previously planned sequences rather than to compute new and context-sensitive sequences. Interestingly, at each stage infants show themselves able to *evaluate* correct sequences even when they cannot *generate* them. Specifically, infants can identify correct sequences for the retrieval of a hidden object long before they spontaneously produce these sequences. Similarly, infants can identify context-appropriate searches after delays of 15, 30, and even 70 seconds long before they produce correct searches at comparable delays.

A salient aspect of the explanations proposed here is that they appeal to problem solving limitations that have already been identified in children and adults. Adults often have difficulty solving physical problems whose solutions depend on moves that are counterintuitive in that they appear to take one farther away from one's goal. Furthermore, adults can be lulled by overall context similarity in applying a previous solution that is no longer appropriate. Finally, in all these instances, adults typically have little difficulty recognizing accurate solutions, even when they have failed to generate them.

The general picture suggested by the present research is, thus, one in which the physical world of infants appears very similar to that of adults: Not only do infants and adults share many of the same beliefs and show many of the same physical reasoning abilities, but these abilities seem limited in the same ways.

Final Remarks

The research presented in this chapter is interesting for three reasons. One is that it yields a picture of infants as budding intuitive physicists, capable of detecting, interpreting, and predicting physical outcomes, which is radically different from the traditional portrayal of young infants as enclosed within a world in which an object is ''a mere image which reenters the void as soon as it vanishes, and emerges from it for no objective reason''(Piaget, 1954, p. 11). Another reason is that it suggests several new directions for research on infants' acquisition and representation of physical knowledge and on the manifestation of this knowledge in tasks calling for manual and non-manual responses. The third reason is that, as we discover how infants attain, represent, and use physical knowledge, we come one step closer to understanding the central issue of the origins of human cognition.

ACKNOWLEDGMENTS

The research reported in this manuscript was supported by grants from the National Institute of Child Health and Human Development (HD-21104 and HD-05951). I wish to thank Judy Deloache and Carl Granrud for their careful and discerning review of the manuscript, and Jerry DeJong and Joe Malpelli for insightful suggestions about the research.

REFERENCES

Anderson, J. R. (1985). *Cognitive psychology and its implications* (2nd ed.). New York: Freeman.

Baillargeon, R. (1986). Representing the existence and the location of hidden objects: Object permanence in 6- and 8-month-old infants. *Cognition, 23,* 21–41.

Baillargeon, R. (1987a). Object permanence in 3.5- and 4.5-month-old infants. *Developmental Psychology, 23,* 655–664.

Baillargeon, R. (1987b). Young infants' reasoning about the physical and spatial properties of a hidden object. *Cognitive Development, 2,* 179–200.

Baillargeon, R. (1991). Reasoning about the height and location of a hidden object in 4.5- and 6.5-month-old infants. *Cognition, 38,* 13–42.

Baillargeon, R. (1992). *The role of perceptual similarity in infants' qualitative physical reasoning.* Unpublished manuscript.

Baillargeon, R., & DeVos, J. (1991). Object permanence in young infants: Further evidence. *Child Development, 62,* 1227–1246.

Baillargeon, R., & DeVos, J. (1992). *Qualitative and quantitative inferences about hidden objects in infants.* Manuscript submitted for publication.

Baillargeon, R., DeVos, J., & Black, J. (1992). *Young infants' reasoning about the use of supports to bring objects within reach.* Unpublished manuscript.

Baillargeon, R., DeVos, J., & Graber, M. (1989). Location memory in 8-month-old infants in a non-search AB task: Further evidence. *Cognitive Development, 4,* 345–367.

Baillargeon, R., & Graber, M. (1987). Where is the rabbit? 5.5-month-old infants' representation of the height of a hidden object. *Cognitive Development, 2,* 375–392.

Baillargeon, R., & Graber, M. (1988). Evidence of location memory in 8-month-old infants. *Cognition, 20,* 191–208.

Baillargeon, R., Graber, M., DeVos, J., & Black, J. (1990). Why do young infants fail to search for hidden objects? *Cognition, 36,* 255–284.

Baillargeon, R., Spelke, E. S., & Wasserman, S. (1985). Object permanence in 5-month-old infants. *Cognition, 20,* 191–208.

Bjork, E. L., & Cummings, E. S. (1984). Infant search errors: Stage of concept development or stage of memory development? *Memory & Cognition, 12,* 1–19.

Bower, T. G. R. (1967). The development of object permanence: Some studies of existence constancy. *Perception and Psychophysics, 2,* 411–418.

Bower, T. G. R. (1972). Object perception in infants. *Perception, 1,* 15–30.

Bower, T. G. R. (1974). *Development in infancy.* San Francisco: Freeman.

Bower, T. G. R., Broughton, J. M., & Moore, M. K. (1971). Development of the object concept as manifested in the tracking behavior of infants between 7 and 20 weeks of age. *Journal of Experimental Child Psychology, 11,* 182–193.

Bower, T. G. R., & Wishart, J. D. (1972). The effects of motor skill on object permanence. *Cognition, 1,* 165–172.

Bremner, J. G. (1985). Object tracking and search in infancy: A review of data and a theoretical evaluation. *Developmental Review, 5,* 371–396.

Bremner, J. G., & Knowles, L. S. (1984). Piagetian Stage IV search errors with an object that is directly accessible both visually and manually. *Perception, 13,* 307–314.

Brown, A. L. (1989). Analogical learning and transfer: What develops? In S. Vosniadou & A. Ortony (Eds.), *Similarity and analogical reasoning* (pp. 369–412). London: Cambridge University Press.

Bruner, J. S., Olver, R. R., & Greenfield, P. M. (1966). *Studies in cognitive growth.* New York: Wiley.

Bushnell, E. W. (1985). The decline of visually guided reaching during infancy. *Infant Behavior and Development, 8,* 139–155.

Butterworth, G. E. (1977). Object disappearance and error in Piaget's Stage IV task. *Journal of Experimental Child Psychology, 23,* 391–401.

Carey, S. (1985). *Conceptual change in childhood*. Cambridge, MA: MIT Press.

Chi, M. T. H., Feltovitch, P. J., & Glaser, R. (1981). Categorization and representation of physics problems by experts and novices. *Cognitive Science, 5*, 121–152.

Clement, J. (1982). Students' preconceptions in introductory mechanics. *American Journal of Physics, 50*, 66–71.

Clifton, Rachel K., Rochat, P., Litovsky, R. Y., & Perris, E. E. (1991). Object Representation Guides Infants' Reaching in the Dark. *Journal of Experimental Psychology: Human Perception and Performance, 17*, 323–219.

Diamond, A. (1985). Development of the ability to use recall to guide action, as indicated by infants' performance on AB. *Child Development, 56*, 868–883.

Diamond, A. (1988). Differences between adult and infant cognition: Is the crucial variable presence or absence of language? In L. Weskrantz (Ed.), *Thought without language* (pp. 337–370). Oxford: Oxford University Press.

Fagan, J. F. (1970). Memory in the infant. *Journal of Experimental Child Psychology, 9*, 217–226.

Fagan, J. F. (1973). Infants' delayed recognition memory and forgetting. *Journal of Experimental Child Psychology, 16*, 424–450.

Flavell, J. H. (1985). *Cognitive development* (2nd ed.). Englewood Cliffs, NJ: Prentice-Hall.

Forbus, K. D. (1984). Qualitative process theory. *Artificial Intelligence, 24*, 85–168.

Fox, N., Kagan, J., & Weiskopf, S. (1979). The growth of memory during infancy. *Genetic Psychology monographs, 99*, 91–130.

Gelman, R. (1990). First principles organize attention to and learning about relevant data: Number and the animate–inanimate distinction as examples. *Cognitive Science, 14*, 79–106.

Gentner, D., & Gentner, D. R. (1983). Flowing waters or teeming crowds: Mental models. In D. Gentner & A. Stevens (Eds.), *Mental models* (pp. 99–127). Hillsdale, NJ: Lawrence Erlbaum Associates.

Gentner, D., & Stevens, A. (Eds.). (1983). *Mental models*. Hillsdale, NJ: Lawrence Erlbaum Associates.

Gentner, D., & Toupin, C. (1986). Systematicity and surface similarity in the development of analogy. *Cognitive Science, 10*, 277–300.

Gick, M. L., & Holyoak, K. J. (1980). Analogical problem solving. *Cognitive Psychology, 12*, 306–355.

Goldberg, S. (1976). Visual tracking and existence constancy in 5-month-old infants. *Journal of Experimental Child Psychology, 22*, 478–491.

Granrud, C. E. (1986). Binocular vision and spatial perception in 4- and 5-month-old infants. *Journal of Experimental Psychology: Human Perception and Performance, 12*, 32–49.

Gratch, G. (1975). Recent studies based on Piaget's view of object concept development. In L. B. Cohen & P. Salapatek (Eds.), *Infant perception: From sensation to cognition* (Vol. 2, pp. 51–99). New York: Academic Press.

Gratch, G. (1976). A review of Piagetian infancy research: Object concept development. In W. F. Overton & J. M. Gallagher (Eds.), *Knowledge and development: Advances in research and theory* (pp. 59–91). New York: Plenum.

Gratch, G. (1982). Responses to hidden persons and things by 5-, 9-, and 16-month-old infants in a visual tracking situation. *Developmental Psychology, 18*, 232–237.

Gratch, G., Appel, K. J., Evans, W. F., LeCompte, G. K., & Wright, J. A. (1974). Piaget's Stage IV object concept error: Evidence of forgetting or object conception. *Child Development, 45*, 71–77.

Gratch, G., & Landers, W. (1971). Stage IV of Piaget's theory of infants' object concepts: A longitudinal study. *Child Development, 42*, 359–372.

Harris, P. L. (1973). Perseverative errors in search by young children. *Child Development, 44*, 28–33.

Harris, P. L. (1983). Infant cognition. In M. M. Haith & J. J. Campos (Eds.), *Handbook of child psychology: Infancy and developmental psychobiology* (Vol. 2, pp. 689–782). New York: Wiley.

Harris, P. L. (1987). The development of search. In P. Salapatek & L. B. Cohen (Eds.), *Handbook of infant perception* (Vol. 2, pp. 155–207). New York: Academic Press.

Harris, P. L. (1989). Object permanence in infancy. In A. Slater & J. G. Bremner (Eds.), *Infant development* (pp. 103–121). Hillsdale, NJ: Lawrence Erlbaum Associates.

Hofsten, C. von (1980). Predictive reaching for moving objects by human infants. *Journal of Experimental Child Psychology, 30*, 369–382.

Holyoak, K. J., Junn, E. N., & Billman, D. O. (1984). Development of analogical problem-solving skill. *Child Development, 55*, 2042–2055.

Hood, B., & Willatts, P. (1986). Reaching in the dark to an object's remembered position: Evidence for object permanence in 5-month-old infants. *British Journal of Developmental Psychology, 4*, 57–65.

Kagan, J. (1974). Discrepancy, temperament, and infant distress. In M. Lewis & A. Rosenblum (Eds.), *The origins of fear* (pp. 229–248). New York: Wiley.

Karmiloff-Smith, A., & Inhelder, B. (1975). If you want to get ahead, get a theory. *Cognition, 3*, 195–212.

Keil, F. C. (1990). Constraints on constraints: Surveying the epigenetic landscape. *Cognitive Science, 14*, 135–168.

Larkin, J. H. (1983). The role of problem representation in physics. In D. Gentner & A. Stevens (Eds.), *Mental models* (pp. 75–98). Hillsdale, NJ: Lawrence Erlbaum Associates.

Lockman, J. J., & Pick, H. L. (1984). Problems of scale in spatial development. In C. Sophian (Ed.), *Origins of cognitive skills* (pp. 3–26). Hillsdale, NJ: Lawrence Erlbaum Associates.

Logan, G. D. (1988). Toward an instance theory of automatization. *Psychological Review, 95*, 492–527.

Luchins, A. S. (1942). Mechanization in problem-solving. *Psychological Monographs, 54*(6, Whole No. 248).

Luchins, A. S., & Luchins, E. H. (1950). New experimental attempts at preventing mechanization in problem-solving. *Journal of General Psychology, 42*, 279–297.

Martin, R. M. (1975). Effects of familiar and complex stimuli on infant attention. *Developmental Psychology, 11*, 178–185.

Mayer, R. E. (1983). *Thinking, problem-solving, cognition*. New York: Freeman.

McCloskey, M. (1983). Naive theories of motion. In D. Gentner & A. L. Stevens (Eds.), *Mental models* (pp. 299–324). Hillsdale, NJ: Lawrence Erlbaum Associates.

Meicler, M., & Gratch, G. (1980). Do 5-month-olds show object conception in Piaget's sense? *Infant Behavior and Development, 3*, 265–282.

Meltzoff, A. N. (1988). Infant imitation and memory: Nine-month-olds in immediate and deferred tests. *Child Development, 59*, 219–225.

Miller, D., Cohen, L., & Hill, K. (1970). A methodological investigation of Piaget's theory of object concept development in the sensory-motor period. *Journal of Experimental Child Psychology, 9*, 59–85.

Moore, M. K., Borton, R., & Darby, B. L. (1978). Visual tracking in young infants: Evidence for object identity or object permanence? *Journal of Experimental Child Psychology, 25*, 183–198.

Muller, A. A., & Aslin, R. N. (1978). Visual tracking as an index of the object concept. *Infant Behavior and Development, 1*, 309–319.

Newell, K. M., Scully, D. M., McDonald, P. V., & Baillargeon, R. (1989). Task constraints and infant grip configurations. *Developmental Psychobiology, 22*, 817–832.

Newell, A., & Simon, H. A. (1972). *Human problem solving*. Englewood Cliffs, NJ: Prentice-Hall.

Nielson, I. (1982). An alternative explanation of the infant's difficulty in the Stage III, IV, and V object-concept task. *Perception, 11*, 577–588.

Piaget, J. (1951). *Play, dreams, and imitation in childhood*. New York: Norton.

Piaget, J. (1952). *The origins of intelligence in children*. New York: International University Press.

Piaget, J. (1954). *The construction of reality in the child*. New York: Basic Books.

Reder, L. M., & Kusbit, G. W. (1991). Locus of the Moses illusion: Imperfect encoding, retrieval, or match? *Journal of Memory and Language, 30*, 385–406.

Rieser, J. J., Doxsey, P. A., McCarrell, N. S., & Brooks, P. H. (1982). Wayfinding and toddlers use of information from an aerial view of a maze. *Developmental Psychology, 18*, 714–720.

Ross, B. H. (1984). Remindings and their effects in learning a cognitive skill. *Cognitive Psychology, 16*, 371–416.

Schacter, D. L., & Moscovitch, M. (1983). Infants, amnesics, and dissociable memory systems. In M. Moscovitch (Ed.), *Infant memory: Its relation to normal and pathological memory in humans and other animals* (pp. 173–216). New York: Plenum.

Schacter, D. L., Moscovitch, M., Tulving, E., McLachlan, D. R., & Freedman, M. (1986). Mnemonic precedence in amnesic patients: An analogue of the AB error in infants? *Child Development, 57*, 816–823.

Schubert, R. E. (1983). The infant's search for objects: Alternatives to Piaget's theory of concept development. In L. P. Lipsitt & C. K. Rovee-Collier (Eds.), *Advances in infancy research* (Vol. 2, pp. 137–182). Norwood, NJ: Ablex.

Siegler, R. S. (1978). The origins of scientific reasoning. In R. S. Siegler (Ed.), *Children's thinking: What develops?* Hillsdale, NJ: Lawrence Erlbaum Associates.

Siegler, R. S. (1983). Information processing approaches to cognitive development. In W. Kessen (Ed.), *Handbook of child psychology: History, theory, and methods* (Vol. 1, pp. 129–211). New York: Wiley.

Sophian, C. (1984). Developing search skills in infancy and early childhood. In C. Sophian (Ed.), *Origins of cognitive skills* (pp. 27–56). Hillsdale, NJ: Lawrence Erlbaum Associates.

Sophian, C., & Wellman, H. M. (1983). Selective information use and perservation in the search behavior of infants and young children. *Journal of Experimental Child Psychology, 35*, 369–390.

Spelke, E. S. (1988). Where perceiving ends and thinking begins: The apprehension of objects in infancy. In A. Yonas (Ed.), *Minnesota symposia on child psychology: Vol. 20. Perceptual development in infancy* (pp. 197–234). Hillsdale, NJ: Lawrence Erlbaum Associates.

Suchman, L. A. (1987). *Plans and situated actions: The problem of human-machine interaction.* Cambridge: Cambridge University Press.

Vosniadou, S., & Brewer, W. F. (1989). A cross-cultural investigation of children's conceptions about the earth, the sun, and the moon: Greek and American data. In H. Mandl, E. DeCorte, N. Bennett, & H. F. Friedrich (Eds.), *Learning and instruction: European research in an international context* (Vol. 2.2, pp. 605–629). Oxford: Pergamon.

Wellman, H. M. (in press). *Children's theories of mind.* Cambridge, MA: Bradford Books/MIT Press.

Wellman, H. M., Cross, D., & Bartsch, K. (1987). Infant search and object permanence: A meta-analysis of the A-not-B error. *Monographs of the Society for Research in Child Development, 51*(3, Serial No. 214).

Willatts, P. (1984). Stages in the development of intentional search by young infants. *Developmental Psychology, 20*, 389–396.

Willatts, P. (1989). Development of problem-solving in infancy. In A. Slater & J. G. Bremner (Eds.), *Infant development* (pp. 143–182). Hillsdale, NJ: Lawrence Erlbaum Associates.

Wiser, M., & Carey, S. (1983). When heat and temperature were one. In D. Gentner & A. L. Stevens (Eds.), *Mental models* (pp. 267–297). Hillsdale, NJ: Lawrence Erlbaum Associates.

Commentary: Extending the Ideal Observer Approach

Velma Dobson
University of Pittsburgh

Throughout the history of research in visual development, a variety of mechanisms have been hypothesized to underlie the developmental changes in vision that occur between birth and adulthood. Bronson (1974), for example, suggested that the visual responses of the newborn are based on subcortical pathways, and that the changes seen in the quality of visual responses during infancy are the result of the maturation of cortical pathways. Maurer and Lewis (1979) also emphasized the importance of cortical maturation. However, they suggested that visual responses in early infancy are mediated by the X pathway to the visual cortex and the Y pathway to the superior colliculus and pretectum, and that the changes in visual responsiveness that occur during infancy are the result of maturation of the Y pathway to the cortex.

The ideal observer approach to visual development, described by Banks and Shannon in their chapter (this volume) and previously by Banks and Bennett (1988), provides an exciting, new way to look at the mechanisms that may underlie the deficits in vision shown by infants. This approach concentrates on the "front end" of the visual system, and reminds us that developmental changes in visual responsiveness may have nothing to do with cortical maturation. They may, instead, be related to maturational changes in the structure of the eye and the photoreceptors that influence visual input long before it reaches visual cortex.

THE IDEAL OBSERVER APPROACH:
NEWBORNS VERSUS ADULTS

To use the ideal observer approach to examine how front end changes in the visual system correlate with developmental changes in visual behavior, one must have information on the structural changes that occur in the eye and the photoreceptors. Until the recent work of Hendrickson and Yuodelis (1984), however, little was known about photoreceptor development in humans. Hendrickson and Yuodelis published a description of the morphology of the human fovea in a newborn infant, in a 15-month-old toddler, in a 45-month-old child, and in an adult. This paper was followed by a more quantitative evaluation of the morphology of the fovea at these ages (Yuodelis & Hendrickson, 1986). These descriptions of the photoreceptor anatomy of the newborn infant, along with previously published information on the gross structure of the newborn eye, provided Banks and Bennett (1988) with the information necessary to apply the ideal observer approach to human infants.

The goal of Banks and Bennett's work was to determine the extent to which structural changes in the eye and in the photoreceptors between birth and adulthood can account for deficits in visual function shown by very young infants. Ideal observer modeling indicates that the morphological immaturity of the eye and the photoreceptors results in a 350-fold difference in photoreceptor efficiency in the visual system of young infants versus adults. As described in Banks and Shannon's chapter and in the Banks and Bennett (1988) publication, this difference in photoreceptor efficiency can account for many of the differences in visual function shown by young infants in comparison to adults. For example, the poor photoreceptor efficiency of the young infant can account for most, but not all, of the differences between color vision in infants and adults, described by Teller and Lindsey in their chapter and in previous publications from Teller's lab (Hamer, Alexander, & Teller, 1982; Packer, Hartmann, & Teller, 1984; Peeples & Teller, 1975; Teller, Peeples, & Sekel, 1978). The infant's poor photoreceptor efficiency can also account for much, but not all, of the reduction in contrast sensitivity seen when newborns' contrast sensitivity functions (Atkinson, Braddick, & French, 1979; Banks & Salapatek, 1978) are compared with those of adults. Finally, the fact that the relation between photoreceptor efficiency and vernier acuity is different from that between photoreceptor efficiency and grating acuity may account for the difference in the rates of development of vernier and grating acuity described by Held in his chapter and in previous publications (Gwiazda, Bauer, & Held, 1989; Shimojo, Birch, Gwiazda, & Held, 1984; Shimojo & Held, 1987). Geisler (1984) showed that, for the ideal observer, vernier acuity improves with the square root of photoreceptor efficiency, whereas grating acuity increases with the quarter root of efficiency. As Banks and Bennett pointed out, this means that the 350-fold change in photoreceptor efficiency between birth and adulthood will produce a much greater change in vernier acuity than in grating acuity, in qualitative agreement with the results of Shimojo, Held, and colleagues.

In summary, Banks and Shannon's chapter emphasizes the importance of including structural changes in the front end of the visual system in any description of possible mechanisms underlying developmental visual changes. It reminds us that changes in photoreceptor structure can affect not only aspects of visual function, such as grating acuity, that are clearly tied to photoreceptor spacing, but also aspects of visual function, such as color vision and vernier acuity, that are usually considered in terms of neural processing.

EXTENDING THE IDEAL OBSERVER APPROACH TO OLDER INFANTS

It is noticeable in Banks and Shannon's chapter that their use of the ideal observer approach to account for empirical data is limited to two ages: newborns and adults. There are several reasons for this. First, if one is interested in modeling development, it makes sense to start with the earliest age at which empirical data can be obtained, which, for infants, is at birth. Second, it makes sense to use the model to predict data at an age at which empirical data are available, and the bulk of the data on the sensory aspects of visual development have been obtained from infants in the first few months after birth. Finally, the ideal observer approach requires knowledge of photoreceptor anatomy, and the only time during infancy for which this knowledge is available is at the newborn stage.

Visual development continues throughout infancy and early childhood. It would be of interest, therefore, to use the ideal observer approach to determine the extent to which front-end structural ocular factors limit visual function after the newborn period. Unfortunately, the only age at which such an analysis is currently possible is 15 months, because, with the exception of the newborn period, 15 months is the only age during infancy or early childhood for which Yuodelis and Hendrickson (1986) presented quantitative information on the anatomy of foveal photoreceptors.

The goal of the present chapter is to use the ideal observer approach to determine the extent to which front-end structural factors may underly any visual deficits shown by 15-month-olds. In areas of visual function where empirical data have not yet been collected for 15-month-olds, the ideal observer approach will be used to suggest future research directions and make predictions about the expected outcomes of this research. Essential to this effort will be data and ideas presented in the chapters by Banks and Shannon, Teller and Lindsey, Aslin, and Held.

THE IDEAL OBSERVER APPROACH AT 15 MONTHS

Calculation of the photoreceptor efficiency of the 15-month-old eye relative to the adult eye requires knowledge of pupil diameter, posterior nodal distance of the eye, photoreceptor aperture, photoreceptor spacing, and efficiency of the photoreceptor outer segment in absorbing incident quanta. These values were summarized by Banks and Bennett (1988) for the newborn eye, the 15-month-old eye, and the adult eye, and are presented here in Table 10.1.

Pupil Diameter and Posterior Nodal Distance

The retinal illuminance provided by a stimulus is proportional to the eye's numerical aperture (pupil diameter divided by the posterior focal length). Because the age-related increases in pupil diameter are similar to the age-related increases in posterior nodal distance (see Table 10.1), the retinal illuminance provided by a stimulus is similar for 15-month-olds and adults, and therefore can be ignored in our calculation of relative photoreceptor efficiency.

Calculation of the Light-Collecting Area of the Retina

To calculate photoreceptor efficiency one must first determine what proportion of the retina is capable of absorbing quanta and producing a neural signal. In Table 10.1, the value for the receptor aperture provides the diameter of the part of the photoreceptor capable of collecting light, and the value for receptor spacing provides the overall diameter of the photoreceptor. The same information is illustrated in Fig. 10.1, with the filled area representing the area of the

TABLE 10.1
Ideal Observer Parameters*

	Central Fovea		
Factor	Neonate	15-Mo-Old	Adult
Pupil diameter	2.2 mm	2.7 mm	3.3 mm
Posterior nodal distance	11.7 mm	14.4 mm	16.7 mm
Receptor aperture	0.35 arcmin	0.67 arcmin	0.48 arcmin
Receptor spacing	2.30 arcmin	1.27 arcmin	0.58 arcmin
Outer segment efficiency (ratio to adult value)	10.25	1.8	
Photoreceptor efficiency (ratio to adult value)	350	4.4	

*From Banks & Bennett (1988)

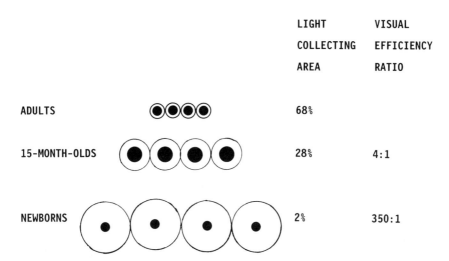

	LIGHT COLLECTING AREA	VISUAL EFFICIENCY RATIO
ADULTS	68%	
15-MONTH-OLDS	28%	4:1
NEWBORNS	2%	350:1

FIG. 10.1.   Schematic representation of photoreceptor spacing in the central fovea of adults, 15-month-olds, and newborns. Outer circles at each age represent photoreceptor spacing; filled inner circles represent effective light-collecting areas.

photoreceptors capable of absorbing quanta and the surrounding circles representing the total photoreceptor area. Dividing the light collecting area by the total photoreceptor area shows that, for the newborn the region capable of absorbing quanta represents only 2% of the area occupied by photoreceptors, whereas the region capable of absorbing quanta is 28% of the total area in 15-month-olds and 68% of the total area in adults.

Outer Segment Efficiency

To calculate relative photoreceptor efficiency, one also needs to know the probability that the quanta that fall on the collecting area will actually be absorbed. The proportion of quanta absorbed is dependent on the amount of photopigment available to absorb quanta, which, in turn, depends on the length of the outer segments of the photoreceptors and on the concentration and extinction coefficient of photopigment in the outer segments. Banks and Bennett (1988) assumed that the concentration and extinction coefficient of photopigment does not differ between infants and adults, and used the relative difference in outer segment length between infants and adults to calculate the relative outer segment efficiency of the newborn infant and the 15-month-old. Their results indicated that the outer segment efficiency of the newborn is about 10 times poorer than that of the adult, and that the outer segment efficiency of the 15-month-old is approximately 1.8 times poorer than that of the adult.

Calculation of Photoreceptor Efficiency

To obtain the relative photoreceptor efficiency of the 15-month-old compared
to the adult, the ratio of the collecting areas at the two ages is multiplied by
the ratio of outer segment efficiency at the two ages. This yields a value of 4.37,
indicating that if a 15-month-old and an adult view the same visual stimulus, approximately four times more quanta will be absorbed by the adult's photoreceptors than by the 15-month-old's photoreceptors. Although the 4-fold difference
in photoreceptor efficiency between the retina of the 15-month-old and the retina of the adult is much less than the 350-fold difference in photoreceptor efficiency between the retina of the newborn and the retina of the adult, the reduced
quantum catch of the eye of the 15-month-old would still affect the amount of
information available for processing in the visual system of the 15-month-old.

What are the implications of the reduced quantum catch of the eye of the
15-month-old? The following pages provide a discussion of the implications of
the ideal observer approach for visual function in the 15-month-old. Aspects of
visual function discussed are those described in the chapters by Banks and Shannon, Teller and Lindsey, Aslin, and Held, and include vernier acuity, grating
acuity, color vision, eye movements, contrast sensitivity functions, and stereopsis.

THE IDEAL OBSERVER APPROACH AT 15 MONTHS: VERNIER VERSUS GRATING ACUITY

Held and his colleagues have compared vernier versus grating acuity development between early infancy and childhood (Gwiazda et al., 1989; Shimojo &
Held, 1987; Shimojo et al., 1984). Their data, shown in Fig. 10.2, indicate that
both types of acuity improve rapidly prior to 15 months and continue to improve
from 15 months into early childhood, with the rate of development being faster
for vernier acuity than for grating acuity.

As already described, Banks and Bennett (1988) suggested that the difference in the rate of acuity development between birth and adulthood for vernier
versus grating acuity is the result of the difference in the relation of photoreceptor
efficiency to the vernier versus the grating acuity tasks. This is illustrated in
Fig. 10.3, which is adapted from a similar figure in Banks and Bennett (1988).
The location of the filled arrows indicates the 350-fold difference in photoreceptor efficiency (absorbed vs. incident photons) between newborns and adults,
and the line indicates the relative improvement in grating acuity (top graph) and
vernier acuity (bottom graph) that are predicted to occur with the change in
photoreceptor efficiency between birth and adulthood. Clearly, the slope of the
line indicating the relative improvement in vernier acuity between birth and adulthood is steeper than the slope of the line indicating the relative improvement
in grating acuity between birth and adulthood, suggesting that the empirical differ-

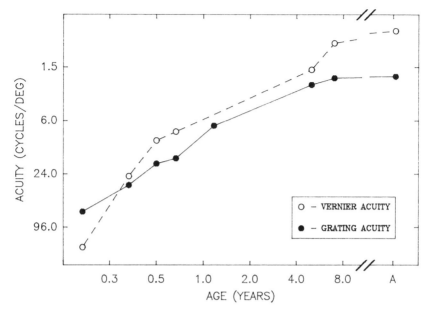

FIG. 10.2. Improvement in vernier and grating acuities as a function of age. Data are replotted from studies by Shimojo et al. (1984), Shimojo and Held (1987), and Gwiazda et al. (1989), in which forced-choice preferential looking procedures were used to measure vernier and grating acuities.

ence that Held and his colleagues found between the rate of vernier acuity development and the rate of grating acuity development may simply be the result of increasing photoreceptor efficiency and not the result of cortical maturation.

A further test of how well front-end structural changes can account for differences in the rate of vernier vs grating acuity development is to locate the photoreceptor efficiency of the 15-month-old on the graphs in Fig. 10.3 (dashed arrows), and then to see whether the predictions that follow from knowing the 15-month-old's photoreceptor efficiency agree with the empirical data shown in Fig. 10.2. The location of these arrows leads to three predictions about the effect of front-end limitations on vernier versus grating acuity development. First, it predicts that both vernier and grating acuity should be worse in 15-month-olds than in adults. Second, it predicts that the change in both vernier acuity and grating acuity between birth and 15 months should be greater than the change in both vernier acuity and grating acuity between 15 months and adulthood. Finally, it predicts that the rate of vernier acuity development between 15 months and adulthood should be more rapid than the rate of grating acuity development during the same age period.

Comparison of these three predictions with the empirical data shown in Fig. 10.2 indicates that, qualitatively, all three predictions agree with the data. It

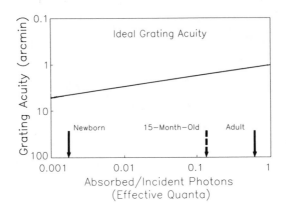

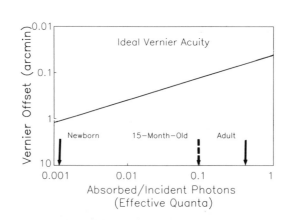

FIG. 10.3. Banks and Bennett's (1988) representation of ideal grating and vernier acuity thresholds as a function of the proportion of incident photons absorbed (photoreceptor efficiency). Location of arrows on the abscissa indicates that the photoreceptor efficiency of the newborn is 350 times poorer than that of the adult, and the photoreceptor efficiency of the 15-month-old is 4 times worse than that of the adult. The graphs predict that (a) both vernier and grating acuity should be worse in 15-month-olds than in adults, (b) both vernier and grating acuity should improve more between birth and 15 months than they improve between 15 months and adulthood, and (c) the rate of vernier acuity development between 15 months and adulthood should be more rapid than the rate of grating acuity development during the same age period. All three predictions are consistent with the data presented in Fig. 10.2. (Replotted and modified, with permission, from Banks & Bennett, 1988.)

would be of interest to know if the agreement between the ideal observer predictions and the data is quantitative, as well as qualitative, to determine whether all of the difference between the rates of vernier and grating acuity development could be accounted for by structural changes in the eye and photoreceptors. According to Banks and Bennett (1988), however, such a quantitative comparison is not possible because of the lack of information about spatial summation areas in children of different ages.

THE IDEAL OBSERVER APPROACH AT 15 MONTHS: GRATING ACUITY AND THE NYQUIST LIMIT

The *Nyquist limit* is an estimate of the limitation placed on acuity by the spacing of the photoreceptors. It provides a theoretical estimate of the finest grating that is resolvable at the photoreceptor level. Table 10.2 shows the Nyquist limit for newborns, 15-month-olds, and adults, as presented by Banks and Bennett (1988), along with empirical grating acuity values for each age. In adults, grating acuity has been measured to be near the Nyquist limit, indicating that the primary limitation on grating acuity in adults is photoreceptor spacing. The measured grating acuity of the newborn, on the other hand, is far below the Nyquist limit, suggesting that the acuity of the newborn is limited by factors other than photoreceptor spacing.

The only study in which grating acuity has been measured in 15-month-olds was reported by Birch, Gwiazda, Bauer, Naegele, and Held (1983). The results indicated that 15-month-olds have an average acuity of 14 c/deg, as measured with the forced-choice preferential looking (FPL) procedure. This acuity value is poorer by a factor of two than the Nyquist limit, suggesting that the acuity of the 15-month-old, like the acuity of the newborn, is limited by factors other than photoreceptor spacing.

Unfortunately, the conclusion that acuity in 15-month-olds is limited by factors other than photoreceptor spacing can be only a tentative conclusion at

TABLE 10.2
Theoretical versus Emperical Estimates of Grating Acuity

Age	Nyquist Limit* (cycles/deg)	Grating Acuity (cycles/deg)
Neonate		
Central Fovea	15.1	1–5
Foveal Slope	20.9	
15-Month-Old	27.2	14
Adult	59.7	50–60

*From Banks & Bennett (1988)

present. This is because adults tested in the Birch et al. study showed grating acuity of 30 c/deg, which, like the grating acuity of 15-month-olds, is a factor of two poorer than the Nyquist limit. In all probability, the acuity value of 30 c/deg found for adults by Birch et al. was an underestimate of acuity due to limitations in the researchers' ability to produce stimuli higher in spatial frequency than 30 c/deg. If so, then the acuity estimate of 14 c/deg for 15-month-olds is probably a true acuity estimate, and factors other than photoreceptor spacing *do* play a role in limiting the acuity of the 15-month-old. However, the alternative hypothesis is that some aspect of the Birch et al. apparatus or procedure had a common effect on 15-month-olds and adults, and reduced the acuity of both by a factor of two. If this hypothesis were true, then elimination of this procedural factor should reveal acuity at the Nyquist limit in both 15-month-olds and adults. Thus, what is needed to determine whether the ideal observer approach can adequately describe grating acuity in the 15-month-olds is a study in which both 15-month-olds and adults are tested with stimuli that allow adults to show acuity values close to 60 c/deg.

THE IDEAL OBSERVER APPROACH AT 15 MONTHS: COLOR VISION

In their respective chapters, both Teller and Lindsey (chap. 2) and Banks and Shannon (chap. 1) have suggested that the poor chromatic discrimination shown by very young infants is probably a manifestation of the 350-fold difference in photoreceptor efficiency between newborns and adults. The finding of a 4-fold difference in photoreceptor efficiency between 15-month-olds and adults suggests that there should be a 2-fold difference between 15-month-olds and adults in the chromatic contrast necessary to make a chromatic discrimination.

Unfortunately, there are no psychophysical studies of color vision in 15-month-olds. Given the difficulty of getting 15-month-olds to keep electrodes attached to their heads for visual evoked potential (VEP) recording, such as that described by Banks and Shannon for younger infants, it is unlikely that the VEP procedure will be useful for studying color vision in 15-month-olds. It is also unlikely that preferential looking (PL) procedures, such as those described by Teller and Lindsey for younger infants, will be useful with 15-month-olds, because they typically require more trials than active 15-month-olds will tolerate. The optokinetic nystagmus technique described by Teller and Lindsey offers an exciting alternative to the VEP and PL procedures, which may be efficient enough and provide stimuli of sufficient interest to allow studies of color vision in 15-month-olds.

THE IDEAL OBSERVER APPROACH AT 15 MONTHS: EYE MOVEMENTS

Photoreceptors in the central fovea decrease in diameter by a factor of four between birth and adulthood. As illustrated in Fig. 10.1, this results in a considerable change in the retinal location of photoreceptors between birth and adulthood. Aslin (1988) has pointed out that the migration of the photoreceptors during infancy presents the infant with an eye movement calibration problem. That is, as illustrated in Fig. 10.1, an eye movement large enough to shift fixation from the leftmost of the four photoreceptors represented in the figure to the rightmost photoreceptor in the newborn will be much larger than an eye movement needed to shift fixation from the leftmost to the rightmost photoreceptor in the 15-month-old or the adult. Aslin has suggested that the visual system of the young infant approaches this calibration problem in a practical fashion, by making multiple short saccades to shift fixation to the new photoreceptor. By later in infancy, the infant seems to have solved the calibration problem and can make saccades appropriate in size for the required change in fixation.

As illustrated in Fig. 10.1, photoreceptor spacing is about twice as large in the 15-month-old as in the adult. This means that the need for recalibration of eye movements as a result of photoreceptor migration toward the center of the fovea exists not only between birth and 15 months, but also beyond 15 months. It would be of interest to examine data on saccadic refixation as a function of age during the first few years of life, to determine whether there are characteristics of the eye movements that might yield information on the method used by the developing visual system to recalibrate eye movement excursion as photoreceptor spacing changes. Unfortunately, virtually all developmental eye movement data are from very young infants, who are typically more cooperative than are 15-month-olds.

THE IDEAL OBSERVER APPROACH AT 15 MONTHS: CONTRAST SENSITIVITY FUNCTIONS

Banks and Bennett (1988) have shown that the front-end changes in the visual system described by the ideal observer approach predict the large downward shift seen in the contrast sensitivity function of the newborn. However, the approach does not predict the empirical finding that the newborn's contrast sensitivity function is shifted leftward, toward lower spatial frequencies. This implies that, as for grating acuity, postreceptoral factors play an important role in limiting contrast sensitivity in newborns.

Ideal observer calculations of the contrst sensitivity function of 15-month-olds predict a downward shift by a factor of two in the high frequency portion of the function. Although empirical contrast sensitivity data are not available for 15-month-olds, Pirchio, Spinelli, Fiorentini, and Maffei (1978) measured the contrast sensitivity functions of one 10-month-old and one 13-month-old with the VEP procedure. Their results indicated that the location of the peak spatial frequency was similar in these 1-year-olds and in adults (i.e., there was no leftward shift in the contrast sensitivity function toward lower spatial frequencies), but the high frequency cut-off (the acuity limit) was a factor of two lower in the 1-year-olds than in adults. Thus, data from these two children are in qualitative agreement with the ideal observer prediction for the performance of 15-month-olds.

One other piece of data presented by Pirchio et al. was that the maximum contrast sensitivity for the 10-month-old was similar to that of the adult. This result is in contrast to the ideal observer prediction that the maximum contrast sensitivity of the 15-month-old should be less than that of the adult. Clearly, more empirical data are needed to allow evaluation of the adequacy of the ideal observer predictions concerning contrast sensitivity at 15 months.

THE IDEAL OBSERVER APPROACH AT 15 MONTHS: STEREOPSIS

As Held points out in his chapter, stereopsis (binocular depth perception) does not appear to be present in newborns. Instead, data from his lab (Birch, Gwiazda, & Held, 1982; Gwiazda et al., 1989) suggest that stereopsis appears rather suddenly when the infant reaches about 4 months of age, after which stereoacuity gradually improves to adult levels by early childhood (see Fig. 10.4).

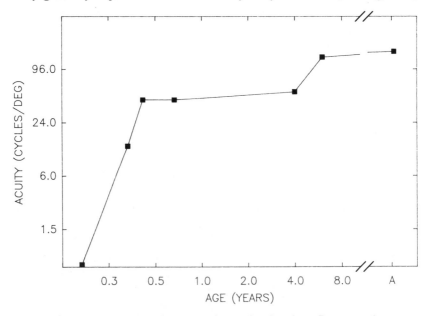

FIG. 10.4.   Improvement in stereoacuity as a function of age. Data are replotted from studies by Birch et al. (1982) and Gwiazda et al. (1989), in which FPL procedures were used to measure stereoacuity. The data show a difference, by a factor of 3.5, between stereoacuity at 8 months and that in adulthood, which is not much greater than the ideal observer prediction of a factor of 2.8 difference between 15 months and adulthood.

Held (1985) has suggested that the onset of stereopsis is dependent on maturation of the binocular cells in visual cortex that are known to mediate binocular vision. The ideal observer approach, on the other hand, reminds us that developmental changes in visual function, even in aspects of visual function that are cortically mediated, may result from structural changes in the visual system unrelated to cortical maturation. That is, it is possible that the empirical changes in stereoacuity seen in Fig. 10.4 are partly or entirely the result of front-end anatomical changes in the eyes and the photoreceptors.

Aslin (1988) has pointed out that there are two structural changes that occur during infancy that would affect binocular vision. The first is the change in interocular separation that occurs as the child's head and face grow. The interocular separation in newborns is about 40 mm, whereas it is about 64 mm in the adult. This means that if an adult and an infant are fixating the same target, point F in Fig. 10.5, and a second target is placed at point P, the angular disparity created on the retina by the second target will be greater in the eyes of the adult than in the eyes of the infant. If the angular disparity is so small that the target remains within Panum's fusion area for the infant, then the infant would not see the target as different in depth from point F and would therefore give no evi-

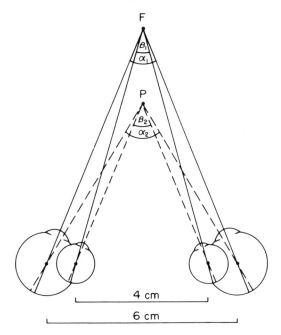

FIG. 10.5. Schematic representation of a newborn (dashed lines) and an adult (solid lines) fixating point F with their foveas. An object placed at point P projects onto noncorresponding points and creates retinal disparity. The magnitude of the retinal disparity is greater in the adult than in the newborn. (Reprinted with permission from Aslin & Dumais, 1980.)

dence of stereopsis. Thus, one hypothesis for why young infants don't show stereopsis is that their reduced interocular difference decreases the retinal disparity produced by stimuli that, to adults, would appear to have depth.

Aslin has done the calculations to make this a quantitative hypothesis. Aslin's results indicate that the smaller interocular separation of the newborn would reduce angular disparity only by a factor of 1.6. Given that the smallest resolvable angular disparity in adults is 2 to 10 arcsec (Berry, 1948), this would predict a stereoacuity of 3 to 16 arcsec in the newborn. A stereoacuity threshold of 3 to 16 arcsec is much smaller than the angular disparities of the targets used in studies that failed to detect stereopsis in very young infants, which means that some factor in addition to interocular separation is needed to explain the lack of stereopsis in very young infants.

A second structural change in the eye that would be predicted to affect stereoacuity development is the increase in photoreceptor packing of the central fovea that occurs during development. Aslin (1988) calculated that the migration and increased packing density of foveal photoreceptors would be expected to improve stereoacuity by a factor of 3.6 between birth and adulthood. This factor, in combination with the newborn's decreased interocular difference, predicts that stereoacuity in the newborn would be 11 to 58 arcsec. Held and his colleagues have reported, however, that the stereoacuity of infants less than 2 months of age is much worse than this, in that they give no evidence of detecting a disparity of 60 arc*min* (Birch et al., 1982; Gwiazda et al., 1989). Thus, changes in photoreceptor spacing and interocular distance cannot account for the very large improvement in stereoacuity that occurs between infancy and adulthood.

Aslin (personal communication, June, 1989) has also calculated ideal observer predictions for the stereoacuity of the 15-month-old. These calculations indicate that the 50 mm interocular separation of the 15-month-old would reduce angular disparity by a factor of 1.28, which would predict a stereoacuity of 3 to 13 arcsec. The factor of 2.2 difference in photoreceptor packing density between the 15-month-old and the adult would further reduce predicted stereoacuity to 6 to 28 arcsec, a factor of 2.8 worse than the stereoacuity of the adult.

As shown in Fig. 10.4, Birch et al. (1982) found a 3.5-factor difference between the stereoacuity of 8-month-old infants and that of adults. This empirical difference between stereoacuity of 8-month-olds and adults is similar enough to the predicted difference of 2.8 between 15-month-olds and adults to suggest that the poorer stereoacuity of 8-month-olds may be due entirely to front-end limitations of the visual system. I look forward to the publication of empirical stereoacuity data for 15-month-olds to see how well the data agree with the ideal observer predictions at that age.

SUMMARY AND CONCLUSIONS

In summary, in all areas of visual function that have been studied, evidence has been found for an improvement in visual function between birth and adulthood. Researchers often attribute this improvement to the maturation of cortical mechanisms, ignoring developmental changes at earlier stages of the visual system. The advantage of the ideal observer approach is that it reminds the researcher that there are many developmental changes that occur distal to any cortical mechanisms. These distal changes in the visual system can have substantial influence on what type of information reaches visual cortex and, in fact, may be responsible for developmental changes in many of the aspects of visual function described in the chapters by Banks and Shannon, Teller and Lindsey, Aslin, and Held.

ACKNOWLEDGMENTS

This work was supported by NIH grant EY 05804. I thank Marty Banks and Dick Aslin for helpful discussions on the ideal observer approach, and Carl Granrud for comments on an earlier version of this chapter.

REFERENCES

Aslin, R. N. (1988). Anatomical constraints on oculomotor development: Implications for infant perception. In A. Yonas (Ed.), *Perceptual development in infancy* (pp. 67–104). Hillsdale, NJ: Lawrence Erlbaum Associates.

Aslin, R. N., & Dumais, S. T. (1980). Binocular vision in infants: A review and a theoretical framework. *Advances in Child Development, 15*, 53–94.

Atkinson, J., Braddick, O., & French, J. (1979). Contrast sensitivity of the human neonate measured by the visual evoked potential. *Investigative Ophthalmology and Visual Science, 18*, 210–213.

Banks, M. S., & Bennett, P. J. (1988). Optical and photoreceptor immaturities limit the spatial and chromatic vision of human neonates. *Journal of the Optical Society of America A, 5*, 2059–2079.

Banks, M. S., & Salapatek, P. (1978). Acuity and contrast sensitivity in 1-, 2-, and 3-month-old human infants. *Investigative Ophthalmology and Visual Science, 17*, 361–365.

Berry, R. N. (1948). Quantitative relations among vernier, real depth, and stereoscopic depth acuities. *Journal of Experimental Psychology, 38*, 708–721.

Birch, E. E., Gwiazda, J., Bauer, J. A., Jr., Naegele, J., & Held, R. (1983). Visual acuity and its meridional variations in children aged 7–60 months. *Vision Research, 23*, 1019–1024.

Birch, E. E., Gwiazda, J., & Held, R. (1982). Stereoacuity development for crossed and uncrossed disparities in human infants. *Vision Research, 22*, 507–513.

Bronson, G. (1974). The postnatal growth of visual capacity. *Child Development, 45*, 873–890.

Geisler, W. S. (1984). Physical limits of acuity and hyperacuity. *Journal of the Optical Society of America A, 1*, 775–782.

Gwiazda, J., Bauer, J., & Held, R. (1989). From visual acuity to hyperacuity: A 10-year update. *Canadian Journal of Psychology, 43*, 109–120.

Hamer, R. D., Alexander, K. R., & Teller, D. Y. (1982). Rayleigh discriminations in young human infants. *Vision Research, 22*, 575–587.

Held, R. (1985). Binocular vision: Behavioral and neuronal development. In J. Mehler & R. Fox (Eds.), *Neonate cognition: Beyond the blooming buzzing confusion* (pp. 37–44). Hillsdale, NJ: Lawrence Erlbaum Associates.

Hendrickson, A. E., & Yuodelis, C. (1984). The morphological development of the human fovea. *Ophthalmology, 91*, 603–612.

Maurer, D., & Lewis, T. L. (1979). A physiological explanation of infants' early visual development. *Canadian Journal of Psychology, 33,* 232–252.

Packer, O., Hartmann, E. E., & Teller, D. Y. (1984). Infant color vision: The effect of test field size on Rayleigh discriminations. *Vision Research, 24,* 1247–1260.

Peeples, D. R., & Teller, D. Y. (1975). Color vision and brightness discrimination in two-month-old human infants. *Science, 189,* 1102–1103.

Pirchio, M., Spinelli, D., Fiorentini, A., & Maffei, L. (1978). Infant contrast sensitivity evaluated by evoked potentials. *Brain Research, 141,* 179–184.

Shimojo, S., Birch, E. E., Gwiazda, J., & Held, R. (1984). Development of vernier acuity in infants. *Vision Research, 24,* 721–728.

Shimojo, S., & Held, R. (1987). Vernier acuity is less than grating acuity in 2- and 3-month-olds. *Vision Research, 27,* 77–86.

Teller, D. Y., Peeples, D. R., & Sekel, M. (1978). Discrimination of chromatic from white light by two-month-old human infants. *Vision Research, 18,* 41–48.

Yuodelis, C., & Hendrickson, A. (1986). A qualitative and quantitative analysis of the human fovea during development. *Vision Research, 26,* 847–855.

11

Commentary: Cheers and Lamentations

Robert S. Siegler
Carnegie Mellon University

Searching for ideas and inspiration for this discussion, I read the concluding chapters from a number of previous Carnegie-Mellon Cognition Symposia. It struck me that most discussants assumed one of two roles: Jeremiah or cheerleader. Like most dichotomies, this one is too simple; all of the Jeremiahs offered some words of praise, and all of the cheerleaders voiced some criticisms. Still, the labels convey the dominant tone of the articles.

The titles alone are revealing. First consider those of the Jeremiahs: "You Can't Play 20 Questions with Nature and Win" (Newell, 1973); "Copycat Science, or 'Does the Mind Really Work by Table Look Up' " (Norman, 1980); "A Garden of Opportunities and a Thicket of Dangers" (Steinberg, 1980).

Perhaps the prototypic Jeremiad was Newell's 20-questions article. The following passage communicates the main theme:

> Still, I am distressed. I can illustrate it by the way I was going to start my comments, though I could not in fact bring myself to do so. I was going to draw a line on the blackboard and, picking one of the speakers of the day at random, note on the line the time at which he got his PhD and the current time (in mid-career). Then, taking his total production of papers like those in the present symposium, I was going to compute a rate of productivity of such excellent work. Moving, finally, to the date of my chosen target's retirement, I was going to compute the total future addition of such papers to the (putative) end of this man's scientific career. Then I was going to pose, in my role as discussant, a question: Suppose you had all those additional papers, just like those of today (except being on new aspects of the problem), *Where will psychology then be?* (Newell, 1973, pp. 283–284)

In contrast to these words of weariness, warning, and woe, those who assume the cheerleader role offer compliments, congratulations, and kudos. Thus, Simon (1980) praised investigators in that symposium for showing "How to Win at Twenty Questions with Nature." Klahr (1984) described the papers in his session on mathematical cognition as offering "An Embarrassment of Number." Finally, Bower (1978) provided a name for this entire genre in his memorable comments:

> This is the first time I have assumed the role of public discussant; I have found it a most disagreeable job. I dislike the role of examining someone's prized writing, looking for possible flaws or things to take issue with or disagree about. . . .
>
> As I grow older and more mellow, I have become increasingly disenchanted with that adversarial view. It leads to devastating criticisms that are terribly destructive of the spirit, self-esteem, and enthusiasm of the parties involved as well as the onlookers. From my perspective, what is good about a conference like this one is that it brings together a community of scholars, many of whom have been friends for years, and who respect and support one another. We depend on one another, not only for intellectual stimulation, but also for emotional support and reinforcement.
>
> This is why the role of critic is so nihilistic and life-denying. I propose that in the future, we dispense with the critic and replace him or her with a Grand Celebrator, a Herald, a Cheerleader, who leaps up to proclaim the depth and originality of the participants' ideas and findings. Such a hornblower would surely make all of us—participants as well as onlookers—feel a lot better about ourselves and the professional life in which we toil. (p. 361)

I find my reactions to the present symposium to be much more those of the cheerleader than those of the Old Testament prophet. Even to someone as far outside the area as I am, the rapidity of progress in this field is striking. The ratio of cheers to lamentations in the discussion below—6 to 2—reflects my overall reaction.

SIX CHEERS

1. For Asking the Big Questions

One of the most impressive aspects of the symposium was the directness with which participants addressed the fundamental issues in the field. What capabilities do infants possess in the first days out of the womb (Granrud)? Which aspects of visual development are due to changes in the eye, and which are due to changes in the brain (Banks & Shannon; Held)? How do infants know that they live in a world of enduring objects and object properties, rather than one in which all is flux (Arterberry, Craton, & Yonas; Baillargeon)? The research presented at this symposium focused directly on these and other fundamental issues about how infants perceive and think about the world.

2. For Interesting Empirical Phenomena

In recent years, studies of infants' perception and cognition have yielded numerous fascinating empirical findings. These have revealed infant competencies that few would have anticipated. Even with the upward revision of expectations that these past reports have engendered, the new discoveries continue to be impressive. Among the most striking reports of early competencies discussed here were Baillargeon's demonstrations that 4-month-olds expect not only objects but the properties of objects to be maintained when the objects pass out of view; Kellman's demonstrations that 4-month-olds can use motion to infer the unity of objects; and Bertenthal's demonstrations of 4-month-olds' ability to perceive biomechanical motion on the basis of point-light displays.

In addition to these demonstrations of early competencies, the symposium included several intriguing examples of relatively abrupt changes in perceptual abilities. Particularly interesting were Held's findings concerning the development of stereopsis and Arterberry et al.'s findings concerning the development of sensitivity to time-dependent information for object properties. These types of discoveries may stimulate insights about underlying physiological mechanisms, a potential that is already being realized in Held's work.

Yet other intriguing empirical contributions might best be viewed as creative reconstruals rather than as new discoveries. Consider Haith's demonstrations that 3-month-olds can form expectations. Haith argued that previous demonstrations of operant conditioning and generalization in very young children did not demonstrate that they could form expectations, whereas his findings did. I don't know if I agree with this argument, but it seems unimportant whether it is right or not. Regardless of whether the previous studies can legitimately be interpreted as arguing for the same conclusion, previous investigators did not interpret their findings in this way. The largest contribution of the work that Haith reported may be the insightful framing of the issue, which makes apparent the significance of the previous as well as the new findings.

3. For Direct Assaults on the Nature–Nurture Issue

Part of the appeal of infancy research to people outside the field is its promise for addressing the nature–nurture issue. Realizing this promise has proved difficult, however, because ruling out all potential experiential interpretations demands working with newborns. Newborns' volatile moods and high ratio of sleeping to waking states have proved daunting even for those accustomed to the general rigors of studying infants.

It is, therefore, especially praiseworthy when researchers are sufficiently motivated that they accept the challenge of working with newborns in order to answer epistemologically important questions. Granrud's work on size constancy in 1- and 2-day-olds provides a model of the research that is possible even with this difficult group. The work compellingly demonstrates that infants are born possessing some degree of size constancy. Such direct confrontation of basic questions evokes memories of the reasons why many of us became interested in psychology in the first place.

4. For Innovative Methods

Historically, increased understanding of infant perception and cognition has often been based on methodological innovations that allow infants to reveal their competencies. The habituation, visual preference, and conditioning paradigms have been especially large contributors. By allowing infants to demonstrate the discriminations that they can make, these paradigms have forced upward revisions of earlier estimates of infants' abilities.

The paradigms also have clear limits in what they can tell us about infants' perception and cognition, however. They are more useful for answering "Can they do X?" questions than for answering questions about "How do they do X?". This limitation, together with the widespread use of these methods, has made it difficult to link up findings about infants' capabilities with findings about children and adults, so as to provide an integrated depiction of development.

Studies presented at this symposium went beyond these standard methods. They utilized to good advantage several approaches that have proved informative in studying older children and adults but that have less often been employed to study infants. Haith used reaction time patterns to examine infants' anticipations of future events; Aslin analyzed eye movements in order to model oculomotor control and to determine what functions might be served by the consistent undershooting of targets that occurs in the first few months; Banks and Shannon formulated mathematical models that allow precise analyses of the sources of development of contrast sensitivity, color vision, and visual acuity. Application of these powerful methods may foreshadow a new burst of progress in our understanding of infants' perception and cognition.

5. For Integration of Neural and Behavioral Data

The field of infant perception has made far more progress than any other area of developmental psychology in integrating neural and behavioral data. The present chapters provided a number of excellent examples. Banks and Shannon's research on contrast sensitivity, Held's work on stereopsis, Teller's investigation of color vision, and Aslin's analyses of oculomotor control are all exemplary in demonstrating how knowledge of anatomy and physiology can help in interpreting behavior. Several of these analyses also suggest intriguing developmental mechanisms, for example, Held's hypothesis concerning the role of segregation of neuronal input in the development of stereopsis and Banks and Shannon's hypothesis that increased density of cones, along with morphological changes in the lengths and shapes of the individual cones, play a large role in producing increasingly acute foveal vision.

6. For a Scholarly Community

As Bower noted in the statement quoted earlier, scholars depend on each other not only for intellectual stimulation but also for emotional support and reinforcement. Those who attended this symposium could only be impressed with the quality of interactions among participants. The sense of shared enterprise and community was evident both among those who presented papers and among those in the field who came just to listen to them. To a degree that is rarely seen, participants were knowledgable about each other's research, understood its strengths and weaknesses, and appreciated the difficulties that had to be overcome to conduct it. There was an alertness to breakthroughs and a willingness to consider their implications for one's own research that is all too rare. The rapid progress in this field may owe as much to the productive and supportive culture as to particular empirical discoveries and methodological innovations.

TWO LAMENTATIONS

Alongside these positive reactions, I have two major concerns.

1. Too Little Attention to How Behavior is Produced

Table 11.1 provides a simple framework for thinking about developmental research. Each of the five types of investigation in it is defined in terms of the most general question that it asks. The questions are ordered from most to

TABLE 11.1
Genres of Infancy Research

---

1. Can infants of age x do task y?
2. How well can infants of age x do task y?
3. How do infants of age x do task y?
4. How does change occur with age in how infants do task y?
5. How does change occur with age in how infants do tasks y, y', y'' . . .?

---

least frequent within the literature (and within this symposium) and also from easiest to most difficult to answer successfully.

The overwhelming majority of infancy research that I have encountered previously, and a high percentage at this conference as well, fits into the first category, "Can infants of age x do task y?" Most of the rest falls into the second category, "How well can infants of age x do task y?" These questions are important ones, and are the obvious first ones to ask. Still, the time may be at hand to go beyond them, to ask how infants do what they do and to model the processes that underlie their behavior.

The lack of attention to how infants perform tasks, as opposed to the simple fact of whether they can perform them, seems to be partially dictated by the traditional methods for studying infant perception and cognition: preference, habituation, conditioning, and reaching paradigms. Each of these methods can indicate that infants discriminate between displays and can provide information about the cues to which they are sensitive. However, none of them yields detailed information about underlying processes, and none provides data that very much constrain models of the processes. Without such models, however, understanding of how behavior is produced must remain severely limited.

Before going further, I should specify what I mean by a model of how behavior is produced. What I have in mind involves at least three facets: input, representations, and processes. That is, models need to specify what the input is, how it is represented, and how the processing system operates on the representation so as to produce behavior. Such models can be evaluated by their success in accounting for a wide range of behavior (e.g., relative and absolute accuracy under various conditions, solution time patterns, specific errors); by their ability to generate correct, nonintuitive predictions; and by their consistency with knowledge of relevant physiology.

This symposium was actually better than the field in general in terms of the prevalence of such models. Banks and Shannon provided a very detailed and comprehensive model of the determinants of visual acuity. Aslin's models of oculomotor functioning and Bertenthal's phase plane trajectory model were also quite well worked out.

Nonetheless, I would like to see more models of how infants perceive and think. One advantage of such models, as Newell (1973) pointed out, is that they help research to accumulate. They allow us to go beyond the question of whether infants can show a particular kind of discrimination and almost force us to consider how the same perceptual-cognitive system can produce successful performance on some tasks yet unsuccessful performance on other, seemingly similar ones.

When the model is realized as a running computer simulation, we can also learn about incongruities among our ideas that we otherwise would be unlikely to detect. I have seen this phenomenon in my own modeling of children's learning of arithmetic (Siegler & Shipley, 1992). The largest stumbling block for the model was in an area that I never would have anticipated: The model had difficulty progressing from very accurate to extremely accurate performance, that is, from roughly 95% correct to 100% correct performance. The difficulty of producing such learning forced us to rethink the model's learning mechanisms and eventually to revise them so that such high-end learning would occur. Without the difficulty that the model encountered, I am quite sure that I never would have recognized the problem with the original formulation.

Such models might be especially useful in this area, because they would allow us to go beyond arguments with dead people. Much infancy research, both in this symposium and in the field in general, is justified on the grounds that it disproves statements by Piaget, Helmholtz, Berkeley, or the Gestaltists. The immediate impression created by such arguments is that the new research is of historic importance. On reflection, however, the justification is also troubling. It is not just that it is unsporting to argue with those who can no longer answer. The more disturbing part is that the vastly greater data base that is available today has not stimulated comparable improvements in the quality of theoretical discussion. Regardless of how great the early theorists were, available data did not allow them to go much beyond their intuitions. Indeed, they could make such bold, unqualified claims precisely because no data were available to contradict them. The clarity of their claims makes them tempting targets for refutation, but only so much progress can be made through this route. There is a reason why physicists no longer argue with Aristotle. At some point, oppositions to the claims of historical figures must give way to arguments over which contemporary model explains the most data and does so most plausibly and parsimoniously.

My point is not that we should stop addressing the *issues* raised by illustrious predecessors. Indeed, the best evidence of their historic stature is that they raised the issues that remain fundamental. Rather, the point is that their speculations about these issues do not provide the worthy focal point that syntheses of currently available evidence could.

I will use Baillargeon's interesting and influential research on object permanence to illustrate the difficulties that even the best examples of such refutational research encounter. Baillargeon began by citing Piaget's claim that infants do not understand object permanence and questioning whether the claim was true. To test Piaget's contention, she developed a basic experimental paradigm that involves presenting infants with situations that appear to violate physical laws regarding the permanence of objects and their properties. She then observes whether the infants look longer at those ("impossible") arrangements than at ones consistent with physical laws. In a series of elegant studies, Baillargeon has found that 3- to 13-month-olds do look longer at many specific types of violations. In so doing, she has provided strong evidence against Piaget's theory of object permanence. Clearly, infants have more understanding of the permanence of objects and their properties than Piaget thought they did.

Just what this understanding involves is not as well addressed, however. Bail-largeon's main theoretical claim is summarized in such statements as: "The results of these experiments thus indicated that, contrary to what Piaget had claimed, infants as young as 3½ months of age represent the existence of oc-cluded objects" (p. 272). This conclusion was based on the evidence that infants "looked reliably longer at the impossible than at the possible event . . . and were surprised at the impossible event" (pp. 271–272).

On the surface, this conclusion seems well justified. Certainly something in the impossible condition is leading the infants to look longer at it. Whether this longer looking indicates that the infants are surprised, however, is far less clear.

An anecdote illustrates the problem. While on my back porch the weekend before the symposium, I saw a bird turn its head 180°, so that it was looking directly back at its tail. I was not surprised that the bird could do this, since I had read that birds possess this capability. I was extremely interested in see-ing it, though. Anyone measuring my looking times would have recorded a very long fixation. The point is that long looking times do not necessarily reflect sur-prise; they can reflect interest, amusement, efforts at remembering, or any num-ber of other reactions.

What difference does it make if we interpret infants' long looking times as indicating that they were "surprised" by what they saw? Not very much, if we believe that the infant's representation of the situation only specifies that some object with a height that tends to remain more-or-less constant is proba-bly behind the barrier; a great deal, however, if we believe that the infant's representation specifies that the previously seen object is definitely behind the barrier, that its height must remain exactly the same, and that any deviation means that an "impossible" event has occurred. Saying that infants can represent and reason about occluded objects only scratches the surface of what is going on in the infant's mind. Thus, the studies clearly demonstrate that Piaget was wrong, but are less clear indications of the perceptual and cognitive processes that are producing the observed behavior.

It is precisely for this purpose—specifying the processes that give rise to observed behavior—that formulating models is most useful. Attempting to model infants' thinking in this situation would almost demand that the modeler con-front such issues as: (a) whether infants of a given age are 100% certain that objects continue to exist or whether they believe it probable but not certain; (b) whether infants believe that the object's properties remain exactly constant or only approximately so; and (c) which transformations infants believe affect the continued existence of objects and their properties and which they believe do not. In cases where available evidence does not allow answers to such ques-tions, such a model would motivate informative experiments that otherwise would be unlikely to be run.

Perhaps the best argument for modeling infant perception and cognition comes from considering the benefits gained when this has been done. In the present symposium, Banks and Shannon's ideal observer approach provided the outstanding example of a well-worked-out model. Its invigorating effects were readily apparent. It stimulated Dobson to consider how older infants' perceptions might be modeled within such a framework, stimulated Held to provide counterexamples of how development of stereopsis and orientation selectivity could not be explained entirely at the retinal level, and stimulated Aslin to wonder how ideal observer models might be applied to studying early oculomotor control. The basic idea of identifying all of the sources of information loss known to occur at one level of functioning, and modeling the best functioning possible if processing at other levels does not result in any further degradation of the information, seems a generally powerful way of studying perception.

In many perceptual and cognitive contexts, the underlying physiology is not sufficiently understood to provide comparably strong constraints. However, in such cases, examining the effects of different processing and learning assumptions on a model's ability to conform to known behavioral data can produce similarly salutary effects. Aslin's simulations of how the development of oculomotor control would vary with differing learning and memory capabilities provide a nice illustration of how modeling can contribute to theoretical progress under these conditions.

2. Too Little Attention to How Change Occurs

Again, the papers in the present symposium were better on this score than the field in general. Nonetheless, only Banks and Shannon's, Aslin's, and Held's papers specified in detail how change occurs on any task, much less how it occurs across a variety of tasks.

It often seems that the implicit logic of most research on infant perception and cognition corresponds to the caricature in Fig. 11.1. In the beginning, an experiment was designed to determine whether infants of a given age could perform a given task. If they could, an effort was then made to determine if yet younger infants also could do so. If infants of the original age could not perform the task, more sensitive tasks and/or measures were developed to determine whether they then could do so. Whatever the outcome, the cycle continued to the present day.

This caricature masks the enormous cleverness and ingenuity that has gone into demonstrating competencies among younger and younger infants. Still, I am bothered by the lack of attention to how change occurs. The logic of such investigations looks ever downward, never upward. When investigators do study older age groups, they tend to look to different concepts and capabilities than the ones they originally examined and to start new downward cycles for these abilities. The result has been conclusions that more closely resemble lists of competencies known to be present at each age than a coherent depiction of development.

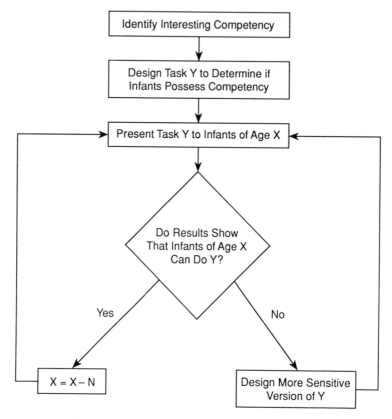

FIG. 11.1.   The agenda underlying most infancy research?

The lack of compelling depictions of change within the contemporary literature seems to be a major reason for arguments with the dead continuing to play
such a prominent role in this field. Much of what made Berekely, Hume, and
Piaget great was that they proposed intriguing (though frequently incorrect) ideas
about change. Until we formulate alternative coherent accounts of change that
have the added virtue of being consistent with available data, theoretical progress
will be limited.

What I would like to see is models that generate both the strengths and the
weaknesses of infants of a given age, and that depict the processes through
which the weaknesses become strengths. For example, I would like to understand the changes between 2 and 3 months that allow 3-month-olds to succeed
on Haith's expectancy tasks, the changes between 10 and 12 months that allow
the 12-month-olds to succeed on Arterberry, Craton, and Yonas's time-
dependent information tasks, and the changes between 4½ and 6½ months that
allow the older infants to succeed on Baillargeon's 80% height violation task.
I would be even happier if the proposed developmental mechanisms accounted

for a number of specific changes. For the time being, however, providing a rigorous explanation for even a single change would be a big step in the right direction.

Again, the models of change processes that have been proposed provide the best arguments for formulating more of them. Banks and Shannon's model is particularly appealing, because it accounts for a large variety of particular changes: changes in contrast sensitivity, grating acuity, and color vision. It does this parsimoniously and elegantly, without invoking a large number of special mechanisms. In doing so, it has shifted the whole framework of the debate about how retinal and postretinal changes contribute to visual development. It also represents a base upon which even more encompassing and detailed models can be built.

Aslin's models illustrate some of the gains that can accrue from constructing models of change processes, even when we quickly decide that the models are wrong. Aslin noted that his models revealed hidden assumptions in his own thinking about the types of information infants use to control their eye movements, the algorithms they use for combining the various types of information, the memory demands of the different algorithms, and the adaptive consequences that undershooting might have for infants. Such recognitions seem likely to lead both to theoretical progress and to interesting new experiments.

The arguments presented in this discussion might evoke the response that modeling performance and change is a desirable goal, but only in the long term. In the meantime, until we can formulate more specific ideas about how behavior is produced and how change occurs, we should learn more about what infants can do at each age.

I have two reactions to this argument. First, my own experience is that the largest impediment to making theoretical progress often is the belief that it is premature to focus on doing so. No matter how well researched an area, there are always further empirical uncertainties to resolve. Given the exceptionally high ratio of empirical findings to data-based theoretical models in this field (and in most of psychology), however, the time seems ripe for greater efforts toward theoretical progress.

Second, there is the Roger Bannister effect. Runners had been flirting with the 4-minute mile for 30 years before Bannister broke the barrier. Yet within a short time, other milers followed his lead, and even ran faster times than Bannister had. By showing that such a feat was possible, Bannister inspired the confidence that allowed others to surmount the barrier as well. Within the present symposium, Banks and Shannon's model may serve the same function. It shows how it is possible to build models of performance and change that are highly constrained, specific, and encompassing.

Even for those who totally disagree with these arguments and think it would be premature to devote substantial effort to modeling changes in infants' perceptual and cognitive capabilities, this symposium included many sources of inspiration. There were any number of examples of excellent research. Perhaps the greatest contribution of a conference like this is that it stimulates everyone to go back to their labs and try harder to learn more. The hope of such renewal is perhaps the best reason for holding such symposia.

ACKNOWLEDGMENTS

Preparation of these comments was supported in part by grants from the National Institutes of Health (HD-19011), the Spencer Foundation, and the Mellon Foundation. Helpful comments on an earlier draft were provided by Carl Granrud.

REFERENCES

Bower, G. H. (1978). Representing knowledge development. In R. S. Siegler (Ed.), *Children's thinking: What develops?* (pp. 349–362). Hillsdale, NJ: Lawrence Erlbaum Associates.

Klahr, D. (1984). Commentary: An embarrassment of number. In C. Sophian (Ed.), *Origins of cognitive skills* (pp. 295–309). Hillsdale, NJ: Lawrence Erlbaum Associates.

Newell, A. (1973). You can't play 20 questions with nature and win: Projective comments on the papers of this symposium. In W. G. Chase (Ed.), *Visual information processing* (pp. 283–308). New York: Academic Press.

Norman, D. A. (1980). Copycat science or does the mind really work by table look-up? In R. A. Cole (Ed.), *Perception and production of fluent speech* (pp. 381–395). Hillsdale, NJ: Lawrence Erlbaum Associates.

Siegler, R. S., & Shipley, C. (1992). *A general model of strategy choice.* Unpublished manuscript.

Simon, H. A. (1980). How to win at twenty questions with nature. In R. A. Cole (Ed.), *Perception and production of fluent speech* (pp. 535–548). Hillsdale, NJ: Lawrence Erlbaum Associates.

Steinberg, E. R. (1980). A garden of opportunities and a thicket of dangers. In L. W. Gregg & E. R. Steinberg (Eds.), *Cognitive processes in writing* (pp. 155–167). Hillsdale, NJ: Lawrence Erlbaum Associates.

Author Index

A

Abelson, K. P., 237, *264*
Abraham, R. H., 198, *212*
Abramov, I., 14, *43*, 51, *72*, 111, 112, *117*
Aggarwal, J. K., 190, 191, *214*
Alexander, K., 17, 18, 21, 26, 27, 30, *44*
Alexander, K. R., 318, *331*
Allen, D., 12, 17, 28–32, 36, *43*, *45*
Allman, J., 123, *170*
Ames, A., 124, *170*
Anderson, J. R., 293, *312*
Ankrum, C., 17, 19, 21, 32–36, *44*, 63, *72*
Anliker, M., 231, *234*
Anstis, S. M., 49, 51, 56, 62, *71*, *72*, 197, *214*
Anstis, T., 114, *118*
Antell, S. H., 226, *233*
Appel, K. J., 301, *313*
Appelle, S., 80, *87*
Arehart, D. M., 257, 261, *263*
Arterberry, M., 143, 145, 155, *173*
Arterberry, M. E., 176, *212*, 215, 218–221, 223, 226, 228, 231, 232, *233*, *234*
Aslin, R., 163, *171*
Aslin, R. N., 93, 94, *116*, *170*, 231, *233*, 236, 251, *263*, 270, *314*, 329, *331*
Atkeson, C. G., 106, *116*
Atkinson, J., 11, 38, 41, *43*, 75, 82, *87*, *88*, 163, *170*, *331*

B

Baillargeon, R., 231, 232, *233*, 270, 271–278, 280–291, 293–299, 303, 304, 308, 309, *312*, *314*
Baker, C. L., 110, *117*
Banks, M. S., 1–3, 5, 6, 8–15, 20, 26, 28–33, 36, 40, 41, *43*, *44*, 48, 63, 70, *71*, 75, 76, 79, *87*, 93, 109, *117*, 216, *233*, 235, *263*, 317–321, 324, 325, 327, *331*
Barbeito, R., 93, *117*
Barlow, H. B., 2, 9, 41, *43*, *45*
Barnes, I., 94, *118*
Baron, R. M., 177, *213*
Bartsch, K., 266, 301–303, 306, *315*
Bauer, J. A., 78, 82–86, *87*, *89*
Bauer, J. A., Jr., 318, 322, 323, 325, 328, 330, *331*
Baumgartner, G., 231, *234*
Bedell, H. E., 93, 115, *117*, *118*
Bennett, P. J., 1–3, 5, 8–11, 13–15, 20, 26, 32, *43*, 48, 63, 70, *71*, 75, 76, 79, *87*, 317–321, 324, 325, 327, *331*
Benson, J. B., 236, 261, *263*, *264*
Berkeley, G., 124, 142, *170*
Bernard, 6

Berry, R. N., 330, *331*
Bertenthal, B. I., 136, *170*, 177, 182, 187,
    190, 192, 195, 197, 199, 201, 204,
    205, 208, 211, *212, 213*
Bertrand, J. A., 86, *88, 233*
Berzins, V. A., 218, *234*
Beverly, K. I., 123, *172*
Biederman, I., 237, *263*
Billman, D. O., 283, *314*
Birch, E. E., 82–85, *87, 88, 89*, 163, *171*,
    231, *233*, 318, 322, 323, 325, 328,
    330, *331, 332*
Bjork, E. L., 301, *312*
Black, J., 294–299, 308, *312*
Blake, R., 85, *87*
Blakemore, C., 1, 16, 41, *43, 44*
Boley, S., 261, *263*
Bolles, R. C., 237, *263*
Bond, E., 143, *170*
Bonds, A. B., 38, *43*
Bone, R. A., 3, *43*
Booth, R. G., 16, *43*
Boring, E. G., 96, *117*
Bornstein, M. H., 1, *45*, 47, 48, 58, 63, *72*
Borton, R., 292, *314*
Borton, R. W., 223, *234*
Bouman, M. A., 87, *89*
Bower, G. H., 270, 286, *312*, 334, *344*
Bower, T. G. R., 270, 292, *312*
Boynton, R. M., 48, 52, 56, *71, 72*
Braddick, O., 11, 38, 41, *43*, 82, *88*, 162,
    170, 318, *331*
Braddick, O. J., 110, *117*
Braunstein, M., 121–124, *170*
Braunstein, M. L., *212*
Bremner, J. G., 266, 305, *312*
Brennan, N. A., 16, *45*
Brewer, W. F., 265, *315*
Bridgeman, B., 107, 109, 114, 115, *117, 118*
Brill, S., 75, 80, 82, *88*
Bronson, G., 317, *331*
Bronson, G. W., 1, 2, *43*, 75, *88*, 102, *117*
Brooks, P. H., 306, *314*
Broughton, J. M., 270, *312*
Brown, A. L., 283, *312*
Brown, A. M., 1, 17, 19, 21, 32–36, *44*, 47,
    48, 63, *71, 72*, 87, *88*
Brown, E., 135, 166, *173*
Bruner, J. S., 302, *312*
Brunswik, E., 122, 128, 142, *170*
Buffart, H., 155, *170*

Bullock, D., 236, *263*
Burgess, A. E., 38, 39, *45*
Burr, D. C., 110, *117*
Burt, P., 110, *117*
Bushnell, E., 149, *173*
Bushnell, E. W., 293, *312*
Butterworth, G. E., 306, *312*

C

Camenzuli, C., 51, *72*
Campbell, F. W., 9, 12, 15, 41, *43, 44*, 80, 81, *88*
Campos, J. J., 136, *170*, 182, 188, *212*, 245, *236*
Canfield, R. L., 246, 247, 249, *263*
Carey, S., 210, *212*, 265, *313, 315*
Carpenter, G. C., 159, *170*
Cathiard, A. M., 86, *88*
Cavanagh, P., 49, 51, 56, 62, *71, 72*, 114, *118*
Chi, M. T. H., 265, *313*
Clarkson, M. G., 85, *88*, 94, *117*
Clavadetscher, J. M., 17, 19, 21, 32–36, *44*,
    63, *72*
Clement, J., 365, *313*
Clifton, R. K., 85, *88*, 94, *117*, 292, 293, *314*
Cohen, L., 155, *170*, 301, *314*
Colleta, N. J., 1, *44*
Collins, D., 237, 238, *263*
Condry, K., 158, 160, 162, 164–167, *171, 172*
Cook, J. E., 17, 19–21, 31–36, *45*
Cooper, R., 226, *234*
Cornsweet, T., 8, *44*
Cornsweet, T. N., 53, *72*
Crabbe, G., 127, *172*
Craton, L. G., 218–221, 232, *233, 234*
Crewther, S. G., 16, *45*
Cross, D., 266, 301–303, 306, *315*
Crowell, J. A., 9, 14, *44*
Cummings, E. S., 301, *312*
Curtis, L. E., 226, *234*
Cutting, J. E., 177, 180, 181, 183–188, 190, 196,
    200, 203, 208, *212, 213*
Cynader, M., 123, *172*

D

Dannemiller, J. L., 1, 41, *43*, 63, *71*
Darby, B. L., 292, *314*
Day, 162, *170*
Davidson, 166

Davis, P., 195, 199, 205, 207, *212*
de Bie, J., 51, *72*
de Courten, C., 86, *88*
Delgado, D. 108, *117*
DeLoache, J., 155, *170*
Derrington, A. M., 38, *44*, 52–54, *72*
DeVos, J., 231, *233*, 273, 274, 283–289, 291, 294–299, 303, 304, 308, 309, *312*
Diamond, A., 291, 300, 302, 305, *313*
Diamond, R., 114, *117*, 210, *212*
Dobson, M. V., 159, *173*
Dobson, V., 1, 12, 14, 38, *43*, *44*, 87, *88*
Doxsey, P. A., 306, *314*
Dumais, S. T., 163, *171*, 231, *233*, 329, *331*

E

Edwards, M. W., 109, *118*
Efron, N., 16, *45*
Epstein, W., 135, *171*, 185, *213*
Estevez, O., 8, *44*
Evans, W. F., 301, *313*

F

Fagan, J. F., III, 143, *171*, 302, *313*
Fantz, R. L., 143, *171*, 239, *263*
Favreau, O. E., 56, *72*
Feltovich, P. J., 265, *313*
Fernandez, 3
Fernandez, L., *43*
Field, J., 94, *118*
Findlay, J. M. 16, *45*, 163, *173*
Fiorentini, A., 12, *45*, 80, *89*, 327, *332*
Fisher, B., 114, *117*
Flavell, J. H., 266, *313*
Flinchbaugh, B. E., 191, *213*
Flom, M. C., 93, *117*
Flynn, J. T., 38, *44*
Fodor, J., 142, *171*, 209, *212*
Forbus, K. D., 277, *313*
Forest, M. G., 86, *88*
Fox, N., 301, 305, *313*
Fox, R., 163, *171*, 206, *212*, 231, *233*
Freedman, M., 301, *315*
Freeman, R. D., 80, *88*
French, J., 318, *331*
Fuchs, A. F., 38, *44*
Fulton, A. B., 41, *44*, 61, *72*

G

Garey, L. J., 86, *88*
Garner, W. R., 188, *213*
Geisler, W. S., 1, 2, 8–11, 13, 14, 21, 39, *43*, *44*, 75, *88*, 318, *331*
Gelman, R., 226, *234*, 265, *313*
Gentner, D., 265, 283, *313*
Gentner, D. R., 265, *313*
Gesell, A., 206, *213*
Gibson, J. J., 91, 109, *117*, 121–124, 128, 135, 142, 145, 147, 148, 156, 167, *171*, 215, 216, 232, *233*
Gick, M. L., 283, *313*
Gilden, D. L., 197, *213*
Glaser, R., 265, *313*
Glass, A. L., 237, *263*
Gleitman, H., 132–134, *172*
Glicksman, M. L., 218–221, *233*
Gogel, W., 158, 159, 168, *171*
Goldberg, S., 270, *313*
Goldman-Rakic, P. S., 245, *263*
Goodman, G. S., 237, 240, *263*
Gordon, J., 14, *43*
Gould, S. J., 178, *213*
Graber, M., 231, *233*, 283, 291, 294–298, 303, 304, *312*
Graham, M., 123, *173*
Granrud, C. E., 143, 145, 155, 161, 166, *171*, *173*, 215, 218–221, *233*, *234*, 293, *313*
Gratch, G., 266, 269, 270, 301, 305, *313*, *314*
Green, B. F., 192, *213*
Green, D. G., 2, 6, *44*
Greenfield, P. M., 302, *312*
Grossberg, S., 236, *263*
Gubisch, R. W., 9, *44*
Gwiazda, J., 75, 80, 82–86, *87*, *88*, *89*, 163, *171*, 231, *233*, 318, 322, 323, 325, 328, 330, *331*, *332*

H

Hainline, L., 14, 16, *43*, *44*, 51, *72*, 111, 112, *117*
Haith, M. M., 95, *117*, 136, *170*, 182, 188, *212*, 236–238, 240, 245, 246, 252, 257, 261, *263*, *264*

Hamaski, D. I., 38, *44*
Hamer, R. D., 17, 18, 21, 26, 27, 30, *44*, 318, *331*
Hansen, R., 61, *72*
Hansen, R. M., 41, *44*
Harris, C. M., 16, *44*, 111, 112, *117*
Harris, P., 94, *117*, *118*, 142, *171*
Harris, P. L., 266, 270, 301–303, *313*
Hartmann, E. E., 17, 18, 21, 24–27, 40, 41, *43*, *45*, 318, *332*
Hatfield, G., 185, *213*
Hazan, C., 240, *263*
Heeley, D. W., 52, *72*
Hein, A., 114, *117*, 126, *171*
Heit, G., 115, *117*
Held, R., 2, 41, *45*, 75, 78, 80, 82–86, *87*, *88*, *89*, 126, 163, *171*, 231, *233*, 318, 322, 323, 325, 328–330, *331*, *332*
Helmholtz, H. von, 108, *117*, 125, 156, 168, *171*
Helson, H., 136, *171*
Hendrickson, A., 3, 14, 16, *43*, *44*, *46*, 93, *119*, 318, 319, *331*, *332*
Hendry, D., 114, *117*, *118*
Hering, E., 92, *117*, *171*
Hess, R. F., 9, 13, *44*
Hickey, T. L., 3, *44*
Hill, K., 301, *314*
Hime, 3
Hirano, S., 3, *44*
Hochberg, J., 122, 135, *171*
Hoffman, D. D., 141, *171*, 191, *213*
Hoffmann, K. P., 109, *117*
Hofsten, C. von, 93, *117*, *121*, *157*, *158*, *160*, *162–167*, *171*, *172*, 236, *264*, 293, *314*
Holyoak, K. J., 237, 261, *264*, 283, *313*, *314*
Hood, B., 270, 292–294, *314*
Howell, E. R., 9, 13, *44*
Hubel, D. H., 38, *44*
Hurvich, L. M., 52, *72*
Huttenlocher, P. R., 86, *88*

I

Ilg, U. J., 109, *117*
Inada, V., 197, *214*
Inhelder, B., 265, *314*

J

Jacobs, D. S., 1, *44*
James, W., 168, 169, *171*, 211, *213*, *314*
Jameson, D., 52, *72*
Jansson, G., 121, *171*
Jennings, T., 261, *263*
Johansson, G., 121–124, 142, 155, *171*, 177, 179–181, 211, *213*
Judd, D. B., 61, *72*
Julesz, B., 231, *234*
Junn, E. N., 283, *314*

K

Kagan, J., 237, *264*, 301, 305, *313*, *314*
Kaplan, G., 123, *171*, 216–219, *233*
Karmiloff-Smith, A., 265, *314*
Kauffman, F., 210, *214*
Kauffman-Hayoz, R., 210, *214*
Kaufman, L., 161, *171*
Kaufmann, F., 140 *171*, 217, 220, 230, *233*
Kaufmann, R., 232, *233*
Kaufmann-Hayoz, R., 140, *171*, 217, 220, 230–232, *233*
Kay, D., 17, *45*, 94, *118*
Kearns, L., 261, *263*
Keating, D. P., 226, *233*
Keil, F. C., 175, *213*, 265, *314*
Kellman, P. J., 127–130, 132–136, 138, 139, 141, 143–145, 147–150, 152, 156, 158, 160, 162, 164–167, *172*, *173*, 176, *213*, 215, *233*, *234*
Kelly, D. H., 41, *44*
Kelso, J. A. S., 199, *213*
Kersten, D., 38, 39, *45*
Kessen, W., 16, *45*, 237, 238, *263*
Kiama, G., 197, *214*
Kiely, P. M., 16, *45*
Kiorpes, L., 16, 41, *43*, *45*, 82, *88*
Klahr, D., 334, *344*
Klein, S., 82, *88*
Knowles, L. S., 306, *312*
Koenderink, J. J., 122, *172*
Koffka, K., 142, *172*
Kol, K., 237, 261, *264*
Kong, R., 114, *118*
Kozlowski, L. T., 203, *213*
Kramer, S. J., 177, 188, 190, 192, 201, *212*
Krauskopf, J. 52–54, *72*
Krinsky, S. J., *44*
Kropfl, W., 231, *234*
Kulikowski, J. J., 41, *44*, 80, 81, *88*

349

Kupfer, C., 16, *44*
Kusbit, G. W., 307, *314*

L

LaBossiere, E., 14, *43*
Landers, W., 305, *313*
Landrum, J. T., *43*
Larkin, J. H., 265, *314*
Larsen, J. S., 3, 6, *45*, 93, *117*, *118*
LeCompte, G. K., 301, *313*
Lee, D., 236, *264*
Lee, D. N., 109, *118*, 122, 123, 168, *172*
Leehey, S. C., 80, 82, *88*
Leeuwenberg, E., 155, *170*
Legge, G., 38, 39, *45*
Lemerise, E., 111, 112, *117*
Lennie, P., 52–54, *72*
Levinson, J., 80, 81, *88*
Lewis, T. L., 16, *45*, 49, 51, 62, *72*, 75, *88*,
    94, *118*, 317, *332*
Lewis, S., 115, *117*
Lindsey, D. T., 48, 49, 51, 56, 58, 61, *72*, *73*
Litovsky, R., 292, 293, *314*
Lockman, J., 215, *234*
Lockman, J. J., 306, *314*
Logan, G. D., 305, *314*
Logothetis, N. K., 85, *88*
Longuet-Higgins, H. C., 122, *172*
Loomis, J. M., 122, 160, *172*
Lotze, R. H., 92, *118*
Loukides, M. G., 139, *172*
Luchins, A. S., 307, *314*
Luchins, E. H., 307, *314*

M

MacArthur, L. Z., 177, *213*
MacArthur, R., 109, *118*
MacFarlane, A., 94, *117*, *118*
MacLeod, D. I. A., 49, 56, *72*
Madigan, M., 16, *45*
Maffei, L., 12, *45*, 80, *89*, 327, *332*
Maier, J., 1, *44*, 87, *88*
Mandler, G., 175, 204, *213*
Mandler, J., 125, *172*
Mandler, J. M., 207, 211, *213*
Manny, R., 82, *88*
Marr, D., 110, *118*, 123, 135, 141, *172*,
    177, 204, *213*, 220, *234*

Martin, R. M., 302, *314*
Martinez, 3
Matin, E., 109, *118*
Matin, L., 109, 118
Matsuo, K., 3, *44*
Mattock, A., 135, 166, *173*
Maurer, D., 16, *45*, 49, 51, 62, *72*, 75, *88*,
    94, *118*, 317, *332*
Mayer, R. E., 293, 307, *314*
McCarrell, N. S., 306, *314*
McCarty, M., 252, 253, 257, *264*
McCloskey, M., 265, *314*
McDaniels, C., 206, *212*
McDonald, M. A., 17, 19–21, 31–36, *45*
McDonald, P. V., 293, *314*
McGuinness, E., 123, *170*
McLachlan, D. R., 301, *315*
McLaughlin, S. C., 114, *118*
Meicler, M., 270, *314*
Meltzoff, A. N., 223, *234*, 302, *314*
Michotte, A., 127, *172*
Miezin, F., 123, *170*
Mill, J. S., 142, *172*
Miller, 6
Miller, D., 301, *314*
Miller, J. M., 114, *118*
Miranda, S. B., 143, *171*
Moar, K., 11, 41, *43*
Mohindra, I., 75, 80, 82, *88*
Mohn, G., 79, *88*
Moidell, B. G., 115, *118*
Moore, C., 200, 203, *212*
Moore, 166
Moore, M. K., 270, 292, *312*, *314*
Morison, V., 81, *89*, 135, *173*
Morrison, R., 200, 203, *212*
Morrone, M. C., 110, *117*
Morrongiello, B. A., 94, *117*
Moscovitch, M., 301, 302, *315*
Moskowitz-Cook, A., 80, 82, *88*
Movshon, J. A., 41, *45*, 82, *88*
Muir, D., 94, *118*
Muir, D. W., 85, *88*
Mullen, K. T., 21, *45*
Muller, A. A., 270, *314*
Mutch, K. B., 218, *234*

N

Naegele, J., 325, *331*
Naegele, J. R., 38, *45*
Nagle, M., 115, *117*

Nakayama, K., 112, *118*, 122, 160, *172*
Nanez, J., Sr., 215, *234*
Nathan, J., 16, *45*
Newell, A., 333, 338, *344*
Newell, K. M., 293, *314*
Nielson, I., 306, *314*
Nisbett, R. E., 237, 261, *264*
Nishihara, H. K., 204, *213*
Norcia, A. M., 12, 15, 17, 28–32, 36, *43*, *45*
Norman, D. A., 333, *344*

O

O'Connell, D. N., 123, 124, 142, 143,
    147–149, *173*, 176, *214*
O'Connell, K. M., 78, 84, 85, *89*
O'Halloran, R., 158, 160, 162, 164, 165, *172*
O'Regan, J. K., 109, *118*
O'Shea, R., 85, *87*
Olver, R. R., 302, *312*
Othman, S., 197, *213*
Owsley, C., 143, 145, 155, *172*, 215, *234*

P

Packer, O., 17, 18, 21, 24–27, *45*, 318, *332*
Pandya, A. S., 197, 199, *213*
Parks, T., 223, *234*
Pearce, D., 109, *118*
Peduzzi, J. D., 3, *44*
Peeples, D. R., 17–20, 25, 36, *45*, 58, *72*,
    318, *332*
Pelli, D., 1, 2, 39, *45*
Pentland, A., 149, *172*
Perlmutter, M., 188, *214*
Perris, E., 292, 293, *314*
Petrig, B., 231, *234*
Pettersen, L., 215, *234*
Phillips, G. C., 81, *89*
Piaget, J., 126, 142, 168, *172*, 175, *213*,
    266, 267–269, 273, 285, 286,
    290–293, 299, 300–302, 308, *314*
Pick, H. L., 306, *314*
Picoult, E., 109, *118*
Pinto, J., 197, 199, 207, *212*
Pirchio, M., 12, *45*, 80, *89*, 327, *332*
Prazdny, K., 122, *172*
Proffitt, D. R., 177, 180, 185, 187, 188, 190,
    192, 201, 204, 208, 211, *212*, *213*

R

Ramachandran, V. S., 197, *214*
Rashid, R. F., 190, *214*
Reder, L. M., 307, *314*
Regan, D., 123, *172*
Reichardt, W., 110, *118*
Rescorla, R., 237, *264*
Restle, F., 155, 184, *170*
Reynolds, H., 216, *233*
Reynolds, H. N., 123, *171*
Richards, W. A., 141, *171*
Rieser, J., 94, *118*
Rieser, J. J., 306, *314*
Roberts, R. J., 187, *213*
Robinson, D. A., 106, 111, *118*
Robson, J. G., 2, 12, 15, *45*
Rochat, P., 292, 293, *314*
Rock, I., 135, *173*, 223, 226, *234*
Roder, B., 149, *173*
Rogers, B., 123, *173*
Ronnqvist, L., 236, *264*
Rose, A., 9, *45*
Rose, S. A., 231, *234*
Ross, B. H., 283, 307, *315*
Ross, J., 110, *117*
Rozin, P., 175, *214*
Ruff, H. A., 152, *173*

S

Sakovitz, L. J., 223, *234*
Salapatek, P., 2, 3, 6, 8, 11, 12, 15, 16, 41,
    43, *45*, 94, *116*, 143, *173*, 235, 251,
    263, 318, *331*
Salinger, W., 114, *117*
Santen, J. P. H. van, 110, *118*
Schacter, D. L., 301–303, *315*
Schall, J. D., 85, *88*
Schank, R. C., 237, *264*
Schlodtmann, W., 92, *118*
Schmidt, 128, 136, *173*
Schneck, M. R., 17, 19–21, 31–36, *45*
Schwartz, S., 114, *118*
Schubert, R. E., 266, *315*
Scully, D. M., 293, *314*
Sekel, M., 17, 19, 20, 25, 36, *45*, 318, *332*
Senden, M. von, 92, *118*
Shannon, E., 28–32, 36, *43*
Shaw, C. D., 198, *212*

Shaw, L., 149, *173*
Shea, S. L., 163, *171*, 231, *233*
Shepard, R. N., 123, 128, 142, 145, *173*
Shimojo, S., 2, 41, *45*, 78, 82–85, *87*, *88*,
    89, 318, 322, 323, *332*
Shioiri, S., 114, *118*
Shipley, C., 338, *344*
Shipley, T. F., 127, 136–137, 138, 139, 141,
    172, *173*
Short, K., 215, *233*
Short, K. R., 128, 130, 132, 136, 143,
    147–150, 152, *172*, 215, *234*
Siegler, R. S., 265, *315*, 338, *344*
Simon, H. A., 293, *314*, 334, *344*
Slater, A., 135, 163, 166, *173*
Slater, A. M., 16, *45*, 81, *89*, *173*
Smith, I. M., 218–221, *233*
Somers, M., 81, *89*, 135, *173*
Sophian, C., 266, 301–303, *315*
Sorknes, A., 218–221, *233*
Spelke, E., 226, *234*
Spelke, E. S., 127–130, 132–136, 141, *172*,
    173, *233*, 266, 270, 271, 294, 308,
    312, *315*
Sperling, G., 110, *117*, *118*
Spetner, N. B., 188, 190, *212*
Stillmann, L., 75, *89*
Spinelli, D., 12, *45*, 80, *89*, 327, *332*
Stacy, E. W., Jr., 237, *263*
Stark, L., 109, 114, *117*, *118*
Starkey, P., 226, *234*
Steinbach, M. J., 107, *118*
Steinberg, E. R., 333, *344*
Stenstrom, 6
Stephens, B. R., 40, 41, *43*
Stevens, A., 265, *313*
Stevens, J. K., 109, *118*
Strauss, M., 155, *170*
Strauss, M. S., 226, *234*
Stucki, M., 210, *214*, 217, 220, 230, *233*
Suchman, L. A., 305, *315*
Sugata, Y., 3, *44*
Sumi, S., 203, *214*
Swets, J. A., 2, *44*

T

Takayama, H., 3, *44*
Tansley, B. W., 52, *72*
Taylor, D., 135, *173*
Teller, D. Y., 12, 16–21, 24–27, 30, 32–36,
    38, *43*, *44*, *45*, 47–49, 51, 56, 58, 61,
    63, *72*, *73*, 318, *331*, *332*

Templeton, W. B., 114, *118*
Thibos, L. N., 80, *88*
Thines, G., 127, *172*
Thorn F. 83, *87*
Thompson, W. B., 218–220, *234*
Tiana, C. L. M., 1, *44*
Titchener, E. B., 142, *173*
Todd, J. T., 123, 131, *173*
Toupin, C., 283, *313*
Troscianko, T., 56, *73*
Tsarsis, S. L., *43*
Tulving, E., 301, *315*
Turkel, J., 111, 112, *117*
Tyler, C. W., 12, 17, *43*, *45*, 56, *72*

U

Ullman, S., 123, 142, 143, 148, *173*,
    177, *214*

V

van der Loos, H., 86, *88*
Van de Walle, G, 166, 167, *172*
van Hof-van Duin, J., 79, *88*
Van Nes, F. L., 87, *89*
Varner, D., 17, 19–21, 31–36, *45*
Vital-Durand, F., 16, *43*, 114, *117*
Volkmann, F. C., 159, *173*
Vosniadou, S., 265, *315*

W

Wagner, S. H., 223, *234*
Wallach, H., 123, 124, 142, 143, 147–149,
    163, 166, *173*, 176, *214*
Wallach, 166
Walls, G., 121, *173*
Walls, G., L., 92, *119*
Walraven, P. L., 8, *45*
Walther, D., 140, *171*, 232, *233*
Warren, R., 123, *173*
Wasserman, S., 270, 271, 294, 308, *312*
Watson, A. B., 2, *45*
Wattam-Bell, J., 41, *43*, 82, *88*, 163, *170*
Webb, J. A., 190, 191, *214*
Weiskopf, S., 301, 305, *313*
Welch, R. B., 93, *119*
Wellman, H. M., 265, 266, 301–303, 305,
    306, *315*

Wentworth, N., 235, 236, 256, 261, *264*
Werner, J., 75, *89*
Werner, J. S., 3, *46*, 188, *214*
Wertheimer, M., 127, 129, 196, *173*
Wertheimer, M., 196, *214*
Wheeler, K., 216, *233*
Wiesel, T. N., 38, *44*
Wikner, K., 94, *118*
Willatts, P., 270, 291–294, 299, *314*, *315*
Williams, D. R., 1, 6, *44*, *46*, 52, *72*
Williams, R. A., 16, *43*
Wilson, H. R., 1, *46*, 79, 81, *89*
Wiser, M., 265, *315*
Wishart, J. D., 270, 292, *312*
Wolfe, J. M., 85, *89*
Wright, J. A., *313*

Y

Yamamoto, Y., 3, *44*
Yonas, A., 94, *118*, 136, 143, 155, 161, *173*, 176, *212*, 215, 218–220, 221, 232, *233*, *234*
Yoshida, H., 82, *89*
Young, D., 109, *118*
Yuodelis, C., 3, 6, *46*, 93, *119*, 318, 319, *331*, *332*

Z

Zuckerman, C., 163, *173*

Subject Index

A

Acuity, 12, 42
  grating, 76, 79–83, 322–326
  nyquist limit, 6, 325, 326
  vernier, 76, 79, 82–83, 322, 325
  sex differences in vernier acuity, 83
  stereoacuity, *see* Stereopsis

B

Binocular vision, *see* Stereopsis
Biomechanical motion
  infant perception of, 181–184, 188–190,
    192–196, 201–203, 208–211
  processing constraints, 175–181, 184–187,
    190–191, 196–199, 203–205, 209–211
  coding theory, 184–190
  knowledge-based constraints, 203–208
  local rigidity, 190–196
  temporal phase relations, 196–203
  vector analysis, 179–184

C

Chromatic vision, 17–37, 42, 326
  chromatic contrast sensitivity, 22, 23, 28
  in color-deficient observers, 29
  chromatic deficiencies, 21, 47–48
  chromatic discriminations, 17–36, 41,
    58–63, 326
    neutral-point tests, 17, 20 25, 36
    Rayleigh discrimination, 21–22, 26–28,
      36, 47–48
    tritan discrimination, 20–22, 31–34, 36,
      48
  chromatic vs. achromatic sensitivity,
    21–25, 63–70
  motion nulling techniques, 49–70
  postreceptoral channels, 22, 52, 53, 55, 56
  stimulus modulation, 57–58
  trichromatic theory, 47–52
Color vision, *see* Chromatic vision
Contrast sensitivity, 8–17, 37, 38, 41, 42,
  327–328

D

Depth perception, 157–168, 216–223, *see
  also* Stereopsis
  kinetic depth information, 216, 230–232
    accretion and deletion of texture,
      216–218, 220, 230–231
    boundary flow, 218–220, 230–231

353

Depth Perception *(Cont.)*
 and motion perception, 157–167
 oculomotor cues, 163, 166
 pictorial cues, 124
Distance perception, *see* Depth perception

E

Ecological optics, *see* Gibson's theory of
   perception
Ecological validity, 122–128
Event perception, *see* Motion perception
Expectation, *see* Future-oriented processes,
Eye, development of, 2–3, 320
Eye movements
 optokinetic nystagmus, 49, 51
 saccadic eye movements, 93–107,
   109–116, 327
  calibration, 93, 94, 114–116, 326–327
  simulations of saccadic calibration,
    95–107

F

Figure-ground, *see* Object perception
Fovea, development of, 3, 4, 320, 321
Future-oriented processes, 235–239
 visual expectation, 239–262

G

Gestalt principles, 127–129, 135, 142
Gibson's theory of perception, 122–123,
   135, 156

I

Ideal observers, 2, 7–14, 22–37, 42, 75–76,
   79, 317–319, 322–331, 341, 343

K

Kinematic information, *see* Motion perception,
   Three-dimensional form

M

Motion perception, *see also* Biomechanical
   motion, Three-dimensional form

and distance perception, 121–123
motion detectors, 110–113
moving observers, 156–168
Motion nulling techniques, *see* Chromatic vision

O

Object Permanence, 231, 265–311, 339–340
 AB search errors, 268–269, 301–306
 manual search tasks, 267–268, 291–294,
   310, 311
 means-end sequences, 292–300, 308
 properties of occluded objects, 273–291
 Piaget's theory, 266–269
Object perception, *see also* Three-dimensional
   form
 boundaries, 137–141
 figure-ground segregation, 220–223
 object unity, 126–141, 168–169
 partly-occluded objects, 129–134, 136
 properties over time, 223–232
 length, 224–226
 number, 226–230
Oblique effect, 80–82
Occluded objects, *see* Object permanence,
   Object perception
Orientation selectivity, 80–82

P

Photoreceptors
 cones, 4–6, 14, 16, 52, 321, 322
 development, 2–8
 rods, 52–53
Piaget, theory of cognitive development, *see*
   Object permanence
Point-light displays, *see* Biomechanical motion
Position constancy, 91, 107–115, 132–135,
   156

R

Retina, *see* Fovea, Photoreceptors
Retinal Disparity, *see* Stereopsis

S

Saccadic eye movements, *see* Eye
   movements

Sex differences, *see* Acuity, Stereopsis
Space perception, *see* Depth perception
Stereopsis, 78, 83–86, 163, 328–330
  binocular disparity, 85, 166
  interocular separation, 329–330
  neural mechanisms, 78, 85
  stereoacuity, 83, 84, 86, 163, 330
  sex differences, 83, 85, 86

T

Three-dimensional form, 141–156, 123,
  168, 169

  kinematic information, 123–126, 141–152,
    155, 168, 169, 176
  kinetic depth effect, 142, 176
  static information, 152–155

V

Visual direction
  developmental plasticity, 93
  innateness, 92–95
Visual Expectation, *see* Future-oriented
  processes